OS/2® 2.1 REXX Handbook: Basics, Applications, and Tips

VNR's OS/2 Series

- **OS/2 Presentation Manager GPI Graphics**
  by Graham C.E. Winn
- **Writing OS/2 2.0 Device Drivers In C**
  by Steven Mastrianni
- **Integrating Applications with OS/2 2.0**
  by William H. Zack
- **The Cobol Presentation Manager Programming Guide**
  by David M. Dill
- **Learning To Program OS/2 2.0 Presentation Manager By Example: Putting the Pieces Together**
  by Stephen A. Knight
- **Comprehensive Database Performance For OS/2 2.0's Extended Services**
  by Bruce Tate, Tim Malkemus, and Terry Gray
- **Client/Server Programming With OS/2 2.1, Third Edition**
  by Robert Orfali and Daniel Harkey
- **Now That I Have OS/2 2.1 On My Computer — What Do I Do Next?**
  by Steven Levenson
- **The OS/2 2.0 Handbook**
  by William H. Zack
- **OS/2 2.X Notebook: Best of IBM OS/2 Developer**
  edited by Dick Conklin, Editor
- **Using Workplace OS/2: Power User's Guide to IBM's New Operating System/2 Version 2.1**
  by Lori Brown and Jeff Howard
- **The Shell Collection: OS/2 2.X Utilities**
  by Steven Levenson
- **Writing OS/2 2.1 Device Drivers in C, 2nd Edition**
  by Steven Mastrianni
- **The OS/2 2.1 Corporate Programmer's Handbook**
  by Nora Scholin, Mark Sullivan, and Robin Scragg
- **OS/2 2.1 REXX HANDBOOK: Basics, Applications, and Tips**
  by Hallett German
- **The OS/2 2.1 Application Developer's Guide**
  by Jody Kelly, Craig Swearingen, Dawn Bezviner, and Theodore Shrader
- **OS/2 and Netware Programming: Using the Netware Client API for C**
  by Lori Gauthier
- **OS/2 V2 Presentation Manager Programming in C++ Using the User Interface Class Library**
  by Bill Law, Kevin Leong, Bob Love, Hiroshi Tsuji, Pub. date: January 1994
- **OS/2 Remote Communications: Asynchronous to Synchronous Tips and Techniques**
  by Ken Stonecipher, Pub. date: January 1994
- **Objects for OS/2 2.1**
  by Bruce Tate, Scott Danforth, Paul Koenen, Pub. date: February 1994
- **C Programming In The OS/2 Environment**
  by Mitra Gopaul, Pub. date: March 1994

OS/2® 2.1 REXX Handbook: Basics, Applications, and Tips

Hallett German

VNR VAN NOSTRAND REINHOLD
New York

Library of Congress Catalog Card Number 93-26343
ISBN 0-442-01734-0

I(T)P Van Nostrand Reinhold is an International Thomson Publishing company. ITP logo is a trademark under license.

Printed in the United States of America

Van Nostrand Reinhold
115 Fifth Avenue
New York, NY 10003

International Thomson Publishing
Berkshire House, 168-173
High Holborn, London WC1V 7AA
England

Thomas Nelson Australia
102 Dodds Street
South Melbourne 3205
Victoria, Australia

Nelson Canada
1120 Birchmount Road
Scarborough, Ontario
M1K 5G4, Canada

International Thomson Publishing GmbH
Königswinterer Str. 518
5300 Bonn 3
Germany

International Thomson Publishing Asia
38 Kim Tian Road, #0105
Kim Tian Plaza
Singapore 0316

International Thomson Publishing Japan
Kyowa Building, 3F
2-2-1 Hirakawacho
Chiyada-Ku, Tokyo 102
Japan

16 15 14 13 12 11 10 9 8 7 6 5 4 3 2 1

Library of Congress Cataloging-in-Publication Data
German, Hallett,
OS/2 2.1 REXX Handbook: Basics, Applications, and Tips / Hallett German —
p. cm. -- (VNR's OS/2 series)
Includes index.
ISBN 0-442-01734-0
1. REXX (Computer program language) 2. OS/2 (Computer file)
I. Title. II. Series.
QA76.73.R24G47 1993
005.26'2--dc20

93-26343
CIP

Project Management: Ray Campbell • Art Director: Jo-Ann Radin-Campbell • Production: mle design, Milford, CT 06460

To the memory of my grandparents —

Lillian & Joseph German   Rose & Maurice Goldstein

"As the rivers full of water
go to make the ocean full,
so may that which is given here
go to the benefit of the departed."

Theravada Buddhist Meditation

Contents

Preface

After completing the *Command Language Cookbook*, I vowed never to write another new book. However, *one month* after the publication of the above book, I was fortunate to finally meet VNR's Executive Editor of Computer Science, the wonderful Dianne Littwin. The meeting took place during the Summer 1992 Windows and OS/2 conference. After a discussion of all sorts of issues, Dianne raised the question, "How would you like to write a book on OS/2 REXX?"

Bells went off in my head. The old gears started moving again. "This is certainly an interesting topic. If I could include third-party software as well…" The result is the book you see before you. I hope it is useful in your creation of OS/2 REXX procedures (i.e., programs both big and small).

Although one author's name is listed on the cover, this book would have never made it to completion without the help of reviewers, vendors, and other kindred spirits.

Comments from the following people resulted in many topics being expanded or clarified. My hat (the one with the OS/2 logo) goes off to:

- Lowell ("Jammin") Mercier of Private Health Care for encouragement.
- Gerry Pauline of Pace University. Gerry is an amazing resource of REXX information. He was a strong influence for Chapter 2.
- The anonymous reviewers who offered many useful suggestions.

Vendor support was an essential part of this book and has been tremendous. (Especially chapters 5 and 6.) These include:

- Carroll Hall of Borland International Inc. for providing a copy of ObjectVision for OS/2.
- Sabrina Schultz of Command Technology Corporation (CTC) for providing a copy of SPF/PC. All SPF/PC screens are reproduced with the permission of CTC.
- DeScribe, Inc. for providing a copy of DeScribe which was used in generating much of this original manuscript.
- Melissa Robertson and the IBM Independent Vendor League for providing IBM software, documentation and hardware in a timely and efficient fashion.
- Mark Hessling of Griffith University for sending a copy of THE. All THE screens are reproduced with the permission of Mark Hessling.
- Kevin Kearney of Mansfield Software Group Inc. for providing a copy of KEDIT for OS/2. All KEDIT screens reproduced in this book are with the permission of Mansfield Software Group Inc.
- Brady Flowers of Oberon Software for providing a copy of TE/2.
- Charles Daney of Quercus Systems for providing a copy of Personal REXX for OS/2 and subsequent updates up to the publication date. All Personal REXX and REXXTerm screens reproduced in this book are with the permission of Quercus Systems. Charles also patiently answered all of my electronic questions in a timely fashion.
- Anthony Green of Ruddock & Associates, Inc. for permission to reproduce the REXXTACY screens.
- Bill Mueller of SourceLine Software Inc. for providing a copy of SourceLink and for permission to reproduce the SourceLink screens.
- Barry Patton and Reed Meseck of Tritus, Inc. for providing a copy of Tritus SPF and updates. They have the most enthusiastic tech support of all vendors encountered for this book!
- Grace Welch, of Watcom; Waterloo, Ontario, Canada; for speedily supplying a copy of VX-REXX.

Thanks goes to the following people who gave permission for original material to appear in this book. These include:

- Eric Giguère (*The REXX Frequently Asked Questions*).
- Timothy Sipples and IBM (*The OS/2 Frequently Asked Questions*).

Other people that I found to be of tremendous help:

- Cathie Dager of Stanford Linear Accelerator Center who provided many good leads for this book and much encouragement for this work.
- Dianne Littwin of VNR was full of enthusiasm for this project. Her production staff excelled at converting this manuscript to the finished product. My thanks to Dianne's assistant, Risa Cohen for patiently putting up with my numerous calls.
- The Coca-Cola Company for continuing to produce Coke Classic, the liquid inspiration behind creating this book.
- Every musician that ever influenced me especially: Pete Seeger, Dave Cousins & the Strawbs, John Cafferty & Beaver Brown, Roderick Falconer, Rita Lee, and Alan Mann.
- WFNX for just "keep on keeping on" and playing the type of music they do. The radio dial never strayed while this work was being created.
- To Jason Dour, for his generosity, great signature file, and appreciation of Annie Lennox.
- Jo-Ann and Ray Campbell, of mle design, for patiently and enthusiastically proofing and laying out the book. I hope when I start my home business, it has half the energy of their company.
- Shakamuni Buddha's teaching and life inspired me through this and other projects.
- Cicely, Stanley and Robbyn German for actively supporting this project.
- Vovo and Mamae Miranda sent prayers and hope from afar. Obrigado.
- To Alessandra and Chelsea German, my daughters, for making sure I didn't forget the important things (such as reading books and playing songs) throughout this project.
- *And most important, my wife, Raquel Miranda German. She patiently put up with my time away from the children and the inevitable house responsibilities. She has my most heart-felt thanks and greatest appreciation.*

Screen images appearing in this publication were captured and processed using the **PrntScrn™ Screen Image Utility**.
This utility is provided by:
MITNOR Software
28411 E. 55th Street
Broken Arrow, OK 74014
(918) 357-1628

Foreword

1993 marks the tenth anniversary of the availability of the first commercial REXX interpreter from IBM. Since that time, REXX has gone on to become one of the most popular programming languages ever, with an estimated one million people who have programmed in REXX.

A REXX interpreter has been included with the OS/2 base operating system since the release of OS/2 1.3. You can use REXX as a replacement for the old BATCH language, as an applications programming language, and as a macro language for REXX-aware applications such as spreadsheets, communications programs, and database programs. Besides conforming to the latest version of the REXX language, the OS/2 version of REXX also includes a number of OS/2-specific extensions. In addition, many other extensions are available commercially and as shareware.

Hal German's book describes all these various uses of the REXX language. The book also includes an overview of the language for novices, and has technical information on enabling the use of REXX within your own applications and extending REXX with functions written in other languages. Rounding out the book is an introspective view of REXX, comparing different implementations of REXX, comparing REXX to other command languages currently available, and discussing REXX programming style issues.

This book is a great source of information on programming with REXX on OS/2.

Patrick Mueller
IBM Software Solutions
Cary, NC

1

A Road Map

A BRIEF LOOK AT OS/2'S HISTORY

In 1987, IBM and Microsoft released version 1.0 of an operating system called OS/2. It was an extremely limited product — especially in its ability to run DOS applications. Yet, these two vendors promised greater things to come. The product was released as a Standard and as an Extended Edition (with communications and database services). Three subsequent releases brought increasingly greater functionality and reliability.

By 1992, Microsoft had withdrawn from developing OS/2 and was using the knowledge gained from that experience to begin creating Windows New Technology (NT) and the Object BASIC command language. That year brought the availability of OS/2 2.0. Its major selling point was the ability to seamlessly run DOS, Windows, and OS/2 (16- and 32-bit) applications simultaneously. With the delay of all Windows NT components until August 1993, and over three million copies of OS/2 2.0 and 2.1 sold at the time of publication, this operating system should continue to do well. (Initial NT reviews have been mixed.)

In May 1993, OS/2 2.1 was released with MS-Windows 3.1 support, enhanced hardware and multimedia support.

An important feature of OS/2, starting with Extended Edition 1.2 and Standard Edition 1.3, was the inclusion of both command line and full-screen REXX interpreters. REXX, which stands for **RE**structured e**X**tended e**X**ecutor, was created by Mike Cowlishaw of IBM in 1979. REXX is a **command language** or **CL**. A command language uses English-like commands and offers the user an easy way to *ask* the operating system to perform one or more tasks. A REXX program is called a procedure, (the term used throughout this book), an exec or, a macro (if it interfaces with an application such as an editor, a macro). OS/2 REXX supports all the features of language version 4.00, described in Mike Cowlishaw's *The REXX Language* (1990b). Note that not all REXX interpreters/compilers are REXX language version 4.0-compliant. Compliant interpreters/compilers include CMS (all), OS/2, SAA, DOS and Windows (all), and TSO.

REXX's success was spurred in part by having been selected as the SAA Procedure Language SAA/PL. SAA or Systems Applications Architecture is a set of IBM-generated procedures and standards designed to provide a common look and feel across operating systems (for their entire product line). The SAA REXX specification is outlined in the document *SAA CPI Procedures Language Level 2 Reference*. Common User Access (CUA) is the underlying basis for OS/2 2.1's Workplace Shell is also part of SAA. Ironically, the future of the whole of SAA is bleak as of this writing. Chapter 2 further looks at the history of REXX. Presently, there are at least 18 REXX interpreters and compilers available on 12 different operating systems including all IBM operating systems, MS-Windows, Amiga, Tandem, Macintosh, and UNIX.

WHAT ARE THE GOALS OF THIS BOOK?

- To offer a one-stop reference, tutorial, and idea book for OS/2 REXX.
  - The goal is to reduce the need to look up information in a variety of IBM, third-party OS/2 REXX and related manuals, some of which is an additional expense. You should never have to say "Where do I look up..." or "How do I do...".
  - This book views OS/2 REXX as a means to develop self-contained applications, interface with third-party software, act as a macro language for XEDIT- or SPF-like editors, perform system utility operations, and much more!
- To review in-depth the major OS/2 REXX interpreters.
  - This includes a discussion of features unique to OS/2 and for each interpreter. Product comparisons will be provided.
- To discuss at length all of the major third-party commercial and shareware software that interfaces with OS/2 REXX.
  - There are at least 100 shareware and commercial editors, communication packages, full-screen development software, and REXX utilities. This book will attempt to provide information on many of these.
- To provide ideas where to look for further information.
  - The Appendices list OS/2 REXX and REXX-related resources: commercial and shareware vendors, electronic bulletin boards (including IBM's), CompuServe locations, and Internet Anonymous FTP sites with OS/2 REXX software.
- To continually revise this book to meet your OS/2 REXX information needs.

– Please take advantage of Appendix A ("Your Turn") and let me know what changes and enhancements you would like to see made to this book.

WHO SHOULD READ THIS BOOK?

This book assumes familiarity with OS/2. If this is not the case, you are urged to read Steven Levenson's and Eli E. Hertz's *Now That I Have OS/2 2.0 on My Computer, What Do I Do Next?* (Van Nostrand Reinhold, 1992).

The following audiences will find this book useful:

- Users who are new to both OS/2 and REXX. This book provides an explanation of the general capabilities of REXX, and shows how to take advantage of features unique to OS/2 REXX.
- Users who are familiar with REXX but not how it works under OS/2. OS/2 REXX features that are non-portable but handy for operating system tasks are documented. This includes casual and full-time REXX programmers.
- System integrators who need to get various operating systems talking to each other. A good part of this effort includes converting REXX procedures between different platforms. The issues involved in doing this are discussed, including porting to non-SAA and REXX language version 4.00.
- Programmers and end-users who want to extend the OS/2 REXX language, by building environments (subcoms), creating function packages, and using third-party software are examined.

HOW SHOULD I READ THIS BOOK?

Two suggested ways to read this book follow: by type of audience and by type of concerns.

By Type of Audience

Section 1.3 described some potential types of audiences for this book. Here is a suggested reading order based on these types:

Audience	Chapter(s)
New OS/2 and REXX users	1, 2, 3, 7
Experienced REXX but new OS/2 users.	3-7
REXX users who want to create portable procedures (programs).	3,7
REXX users who want to extend OS/2 REXX capabilities.	3, 6, 7

By Type of Questions

New and experienced REXX users will usually ask the following questions when starting to use OS/2 REXX:

Question	Chapter(s)
What is the REXX Language?	1
When should I use REXX to develop an OS/2 application?	3,7
What are the unique features of OS/2 REXX?	3-5
Which OS/2 REXX interpreter should I use?	3,5
What IBM REXX extensions are available?	3-4
How can I extend the REXX language under OS/2?	5-6, I
How can I interface REXX with third-party shareware and commercial software?	5-6, I

THE APPROACH USED IN THIS BOOK

Chapter 2 gives an overview of the "standard" REXX command language (i.e., language version 4.00). The reader, having read Chapter 2, will have the framework to learn how to take advantage of OS/2 REXX unique features. Mention of the forthcoming ANSI REXX standard is also included.

Chapter 3 and 4 present the IBM OS/2 extensions to the REXX Language. Chapter 3 focuses on the OS/2 REXX interpreter, while Chapter 4 looks at other IBM OS/2 products including the exciting Visual REXX and interfacing with Communications Manager.

Chapter 5 and 6 looks at third-party alternatives and extensions to the IBM REXX interpreter. Chapter 5 reviews a third-party REXX interpreter and Chapter 6 examines third-party REXX-related software.

Chapter 7 wraps up the book by looking at some advanced and miscellaneous REXX issues such as REXX programming style, portability, and application development.

The *Appendices* lists additional REXX resources and a look at Watcom's VS-REXX.

Here is a possible procedure on how to use this book when developing a OS/2 REXX application:

Steps	Chapter	Section
What type of application do I have?	7	Application Development Using REXX
Should I code the application in REXX?	7	Which Command Language Should I Use?
Which tasks does the application need to perform?	7	Application Development Using REXX
Which REXX commands correspond to these tasks?		Application Development Using REXX
– Standard IBM OS/2 REXX interpreter	3	
– Third party OS/2 REXX interpreter	5	
– Standard IBM OS/2 REXX Extensions	3,4	
– Third-party OS/2 REXX Extensions	5,6, I	
Are there other concerns?	7	Other REXX Concerns
– Portability	7	
– Programming Style	7	
– Naming Conventions	7	
– Other Concerns	7	
Code the Application		

Figure 1-1. A general method for developing command language (CL) applications

The reader is urged to read my 1992 book *Command Language Cookbook* (German, 1992) for an extensive treatment of this topic and to see how this approach is used with other command languages.

SOFTWARE VERSIONS USED IN THIS BOOK

All efforts were made to keep this book as current as possible. These were the version numbers at the time of publication:

Product	Vendor	Version
EPM (Enhanced Editor)	IBM (Bundled with OS/2 2.0)	5.51 (The 2nd version)
KEDIT	Mansfield Software	5.0 (32-bit version)
ObjectVision for OS/2	Borland International	2.0
OS/2 Extended Edition	IBM	1.0
OS/2 LAN Manager Utilities	IBM	1.0
OS/2 REXX & PMREXX	IBM (Bundled with OS/2 2.1)	2.1
Personal REXX for OS/2	Quercus Systems	3.0
REXXTACY	Ruddock & Associates	2.0
SourceLink	SourceLine	2.0B
SPF/2	Command Technology Corporation	3.0
TE/2	Oberon	1.23
THE	Mark Hessling	1.1
Tritus SPF	Tritus Inc.	1.24
Visual REXX	IBM	1.0
VX-REXX	Watcom	1.1

REFERENCES

Cowlishaw, M.F. 1990a "REXX 4.00" in *Proceedings of the REXX Symposium.*

Cowlishaw, M.F. 1990b *The REXX Language: A Practical Approach to Programming* 2nd ed. Englewood Cliffs, N.J.: Prentice-Hall.

German, Hallett 1992 *Command Language Cookbook for Mainframes, Minicomputers, and PCS*. New York: Van Nostrand Reinhold pp. 1-23, 71-142, 307-342.

Green, Linda Suskind 1992 "Rexxbits" *In Proceedings of the REXX Symposium for Developers and Users*, Stanford Lincar Accelerator Center Stanford University, Stanford, CT pp. 56-99.

IBM Corporation 1991 *SAA CPI Procedures Language Level 2 Reference* (SC24-5549).

2

REXX Essentials

This chapter will provide an overview of the standard REXX language as it stands today, including the forthcoming ANSI REXX standard. The current language version is 4.00 and is largely defined by Mike Cowlishaw's second edition of *The REXX Language*. Most REXX interpreters and compilers are compliant with this version, including all OS/2 REXX interpreters.

A review of the characteristics of command languages is also presented. This will provide a framework to easily comprehend the underlying structure of the REXX language and to quickly build REXX-based applications.

WHAT IS A COMMAND LANGUAGE?

REXX, among other things, is a **command language** (**CL**). Command languages are also called scripting languages, shell languages, control languages, and much more. A more extensive look at command languages is presented in German 1992. Although some view them as not for "serious" programming, command languages are widely available on nearly all operating systems and environments. The result is millions of computer users throughout the world daily using command language programs to perform various utility and system operations. Mike Cowlishaw estimates that there are over 10 million users with REXX accessible to them. REXX is not just a command language used internally at IBM, but the most popular programming language, with more than 5 million lines of code.

For this book, we will use the following definition for command language: ***a programming language consisting of a series of high-level, English-like commands entered interactively (e.g., a keyboard, mouse, or other input device) or non-interactively (that is created with an editor, saved in a file, and executed in foreground or background).***

An interpreter or compiler for the command language then determines which user-specified operating system tasks to perform and processes them using corresponding task values.

Command languages have the following characteristics:

- **Command languages are almost always interpreted languages.** This means the Command Line Interface or Command Line Interpreter (CLI) scans the syntax of each command, performs any necessary symbolic substitution, and executes the command language program **every time a command language program is invoked**. This makes command languages ideal for new users because they can immediately verify their results. Application developers will also like command languages because they can build application or application prototypes — FAST. Note that REXX is one of the few command languages available as a compiler. (Available for CMS and TSO.)
- **Command languages are usually executed in the foreground.** This means when a command language program is executing, usually you are unable to run anything else. Under OS/2, REXX programs can either run in foreground simultaneously along with other programs or in background. The result is an increase in overall system productivity.
- **Command languages are composed of English-like verbs describing the task to be performed.** REXX is typical with commands or instructions containing keywords such as SAY, PARSE, and PULL. These keywords may be accompanied by a variable number of parameters, sub-keywords, and modifiers that further define the task to be performed.
- **Command language programs either directly include operating system commands such as OS/2 batch languages, or indirectly includes them through a particular command language such as REXX's ADDRESS instruction.** In addition, OS/2 REXX provides built-in functions to emulate system commands. For example, the SysCls function emulates the CLS command to clear the screen.
- **Command languages usually provide the system capability for users to extend the language through subprocedures, functions, and interfaces to external environments.** The means to do this with OS/2 REXX is discussed throughout the book.

Why REXX?

REXX is one of the most popular command languages appearing on a variety of platforms. It was created to provide new and experienced users with a simplified, yet powerful version of PL/I. REXX programs are called **procedures** (the term used throughout this book) **execs**, or **macros**. Table 2-1 lists the types of audiences attracted to REXX and some reasons for this interest:

Table 2-1 Type of REXX Users and Reasons Why they Use It.

Type of REXX Users	Reasons Why They Use REXX
New & Casual Users	Only a few rules to learn before creating "ready-to-run" programs. So, they can concentrate on programming instead of syntax. English-like command keywords. String, date/time capabilities
Advanced Users (full-time)	Flexibility Wealth of flow control statements. "Data type" determined by value. Symbolic substitution.
Application Programmers	Easy means to process operating system commands within a REXX procedure. High portability to a variety of IBM and non-IBM operating systems. The REXX language is not dependent on a computer's hardware or software. (Although REXX extensions may be written to take advantage of both.) Good interfaces to editors, and third-party applications. Various means to extend the REXX language.

Note that the above typology is far from perfect — some of the reasons that application programmers may like REXX could also apply to advanced REXX users. However, the above reasons do show some of the strength, flexibility, and ease-of-use characteristics of the REXX language. The next section looks at more detail at these characteristics in more detail.

Characteristics of REXX

The following is a detailed look at the major characteristics of the REXX language.

- REXX is flexible.
  - Adaptation of the REXX language to whatever your programming style. This includes: using lower, upper, or mixed case in REXX statements, and a free-formatting nature that allows for generous use of blanks in REXX statements. REXX also allows statements to be placed on one line or several lines.

- After learning a few rules, the beginning REXX programmer is capable of creating "ready-to-run" procedures. There are a variety of reasons for this. Most limits are imposed by your REXX implementation rather than the REXX language. For example, Cowlishaw (1990a) specifies no limitation on the number of CALL arguments, but OS/2 has a maximum of 20. Another reason is that an English-like language makes it easy to begin learning REXX. REXX does many things for you — such as declaring variables and opening files. Finally, REXX employs flexible data types. To REXX, all data is seen as character strings. It will perform mathematical operations on values that look like numeric characters. Thus, SAY 2+2 and SAY '2' +2 yields the same result! This reduces the number of problems in performing string and numeric operations.

  The REXX language is small and is being purposely kept that way. A language with only 20 major keywords to learn will be attractive to developers and programmers.

- REXX provides a structure that is largely independent of hardware and operating system. This includes: The ADDRESS instruction that provides an easy-to-use interface to the operating system and external environments. A general model provided by Cowlishaw (1990a) specifies the following: characters and file input/output, stack or external data queue operations (used by the PUSH, QUEUE, and PULL instructions), and external variable pools such as the SAA variable pool interface (VPI).

- REXX is scalable, from beginning users (even children) to full-scale programmers, one language serves all.

The Components of REXX

Every command language, including REXX, has five major components. Table 2-2 lists these components, their corresponding functions, and **standard** REXX statements all of which are included in OS/2 REXX. There are many statements specific to one or more REXX implementations that can also perform these tasks. An example is the EXECIO instruction for File I/O is supported for CMS, DOS (all), and TSO. These are not discussed here and can be found in German (1992). Note that this includes every standard REXX statement.

Table 2.2 Components, Functions & Standard REXX Statements

Components	Functions	REXX Instructions
Input/Output	Output to screen, printer, file	SAY
	Input from a keyboard or command line.	PULL, PARSE ARG
	File Operations	Functions: CHARIN, CHAROUT, LINEIN, LINE-OUT, LINES, STREAM
	Stack Operations	PULL, PUSH, QUEUE, QUEUED (function)
Flow Control	Conditional flow control	IF-THEN-ELSE, (other formats) SELECT WHEN (other formats)
	Loop Testing/ Processing	Iterative DO, DO-UNTIL, DO-WHILE, DO (other formats), DROP ITERATE, LEAVE, NOP
	Exception handling	CALL, SIGL (special variable), SIGNAL
	Exit/ Return code handling	EXIT, RC (special variable), RETURN
	Array Operations	Compound symbols
General Features	Debugging/Trace Facility	TRACE (function and statement)
	Symbolic Substitution	INTERPRET (not in compilers) VALUE (function)
	Labels	Label name:
	Non-portable Global Options	OPTIONS
	Numeric Format	NUMERIC
	Interpreter Version	PARSE VERSION
Interfaces	Internal Interfaces	Function name CALL, CALL ON, PROCEDURE, RESULT and SIGL (special variables)
	External Interfaces	ADDRESS
Built-In	Functions	60+ built-in functions: String operations, Bit operations, Utility operations, Date operations, Time operations
	Variables	3 Special Variables: RC, RESULT, SIGL

Please feel free to refer to Table 2-2 while reading this book and developing REXX applications. Also, see Chapter 7 for additional information.

What are Typical REXX Applications?

The following are some of the types of applications using REXX.

- Preprocessor for a compiler
- Extend the capabilities of an operating system command or perform system operations such as a customized backup
- Utility operations such as returning an encrypted string

- Perform tasks on startup or login/logout to a LAN/ remote host
- Self-contained application such as a report generator
- Front-end to another application performing housekeeping tasks
- Commands for XEDIT, ISPF or some other application
- Text-based and other types of games. O'Hara and Gomberg (1985) have documented on building checkers and other games

REXX is limited only by imagination and time. As Ross Perot said in the 1992 American presidential election — just do it!

A History of REXX

The origin of REXX reflects the characteristics of the language. Here is a brief look at the history of REXX. See Cowlishaw (1990b) and Green (1992) for more information.

During his spare time at the IBM Laboratories near Hursley, England (also the birthplace of OS/2 Presentation Manager), Mike Cowlishaw worked on a simplified, yet powerful version of the PL/I language. It was then called REX (REformed eXecutor.) He then placed a note in the Tools section (which deals with tools' development on the VM platform) of IBM's internal VNET network asking for impressions of REX. Many replies came back. This was followed by the development and rigorous testing of over 30 versions between 1979 and 1982 —REXX 2.00 in 1980, 2.5 in 1981, and 3.00 in 1982. REXX is one of the few programming languages ever successfully developed by an electronic committee.

1982-1986 was the second phase of the REXX language. This period saw availability of documentation and the first commercial implementations. Highlights included:

- The first public interpreter, released in 1983 as part of VM/SP (Virtual Machine/System Product) for CMS (Conversational Monitor System). REXX soon replaced EXEC2 as the preferred command language for CMS.
- The two "classic" REXX books by O'Hara and Gomberg, and Mike Cowlishaw were published in 1985 featuring REXX 3.50. Mansfield Software also started selling Personal REXX for DOS that year.

From 1987 to the present marked the third period of the REXX language called the popularization and standardization stage. This included:

- IBM selected REXX as the SAA procedures' language in 1987. This is mentioned in Chapter 1.
- IBM producing the first REXX compiler (for VM).
- Many other REXX implementations become available. Here is a list of just some of these:

- Two more DOS REXX interpreters (Kilowatt Software and Tritus Inc.) start being sold.
- Two REXX interpreters for MS-Windows (Kilowatt and Quercus Systems) begin distribution. Quercus took over the development of Personal REXX from the Mansfield Software Group.
- ARexx becomes bundled with the Amiga Operating System
- REXX becomes available on the Macintosh.
- Three REXX interpreters, two in the public domain, became available for UNIX.
- And most important to you, REXX becomes bundled with OS/2 2.0.

Other significant activities include REXX being elevated to a project at the SHARE (IBM Users' Group), the first annual REXX Symposium held in 1990, and the formation of the ANSI REXX standard committee (X3J18) in 1991. The first version of the standard is to be finalized in 1994. It will emphasize means to make the REXX language more portable and less ambiguous. A second version of the standard, slated for release in 1996, will focus on enhancements to the REXX language.

What can we conclude from this?:

- *REXX did not happen overnight.* It was part of a conscious process to formulate a programming language. Green notes that Mike Cowlishaw spent over 4000 hours developing REXX before the first interpreter was shipped! (Green, 1992.) This means all the major bugs have been resolved and the language design was well in place long before the first commercial implementation.
- *The number of available REXX interpreters and compilers has dramatically increased in recent years, and should continue to do so.* Over 18 REXX interpreters and compilers are in existence on over 12 different operating systems.
- *The amount of REXX documentation and third-party support is also increasing.* Over 50 third-party books and 70 user group presentations are available on REXX. Hundreds of third-party software now provide REXX interfaces.

As to the future of REXX, it looks quite strong heading towards its fifteenth year. REXX will continue to be ported to other operating systems. REXX interpreters and compilers will be modified to support such extensions as communication libraries and object-oriented programming. A look at future REXX trends are presented in Chapter 7.

GROUND RULES OF REXX

This section attempts to provide the basic skeleton of the REXX language structure as simply as possible. It's always good to start with a road map of where we're going. Figure 2-1 does just that by showing the overall structure of a REXX program. The forthcoming

ANSI REXX standard is expected to include a very detailed series of syntax diagrams using BNF (Backus Normal Form). These will be of interest to those wanting more information on the structure of REXX syntax.

A **procedure** (REXX program or macro) is comprised of a series of **clauses,** also called statements, which take up one or more lines. Each line (clause) is scanned every time the program is executed. There are five types of clauses. Each clause is comprised of **tokens** that may form **expressions**. *Tokens* are types of data such as strings, symbolic variables, and operators that are delimited by blanks. Expressions are sets of data that an explicit arithmetic, string, Boolean, or relational operation(s) are to be performed on. Clauses may implicitly or explicitly end with one of four types of delimiters.

The remaining subsections will deal with each of these components: clauses and delimiters, tokens, expressions, operators. Feel free to refer to Figure 2-1 while reading them.

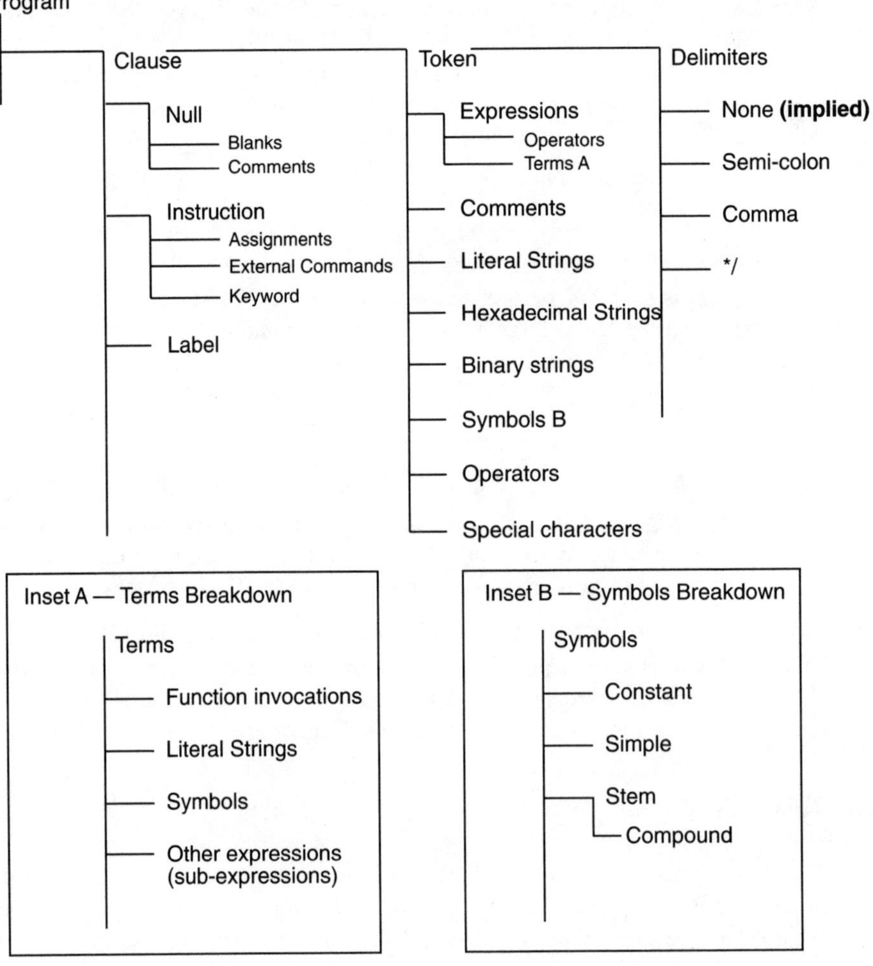

Figure 2-1 REXX General Structure (with two insets)

Overview of Clauses (Statements) and Delimiters

Clauses: As mentioned in the previous section, the foundation of all REXX programs is the **clause**. A clause or statement may take up one or more lines. The interpreter works on one clause at a time and scans them left to right. The components of clauses, such as tokens and expressions, will be discussed in succeeding sections. The following are some of the characteristics of clauses:

- *The minimum/maximum length of a REXX clause is dependent on the interpreter/compiler*. Note that the OS/2 maximum clause length is 500 and the Quercus Personal REXX clause length is 1000. This in part because Cowlishaw (1990) has reserved error message #12 to notify users that a particular REXX compiler's or interpreter's maximum clause length has been surpassed. The specific limit should be part of the error message. This is true for Quercus's interpreter but not IBM's. No minimum or maximum clause length is specified by Cowlishaw.
- There are three major types of clauses:

  null clauses (such as comments, labels, and blank lines, generally these are not processed by the REXX interpreter/compiler)

  labels (to identify subroutine, function, and exception handling [SIGNAL] definition locations), and

  instructions (These are "action clauses" that are not ignored by the REXX interpreter/compiler such as assignment statements, keyword statements and external command statements.)

  There are five subtypes of REXX clauses:

  - Comments and blank lines "whitespace": These are also called **null** or the *ignore it* **clauses**. It is commonly believed that these lines do not effect the processing time of a REXX procedure. In reality, they do have some effect on certain REXX implementations. I found that comments and blank lines did have some effect under OS/2 REXX, such as being with a loop, for larger procedures but nothing conclusive was found. Comments can also be processed by the TRACE instruction or function. Space cruncher programs that automatically remove white space and comments can be easily created or obtained.

A comment line begins with a /* and ends with a */. OS/2 REXX *requires* that a comment *usually* containing the word REXX, **be placed on the first line and start in column one**. If that is not done, the REXX clauses are seen as OS/2 system or batch commands. Note that REXX interpreters/compilers on other operating system require the word REXX in that first comment. No semicolon, as an end-of-clause delimiter is required as an end of clause delimiter. OS/2 accepts the */ placed on a different line other than the one containing the /*. So, a comment can be placed on multiple lines and be of any size. Comments can be nested (i.e., comments within comments) or placed after an instruction on the same line. The issue of commenting styles in REXX is reserved for Chapter 7. Here are some examples of null clauses:

Note: If running these examples, please do not include the explanatory text in parentheses.

Blank line with a comment

```
        /* A comment */
```

Comment to identify a file as a REXX program.

```
/* */ (Minimum required starting in column 1, line 1)
OR /*rexx*/ OR /* REXX*/
OR /*   A ReXX Program */
(Place in column 1, line 1. Comment may contain the word REXX in any case.)
```

Comment on three lines

```
/* This is a comment
That is on
Three lines */
```

A nested comment

```
/*Comment /* A nested comment */ */
```

- The *label clause*: Used to provide in-program commenting to delineate blocks of clauses by some criteria, usually the function of the code block. It may also mark the start of a block of clauses that can be invoked as a function, subroutine, or SIGNAL/CALL error routine. No semicolon is required. See the section "Other Concerns" in this chapter for further information on CALL, SIGNAL, function, and subprocedures. Note that the label name is immediately followed by a colon, 2) the label name can be in any case, there is usually no maximum limit, and TRACE L /TRACE(L) will show all the labels processed by a procedure. The following are examples of labels:

Lowercase Label

```
itbroke:
```

Uppercase Label

```
ITBROKE:
```

Label with Underscores

```
it_broke:
```

Label as a number

```
1.25:
```

- *The Assignment (or sometimes called the "equals") clause*: Takes a variable, in REXX terminology — a symbol with a value, and gives it a new value (in REXX terminology — an expression) and places that value somewhere in the computer's memory. Because a REXX symbol always has default values of their names (actual or derived) in uppercase, assignment statements are not always necessary. The succeeding subsections will talk in detail about symbols and expressions. Here are some examples of both valid and invalid assignment statements:

Valid Assignment Statements

```
Name = "Ron Rex"        /* String value */
Age = 15                /* Numeric value */
a.name = "Ron Rex"      /* Compound symbol (element "name" in array "a") */
a. = "Ron REX"          /* Assign value to stem (every element of array) */
```

Invalid Assignment Statements

```
99 = 200                /* Can't have numbers as symbol names */
.Name = "Ron Rex"       /* Can't have a symbol name start with a period */
                        /* Both return error 31 */
```

- *Keyword (or REXX Commands) Instructions*: This clause(s) performs the action requested by an instruction. The instruction will contain one or more of the near thirty REXX **keywords** in any case. Instructions may be nested, especially within flow control structures such as IF-THEN-ELSE, DO-WHILE-END, etc., and contain subkeywords such as PARSE VERSION. No semicolon is required.
- *External commands.* Any string that is not understood by the REXX interpreter/compiler is viewed as an **external command** and is passed to the default, usually the operating system's command line interpreter such as OS/2's CMD.EXE or current environment. The special system variable RC holds the return result code sent back by the external environment to the REXX interpreter from the last command processed. External commands are discussed in Chapters 3 and 4 including sections on the ADDRESS instruction/ the environment model and on creating your own environment.

Delimiters: Although REXX minimizes the need to use punctuation, there are still times when it is needed. Here is a list of REXX clause delimiters and suggestions on when to use them:

Table 2-3 REXX Clause Delimiters

Delimiter	Character	When to Use
Semicolon	;	End of clause (optional)
		Separate multiple clauses (required)
Colon	:	Marks end of label. Semicolon implied.
Comma	,	Continuation of clause on one or more lines
Asterisk-Slash	*/	Marks end of a one-line or multiline comment
None	None	End of clause

Tokens

The major component of clauses are tokens. Tokens are types of data such as strings, symbolic variables, and operators that are delimited by blanks. Comments are also considered tokens. These are discussed in the Clauses and Operators section in this chapter. Let's look at each of these:

Strings: The following are the major type of REXX strings:

- **Literal (non-interpreted) strings** take up no more than one line containing between 0 and 250 characters for most REXX implementations (including OS/2). The ANSI REXX committee have discussed increasing the maximum limit of literal strings but no increase over the current limit of 250 has yet been agreed upon. Here are some rules about literal strings:
  - *Syntax:* Comprised of any valid characters, including numbers, and are placed *between at least one set* of matching single or double quotes.
  - *Quotes:* A literal string may contain any number of matching sets of single and double quotes. There are two exceptions: To produce the single quote as a character in a literal string enclosed by single quotes, use two single quotes at the desired location. (The same is true for producing a double quote as a character in a literal string enclosed in double quotes. And, to produce a single quote in a literal string enclosed by double quotes or a double quote in a literal string enclosed by single quotes, then no additional single/double quotes are needed.

Some examples of literal strings:

Single quote in a double quoted string

```
"There's no sleep for us tonight"     /* Only one single quote needed */
```

Null string

```
"" or ''
```

Double quote within a double-quote string

```
"Use two double quotes to produce one "" "
```

- Hexadecimal and binary strings are special cases of literal strings. Both types of strings include special characters to be enclosed in either single or double quotes followed by the suffix b/B (for binary) or x/X for hexadecimal. These strings are then packed. Note that the special characters are 0-9,A-F (any case) for hexadecimal strings and 0-1 for binary strings. Blanks may be optionally added to either type of string at the appropriate location to enhance readability. Hexadecimal strings are useful in representing double-byte characters. Double-byte characters, part of SAA, are used to represent Japanese (Kanji), Korean, and Chinese character sets. Note that the OPTIONS EXMODE allows the double-byte characters in mixed strings processed by characters or bytes [default]. OPTIONS ETMODE enables double-byte character processing, this is not the default. These are discussed further in the section, "Nearly portable REXX features in OS/2," found in Chapter 3. The following are examples of hexadecimal and binary strings:

Hexadecimal string with blank

```
'e1 b8'x
```

Hexadecimal string with no blanks

```
'bacd'X
```

Binary strings

```
'11111110'b
```

Symbolic Variables: Symbols are a key part of any REXX procedure. They provide the REXX programmer a means to create and modify variables with specified or calculated values. Symbols include labels and keyword instructions and simple or compound symbols which are discussed below.

Symbol ground rules: Table 2-4 summarizes the essential symbol ground rules:

Table 2-4 Symbol Ground Rules

Area	Rule
First character of symbol name	A-Z, a-z (changed to uppercase by the interpreter), !, ?, _, and. (for decimals/constant symbols).
Any other characters of symbol	The same as 1 and all numeric (0-9)
Length of symbol name	Cowlishaw recommends a minimum of 50 characters but OS/2 supports up to 250 characters. The minimum symbol length of 250 is likely to be approved by the REXX ANSI committee.

It is recommended to use the SYMBOL built-in function to test what type of symbol an expression is and if a symbol name is invalid. This is discussed in the section called "Symbolic Operations."

Constant and Simple Symbols: There are two major categories of symbols: *elementary symbols* which are single variables each holding a value that may or may not be modifiable, and *complex symbols* which are a set of related elementary symbols each holding a value.

The following is a brief look at the two types of simple symbols (constant symbols and simple symbols):

- *Constant symbols* contain a non-modifiable numeric value that is usually either whole numbers (e.g. 1), decimals (e.g. 1.33), or exponents (e.g. 1e10+3, 1e3 OE, 1E3 are all equivalent.) Negative exponents are supported by REXX as well.) Even though they may look to you like numbers, to REXX, constant symbols are still character strings. So, while constant symbols may start with a number or period, any alphabetical character (i.e., a-z, A-Z) may follow, such as 9a9. Note that for REXX interpreters, including OS/2, the default is 9 significant digits for numeric symbols. This can be modified by the DIGITS function.

- *Simple symbols* may only start with alphabetical characters, question marks, exclamation points, and underscores. They may be modified during the processing of the procedure. In other words, symbols create/modify a variable and give it a new value, in REXX terminology — an expression, and, place that value somewhere in the computer's memory. Because a REXX symbol always has the default value of its name (actual or derived) in uppercase, assignment statements to initialize are not always necessary. Examples of valid symbol names include abc, ABC, A12, ?BC, !BC, and _BC.

Compound Symbols and Stems: One of the more powerful features of REXX is compound symbols. They can be thought of as two or more simple symbols concatenated together by periods. These simple symbols can be assigned a value (character, string, or numeric) before being used in a compound symbol name (i.e., y=27; t.y=18 — translates to t.27 has a value of 18). Here are the typical components of a compound symbol:

Components of a Compound Symbol

```
a.1

⇕ ⇕

1 2

Key
1= stem (a. Period separates symbols)
2 = 1 (tail)
```

The **stem**, first simple symbol name and period, is the identifier for the entire "array." It is also a symbol type in its own right. Like simple symbols, a lowercase name is converted by the REXX interpreter to uppercase. The **tail**, remainder of the compound symbol name, identifies the unique "element" in the array. It may be composed of either unsigned constant symbols, simple symbols, or null values. The following are some traps/misconceptions to avoid:

- Thinking that the tail is an indicator of the size of the array or the position of the element in the array. Alphabetical tails (such as a.bob) are valid.

- Thinking that you can perform array (incremental count) operations on a compound symbol with a name containing two consecutive numbers separated by periods, such as a.1.1. Note that many of the compound arrays mentioned in Chapters 4-6 depend on this feature. However, only up to the first period is required by Cowlishaw.

- Thinking that the values of simple and compound symbols used in a internal function or subroutine are local and not "known" by the main procedure. The opposite is true. Use the PROCEDURE EXPOSE to control if a simple or compound symbol is local to an internal subprocedure/function or global to the entire procedure. See the section on subprocedures and functions for an example of this.
- Not realizing that the 0 element of the "array" is reserved for many REXX applications to contain the number of elements in the array. This convention will also be included in the forthcoming REXX standard.

Here are some examples of compound symbol operations:

Assign an initial/new value to the stem

```
a. = 10 /* Assigns 10 to all compound symbols with the a. stem. */
        /* Overwrites any existing values. */
```

Assigning values to a compound symbol "array"

```
        /* For all REXX versions */
val = 0
do loop_cntr = 1 to 10
        a.loop_cntr = val + 10 /* a.1 = 10, a.2 = 20...*/
        val = val+10
end

        /* For REXX 4.00 interpreters (like OS/2) and compilers */
val = 0
do loop_cntr = 1 to 10
        ret = value('a.'loop_cntr,(val + 10)) /* a.1 = 10, a.2 = 20...*/
        val = val+10
end
```

Retrieving values from an array

```
do loop_cntr = 1 to 10
        say a.loop_cntr/* OR for REXX 4.00 – say value('a.'loop_cntr) */
end
```

Uninitializing compound symbols

```
drop a. b.6             /* uninitializes stem and compound symbol "element" */
      OR
drop_list = 'a. b.6'    /* REXX 4.00 only. First create a drop (or indirect) list */
drop(drop_list)         /* Then drop (uninitialize) the symbols specified by the */
                        /* drop list */
```

Operators: Operators are discussed in the following section named "Operators."

Expressions

Expressions are sets of data that an explicit arithmetic, string, Boolean, or relational operation(s) are to be performed on. One or more expressions may be found in a REXX clause. Expressions are comprised of one or a series of **terms** ("the data") and usually one or more **operators** ("how to manipulate the data"). The remainder of this section will look at valid term types, while the next section looks at REXX operators and operator processing.

Terms are comprised of the following:

- Tokens
  - Numeric (constant) symbols
  - Simple and Compound Symbols
  - Hex and Binary Strings
  - Literal strings (i.e. characters in single or double quotes)
  - Functions such as time('e') to get the elapsed time. 'e' is the expression (literal string)
  - Null strings
- Special characters
  - Parentheses to specify the user-desired order of processing the expression components. (The default order is left to right.) Expression components in parentheses are called subexpressions.
  - Comma to separate parameters in functions and to note that a line is being continued.

Operators

REXX includes a wealth of operators that can be used in expressions. This section reviews the major REXX operators and their precedence. The following shows the four types of operators (mathematical, string concatenation, Boolean, and relational operators) and how they appear under OS/2. See the previous section to learn what are the valid types of terms.

Mathematical Operators	Note: Prefix operators deal with only one term while other operators deal with multiple terms + (Add), - (Subtract), * (Multiply), /(Divide), %(Returns integer part of division), // (Returns positive or negative remainder), ** (Exponential), Prefix - (Negate the number), Prefix + (Positive number [keep as is])
String Concatenation	*Blank between two strings* — blank is retained after evaluation. *No blank between strings or* || — blank is not retained after evaluation
Boolean Operators	Note: Use these operators with character strings (terms) that have an initial or derived value of 1(true) or 0 (false). The result after processing is also 1 or 0. & (AND) — Returns 1 if both terms are true. | (IOR — Inclusive OR) — Returns 1 if at least one term is true. && (XOR — Exclusive OR) — Returns 1 if only one term is true. “ or \ (latter for OS/2 and ANSI REXX) A prefix operator (NOT) that returns the Boolean value opposite what the was the term’s initial or derived Boolean value. (i.e. A result of 1 if initially 0. A result of 0 if initially 1.)

Trap: The NOT sign **MAY NOT BE PORTABLE** to REXX interpreters on other operating systems. The ¬ is also used on some REXX interpreters.

Relational Operators

Note: Similar to Boolean operators, all relational operators result in 1 (true) or 0 (false). Note that character equivalents (such as EQ for =) are not supported in the REXX language.

= (tests if two terms are equal),

\= OR “= (tests if two terms are not equal)
Note: ><, <>, and ¬ = are equivalents on some REXX interpreters.
> (left term is greater than the right term)

< (left term is less than right term)

> = (left term is greater than or equal to the right term)

< = (left term is less than or equal to right term)

Note: The following are called strict relational operators. That is because they compare strings (They are not valid for all “data types.”) character or character for an exact match or not.

== (True if an exact match)

\ == or “== (True if not an exact match)

The REXX interpreter scans an expression from left to right unless it contains subexpressions, a set of terms and operators that are enclosed in a set of parentheses. The subexpression is evaluated first. So, in most cases, it is probably not necessary to know the precedence of REXX operators. However, when debugging why an expression produced an unexpected result, it may be helpful to review the following precedence table:

Table 2-5

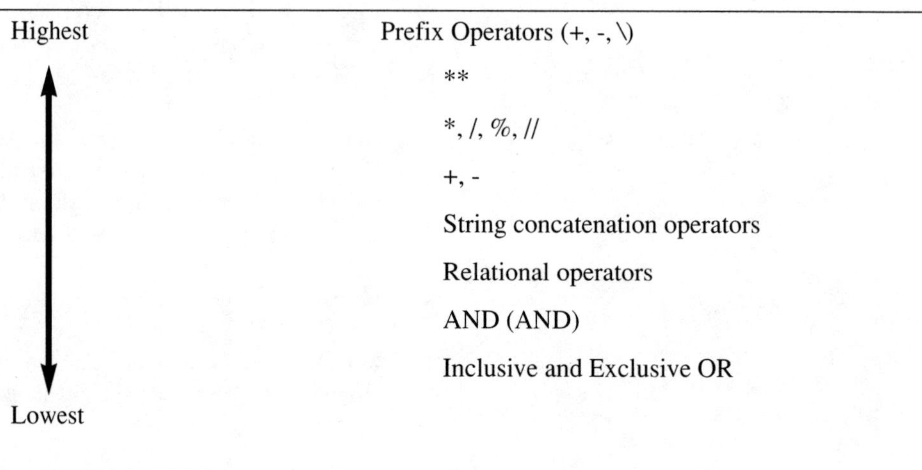

Highest	Prefix Operators (+, -, \)
↑	**
	*, /, %, //
	+, -
	String concatenation operators
	Relational operators
	AND (AND)
↓	Inclusive and Exclusive OR
Lowest	

Flow Control Operations

Note: Before looking at this section, it may be helpful to review the previous section on REXX operators.

Four of the major types of flow control structures/keywords are discussed below:

- conditional flow control,
- loop testing,
- flow control "action" instructions, and
- exit and return code handling.

Another type of flow control statement, exception handling is discussed in its own section near the end of the book.

Conditional Flow Control: Conditional flow control structures, namely IF and SELECT, test to see if one or more conditions are true. Once the condition is met, then one or more actions are performed. Unless enclosed in some kind of a DO loop, conditional flow control structures are only processed once.

Table 2.6 are some of the more popular forms of the IF statement: Note that there are many variants not shown. This includes having condition[1] being multiple conditions joined together by AND/OR, a null THEN (no action), nested THENs, and a null else (ELSE NOP)

Table 2-6 Conditional Flow Control Structures

Format	Syntax	Example
1 condition	IF condition1 THEN action1	IF age > 25 THEN say 'hi'
1 condition, multiple actions	IF condition1 THEN DO action1 action2 END	IF age> 25 THEN DO say 'age = ' AGE say 'To be 18 again' END
2 conditions (standard)	IF condition1 THEN action1 ELSE say 'F'	IF sex = 'M' THEN SAY 'M' ELSE action2
2 conditions, multiple actions	IF condition1 THEN DO action1 action2 END ELSE DO action3 action4 END	IF menuchoice = 1 THEN DO function1(someparms) exit 1 END ELSE DO function2 (someparms) exit 2 END
3 conditions, multiple actions	IF condition1 THEN DO action1 action2 END ELSE IF condition2 THEN DO action3 action4 END ELSE IF condition3 THEN DO action5 action6 END	IF menuchoice = 1 THEN DO function1(someparms) exit 1 END ELSE IF menuchoice = 2, THEN DO function2(someparms) exit 2 END ELSE IF menuchoice = 3, THEN DO function3(someparms) exit3 END

Table 2-7 are the more popular forms of the SELECT statement:

Table 2-7 Select Statements

Format	Syntax	Example
3 conditions, 1 action	SELECT WHEN condition1 THEN action1 WHEN condition2 THEN action2 OTHERWISE action3 END	SELECT WHEN AGE>=25 THEN AGE_D ="Young at heart" WHEN AGE<25 THEN AGE_D = "Young" OTHERWISE AGE_D = '?' END
3 conditions 2 actions	SELECT WHEN condition1 THEN DO action1 END WHEN condition2 THEN DO action2 OTHERWISE action3 END	SELECT WHEN AGE>=25 THEN DO AGE_D = "Young at heart" say AGE_D END WHEN AGE<25 THEN DO AGE_D = "Young" say AGE_D END OTHERWISE AGE_D = '?' END

Some additional tips on SELECT structures:

- THE OTHERWISE case does not need a DO-END structure for multiple actions.
- SELECTs can be as sophisticated as desired, but not necessarily admired!

This includes nesting SELECTS, using IF-THEN-ELSE, and all forms of the DO instruction.

Loop Testing: REXX has more formats of the DO structure than any other programming structure, as well as being combined with conditional flow control structures such as IF-THEN-ELSE and SELECT. In Table 2-8 are some of the more popular formats: Note that DO-TO-BY-FOR-UNTIL, DO-TO-BY-FOR-WHILE and the ultimate DO structure of DO-TO-BY-FOR-WHILE-UNTIL are not shown. FOR indicates how many times to loop through a DO loop (like the simplier DO expression shown. Also note that TO and BY values can include negative or decimal numbers.

Table 2-8 DO Structures

Format	Syntax	Example
DO-FOREVER-END DO-FOREVER-WHILE-END DO-FOREVER-UNTIL-END	DO FOREVER IF condition1 THEN LEAVE END OR DO FOREVER WHILE \= condition1 END OR DO FOREVER UNTIL condition1 END	DO FOREVER IF ANSWER="EXIT" THEN LEAVE END DO FOREVER WHILE ANSWER \= "EXIT" END DO FOREVER, UNTIL ANSWER = "EXIT" END
DO expression-END	DO expression END (expression has an actual or derived value of a whole number.)	DO 6 say 'processed 6 times' END
DO-TO-END	DO sym = min TO max END sym = counter symbol min = minimum counter value max = maximum counter value	DO X = 1 TO 6 SAY X /* Writes 1-6*/ END
DO-TO-BY-END	DO sym = min TO max BY inc END sym = counter symbol min = minimum counter value max = maximum counter value inc = increment (default of 1)	DO X = 1 TO 6 BY 2 SAY X /* Writes 1,3,5 */ END
DO-TO-BY-FOR-END	DO sym = min TO max BY inc FOR *cnt* END sym = counter symbol min = minimum counter value max = maximum counter value inc = increment (default of 1) cnt = number of times to process loop	DO X=1 TO 6 BY 2 FOR 2 SAY X /* Writes 1,3*/ /* Loops twice */ END

Table 2-8 Continued

Format	Syntax	Example
DO-TO-BY-WHILE	DO sym = min TO max BY inc WHILE condition END sym = counter symbol min = minimum counter value max = maximum counter value inc = increment (default of 1)	DO X=1 TO 6 BY 2, WHILE AGE = 25 SAY X /* Writes 1,3,5 if age is 25 */ END
DO-TO-BY-WHILE	DO sym = min TO max BY inc BY condition END sym = counter symbol min = minimum counter value max = maximum counter value inc = increment (default of 1)	DO X= 1 TO 6 BY 2, UNTIL AGE = 25 SAY X /* Writes 1,3,5 if age not 25 */ END

Flow Control Action Instructions: There are some addition keywords that are useful in the "action" or THEN part of the flow control statement. These are:

Table 2-9 Flow Control Action Instructions

Keyword	What it does
CALL *program parameters*	1. Invokes a general or exception handling subroutine.
Where program is a general or exception-handling subroutine. Where parameters are one or more parameters to be passed to the subroutine.	2. If the subroutine is completed successfully, then the program returns to the CALL instruction that invoked it. An optional result value may also be passed back from the subroutine. (Note: For more information, read the sections on "Exception Handling" and "Function/Subprocedures" later in this chapter.)
ITERATE (Use only in a DO structure)	1. Stops processing the remaining statements in the "current loop" of a DO-END structure.
	2. Increments/decrements any DO "counter" symbols.

Table 2-9 Continued

Keyword	What it does
	3. Returns to the "top" of the same DO-END structure and processes the next iteration or "loop."
LEAVE (Use only in a DO structure)	1. Stops processing the remaining statements in the "current loop" of a DO-END structure
	2. Processes the next instruction following the DO-END structure.
NOP	1. Performs no action.
	2. Continues to next statement in the flow-control structure.
SIGNAL *label_name*	1. Exits flow control structure and goes to signal (error handling) routine.
Where label_name is the label locating the start of the signal function	(Note: For more information, read the section on "Exception Handling" later in this chapter.)

Exit and Return Code Handling: The following summarizes the REXX's exit and return handling capabilities:

EXIT expression Expression is any valid REXX expression (such as numeric or character strings). Note: If uncertain what constitutes an expression, then review the earlier section on expressions.	Ends a procedure or function/subroutine. A specified or calculated return value (such as the value of the special variable RC [which is the result of the last value processed]) may also be specified

RETURN *expression* Expression is any valid REXX expression (such as numeric or character strings)	1. Returns from a function or subprogram to the main "part" of the PROCEDURE. An optional return value may also be specified.
Note: If uncertain what constitutes an expression, then review the earlier section on expressions.	Note: For more information, read the section on "Functions/Subprocedures" later in the chapter.

INPUT/OUTPUT OPERATIONS

REXX is not just a command language that deals with numbers and character strings. It provides the means to interface with a computer's screen, keyboard, command line, or files. The following sections tell you how to do just that.

Screen Operations

The most common way in REXX to write to the default output stream is to use the SAY instruction. In chapters 4-6, some non-standard full-screen extensions are discussed.

SAY for prompting input:

```
say "What is the operating system of this computer?"
pull os /* get value (in uppercase) */

                                SAY for menus
say '##############################################'
say '# Please select (1) of the following:        #'
say '# 1. Time card application                   #'
say '# 2. Project timeline application            #'
say '##############################################'
pull menu_choice /* get value */
```

SAY combining symbol and strings

```
say 'x=' x 'y=' y
/* Displayed x= 26 y= zoo */
```

Here are some formats of SAY:

Keyboard Operations

The PULL, really *PARSE UPPER PULL*, is a common way to capture input while a REXX procedure is being processed. How to capture input from the command line is discussed in the following section. Chapters 4-6 show additional ways to capture input. Here are some tips about the PULL instruction:

- This command converts all text to upper case, use PARSE PULL to capture mixed case input.
- A typical format is PULL *symbol¹ symbol²... symbolⁿ*. Symbol¹ will contain the input value from the first character up to the first blank. If specified, Symbol² will contain the input value from one character past the first blank until the end of the input value (if symbol³ is not specified) or up to the third blank in the input value (if symbol³ is specified.) For example:

```
Say 'What is your first and last names? (No middle name)'
pull first last
/* So first could be JIM [up to first blank] and last */
/* could be HALL [one past second blank to end of input string */
```

- An alternative form is PULL template. The values of template are discussed in the next section.

Capturing Command Line Values (An Overview of REXX Parsing Capabilities)

There are two major ways to capture user input. One way, capturing input while a REXX procedure is processing, was discussed in the last section. In the following section, we will discuss the other approach of capturing input from the command line values that are passed to the REXX procedure on invocation.

Entered from the command line:

```
REXX procl Spring is here
              ⇕     ⇕  ⇕
      arg     a     b  c (parsing by blanks)
```

Note: REXX may be a command to invoke the REXX interpreter, procl the name of a procedure and *Spring* is here the command line input parameters.

The following example shows the relationship between the command line and what ARG captures:

The remainder of the section will include an explanation of a major strength of REXX — its **parsing** capabilities. That is the ability to break up a string into two or more specified substrings. Note that any of the following parsing capabilities can be used by the ARG, PARSE, and the PULL instructions (see the previous section).

The parsing **template** provides the REXX interpreter with a set of directions on *how to parse a string* entered on the command line and *which symbols* will store the resulting substrings. String parsing methods include parsing by blanks (usually for words), parsing by character or substrings (for strings and substrings) and character position (when the string to be parsed has a variable length). The following are examples of various parsing templates:

By Blanks

```
arg a b c
        /* If THE NEXT GENERATION was the string entered on the command */
        /* line when the procedure was invoked, then a has a value of THE */
        /* b a value of NEXT and c of GENERATION. Leading and trailing */
        /* blanks are removed. */
```

By Character (Not from Symbol)

```
arg hours ':' minutes ':' seconds
        /* If 12:10:01 was entered on the command line when the procedure */
        /* was invoked, then hours has a value of 12, minutes has a */
        /* value of 10 and seconds has a value of 01. */
```

By Character (from Symbol)

```
colon = ':'
arg hours (colon) minutes (colon) seconds
        /* Same result as the previous example. Character delimiter of : */
        /* (colon) assigned to a symbol named colon. Put the symbol */
        /* name in parentheses. */
```

By Absolute (No + or -) Column Position

```
arg first 4 second =8 third
        /* If 099-55-5555 was the string entered on the command line when */
        /* the procedure was invoked [such as a social security number]. Then */
        /* symbol first would have a value of 099, second of -55 - and third of */
        /* 5555.. The equals sign is another way to denote absolute */
        /* column position. */
```

By Relative (+ or -) Column Position

```
arg first 4 second +4 third
        /* Same as last example. +4 means 4 from the last column */
        /* specified. In this example, that is the same as an absolute column */
        /* position of 8 */
```

By Absolute or Relative Column Position — Use of Symbol

```
absolute1 = 4; relative1 = 4
arg first =(absolute1) second +(relative1) third
        /* Same as last example. Symbol name in parentheses may be */
        /* prefixed by an equals (absolute) or plus/minus (relative) sign */
        /* denoting absolute or relative column position. */
```

The following are some tips and traps when parsing REXX command line strings:

- *If there are more symbols than command-line values*, then the extra symbols are assigned a null value. If the user input doesn't match the parsing pattern/template, then the command line string is assigned to the symbols left of the pattern. All other symbols in the template have null values. If there are more substrings than symbols, then REXX assigns the remainder of the string to the last symbol.
- ARG is an alias for PARSE *UPPER ARG* which converts all input to uppercase. Using PARSE ARG will retain mixed and lowercase. Leading blanks are dropped for both PARSE ARG and PARSE UPPER ARGS.
- A period can be used to create a "dummy" or place holder symbol. An example of this is retrieving the third word in a command line by bypassing the first two words

```
arg.. c
        /* First two words are ignored. Third word is assigned the symbol c */
```

- A period at the end of a parsing template acts a "garbage collector" and eliminates capturing additional input.

```
arg. b.
        /* Captures only the second word. The last period excludes any */
        /* additional input. */
```

- ARG A B C is **not** the same thing as ARG A,B,C. The first instruction parses one string into three symbols. The second parses three strings.

However, they can be combined together.

```
arg A B, C, D
/* First string is split between A and B, the remaining two strings */
/* are assigned to C and D */
```

- Use the ARG (*argument_number,flag*) built-in function to determine if an argument was passed from the command line or a function/subprocedure. Using the optional *flag* argument — E for exists or O for omitted — argument not present. (Returns 1 if flag is true, 0 if false)

File Operations

There are two major approaches that current REXX interpreters/compilers use to process files.

- Using the CMS-based **EXECIO** command to read, write, and update *records.* AmigaDOS, CMS, MS-DOS (Kilowatt and Quercus), OS/2 (Quercus), and TSO and all support this command with varying syntax.
- Using Cowlishaw's file I/O model (1990a, pp 139-145) that emphasizes reading/writing lines or characters from a named *stream* of data such as from a modem or a file, into REXX symbols. Two types of streams are supported in REXX: *persistent streams*, such as a file, which allow resetting the read/write pointer position, and *transient streams*, such as a pipe or standard output, usually your terminal, which allows sequential reads/writes but not resetting the pointer position. This approach is also part of the SAA Procedure Language Specification. It is supported by AmigaDOS (with slightly different commands), MS-DOS (both interpreters), OS/2 (IBM and Quercus), UNIX (Uni-REXX), and the forthcoming ANSI REXX standard. The remainder of this section will focus on this approach.

The following lists the standard REXX "built-in" functions used to support this approach: (Syntax is for IBM OS/2 unless otherwise stated.) The input/output area is one area that the forthcoming REXX standard will be enhancing. This tentatively includes: GivenCharin(stream_name,stream_function) with stream_function being either CHARIN, LINEIN, or STREAM. GivenCharin will set the stream's condition. It will return these compound symbols: 1-2) CharPosition.stream_name and LinePosition.stream_name with stream_name the name of the stream specified by the GivenCharin function. This represents the position in the specified stream (0 — not used, 1 — start of stream). 3)

ThisCharacter.stream_name is the next character to be read from the stream stream_names. A null string is a valid value. And 4) This Exception.stream_name will be the condition of the stream stream_name.

Values include READY (able to return a character), NOTREADY (unable to return a character due to being at the end of a stream), ERROR (unable to return a character), and SYNTAX (invalid stream operation such as an invalid starting position or length).

Other changes are planned as well for both the forthcoming and future versions of the REXX standard.

CHARS

Function: Returns the number of characters still in the input stream (including end-of-clause delimiters)

Syntax: CHARS(*stream_name*)

Stream_name is an optional argument and is the name of the queried stream. For IBM OS/2, STDIN: (standard input stream usually the keyboard) is the default.

Example: CHARS(a.txt) Returns 1 or >1 if the input stream is not empty.

Returned Values: 0 — No characters still in the input stream. (The NOTREADY condition.)

1 — One or more characters are left in the input stream. In some cases (i.e., For both IBM OS/2 REXX and Quercus's OS/2 Personal REXX, OS/2 device drivers [like LPT1:] and the STDIN: stream), an exact number of characters cannot be obtained, so 1 is used to indicate a full or partially full input stream.

>1 — (if supported such as Quercus OS/2 REXX) the actual number of characters left in the input stream.

CHARIN

Function: Positions the read "pointer" in the input stream and reads a specified number of characters (including end-of-clause delimiters).

Syntax: CHARIN(*stream_name, stream_start_position, length_of_read*)

Stream_name is an optional argument and is the name of the stream to read. For IBM OS/2, STDIN: (standard input stream, usually the keyboard) is the default.

Stream_start_position will override the default "pointer" position (which is the current read position) with an explicit position (a positive whole number). A difference worth mentioning between IBM OS/2 REXX and Quercus OS/2 REXX. IBM uses the same "pointer" position for both read and write operations. However, Quercus maintains different "pointers" for tracking read and write positions — as suggested by Cowlishaw(1990,140). Be aware of this when porting OS/2 REXX code to different operating systems!

Length_of_read will override the default of one character being read from the input stream with a specified number of characters. (Expressed as a positive whole number.)

Note: A length of 0 is useful in repositioning the read "pointer" position to the stream_start_position value. It also reads no characters and returns a length of 0.

Example: CHARIN(,,4) Could return ABCD from keyboard (STDIN stream)
Returned Values: The character(s) found at the specified location in the input stream.

CHAROUT

Function: Positions the write "pointer" in the output stream and writes a specified number of characters (including end-of-clause delimiters).

Syntax: CHAROUT(*stream_name,"output_string", stream_start_position*)

Stream_name is an optional argument and is the name of the stream to read. For IBM OS/2, STDOUT: (standard output stream, usually the monitor screen) is the default.

"output_string" is an optional argument and is a valid REXX string (including null strings) that are to be written to the specified or default output stream.

Stream_start_position will override the default "pointer" position (which is the current write position) with an explicit position (a positive whole number). A value of one points to the beginning of the stream.

Note: Specifying no *stream_start_position* and no *"output_string"* is useful in repositioning the write "pointer" position to the end of the stream. It also writes no characters and returns a value of zero.

Example: *CHAROUT(,"Happy Holidays",)* Writes "Happy Holidays" to the standard output stream starting in the default write position. For this case only, CHAROUT is the equivalent of the SAY instruction. Returns 0 (no characters left to write to the output queue.)
Returned Values: The number of remaining characters (including end-of-clause delimiters) that have not been written to the output stream after the CHAROUT instruction is processed. 0 is usually returned because most CHAROUT operations usually write all specified characters to the output stream.

LINES

Function: Returns the number of lines still in the input stream (including end-of-clause delimiters). Useful in debugging CHARIN/LINEIN operations.

Syntax: LINES(*stream_name*)

Stream_name is an optional argument and is the name of the stream to read. For IBM OS/2, STDIN: (standard input stream, usually the keyboard) is the default.

Example: LINES() — Returns 0 (no lines remain in the input stream) for the standard input stream.

Return Values: 0 — No lincs remain in the input stream or the read "pointer" position is at the end of the stream.

1 — One or more lines remain in the input stream. If an OS/2 device is specified as the stream name, such as LPT1:, then 1 is always returned.

LINEIN

Function: Positions the read "pointer" in the input stream and reads a specified number of lines, including end-of-clause delimiters. For Quercus REXX, the line length cannot be any greater than a thousand characters.

Syntax: LINEIN(*stream_name, line_number, line_count*)

Stream_name is an optional argument and is the name of the stream to read. For IBM OS/2, STDIN: (standard input stream, usually the keyboard) is the default. Stream_name is usually a file name or a named pipe (created by a non-REXX program.)

Line_number is an optional argument that overrides the current read line "pointer" value, usually the current read position. For both the IBM and Quercus REXX interpreters, the only valid value is 1 (start of the stream) or no value (designated by a comma). REXX interpreters on other platforms may have *line_number* values of greater than 1.

Line_count is either 0 (Reads no lines) or 1, reads in one line at the current read "pointer" position.

Example: *LINEIN('abc.txt',1)* Reads one line at the current read "pointer" position from the file (stream) named abc.txt.

Return Values: The line read OR a null string (no line read).

LINEOUT

Syntax: *LINEOUT(stream_name," output_string" , line_number)*

Stream_name is an optional argument and is the name of the stream to read. For IBM OS/2, STDOUT: (standard output stream, usually the monitor screen) is the default. *Stream_name* is usually a file name or a named pipe (created by a non-REXX program.)

"output_string" is an optional argument and is a valid REXX string (including null strings) that are to be written to the specified or default output stream.

line_number will override the default "pointer" position (which is the current write position) with an explicit position (a positive whole number). For both IBM and Quercus REXX, the only valid value is 1, which points to the beginning of the stream.

Example: LINEOUT('a.txt','Now What?') — Writes to a.txt at the current "write" pointer position the string "Now what?"

Here are some additional tips while performing file operations:

- You can also use the STREAM function to determine the result of the last CHARIN, CHAROUT, LINEIN, OR LINEOUT operation. This is discussed in Chapter 3.
- It is common practice to place LINEIN, LINEOUT, CHARIN, and CHAROUT in a subroutine, invoked by the CALL instruction. Any return codes or values are then placed in the special (system) variable of RESULT.

```
call charout "a.txt", "aline", 1    /* Write out to a.txt the string "aline" starting */
                                    /* in column 1.*/
```

- It is also common practice to assign a file name to a symbol and use that symbol in the above built-in functions. If the file name is changed, then you only then have to change one line instead of many.

```
file_name = "a.txt"
charout(file_name,"aline",1)
```

- There are several other ways to perform the same operations: PARSE PULL (or PULL) can also capture character or line input from the standard input stream, and PARSE LINEIN or PARSE VALUE LINEIN. The advantage of using over LINEIN is the capability of additional line parsing using the various methods discussed in the previous section on "Capturing Command Line Values."

```
PARSE VALUE LINEIN('a.txt') with first_name last_name
/* Parses the line in a.txt into two variables */
```

- It is good practice to explicitly close a stream (such as a file) when you are done using it. Failure to do this may lead to unpredictable results the next time the file is used. Also use the complete file specification including drive and subdirectories — you may not be always running the procedure from the same directory.
- Compound symbols are very useful in performing file operations

```
file1 = 'c:\a.txt' /* Captures all the lines in a file to a compound symbol */
cnt = 1
do while lines(file1) > 0 /* While not at end-of-file */
        a.cnt = linein(file1)
        cnt = cnt + 1
end
```

"TYPE" OPERATIONS

Symbolic operations (Using INTERPRET, SYMBOL, and VALUE): The previous section discussed "Tokens" in depth simple and compound symbol operations. This section will discuss some additional symbolic operations that can be performed using the VALUE and SYMBOL functions and the INTERPRET instruction.

Using REXX to generate REXX clauses

Approach #1 The INTERPRET instruction is the "older" approach to use. It is discouraged for portability because it is not available for REXX compilers, such as CMS. INTERPRET *expression*, with *expression* being any valid REXX expression up to 64,000 characters, will symbolically create and then execute zero or more REXX clauses at runtime provided that the following rules are complied with:

- Only a **complete** flow control structures are valid (i.e., A DO with an END). Only then will a LEAVE or ITERATE instruction be acceptable within a DO flow control structure.
- Labels should not be part of an *expression* because they will be ignored.
- A PROCEDURE instruction should not be the first clause of *expression*, since the variable scope is ambiguous.

- A SIGNAL call within *expression* will cause a jump to the SIGNAL label and then immediate termination of the INTERPRET statement. However, a subroutine or function will continue to process the INTERPRET *expression* after it has completed.
- Semicolons are only required for *expressions* with multiple clauses. Do note that the REXXTRY REXX procedure that is part of OS/2 is nothing more than a glorified INTERPRET statement. It allows you to try REXX statements without fear of "crashing."

  Using the TRACE function or instruction will help in debugging INTERPRET *expression* problems.

Approach # 2. The "newer" approach, available in REXX 4.00 is using the **VALUE** built-in function. Unlike INTERPRET, it is available on all REXX interpreters/compilers that support REXX 4.00. It can be used to dynamically create symbols (including using nested symbol names). Use INTERPRET only if multiple clauses needed to be created.

```
aa = 1
bb = value('aa')        /* Returns 1 [the value of aa]. */
say value(aa,2)         /* Returns old value of aa */
say bb                  /* Returns 2 */
```

Testing a Symbol: The SYMBOL built-in function can test what type of symbol an expression is and see if a symbol name is invalid. It returns one of three values: BAD (invalid REXX symbol name), VAR (variable — initialized symbol), and LIT (Literal string — all other symbols).

```
Symbol examples
K=88 /* Only symbol defined*/
say symbol('K')        /* Returns VAR - has a value */
say symbol('Q')        /* Returns LIT - uninitialized symbol */
say symbol('&88')      /* Returns BAD - invalid symbol */
```

Numeric Operations: REXX's numeric capabilities are a major strength. Coffee's (1992) recent article on a computer's computational capability concludes by mentioning the infinite precision approach used by REXX as an approach that generates accurate results in a reasonable amount of time. Here is a summary of numeric operations available for REXX:

- In REXX, numbers are really character strings that "resemble numbers." Thus SAY 2+2 and SAY '2' +2 yields the same result!

- In additional to being expressed as positive/negative whole numbers (e.g. 1) or integers (e.g. 2.16), REXX numbers can be expressed also in exponential format (1e+3 or 1000).
- REXX rounding is dependent on the NUMERIC DIGITS/FUZZ settings. This will affect any pertinent built-in function values. Normal rounding rules are followed.
- Useful instructions/functions include:

Table 2-10

Name	Purpose	Example
ABS(number)	A built-in function that returns the absolute value of a REXX *number*.	SAY ABS(-1) /* Returns 1 */
DIGITS()	A built-in function that returns the current value of NUMERIC DIGITS.	SAY DIGITS() /* Returns 11 so the */ /* default of 9 was */ /* overridden */
FORMAT(*number*, *integer*, *decimal*)	A built-in function that rounds a number. If the *integer* or *decimal* argument is supplied, then the *number* is reformatted	SAY FORMAT(5.5,3,3) /* Results in 5.550 */
FORM()	A built-in function that returns the current setting of NUMERIC FORM — either SCIENTIFIC (default) or ENGINEERING.	SAY FORM() /* Returns, ENGINEERING */
FUZZ()	A built-in function that returns the current value of NUMERIC FUZZ	SAY FUZZ() /* Returns 1 */
MAX(*number[s]*), MIN(*number[s]*)	A built-in function that returns the highest (if MAX) or lowest (if MIN) for one or more *numbers*	SAY MIN(-1,2,0,88) /* Returns -1 */

Table 2-10 Continued

Name	Purpose	Example
NUMERIC DIGITS *value* *Value* is a whole number. The value of NUMERIC FUZZ is always less than the value of NUMERIC DIGITS. If no *value* is specified, then the default (9) is used.	An instruction that sets the numeric precision for **ALL** REXX numeric operations. The default is 9. (more digits are rounded /truncated). The *value* selected may affect performance. See the DIGITS function earlier in this table.	NUMERIC DIGITS 3
NUMERIC FORM *format* *Format* is either SCIENTIFIC (default) or ENGINEERING. If no *format* is specified, then the default (SCIENTIFIC) is used.	An instruction that sets the numeric format for **all** REXX numeric operations. See the FORM function earlier in this table.	NUMERIC FORM, ENGINEERING
NUMERIC FUZZ value If no value is specified then the default of 0 is used.	An instruction that sets the "fuzz value." — this determines how precise REXX is during numeric comparisons. This number (always less than the DIGITS value) changes rounding operations so there are DIGITS() -FUZZ() significant digits. See the FUZZ function earlier in this table.	NUMERIC FUZZ 1
RANDOM(*low*, *high*, *seed*)	A built-in function that returns a random number within a range a numbers (if *low* or *high* is specified). An optional *seed* may also be specified.	SAY, RANDOM(0,4,11111) /* Returns 2 */
SIGN(*number*)	A built-in function that returns the sign of *number*. Returns -1 (number is negative), 0 (number is zero), 1 (number is positive)	SAY SIGN(-5) /* Returns -1 */

Table 2-10 Continued

Name	Purpose	Example
TRUNC(*number*,*digits*)	A built-in function that rounds a *number* and returns the integer part and the *digits* number of decimal digit.	SAY TRUNC(18.25,1) /* Returns 18.3 if */ /* DIGITS() =3. Else */ /* Returns 18.2 if */ /* DIGITS() = 9 */

- If additional built-in functions are required, then consider either EVX, RXMATH, or Quercus OS/2 REXX — all of which supports transcendental and algebraic functions. EVX and RXMATH are also copyrighted freeware that has been ported to many REXX platforms (such as OS/2) and are discussed in Appendix G.
- Note that rounding may take place before arguments for ABS, DATATYPE, MIN, MAX, SIGN, and TRUNC are evaluated. This may give different result for earlier REXX implementations than language version 4.00.
- Additional information on REXX mathematical rules can be found in Cowlishaw (1991).

String Operations

REXX excels over other command and programming languages in terms of its string handling capabilities. Here is a summary of the major features: REXX includes only 60 built-in functions with half dedicated to performing operations on substrings, words, and extensions. These include: (Not shown are COPIES (Returns an output string containing 1 or more copies of the input string), OVERLAY (Returns the input string replaced with a new string for part or all of the input string), REVERSE (Returns a reversed input string), SPACE (Returns the input string padded with 0 or more blanks between each word in the string),SUBWORD (Returns "partial words" within an input string), WORDINDEX (Returns location of word within input string), VERIFY (Returns if an input string is comprised of characters from another string). Check the OS/2 REXX help file on how to use these.)

Table 2-11 String Justification

Function Name	Purpose	Example
Note: Input_string is a string the built-in function will manipulate.		
CENTER(*input_string*, *length*, *pad_char*) Also called CENTRE	Produces: — left-justified (if LEFT) OR — right-justified (if RIGHT)	SAY CENTER("Wrong, Way",11,'+') /* Result:+Wrong Way+ */
LEFT(*input_string*, *length*, *pad_char*)	OR — centered (IF CENTER) output string of a specified length that may be padded: — with leading [if RIGHT] — trailing blanks[if LEFT] — leading/trailing blanks (if CENTER)	LEFT("Wrong Way", 12,'+') /* Result, Wrong Way+++ */
RIGHT(*input_string*, *length*, *pad_char*)	— OR some other character if *pad_char* is specified.	RIGHT("Wrong Way", 12,'+') /* Result: +++*Wrong Way* */
Length = The length of the output string		
Pad_char= If the output string is less than the required *length*, then pad using this character		

Table 2-12 String/Word Search

Function Name	Purpose	Example
POS(*search_string, input_string, location)*	Returns the location of the first (if POS) or last (if LASTPOS) occurrence of *search_string* in *input_string*.	SAY POS('OS/2', 'More OS/2 than OS/2') /* Result: Returns 6 */
LASTPOS(*search_string, input_string, location*)	A value of 0 means the search_string was not found.	LASTPOS('OS/2', 'More OS/2 than OS/2') /* Result: Returns 16 */
WORDPOS(*search_string, input_string, location*)	WORDPOS returns the word number of *search_string* within *input_string*.	WORDPOS('OS/2', 'More OS/2 than OS/2') /* Result: Returns 2 */
Search_string = REXX string to look for. *Input_string* = *String* to search. *Location* = *Position* to start searching from. Values range from 1 (string start) to the whole number representing the string end.		

Table 2-13 String/Word Length

Function Name	Purpose	Example
LENGTH(*input_string*) WORDLENGTH(*input_string, word*) Word = word in *Input_string* to get length	Returns the length of an *input_string* (if LENGTH) or a specified word in *input_string* (if WORDLENGTH)	SAY LENGTH('The The') /* Result: 7*/ SAY WORDLENGTH(, 'Tons of gifts',2) /* Result: 2 (length of *of*) */

Table 2-14 Delete Words or Characters

Function Name	Purpose	Example
DELSTR(*input_string, location, length)* DELWORD*(input_string, location, length)* *location* = start of string (DELSTR) or word (DELWORD) to delete *length* = how many characters to delete	Deletes part of *input_string* starting at location (which is either a word or character) for a length of length.	SAY DELSTR('I am, here',2,3) /* Result — I here */ SAY DELWORD('I am, here',3,4) /* Result — I am */
STRIP(*input_string, flag, strip_character*)	Trims blanks or the *strip_character* from the *input_string* according to the flag.	SAY STRIP(' rod ') /* Result: *rod* (no */ /* leading or trailing */ /* blanks) */

Table 2-14 Continued

Function Name	Purpose	Example
flag = character to trim: l/L (leading), t/T (trailing), or b/B (both — the default) *strip_character* = if not specified, then blanks are the character to eliminate. Otherwise, trim *strip_character* if it appears in input_string.		

Table 2-15 Verify/Compare Characters and Strings

Function Name	Purpose	Example
ABBREV(*input_string, search_string, length*) *Search_string* = String compared to *input_string*. *length* = *number* of characters to compare	Compares *search_string* to *input_string*. This returns 1 if the two strings match and optionally specify that search_string's *length* is not longer than input_string's [Null string always returns this.] Otherwise 0 is returned. This function is useful for validating user input where the user may enter either an abbreviated or full form of a string.	SAY ABBREV('Exit','E') /* Result — 1 (match) */
COMPARE(*input_string[1], input_string[2], pad_character)*	Compares *input_string[1]* to *input-string[2]*. Returns 0 (exact match), >0 (non-match: position of first character in *input_string[2]* not the same as *input_string[1]*).	SAY, COMPARE('oats','ox') /* Result — 2 (first., character in, input_string[2] not the, same as input_string[1]) */

Table 2-15 Continued

Function Name	Purpose	Example
	A *pad_character* (to override the default of blank) is used to pad characters necessary to make the input strings the same size when compared.	
DATATYPE (*input_string, flag)* *flag* = Type of data to check for: A (must be a-z/A-Z/0-9) B (must be 0/1) C (must be partial or full double-byte character string) D (must be full double-byte character string) Note: C and D can be found on SAA REXX implementations only. L (must be a-z) M (must be a-z/A-Z) N (must be 0-9) S (must be valid REXX symbol name. Cowlishaw specifies lowercase only. Quercus and IBM OS/2 REXX can be in any case)	Tests if *input_string* matches the "type" criteria of *flag*. If *flag* specified, returns 1 (if match), 0 (if no match). If flag is not specified, then returns NUM (must contain only 0-9, blanks, or decimals), or CHAR (all other strings that are not NUM)	SAY DATATYPE('88') /* Result NUM */ SAY DATATYPE('88',L) /* Result 0 (not a */ /* lowercase letter) */

Table 2-15 Continued

Function Name	Purpose	Example
W (must be whole number [no decimals])	Useful for user input validation.	
X (must be hexadecimal number)		

Table 2-16 Other Useful Functions

Function Name	Purpose	Example
WORDS(*input_string*)	Returns the total number of words in *input_string*. Words are separated by blanks. 0 is returned if no words are found.	SAY WORDS('See a') /* Result — 2 */
TRANSLATE(*input_string*, *conversion_list*, *character_list*) *Conversion_list* — list of corresponding characters to convert to.)	Compares characters in the *input string* to those in the *character list* and converts to the corresponding character in the *conversion list*.	SAY, TRANSLATE('lower') /* Result — LOWER */ SAY, TRANSLATE('ZBBC', 'UYGL', 'ZBCQ')
Character_list — list of characters to compare against.	(i.e,. the second character in the *character list* is converted to the second character in the *conversion_list*) Just the *input_string* alone returns the *input_string* in uppercase. Use this function to reverse/manipulate strings or change to uppercase/lowercase.	/* Result — UYYG */ /* (Z is converted to U */ /* B to Y, and C to G) */

Table 2-16 Continued

Function Name	Purpose	Example
INSERT(*insert_string, input_string, position*)	Inserts *insert_string* in *input_string* starting in *position.*	SAY INSERT('%','you',2) /* Result *yo%u* */

Tips

- Combine built-in functions to perform string operations:

```
if substr(var1,1,(length(var1)-4)) == 're'...
      /* Uses length to supply length for SUBSTR */
```

- See the section "Text Case Operations" later in this chapter on how to manipulate the case of text.

"Type" Conversions

Use the following table in determining which function to use to perform "type" conversions, when using two functions together, minor conversion differences may result:

Table 2-17

From → To ↓	Binary	Character	Decimal	Hexadecimal
Binary	———	X2B(C2X)	X2B(D2X)	X2B
Character	X2C(B2X) or D2C(C2X)	———	C2D	X2C
Decimal	X2D(B2X) or C2D(B2X)	C2D	———	X2D
Hexadecimal	B2X	D2X	C2X	———

Text Case Operations

Here are some tips when performing text case operations:

- ARGS and PULL and TRANSLATE (input_string only) will translate text to uppercase. Use PARSE ARG, PARSE PULL, and TRANSLATE (conversion_list in lowercase) to retain lower and mixed case of a string.
- Use DATATYPE with the L (Lower-case), U (Upper-case) and M (Mixed-case) to determine the case of an input_string.

Date/Time Operations

Tabel 2-18summarizes common date and time formats in REXX:

Table 2-18

Date Function	Purpose	Example
Date('B')	Number of days since the base date of 1/1/01. Replaces the Date('C') format that is still used by Quercus OS/2 REXX.	727634

Table 2-18 Continued

Date Function	Purpose	Example
Date('D')	Number of complete days so far the current year.	72
Date('E')	European date format (dd/mm/yy)	13/03/93
Date('L') **OS/2 only**	Uses the language (local) date format of dd Month yyyy	13 March 1993
Date('N') or DATE()	Uses the default date format of dd Month yyyy	13 March 1993 (maybe)
DATE('O')	Uses the format of yy/mm/dd.	93/03/13
DATE('S')	Uses the format of yyyymmdd. Good for date comparisons.	19930313
DATE('W')	Capitalized day of the week. Good for reports.	Saturday
Time('C')	Returns time in a 12 hour format of hh:mm:td (with td being am or pm)	9:44pm
Time('E')	Returns time elapsed from last Time('E') or Time('R'). (Time('R') resets the timer to 0.)	5.080000 (seconds, hundredths of seconds.) For OS/2, the returned value always has 4 trailing zeros. Also true for Time('L') — current time in the same format.
Time('H')	Returns the hour in a 24 hour format.	21
Time('N') or Time()	Returns the time in a 24 format of hh:mm:ss.	21:44:38 (maybe)

OTHER REXX CONCERNS

Function/Subprocedures: An easy way to extend the REXX language is by creating individualized **subprograms.** Subprograms are "modules" of REXX code that perform a series of tasks and return a result. They may reside in the same procedure that it is invoked (internal subprograms) from or in a different procedure (external subprograms). The following discusses the two different types of subprograms.

Functions

To process a function, two parts are needed:

- The **function definition**.
  - A *label* with the same name as the function marks the start of the function definition.
  - A *RETURN* instruction (passes a result to the "main" part of the procedure) *always* marks the end of the definition. A null value (RETURN '') is valid.
  - An *ARG* (translate arguments to upper case) or *PARSE ARG* (retain case) instruction is usually used to both set the number of expected arguments on invocation of the function and define the symbols to hold the values passed on function invocation.
  - Note that an internal user-defined function is always invoked before a built-in function of the same name. To override this order, place the function name in quotes. Then, the built-in function will be processed.
  - A function may use a PROCEDURE (hides symbols used in a subprogram from the 'main' procedure) or PROCEDURE EXPOSE. (Allows specified symbols to be available to the 'main' procedure. The local symbols are dropped after a RETURN instruction is invoked.) Note, the default is the symbols used in internal subprograms (functions and subroutines) are known by the "main" part of the procedure.
- The **function invocation**:
  - The function invocation can be part of any valid REXX expression.
  - They are invoked with the same format used by REXX built-in functions, that is a *function name* immediately followed by parentheses. Enclosed in the *parentheses* are zero to twenty REXX expressions (also called *arguments*) that are separated by commas.
  - After the function has completed processing, the result is returned to the function invocation line and simulates replacing the same. This result is usually assigned to a symbol.

– The special (system) variable SIGL will contain the line number in the "main" procedure which invoked the internal function.

Here is an example to show the major elements of an internal function:

Table 2-19 Major Elements of an Internal Function

Statement	Location	Comment
/* REXX*/	"Main" part of REXX procedure (start) --|	
q=10	| | |	/* Value used as */ /* argument in function */
other REXX clauses	| |	
b= addit(1,2+1,q)	Function | Invocation | with 3 | arguments |	/* Arguments — */ /* explicit (1) */ /* calculated, (2+1) */ /* and a symbol — */ /* Returns 14 */
say b	display | function | result	
exit	"Main" part | of the | procedure | (end) -- |	/* If not there, would */ /* process all functions */ /* without having been */ /* explicitly invoked */
addit:	Function definition (start) -- |	/* Label with function */ /* name */
procedure	| | |	/* Old a, b, and c are */ /* dropped. Unknown */ /* "main" procedure */
arg a,b,c	|	/* define symbol names */
return a+b+c	function | definition | (end) --|	/* Required */

Subroutines

Subroutines and functions have the following differences:

Table 2-20 Subroutine and Functions Differences

Area	Function	Subroutine
Invocation	As part of expression containing the function name.	A CALL instruction containing the subroutine name.
Arguments	Enclosed in parentheses immediately after the function name and separated by commas. Many operating systems have no more than 20.	Immediately follows the subroutine name and separated by commas. Most operating systems (including OS/2) allow no more than 20.
Result	Returned to the invocation statement. A RETURN instruction **must** be accompanied with a value and be part of the function.	Placed in the System (special) variable called RESULT. This contains the value of any expression in the RETURN instruction.
		A RETURN statement may be accompanied with a value and be part of the subroutine.

To process a subroutine, two parts are needed.

- The **subroutine definition**.
  - A *label* with the same name as the subroutine marks the start of the subroutine definition.
  - A *RETURN* instruction (passes a result to the "main" part of the exec) *usually* marks the end of the definition. A null value (RETURN '') is valid. If the RETURN instruction includes a REXX expression, then it is assigned to the special (system) variable named RESULT.

- An *ARG* (translate arguments to upper case) or *PARSE ARG* (retain case) instruction is usually used to set both the number of expected arguments on invocation of the subroutine and define the symbols to hold the values passed on subroutine invocation.

- A subprocedure may use a PROCEDURE (hides symbols used in a subprogram from the 'main' procedure) or PROCEDURE EXPOSE. (Allows specified symbols to be available to the 'main' procedure. The local symbols are dropped after a RETURN instruction is invoked.) *If you are not careful using these statements, you may have one of the following two unexpected results*: The symbol in a subprocedure is not known to the main procedure when it should be. Or, a symbol in a subprocedure is known to the main procedure when it shouldn't be.

Note, the default scope symbols used in internal subprograms (functions and subroutines) are known by the "main" part of the procedure. The opposite is true for symbols used in external procedures. **PROCEDURE must be the first instruction after the label marking the start of the function/subprocedure definition.**

- The **subprocedure invocation**:
  - They are invoked with the CALL keyword immediately followed zero or more REXX expressions (also called *arguments*) that are separated by commas. OS/2 allows a maximum of twenty arguments. It then invokes an internal or external subroutine.
  - After the subroutine has completed processing, any value passed with a RETURN instruction are assigned to the special (system) variable RESULT.
  - The special (system) variable SIGL will contain the line number in the "main" procedure which invoked the internal subroutine **only** if a PROCEDURE EXPOSE SIGL is included in the subroutine.
  - Do not confuse the REXX CALL instruction with the OS/2 CALL statement. The former invokes internal/external subprocedures while the latter invokes external batch (.CMD files) which may be REXX procedures. There is a subtle difference between IBM and Quercus REXX. IBM will only allow REXX procedures to be processed as operating system commands only if invoked by the OS/2 CALL statement. On the other hand, Quercus REXX will implicitly invoke REXX procedures as system commands.

Table 2-21

<table>
<tr><th>Statement</th><th>Location</th><th>Comment</th></tr>
<tr><td>/* REXX*/</td><td>“Main” part of REXX procedure</td><td></td></tr>
<tr><td></td><td>(start) -- |</td><td></td></tr>
<tr><td>q=10</td><td>|</td><td>/* Value used as */.</td></tr>
<tr><td></td><td>|</td><td>/* argument in function */</td></tr>
<tr><td></td><td>|</td><td></td></tr>
<tr><td>other REXX clauses</td><td>|</td><td></td></tr>
<tr><td></td><td>|</td><td></td></tr>
<tr><td>call addit 1,2+1,q</td><td>Subroutine |</td><td>/* Arguments — explicit */</td></tr>
<tr><td></td><td>Invocation |</td><td>/* (1), calculated, (2+1) */</td></tr>
<tr><td></td><td>with 3 |</td><td>/* and a symbol value */</td></tr>
<tr><td></td><td>arguments |</td><td></td></tr>
<tr><td>say RESULT</td><td>|</td><td>/* Returns 14 */</td></tr>
<tr><td>exit</td><td>“Main” part |</td><td>/* If not there, would */</td></tr>
<tr><td></td><td>of the |</td><td>/* process all */</td></tr>
<tr><td></td><td>procedure |</td><td>/* subroutines without */</td></tr>
<tr><td></td><td>(end) -- |</td><td>/* having been */</td></tr>
<tr><td></td><td></td><td>/* explicitly invoked */</td></tr>
<tr><td>addit:</td><td>Subroutine definition</td><td></td></tr>
<tr><td></td><td>(start) -- |</td><td>/* Label with subroutine */</td></tr>
<tr><td></td><td></td><td>/* name */</td></tr>
<tr><td></td><td>|</td><td></td></tr>
<tr><td>procedure</td><td>|</td><td>/* old a, b, and c */</td></tr>
<tr><td></td><td>|</td><td>/* dropped. Unknown to */</td></tr>
<tr><td></td><td>|</td><td>/* “main” procedure */</td></tr>
<tr><td>arg a,b,c</td><td>|</td><td>/* define symbol names */</td></tr>
<tr><td>return a+b+c</td><td>subprocedure |</td><td>/* Placed in RESULT */</td></tr>
<tr><td></td><td>definition |</td><td></td></tr>
<tr><td></td><td>(end) -- |</td><td></td></tr>
</table>

- In summary, the above example could be called one of two ways:

```
b = addit(1,2+1,q) /* As a function */
call addit 1,2+1,q /* As a subroutine */
```

Exception Handling

An important part of any command language is its ability to handle exceptions — both unexpected and expected errors from syntax, invalid expressions and much more. The rest of the section discuses this important topic.

Pre-REXX 4.00 specification: It is important to review what were the exception handling capabilities in REXX Language version 3.5 (Cowlishaw, 1985) as opposed to language version 4.00 (Cowlishaw, 1990a). Doing this will help you in porting REXX code to interpreters supporting the older language version and show how to enhance ported REXX procedures to take advantage of the latest features.

Signals: SIGNALS were the main means of providing exception handling. *This is not a GOTO and should not be used to break out of a SELECT or DO structure.* To process a signal, two parts were needed:

- **Signal routine definition**
  - A *label* with the same name as the SIGNAL routine marks the start of the SIGNAL routine definition.
  - The system (special) variable SIGL contains the number of the line that invoked the signal routine (i.e. a SIGNAL ON or SIGNAL VALUE instruction)
  - The SIGNAL routine may do any of the following:

    a. Set things as you found it.
       1) Close all files.
       2) Remove all temporary files.
       3) Reset appropriate environment variables.
       4) Purge the data stack.

    b. Display information to the user on what happened:

       1. Printing out the error may be helpful in debugging a problem

```
say 'The error was' errortext(rc)
```

2. Printing out the line and line number that invoked the SIGNAL routine:

```
say 'The error was on line' sigl 'which is' sourceline(sigl)
```

3. Print out the values of the procedure at the time. The user can give this to the exec's creator/maintainer for debugging.

```
say 'Date:'date() 'Time:'time()
      say 'a =' a 'b=' b /* and so forth */
```

4. The special (system) variable RC holds the non-zero return code for SIGNAL ON ERROR, FAILURE, and SYNTAX. Since the value of this variable is volatile (will be reassigned if the subroutine has an operating system or any command invoked through the ADDRESS instruction), it should be captured early in the signal routine. Note this problem will be less likely to happen to REXX interpreters/compilers complying with the forthcoming REXX standard. The 1996 Standard will likely include a new system (special) variable called RS which will be used instead to capture the result of processing of the ADDRESS instruction.

```
ERROR: /* Error signal subroutine */
      say 'Return Code = ' rc
```

- The termination of the procedure (with the EXIT expression instruction) or if possible, a return to the "main" part of the procedure with a RETURN expression instruction if possible, returns to the line in the "main procedure" after the one invoking the SIGNAL routine.

- **Invoking the signal routine**:
  - This is usually part of a flow control structure such as IF or SELECT.
  - Invoked by one of three ways:

    SIGNAL *label_name* — Invokes a signal with that label name. Useful (along with SIGNAL VALUE) to branch to another location within an procedure. [Not necessarily for error-handling.]

```
signal dizzy          /* goto the SIGNAL routine named dizzy. */
     dizzy:...        /* later in the same procedure — the signal routine */
```

SIGNAL *symbol* — Invokes a SIGNAL with that symbol name. SIGNAL *symbol* is useful when the label to be selected is to be determined at run time (such as selected one of several possible CALLs.) No return to the "main" procedure is possible.

```
name = 'dizzy'                /* default SIGNAL routine */
if age = 200 then do
    name = 'tizzy'            /* overrides default SIGNAL routine */
    signal value name         /* goes to the tizzy SIGNAL routine */
end
tizzy:                        /* Later in the procedure */
                              /* the tizzy SIGNAL routine */
```

SIGNAL ON *condition*. Invokes a SIGNAL routine if a particular exception condition takes place. *The SIGNAL routine has the same name as the condition.* Conditions include: ERROR (non-zero return codes), FAILURE (non-zero return codes), HALT (on pressing control (cntrl)-break), NOVALUE (uninitialized value), and SYNTAX (REXX syntax/symbolic substitution error).

- SIGNAL OFF disables error-handling on all conditions. SIGNAL OFF *condition* disables error-handing for the ERROR, FAILURE, HALT, NOVALUE or SYNTAX *condition.*
- SIGNAL on NOVALUE is useful when developing large, complex applications with many subroutines.
- If Ctrl and Break (and sometimes Enter) keys are pressed together, most REXX procedures will complete processing the current clause and then exit the procedure. This is only recommended for emergencies because it forces an exit and may lead to unpredictable results.

REXX 4.00 Specification: REXX 4.00 exception handling consists of the above plus the following:

- A new exception condition of NOTREADY. This is primarily used to handle error and failure conditions for stream (file/pipe) operations. See the earlier section on "File Operations" to see how this error occurs.
- CALL can now do error sequences as well as SIGNAL. The syntax is nearly identical (CALL ON SYNTAX). Here is a comparison:

Table 2-22

CALL ON	SIGNAL
• REXX 4.00 and later	• All REXX versions
• Controlled exit – Can have CALL ON/OFF or SIGNAL ON/OFF in subroutine and won't effect the "main procedure." – Normal procedure processing can resume on completion of subroutine.	• Abnormal error conditions - Can have CALL ON/OFF or SIGNAL ON/OFF in subroutine and won't effect the "main procedure." - Normal procedure processing cannot resume on completion of subroutine.
• RESULT symbol ignored. - Must be internal to procedure. - Probably uses more resources than SIGNAL.	• Does not affect RESULT - Must be internal to procedure.

- You can now use a label name that is different than the error condition. This is both for SIGNAL ON and CALL ON.

```
/* Use a different name */
/* Use swab instead of syntax for labelname */
      call on error name swab
(later in program)
      swab: /* for error — document for others to know this */
      say 'you had an error problem on line' sigl
      return
```

Debugging REXX Procedures

Generally speaking, most REXX compilers/interpreters offer a command-line (i.e. non-full-screen) trace facility. One exception is OS/2 which has two full-screen REXX facilities called PMREXX and RXD. PMREXX is discussed in Chapter 3. It is more than adequate in resolving those inevitable REXX processing problems.

Non-interactive tracing: Non-interactive tracing is the process of running the TRACE instruction or function without interruption (i.e., no additional TRACE commands while the initial TRACE instruction/function).

TRACE *flag* or TRACE(*'flag'*)
Where *flag* is one of the following value.

Table 2-23

Flag	What It Does
A	Traces each clause *before* execution.
C	Traces operating system commands*before* execution. Non-zero return codes are displayed. **This is a frequently used option.**
E	Traces operating system commands *after* execution **only** if they produce non-zero return codes. **This is a frequently used option.**
I	Traces all clauses *before* execution. However, it additionally shows *all* of the levels of symbolic substitution that a clause will go through before it is processed. It is extremely useful for debugging INTERPRET and VALUE statements. **This is a frequently used option.**
L	Traces only the labels processed *during* execution. This is useful as a first step to see "where the problem resides."
N	Nearly identical to E. But traces operating system commands with *negative* return codes. This is the default.
O	**Disables all tracing.**
R	Traces all clauses *before* execution. However, it additionally shows only the *last* level of symbolic substitution that a clause will go through before it is processed.

Interactive Tracing: Interactive tracing allows the user to perform "trial and error" debugging on those harder to solve problems. The user can enter a trace command, see the result, and re-enter another trace command.

- To enable interactive tracing, enter a TRACE ? or a TRACE('?') built-in function. It may be immediately followed by one of the TRACE flags listed above. Each clause is then traced and then interpreter usually pauses for user input. Exceptions are flow control instructions such as DO or END, THEN, and ELSE.
- To disable interactive tracing, re-enter a TRACE ? or TRACE O or TRACE.
- Interactive tracing also allows some additional commands for the TRACE instruction not the TRACE function.

  TRACE *number* — A positive whole number indicates the number of trace pauses (Basically a pause occurs after each pause is traced. See point one above) that are bypassed.

  TRACE *-number* — A negative whole number that allows tracing disabled for *number* of clauses.

IBM/Quercus Extensions: Quercus REXX has the following extensions:

- Placing a prefix of $ before any of the TRACE *flags* listed earlier will directly trace output to a printer.
- Supports the CMS TRACE command of *!*. This turns on or off the processing of any operating system commands. It is not supported by the IBM OS/2 REXX interpreter.
- A SET RXTRACE=N (the default) or to some other TRACE *flag* will set the initial default trace setting for all processed REXX programs. **Note that IBM OS/2 REXX only recognizes ON as a valid value for RXTRACE (i.e., turns on interactive trace for PMREXX and command-line REXX).** Interactive tracing is also supported. This also can be done at run-time with a /TR*flag* following the command to invoke the REXX procedure (PREXX30).
- In interactive mode, supports = to reprocess a clause. This is not supported by IBM OS/2 REXX. It is included as part of "standard REXX."
- For both IBM and Quercus OS/2 REXX interpreters, it may make sense to redirect output and errors to a file such as (IBM — REXX TRYIT.CMD 2>a.dbg or Quercus — PREXX30 TRYIT.CMD>a.dbg)
- How to list error messages and other on-line documents is listed in the section "Getting On-line Help about REXX" in Chapter 3. A list of error messages and what to do about them can be found in Appendix B. Note that list will likely be modified for the forthcoming ANSI REXX standard.

General Debugging Tips

- See the previous section on "Exception Handling" on using special variables RC, RESULT, and SIGL to help debug REXX problems.
- Use an approach similar to the following:

  STEP 1. What happened? Describe what happened and what was supposed to happen. List all error messages.

  STEP 2. Gather more information about the problem. Where did the problem occur? On invocation? In an function/subprocedure? In an ADDRESS instruction? In another procedure?

  - Use TRACE L to see which labels were processed.
  - a. Perhaps followed by a TRACE I (see immediate steps) or TRACE R (final step only) on the section in question to resolve symbolic substitution questions, and

    b. Or examining symbols for their values at the time of the problem. SAY 'A is' a OR SAY value(a), and

    c. Seeing if the interpreter processed certain statements. (i.e. say 'got in DO-loop'), and

    d. Examine special variables RESULT, SIGL, and RC, and

    e. Do a PARSE VERSION to capture the language version/interpreter version (maybe), and

    f. FOR OS/2 only: Do a SYSLEVEL command to check which version of OS/2 that you have. This will be useful if you need to contact IBM Tech Support.
- Use Interactive Tracing.

  STEP 3 Make an educated guess what a problem is and provide a way to test it.

  STEP 4 Perform the test. It works, there is no need to go further. Otherwise, perform STEP 2 through 4 as many times as necessary.

Example

The trace facility output does take some getting used to. Here is an example:

```
The procedure:
        trace i /* Intermediate steps shown as well */

        s=('This has seven words in this sentence')
```

```
        call separse s
        say 'Result is' Result
        exit
        separse: parse arg st
        cnt=words(s)
        do a=1 to cnt
        cv.a=word(s,a)
        end
        do a = 1 to cnt
        say cv.a
        end
        return cnt
With Trace on (Some repetitive loops are not shown)
        2 *-* s=('This has seven words in this sentence') /* original line */
        >L> "This has seven words in this sentence" /* line as a literal */
        3 *-* call separse s
        >V> "This has seven words in this sentence" /* contents of s */
        6 *-* separse:
        6 *-* parse arg st
        >>> "This has seven words in this sentence" /* value of st */
        7 *-* cnt=words(s)
```

```
>V> "This has seven words in this sentence"

>F> "7"

8 *-* do a=1 to cnt

>L> "1"

>V> "7" /* value of cnt */

9 *-* cv.a=word(s,a)

>V> "This has seven words in this sentence"

>V> "1"

>F> "This" /* Result of function */

>C> "CV.1" /* Name of compound symbol after substitution */

10 *-* end /* cv.2 — cv.6 left out */

9 *-* cv.a=word(s,a)

>V> "This has seven words in this sentence"

>V> "7"

>F> "sentence"

>C> "CV.7"

10 *-* end

10 *-* end

11 *-* do a = 1 to cnt

>L> "1"
```

```
        >V> "7"
        12 *-* say cv.a
        >C> "CV.1"
        >V> "This"
This /* Final value of CV.1 */
        12 *-* say cv.a
        >C> "CV.7"
        >V> "sentence"
sentence /* Final value of CV.7 */
        13 *-* end
        13 *-* end
        14 *-* return cnt
         >V> "7"
        4 *-* say 'Result is' Result
        >L> "Result is"
        >V> "7"
        >O> "Result is 7" /* Result's value */
Result is 7 /* The final result of the SAY */
        5 *-* exit
```

REFERENCES

American National Standard for Information Systems 1992 Programming Language REXX ANSI /HTI B173.8-1991.

Coffee, Peter 1992 "Myths of Computer's Math Skills is Widespread and Dangerous" *PC Week* December 7 pp. 105,129.

Cowlishaw, M.F. 1985 *The REXX Language: A Practical Approach to Programming* 1st ed. Englewood Cliffs, N.J.: Prentice-Hall.

Cowlishaw, M.F. 1990a *The REXX Language: A Practical Approach to Programming* 2nd ed. Englewood Cliffs, N.J.: Prentice-Hall.

Cowlishaw, M.F. 1990b "REXX 4.00: For Developers and Users" Proceedings of the REXX Symposium for Developers and Users pp. 7-32.

Cowlishaw M.F. 1991 "Notes on REXX Arithmetic Rules" pp 1-5.

Cowlishaw. M.F. 1992 "REXX — The Future" Proceedings of the REXX Symposium for Developers and Users pp. 6-13.

German, Hallett 1992 *Command Language Cookbook for Mainframes, Minicomputers, and PCS*. New York: Van Nostrand Reinhold pp. 1-23, 71-142, 307-342.

German, Hallett 1992 "SAS Problem Solving Looks East" Proceedings of the Northeast SAS Users' Group. pp. 227-230.

IBM 1991 *IBM OS/2 Procedures Languages 2/REXX User's Guide* S01F-0272-00.

IBM 1991 *IBM OS/2 Procedures Languages 2/REXX Reference* S01F-0271-00.

Quercus Systems 1991 *Personal REXX User's Guide* Version 3.0.

Quercus Systems 1992 "Personal REXX 3.0 for OS/2: Beta Test Notes — Beta version 3.".

3

OS/2 REXX: Unique Features

The previous chapter looked at "standard" REXX with some OS/2 differences noted. For those not familiar with REXX, this provided an important knowledge base for the current and following chapters. From here on, we will be examining what is commonly thought of as "OS/2 REXX". This chapter deals with "standard OS/2 REXX" — that is, nearly portable and unique features of OS/2 REXX. Chapters 4 through 6 and Appendix I will mention IBM and third-party extensions to the REXX language. So let's get started!

NEARLY PORTABLE REXX FEATURES

OS/2 REXX has several instructions that are nearly portable to other REXX implementations. These include features that are part of the SAA standard but not "standard REXX" and OS/2 REXX instructions that are part of "standard" REXX but have slightly different arguments or output.

Part of SAA But Not "Standard REXX"

The OPTIONS instruction is part of "standard REXX". However, any of the settings changed by the statement are usually not portable. These settings are added to the REXX interpreter or compiler to provide a means to change the overall REXX processing for some special circumstances. Here is some additional information about the OPTIONS instruction.

- The OPTIONS keyword is followed by a blank and a literal string being one or more settings, separated by blanks. (i.e., OPTIONS 'etmode exmode')

- Since the OPTIONS settings are mainly for special processing, they are turned off by default. If invalid or unknown by the interpreter/compiler, they are evaluated but ignored by the REXX implementation.
- The following settings are valid under OS/2 REXX interpreters:

Setting	OS/2 Interpreter	What It Does
ETMODE	IBM and SAA REXX	Enables/disables double-byte characters.
NOETMODE (default)		Generally, is the first option setting specified and first instruction when used.
EXMODE NOEXMODE (default)	IBM and SAA REXX	Determines if a double-byte string will be processed as one "character" or as two "characters" (EXMODE). (See note below.)

Note: the Double-byte character set (DBCS) is part of the SAA standard. It is provided to display and process languages like Japanese (Kanjii), Korean, and Chinese — languages that cannot be displayed in the standard single-byte character set of 256 characters. Taking advantage of double-byte characters require a special terminal. The character set includes X'4040 (blank) and X'41' through X'FE'. For ASCII operating systems (such as OS/2), no enclosing set of characters are needed, just make sure the first byte of the double-byte character always holds the correct country value. SAA includes some following additional functions to process double-byte characters (particularly) on EBCDIC-based hosts.

- Place an OPTIONS statement near the top of an procedure, so you can easily find it and change it if needed.
- All of the above settings are saved across subroutines/functions.

Slightly Different Than Standard REXX

ADDRESS: An important part of any command language is the ability to interface with the operating system and external environments (i.e., not part of the interpreter/compiler or the operating system — usually an application). REXX provides several ways to handle this. Before exploring these approaches, it is helpful to understand the "environment model" underlying them.

The "Environment Model"

For each clause being processed, a REXX interpreter/compiler goes through a process similar to the following. Note by not having knowledge of external commands, the REXX interpreter/compiler makes processing these commands operating-system independent.

Step 1. Get the clause.

Step 2. Is it a valid REXX clause?

IF YES, then continue processing, performing normal processing (syntax checking, symbolic substitution, perform string and mathematical operations)

IF NO, is it a valid external command, does it have one of these formats?

a. One or more lines each with a command in quotes (literal string).

b. A REXX ADDRESS instruction accompanied by a external command in quotes (literal string).

c. One or more lines each with a command in quotes (literal string). This block of external commands begins with an ADDRESS instruction on its own line.

- IF YES, continue to STEP 3
- IF NO, issue an error message.

STEP 3. Perform any symbolic substitution and pass the character string to the command processor (CP) for the external environment specified by the ADDRESS instruction. If there is no environment specified, then it is passed to the default command processor — usually the one for the operating system. (For OS/2, that would be CMD.EXE.)

STEP 4. The specified or default external environment processes the command. A well-behaved environment will pass back " a return code" that is stored in the system (special) variable RC. A zero return code means successful processing. The REXX interpreter/compiler then processes the next interpreter/compiler. Exception handling can be handled by a SIGNAL ON ERROR/FAILURE or CALL ON ERROR/FAILURE routine.

The ADDRESS Instruction

The ADDRESS instruction in addition to the stream operations, discussed in the previous chapter, are the two major enhancements to the REXX language planned in the forthcoming standard. Here are a summary of the changes.

- The result of an external command's processing will be placed in a new special variable called RS. Valid values are 0 (worked successfully) 2 (error such as syntax) and -1 (failure). Exception handling and tracing should also be supported. A recent decision by the committee was to delay implementing this until the 1996 version of the REXX standard.
- Allowing the ADDRESS instruction to be another means to access and manipulate streams, symbols, compound symbols, and stacks. Under consideration is adding an IN location with location being STDIN — standard input or QUEUE — stack, and a TO location with location being STDOUT — standard output, QUEUE and PUSH — stack operations, STREAM name and STEM stem. Additional keywords have also been suggested. Both areas have been designated for further enhancements or "bastardizations" depending on your point-of-view, in the second version (1996) of the REXX standard.

Here is an overview of the ADDRESS instruction as it currently stands.

1. The basic forms of external commands (mentioned previously) are:

Single command to the current environment

```
'dir c:\os2'
```

Multiple commands to the current environment

```
'ver'
'syslevel'
```

ADDRESS to OS/2 command processor (CMD.EXE) followed by a single command.

```
ADDRESS CMD 'dir c:\os2'
/* Same as the earlier example if CMD (OS/2) is the current environment */
```

ADDRESS to OS/2 command processor (CMD.EXE) followed by multiple commands.

```
ADDRESS CMD
'ver'
'syslevel'
/* Same as the earlier example if CMD (OS/2) is the current environment */
```

2. Use the ADDRESS function or PARSE SOURCE to process sequences only if a certain environment is active.

```
select
      When address() = 'CMD' then do
        OS/2 command
        another OS/2 command
      end
      when address() = 'DOS' then do
        DOS command
        another DOS command
      end
      otherwise
        say 'environment is' address()
end
```

3. Specifying ADDRESS by itself resets the environment to what it was before the last ADDRESS instruction was invoked. Therefore, to minimize errors when porting procedures and as a good coding habit, get used to explicitly specifying the environment an external command should be used with. Specifying ADDRESS environment_name will make this the active environment.

4. Table 3-1 lists some environments that can be used with OS/2:

Table 3-1

Environment Name	External Environment Description
CMD	The default external environment of the OS/2 command processor — CMD.EXE. This is part of "Standard OS/2 REXX." A null string for environment name (i.e. '') will do the same thing.
CPICOMM	The SAA common environment especially used with communications.
ISPEXEC	Tritus Inc.'s Tritus SPF edit macros. The same environment name is also valid for processing VGET, VPUT and SETMSG using Command Technology Corporation's SPF/2.
ISREDIT	Edit macros using either Command Technology Corporation's SPF/2 or Tritus Inc.'s Tritus SPF edit macros.
KEDIT	Mansfield Software's KEDIT (a full-screen editor patterned after XEDIT) edit macros and profiles.

Table 3-1 Continued

Environment Name	External Environment Description
REXXTERM	Quercus Software's REXXTERM asynchronous communication macros and profiles.
TE2	Oberon Software's TE/2 asynchronous communication macros.
THE	Mark Hessling's THE edit macros.
VISION	The external environment to process Borland International's OBJECTVISION REXX macros.

- There are other types of REXX-external interfaces. These include:
  - Registering external functions to be seen by OS/2 REXX as ordinary built-in functions. This is discussed in the section "External Functions" later in the chapter.
  - Running REXX execs directly from an external application. For example, being able to run REXX macros with an .ERX extension under the OS/2 Enhanced Editor, by entering RX *macroname* at the editor's command line. A more generic approach in using a REXXSTART call and setting up your own subcommand handler is discussed later in the chapter.
- Many IBM and Personal REXX built-in functions simulate OS/2 commands. These are discussed later in this chapter as well as Chapter 5. Consider using them instead of "branching to OS/2" using the ADDRESS instruction.
- Use return codes from external commands to avoid needless processing of commands:

```
address cmd
' dir c:\bad.txt'
      if rc = 0 then 'del c:\bad.txt' /* don't delete file unless it exists */
```

- You can use symbolic substitution or the ADDRESS VALUE keyword to change an environment:

```
x = 'CMD'
interpret address x 'TIME'
```

The following two instructions, PARSE SOURCE and PARSE VERSION, can supply additional information about a procedure or REXX interpreter.

Unfortunately, the output from these commands has not been standardized. So output may vary across REXX implementations. This is a problem recognized by the current REXX standards committee and may be specified in the 1996 standard.

PARSE SOURCE

A quick way to learn information about an unfamiliar procedure is to run the PARSE SOURCE instruction. A sequence similar to the following will help you parse the output from PARSE SOURCE:

```
parse source with os etype proc_name
say '***********************************************************************'
say '   Operating System    Type          Procedure Name'
say '   'os '               ' etype '     ' proc_name
say '***********************************************************************'
```

Both the IBM and Quercus REXX interpreters produces:

```
***********************************************************************
       Operating System    Type          Procedure Name
       OS/2                COMMAND       C:\EXECS\FIRST.CMD
***********************************************************************
```

In addition, to COMMAND, etype could also be FUNCTION or SUBROUTINE. The Procedure name returned will be the complete file name including drive name and directory/subdirectory name(s). You can then use the symbol containing the value of the operating system and then perform sequences that are operating-system specific.

```
if os == 'OS/2'...
```

PARSE VERSION

If you are unsure of the version number or REXX language version number, the PARSE VERSION instruction may supply you with this information. You want to use a sequence similar to the following to parse the output from PARSE VERSION:

```
parse version lang version idate
say '*************************************************************'
say '   Language     Version       Implementation Date'
say '   'lang. '     'version'     ' idate
say '*************************************************************'
```

IBM OS/2 REXX produces:

```
*********************************************************************
       Language       Version       Implementation Date
       REXXSAA        4.00          08 July 1992
*********************************************************************

Quercus OS/2 Personal REXX produces:
*********************************************************************
       Language            Version       Implementation Date
       REXX /Personal      4.00          8 Feb 1993
*********************************************************************
```

In the examples given, the version refers to the REXX language version, not the OS/2 interpreter version. The date refers to the release date of the REXX interpreter/compiler. The non-standard built-in function PRXVERSION returns the current version of the OS/2 Quercus Personal REXX interpreter — currently 3.02.

STREAM

The stream built-in function is part of the 4.00 REXX Language specification but all of the subcommands are not. However, only IBM/Quercus OS/2 REXX and Kilowatt REXX (Windows, MS-DOS) support it. Many of the basic file/stream functions, such as CHARIN, provide the same information. At this writing, the ANSI REXX committee is considering other built-in functions that will basically replace this command. So, you may want to think twice before using this instruction in a production procedure.

Here are some typical operations of the Stream function:

Stream Information

```
say stream('a.txt','S')
OR
say stream('a.txt.'D')
/* Returns current stream status: READY, NOTREADY, ERROR, or UNKNOWN */
/* The D flag may give addition text for known errors (i.e. NOTREADY or */
/* ERROR states. The state name is followed by a colon [i.e. NOTREADY:]).*/

Note:   The actual commands (after the C flag) are non-portable.
        These commands are for streams that may be files, named pipes, or
        serial ports. They do not open a file to do these operations.

say stream('a.txt','c','query exists')    /* Returns complete file name if exists or */
                                          /* null string if non existent. Other commands */
```

```
        /* are query size (returns file size in bytes) */
        /* and query time (returns file creation date */
        /* and time */

                                Stream Operations

Note: The actual commands (after the C flag) are non-portable.)

stream('a.txt','c','OPEN')        /* Opens Read and Write to a stream */
OR
stream('a.txt','c','OPEN READ')   /* Opens Read-only to a stream */
OR
stream('a.txt','c','OPEN WRITE')  /* Opens Write-only to a stream */
                                  /* Returns READY if OK */

stream('a.txt','c','CLOSE')       /* Closes a stream. Returns READY if ok */

stream('a.txt','c','SEEK +2')
        /* Relocates the read/write pointers 2 characters */
        /* beyond the current position */
        /* Returns READY if ok */
        /* Seek may be followed by a positive number, */
        /* Negative number (characters backwards) */
        /* = (beginning of the stream), < (end of the stream) */
```

OS/2 REXX UNIQUE FEATURES: BASICS

This section looks at basic OS/2 REXX operations.

Invoking OS/2 REXX

No two REXX interpreters/compilers are invoked the same way, nor does the forthcoming REXX standard plan to change this. OS/2 REXX procedures can be processed in a variety of ways. The following looks at all of them.

Foreground Processing

The "traditional" view of foreground processing is when a command language program is executing, you are usually unable to run anything else, such as under MS-DOS. However, under OS/2, more than one program can run simultaneously in the foreground, called pre-emptive multitasking or pre-emptive time slicing. While the programs are processing, you can easily switch between them if needed. The result is an increase in overall system productivity.

The following describes the format of OS/2 REXX procedures:

- REXX procedures are ASCII "plain text" files that are readable by any line or text editor or file browser available for OS/2.
- REXX procedures have an extension of .CMD, the same as OS/2 batch files. To help the OS/2 command processor (CMD.EXE) distinguish between the two types of files, a comment (usually containing the word REXX (in any case) for portability and to make sure that PMREXX and the OS/2 REXX interpreter will work) must be appear in the procedure starting in column 1, line 1 (e.g. /*REXX*/). Failure to do this results in a SYS1041 error message of "The name specified is not recognized as an internal or external command, operable program, or batch file." All of the other clauses in the procedure may start in any column.

There are several ways to invoke a REXX procedure in foreground:

1. From the command line.
2. From a OS/2 batch (.CMD) file.
3. From the OS/2 Workplace Shell via an icon.

Invoking Quercus OS/2 Personal REXX will be discussed in Chapter 5. There is another approach that may sometimes be needed — that is the ability to run OS/2 on a minimum OS/2 (non-Workplace shell) system. Here are some tips on doing this:

- You must load REXXINIT.DLL in a process that is always running. If the process terminates, this will not work! This is generally done by creating a program that on startup loads REXXINIT.DLL (using the DosLoadModule call) and then invokes CMD.EXE as a child process (using the DOSExecPgm call). This could be called MINREXX.EXE.
- Then change CONFIG.SYS to read PROTSHELL=C:\MINREXX.EXE, Reboot OS/2, this should now work.

From The Command Prompt (C:\)

Here are some examples how to do this:

The complete procedure name

```
grapes.cmd

/* Processes a REXX procedure named grapes.cmd in the current directory */
/* or path. Using the complete file specification (i.e. c:\myexecs\grapes.cmd) */
/* may avoid later problems. In all of the examples, the procedure name may */
/* be accompanied with various arguments*/
```

The implied procedure name

```
grapes

/* Processes a REXX procedure named grapes.CMD in the current */
/* directory or path. TRAP – the default process order is to first invoke */
/* GRAPE.COM, then GRAPE.EXE, then GRAPE.CMD. So, try give */
/* your unique names to avoid "the wrong file was processed" problem. */
```

Using the CMD command

```
cmd /cgrapes.cmd

/* Explicitly invokes CMD.EXE to process the REXX procedure, Creates a */
/* second command processor if /C is used. */
```

Using the START command

```
START "REXX Procedure" /k grapes.cmd

/* Can be used to invoke the procedure on startup or place in STARTUP.CMD */
/* Creates a new window called "REXX Procedure." The directory is then */
/* listed and the new window is not closed on completion */

/* Used instead of a batch file to invoke a program. Useful options */
/* include: */
/* /C or /K – executes a program without invoking a new command */
/* processor (CMD.EXE). /C closes the window or application when */
/* processing is done. /K (default) does not. If /PM (Presentation Manager) */
/* but not .CMD files or /FS (full-screen) is used, then the session is */
/* implicitly run in foreground. /F explicitly does this */
```

From An OS/2 (.CMD) Batch File Or OS/2 Prompt.

Using the OS/2 CALL command to invoke a REXX procedure as an OS/2 command.

```
CALL grape 'giant' 88 /* Two arguments */
/* After processing, the procedure processes the next command in the file */
```

NOTE: CALL cannot include pipe (|) and output redirection (>,>>) operators.

From the OS/2 Workplace Shell via an Icon.

- Find the icon and double-click on it. You may be prompted for additional arguments. The procedure is then processed.
- To create an icon, follow the following process:

STEP 1: Go into the *Templates* folder and drag and drop a *Program* icon onto the desktop. The *Settings* display will appear.

STEP 2: Click on the "General" tab. Change the Title to a Description of the Procedure.

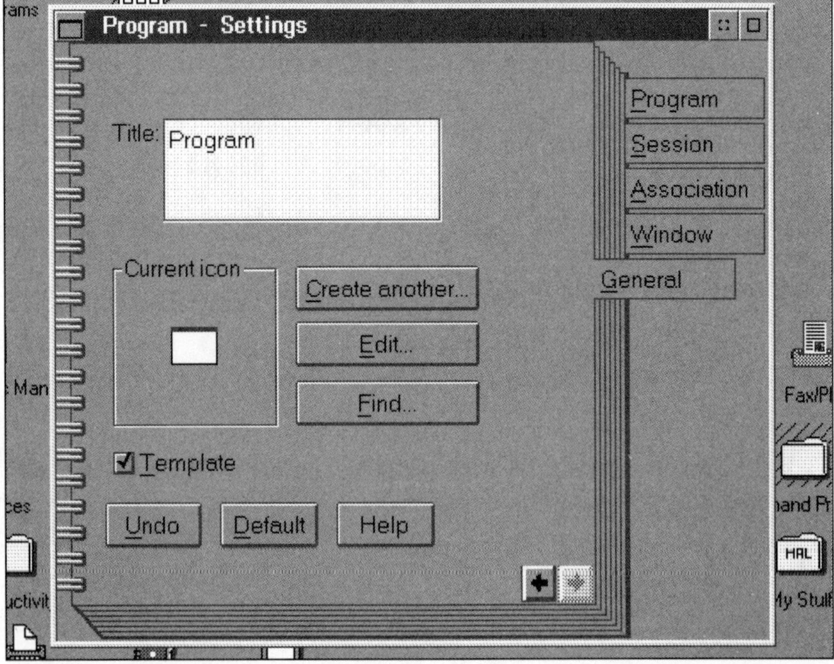

Figure 3-1 Program — Settings (General)

STEP 3: Click on the “Program” tab. Add the *Path and File Name*, a *question mark* if you want to be prompted for arguments at run-time, and the *working directory* which is usually the same as the Path. (See Figure 3-2.)

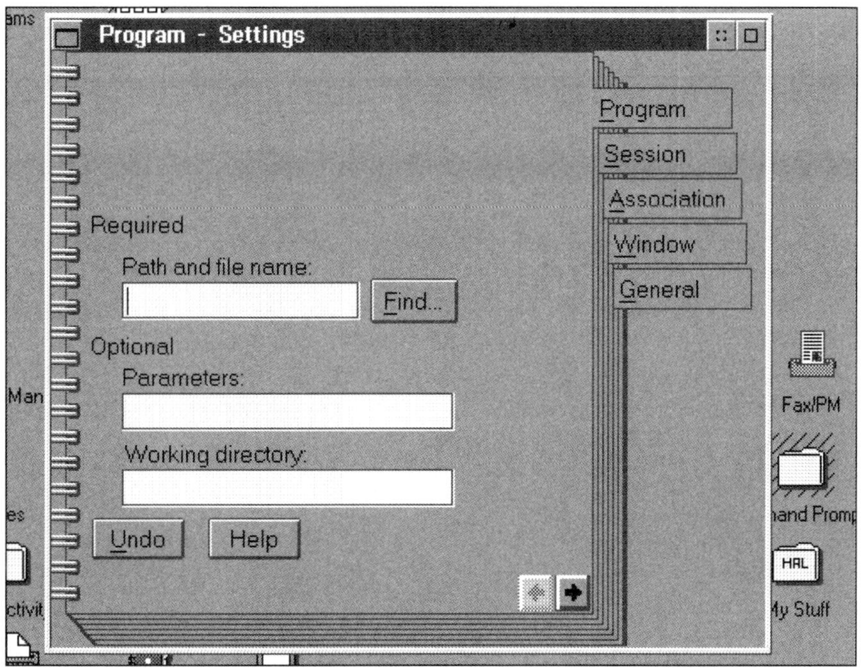

Figure 3-2 Program — Settings (Program)

STEP 4: Click on the icon in the top left. Select Close (last menu choice).

Your new icon has been created!

Background Processing

OS/2 is one of a few operating systems that allows REXX procedures to be run in the background. However, with OS/2’s ability to run several programs simultaneously in the foreground, the advantage becomes less apparent.

Use the DETACH command to do this.

```
DETACH grapes /* Runs grapes.cmd in the background. Returns a */
/* confirmation message similar to - The process identification */
/* number is 88. */
```

Notes

1. Pipes (|) and redirection (< or >) operators are allowed in a DETACH command or a program invoked by a DETACH command.
2. Do not include REXX instructions that prompt for user input or display to the screen (such as PARSE PULL or PULL, SAY) while running a REXX procedure in background. A PARSE PULL/PULL that is tied with a specified queue IS valid.
3. Note that another copy of CMD.EXE is needed to run OS/2 internal commands such as DIR. This will use additional memory.

Behind The Scenes

This section takes a brief look at some of the events that go on while an REXX procedure is processing. OS/2 REXX, included with every copy of OS/2 2.1, uses a 32-bit interpreter. This results in a 40% to 60% performance increase over the 16-bit REXX interpreter included with OS/2 1.3. The following are some of the technical characteristics of the OS/2 2.1 REXX interpreter:

- **Fully re-entrant.** In addition to OS/2 supporting multiple **processes** (an executing copy of a program) simultaneously, a single process can have multiple **threads** (i.e., execution of a set of sequences in a program) running simultaneously! So one thread could be reading input from program[1], another thread could be performing file operations on that same program[1], etc. This means it is highly likely that the same sequence, such as a REXX function, may be simultaneously executed by multiple threads — or that a sequence of code in a program is **re-entrant**. Thus, one thread may, briefly and without serious consequences, be pre-empted while another thread "re-enters" and executes the same sequence.
- Supports the processing of multiple threads for a single REXX procedure. This will result in overall faster execution and response times for REXX procedures.
- Storing OS/2 procedures as tokenized images. The following is from Eric Giguère's *Frequently Asked Questions about REXX* and reprinted with permission:

Why does my OS/2 REXX program run more quickly the second time?

When you run a REXX CMD file for the first time after you modified it, the REXX interpreter will actually store a tokenized version of the program on disk alongside the source version using the OS/2 extended file attributes. (AUTHOR's NOTE: Extended attributes allow OS/2 users to attach additional information to a file such as a long comment about a file. They are identified by a name and cannot be anymore than 65536 bytes. This topic is returned to later in the chapter in the REXXUTIL section.) You can see how big the tokenized version is by using the /N option (Author's Note: /N displays the directory listing in a High Performance File System format which will show the space taken up by extended attributes.) on the DIR command:

```
dir say.cmd
SAY           CMD    22     6-11-92                  8:34a

dir /n say.cmd
6-11-92       8:34a  22               317            SAY.CMD
                                      ⇕
```

Author's Note: Space taken up by the extended attribute.

If a tokenized version exists AND you haven't modified the file, REXX will load the tokenized version instead of rereading the source.

- The bulk of REXX resides in dynamic link libraries. A Dynamic Link Library (DLL) is one means for multiple OS/2 processes to share resources. (Note that you cannot create a DLL from REXX.) It is a set of functions stored in executable files. The REXX DLL's usually reside in the C:\OS2\DLL directory. These include:
  - REXXINIT.DLL (REXX initialization routines — processed only on OS/2 startup. It initializes the REXX queues, function/subcommand/exit definitions);
  - REXXAPI.DLL (REXX external functions/subroutines);
  - REXX.DLL (The REXX interpreter including all built-in functions and instructions); and
  - REXXUTIL.DLL (additional OS/2 REXX built-in functions).

PMREXX (Presentation Manager REXX)

PMREXX is a full-screen application that invokes the REXX interpreter. It is not the REXX interpreter itself. Note that source is included in the REXX samples directory of the OS/2 Toolkit. It offers the following advantages over the command-line REXX interface:

- A full-screen editor where one can modify a REXX procedure and then immediately execute it all within PMREXX. The normal editor capabilities, changing fonts, and scrolling are supported.
- The ability to cut and paste text from MS-DOS, MS-Windows, and OS/2 applications.
- Multiple windows during procedure execution for input and output.
- And probably the most important, the ability to perform full-screen tracing. Although RXD, a full-screen debugger created by Patrick Mueller at IBM (copyrighted freeware), is now also available.

Invoking And Ending PMREXX

PMREXX is invoked from the OS (C:\) prompt by entering:

```
PMREXX flag procedure_name arg1..argn

flag (Usually none. /T will invoke interactive tracing or set the environment
variable RTXTRACE to ON – a SET RXTRACE=ON statement.)

procedure_name (Name of the REXX procedure. May be fully qualified [drive and
directory/subdirectory] or leave off the .CMD extension. The procedure must start
with a comment in column 1, row 1.)

arg1..argn – The various arguments to used by the REXX interpreter when the
procedure is processed.
```

Figure 3-3 is the screen that appears: (In this example, the output generated from a say 'hello world' instruction.)

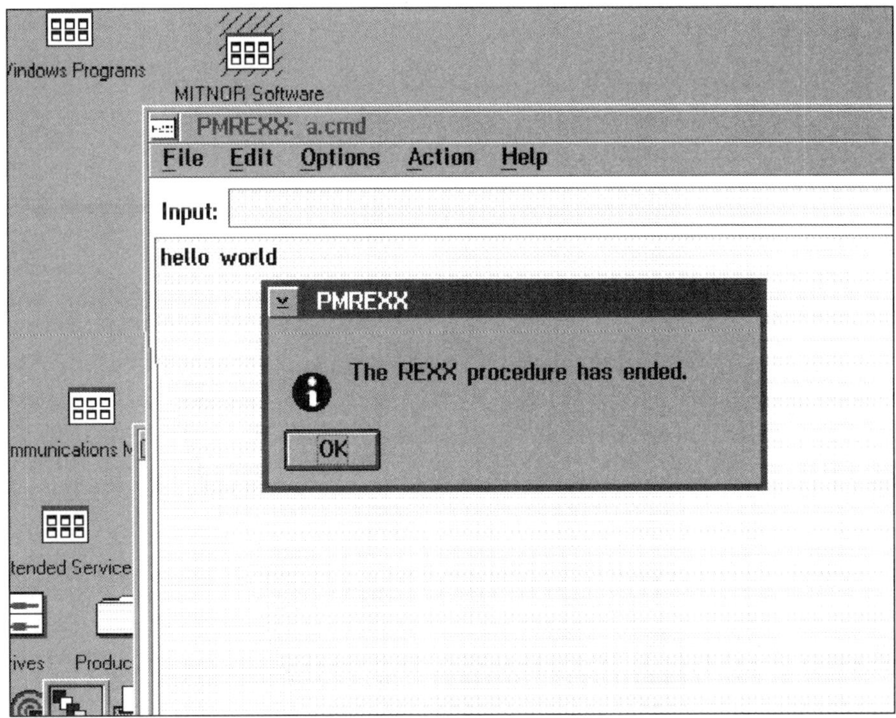

Figure 3-3 PMREXX General Screen

To exit PMREXX. Select the Exit option under the File Menu (or press F3). The following return codes are given by PMREXX: 0 (successful processing), 1 (Window class registration error — perhaps a corrupted PMREXX.EXE). 3 (REXX procedure name was not specified). All other non-zero return code (REXX error and PMREXX window not displayed.)

Editing Operations

Part of the attraction of this product is the good edit capabilities. In Table 3-2 are some other useful operations and the menu selection to execute them:

Table 3-2

Operation	Menu Selection
Copy a block of text (or the entire procedure or output) into another application (such as an editor).	1. Hold down the left mouse button to highlight the desired block of text. 2. Select *Edit* on the main menu and then select *Copy from focus window* to save the highlighted text to the clipboard. (Choose *Select All* under the Edit menu to save the entire procedure or output.) 3. Open the other application. Select Paste (or *Paste Lines*) from the menu and the REXX procedure or output will be pasted.
Erase everything in the output windows.	Select *Edit* on the main menu and then select *Clear*.
Paste a block of text from another application (such as an editor)	1. From the other application, highlight a block of text and select *Copy*. This will place the text in the clipboard. 2. From PMREXX, Select *Edit* on the main menu and then *Paste* to *Input*. The text will be pasted into the Input window.
Process command in the Input Window.	Press Enter
Retrieve the previous input line.	Press the up arrow until the REXX clause appears.
Save the Procedure	1. Select *File* on the main menu and then select *Save* (to save with the current name) or *Save As* (to save under a new name).

Tracing A REXX Procedure

Here are some tips in using the trace facilities of PMREXX:

1. Select /T to initially invoke interactive tracing when PMREXX starts. Or Select *Interactive Trace* under the *Options* menu. The third way to do this is to issue the

following statement from your CONFIG.SYS or the OS/2 command-line — SET RXTRACE=ON.

2. Under the *Actions* menu, the following selections are available.

Action	Menu Selection
Disables tracing	*Interactive Trace (click to deselect)*
Stop all processing of an exec.	*Halt procedure*
Traces last clause (Same as = command).	*Re-do the last clause*
Traces next clause (Same as TRACE 1 or =	*Trace next clause*

Don't forget to use the on-line help under the Help menu if you have any questions about PMREXX. Select the "General Help" option under the HELP menu. Then press the Index key, Figure 3-4 appears:

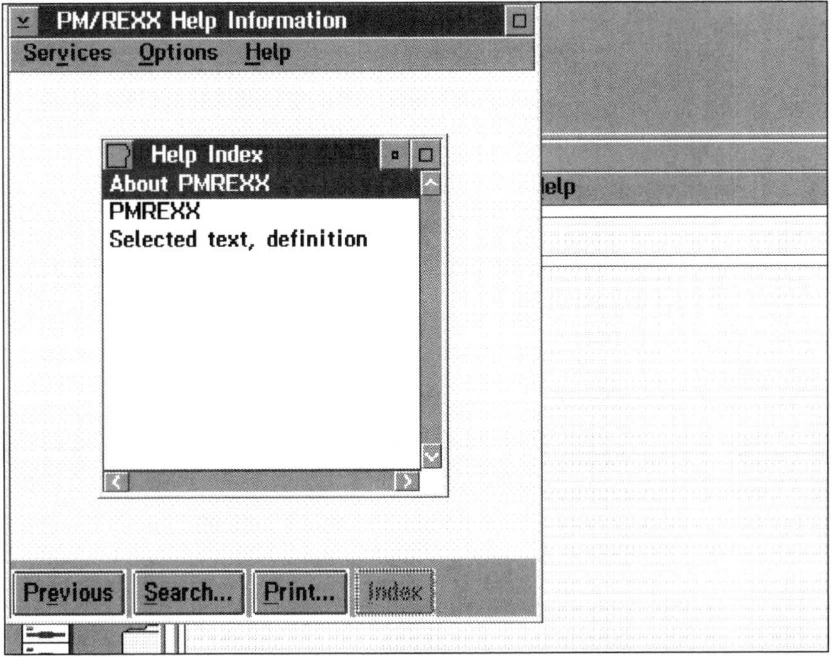

Figure 3-4 PMREXX Help Screen

Some extended OS/2 built-in functions (part of RexxUtil) such as RxMessageBox need a full-screen window in order to run. The full-screen window can be created by either using the OS/2 START command (on startup) or using PMREXX.

Be aware that input/output operations will behave differently under PMREXX. (In which use input/output windows.) In some cases, you may have to fall back to processing a procedure from the command line. Scrolling is also 'jerky.'

REXXTRY — The REXX Testing Ground

If you are unsure if a REXX clause is valid or what it will do, try the REXX "mini-interpreter" — REXXTRY. REXXTRY is not another REXX interpreter interface but a REXX procedure that is a glorified INTERPRET clause. It is useful for processing only a few clauses at a time. Here is a simplified version of the same thing:

```
do forever                   /* Keep going until EXIT is entered */
       Say 'Rexxtry:'        /* Give a prompt so the user knows to put in */
       parse pull rexx_line
                             /* Capture user input and assign to symbol rexx_line */
       interpret rexx_line /* Perform symbolic substitution and then execute */
end
```

1. Two versions of REXXTRY are also supplied with the Quercus OS/2 REXX Interpreter.
2. To invoke REXXTRY enter:

```
REXXTRY REXX_expression
Where REXX_expression is any valid REXX clause such as say "REXX is fun"

OR

PMREXX REXXTRY REXX_expression (full-screen processing)
```

3. Once in REXXTRY, you may enter any of the following (in addition to one-line REXX commands:
   a. Call Show displays the values of PARSE VERSION, PARSE SOURCE, and the special (system) variable RESULT.
   b. ? displays how to use REXXTRY (on-line help). Call Tell will do the same thing.
   c. = reprocesses last line

REXXTRY shows the power of REXX in generating additional REXX code and then executing it. Take the time to look through the code — it is well documented! This will also work under CMS, OS/400, and TSO which will use the operating system-specific code thrown in.

Getting On-Line Help About REXX

Here are some ways to access on-line documents about REXX while in OS/2:

REXX error messages reside in two files both which are usually found in the C:\OS2\SYSTEM directory.

- Entering HELP REXXnnn will allow you to access messages in the first file — REX.MSG (with nnn being a number from 0001 to 0125). These are general REXX help messages and correspond to the error messages 1-49 listed in Cowlishaw's The REXX Language, plus additional error messages. Unfortunately, they do not list the OS/2 interpreter limits when a maximum limit is exceeded. The Quercus OS/2 Personal REXX interpreter does. A list of error messages (and what to do when they occur) can be found in Appendix B. Note that REX.MSG is mostly a text file and can be browsed with an editor. These error numbers are likely to change because of the forthcoming ANSI REXX standard and future enhancements to OS/2 REXX.
- The second file is REXH.MSG. It contains a detailed explanation of what caused the error and some possible remedies. It can also be browsed with an editor.

Note that a OS/2 batch file (HELP.CMD) is processed each time you enter help. Look at this file to see why REXX exceeds the batch language. At least 23 lines are spent trying to the equivalent of this: (10 lines)

```
arg on_off            /* Set to upper case*/
select
when on_off = "ON" then address cmd "prompt $p$g" /* Change prompt */
when on_off = "OFF" then do
       "cls"
       "prompt"
end
otherwise "helpmsg"  /* Invoke OS/2 help */
end
exit
```

Please read the section on "Debugging REXX Procedures" in Chapter 2 to learn more on how to debug REXX problems.

On-line REXX help is also available. This can be accessed one of two ways:

From the Workplace Shell:

1. Click on the Information icon
2. The Information window appears
3. Click on the Book icon named "REXX Information"
4. The Contents windows appears

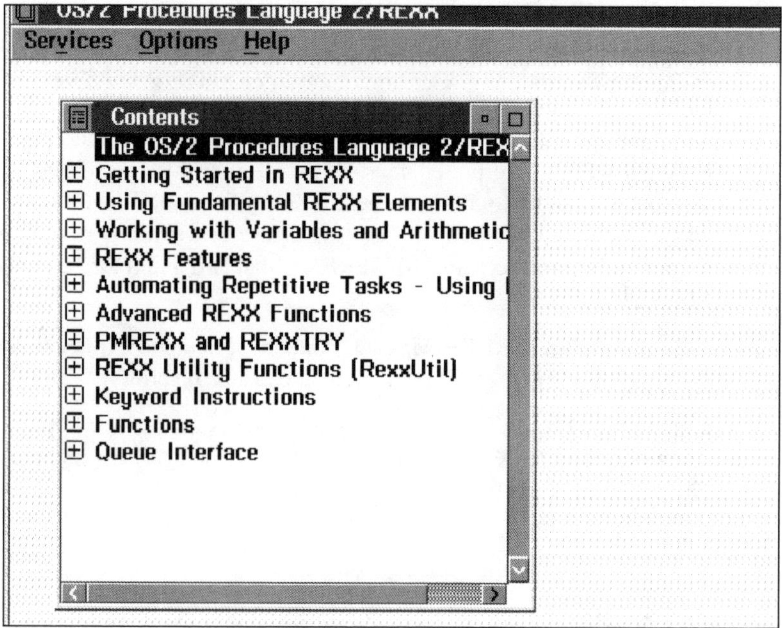

Figure 3-5 REXX General Help Screen

5. Click on the topic that you want or the plus to see secondary topics.
6. Select the Exit Option under the Services menu or F3 to exit.

From the command prompt enter VIEW REXX.INF. (Location is part of the path.)

- There are third-party INF files that also include REXX implementations on other operating systems. SAAREXX.ZIP is a shareware package that does this. It contains the source and the .INF file. A text copy of REXX.INF is available on

CompuServe and the Internet. Look for the name of RXINFO.ZOO or RXINFO.ZIP. The REXX API describes how to create an external function/subroutine and additional information is also available from IBM as an .INF file called REXXAPI.INF. It is located in the Professional Development Kit (PDK).

- BookMaster READ/2 is a useful document browsing utility that can be found in the Professional Development Kit is . READ "text" (really formatted versions of IBM software manuals) files end with a .BOO extension. One such file, included on the PDK, is the REXX User's Guide by the name of S10G6269.BOO. This offers more of a REXX tutorial than REXX.INF. READ is also available on other IBM platforms offering some portability.

OS/2 Environment Variables

OS/2 Environment Variables are the equivalent of global variables for REXX interpreters on other platforms such as CMS. They provide values that can be accessible for all OS/2 processes. Here is a brief look at how to perform environment variable operations using the OS/2 batch (.CMD) language.

- Values are assigned by the OS/2 SET system command which has the format SET *var_name=value*. If *value* is null, then the environment variable is reset. It can be used from the command line or CONFIG.SYS.
- Entering just SET will display the values of all current environment variables.
- If using the environment variable name in any other OS/2 batch statement, then enclose it in % (such as %TOD%). These include ECHO (display the value such as ECHO %TOD%) and IF (for command-line validation testing such as IF "%MONITOR%"=="VGA").
- Note that environment variable names are *always* converted to uppercase.

Table 3-3 lists some of the environment variables used by OS/2.

Table 3-3

Variable	What It Does
BOOKMGR/READIBM	Environment variables used by BookManager Read/2
BOOKSHELF	Directories where .INF files used by the VIEW command (such as the OS/2 and REXX command references) resides. One such directory is usually C:\OS2\BOOK.

Table 3-3 Continued

Variable	What It Does
COMSPEC	The location and name of the current command processor. For OS/2, the value is C:\OS2\CMD.EXE.
DPATH	The search path for data files. The equivalent of DOS's APPEND command. Can be modified by the *DPATH=newpath* /E is issued.
EMPATH	The location of EPM (Enhanced Editor) and .ERX/.E files.
HELP	The location of OS/2 Help (.HLP) files. These are stored in the C:\OS2\HELP directory (among others).
RXQUEUE	The name of REXX queue to be used with the RXQUEUE external command.
RXTRACE	Turns on interactive tracing for both command-line and PMREXX.
USER_INI/SYSTEM.INI	Sets the location of the User (OS2.INI) and System INI files (OS2SYS.INI)
PATH	Search path of all .CMD, .COM, and .EXE files. This can be modified by the PATH command
PROMPT	Modified the command line prompt. One common prompt is pg (display the current directory and the greater than sign.)

Here are the various OS/2 environment variable operations that REXX can perform.

- Chapter 2 showed how the VALUE built-in function could be used to retrieve a symbol's value or assign a symbol an initial or new value. Under OS/2, if a VALUE function statement explicitly or implicitly (through symbolic substitution) includes the literal string 'OS2ENVIRONMENT' as its third argument, then the REXX procedure can also manipulate environment variables. This argument is generally reserved for external global variables. Typical operations include retrieving the values of one or more active environment variables or assigning initial/new values to environment variables:

Viewing the value of a specific environment variable

```
                    say value('help',,'OS2ENVIRONMENT')

                                  OR
                         osenv = 'OS2ENVIRONMENT'
                         say value('help',,osenv)
/* Should return C:\OS2\HELP */
```

Setting the value of an environment variable

```
                      helpx = 'c:\os2\help;c:\myhelp'
                  say value('help',helpx,'OS2ENVIRONMENT')
/* Help now has a value of c:\os2\help;c:\myhelp. But displays old value */
/* of c:\os2\help */
```

- Invoking VALUE as a subroutine will allow for better exception handling and stores the result (PATH of current help directories) in the system (special) variable RESULT.

```
call value help,,'OS2ENVIRONMENT'
```

- Note that if VALUE returns null, then the environment variable is defined: (Here is a subroutine that tests if an environment variable is valid.)

```
call envtest test    /* Is test a valid environment variable? */
                     /* Display result in English */
if Result = 0 then say 'Environment variable does not exist'
      else say 'Environment variable 'test' exists'
exit
/* Later in the procedure...*/
envtest: procedure   /* makes all variables local */
arg envar            /* set to uppercase */
if value(envar,,'OS2ENVIRONMENT') = ' ' then return 0 /* Does not exist */
      else return 1
```

- Note that any environment variables set within a REXX procedure changes the "master" environment. Thus, using the above approach will cause global changes that may affect other REXX procedures and batch files. Fortunately, OS/2 has a way to enable/disable local environment variables on the fly. This is done by either using the SETLOCAL/ENDLOCAL OS/2 commands or the REXX built-in instructions. (One limitation of using REXX is that only one SETLOCAL can be active at a time.)

If SETLOCAL is invoked when using either approach, then a copy of the environment is saved. This includes all environment variables, the active disk drive and directory/subdirectory. Any environment variables can then be temporarily changed using the VALUE built-in function. Then the stored SETLOCAL settings are restored by either issuing an ENDLOCAL or the procedure completes processing (i.e., an implied ENDLOCAL).

Note that the REXX SETLOCAL/ENDLOCAL returns 1 if successfully processed (i.e., the environment was saved or restored), 0 (if not).

For example:

```
/* help = "c:\os2\help". Temporarily change this to look at different */
/* help files */
ret_code = setlocal() /* Settings saved. Returns 1 for successful */
/* processing. */
newhelp='c:\os2\temphelp'
say value(help,newhelp,'OS2ENVIRONMENT')
        /* Temporarily sets the help environment variable to */
        /* c:\os2\temphelp. Displays c:\os2\help */
        /* Perform any help operations.....*/
ret_code=endlocal() /* Restores c:\os2\help and old environment */
```

Queue Operations

Besides writing/reading data from a file (stream), REXX can manipulate an *external data queue*. (This is the term used in the REXX ANSI standard. Sometimes called a buffer, data buffer, data queue, queue, data stack, the stack, program stack or input stack. (There is a name for each day of the week!). Standard REXX specifies the commands to be used with the **data queue** — the generic term that will be used in this book. This section deals with how to perform queue operations using REXX instructions/built-in functions. See the section OS/2 Unique Features: Advanced on how external programs can access REXX variables, data queues, and more!

Types Of Queues

OS/2 allows REXX execs to manipulate three different types of queues:

- **Session queues:** A session queue with the intriguing name of SESSION is created when an OS/2 session is invoked **and** data is put into it. This is the default queue available to all active processes for querying and other operations. OS/2 oversees the management of this queue.

- **Detached session queues:** a detached session queue is created when a DETACH command with a REXX procedure is invoked and data is put into it. This queue has a unique system-generated name. OS/2 oversees the management of this queue.
- **Private queues:** A private queue, used for the majority of REXX operations, is a uniquely user- or system-named queue that is accessible only if **explicitly invoked**. *The REXX programmer is responsible for managing this queue* — including avoiding queue conflicts between procedures, explicitly deleting the queue (not OS/2), etc.

Both queues are composed of data elements. An **element** is a character string ranging between 64 and 65535 bytes that takes up one "slot" or "line" in the data queue. The forthcoming ANSI REXX standard may change this. Already the standards committee has already agreed to a data queue length of 256 because of CMS.

Private Queue Management

Queue management is an important part of queue operations. The RXQUEUE function used to do this is only used on OS/2.Here are the typical queue management operations. This is not to be confused with the RXQUEUE command that can be issued from within a .CMD file or the command line. Here are the typical queue management operations:

Create a system-named private queue

```
queue_name = rxqueue('Create')
/* Queue_name holds the system-generated unique name of the queue if */
/* successful such as S20Q0315753040 */
```

Create a user-named private queue

```
queue_name = rxqueue('Create','Idaho')
/* Queue_name holds the user-generated unique name of the queue (IDAHO) */
/* if successful. A return code of 5 means an invalid queue_name */
```

Delete a private queue

```
ret_code = rxqueue('Delete','Idaho')
/* Deletes the 'Idaho' queue A return code of 0 means successful processing. */
/* A return code of 9 means a non-existent queue. If the 'Idaho' queue exists, */
/* then a system-generated name will be used instead */
```

What is the active queue?

```
act_queue = rxqueue('Get')
/* Returns name of active queue such as SESSION */
```

Assigning a new active private queue

```
new_active = rxqueue('Set','Colorado')
/* Returns the name of the formerly active queue. 'Colorado' is now the */
/* active queue. Returns a 5 if the queue_name is invalid. Returns a */
/* 9 if the new active queue_name does not exist. */
```

The RXQUEUE function operates on the REXX queue indicated as a value of the RXQUEUE environment variable or the SESSION queue — if the environment variable is not specified. Here is the syntax of RXQUEUE:

```
RXQUEUE queuename/flag
where queuename = the name of the queue.
     flag = CLEAR (empties the specifies queue), FIFO (places lines on the
       bottom of the specified REXX queue), LIFO (places lines on the top
       of the specified REXX queue).
```

An interesting piece of Shareware was created by Jay Tunkel of IBM called SERVER.CMD. It shows how to use RXQUEUE to provide interprocess (i.e., across applications) communications.

Queue Transaction Operations

OS/2 Queue Transaction Operations (i.e. reading from or writing to a queue) uses standard REXX instructions. These are listed below in Table 3-4.

Table 3-4

REXX Instruction	Where in the Queue	Order in Which Retrieved
PUSH *expression*	Top of queue (most recent elements)	First data element retrieved.
QUEUE *expression*	Bottom of queue (oldest elements) of queue was pushed.	First element retrieved unless an element near the top
PULL parse_ins (converts text to uppercase)	Doesn't apply — retrieve only.	Top element retrieved (most recent)

Table 3-4 Continued

REXX Instruction	Where in the Queue	Order in Which Retrieved
(IBM OS/2 REXX gives a ? prompt, Quercus does not.) See the section on "Parsing command line input" for an explanation on *parse_ins*.		

Here is the order for pulling data elements:

- First element PUSHed, second element QUEUEd OR both elements QUEUEd —> First element retrieved first, second element retrieved second.
- First element QUEUEd and second element PUSHed OR both elements PUSHED —> Second element is retrieved first, first element is retrieved second.

Use the QUEUED built-in function to tell you number of the lines left in the active queue.

Retrieve a set of data from a queue

```
name = rxqueue('Create') /* Create private queue */
rc = rxqueue('Set',name)
qnum = queued()
cnt = 1
Do while queued() > 0 /* assumes data already on the queue */
       pull line.cnt  /* Retrieve all lines and place in a compound */
/* symbol */
       cnt = cnt +1
end
rc = rxqueue('Delete',name) /* Cleanup queue */.
```

Write a set of data to a queue

```
name = rxqueue('Create') /* Create private queue */
rc = rxqueue('Set',name)
do cnt = 1 to 100 /* writes out the numbers 1 to 100 to a data queue. */
```

```
        queue cnt
end
rc = rxqueue('Delete,name) /* Cleanup queue */.
```

Additional Built-in Functions

OS/2 REXX includes five additional built-in non-portable functions as part of the standard package. Note that Quercus REXX supports all of these as well. Three of these will be discussed in this section. (SETLOCAL and ENDLOCAL were reviewed in the earlier section on "Environmental Variables.")

The Poor Man's/Woman's Multimedia — The Beep Built-in Function

If you are looking for a brief computing diversion, perhaps the BEEP built-in function is for you. Often used as part of a subroutine, it has two arguments, the frequency (37-32767 Hertz), and duration (1-60000 milliseconds). A null string means that your note(s) were successfully played.

```
/* Here is part of "Mary Had a Little Lamb" */
/* Not shown: middle B — 494, C— 262, D — 294, E — 330 */
freq.1 = 440 /* A */
freq.2 = 392 /* G */
freq.3 = 349 /* F */
freq.4 = 392
freq.5 = 440
freq.6 = 440
freq.7 = 440
freq.8 = 392
freq.9 = 392
freq.10 = 392
freq.11 = 440
freq.12 = 523 /* C */
freq.13 = 523
duration = 600 /* one second for the entire "array" */
do cnt = 1 to 13
       call beep freq.cnt, duration.cnt
end
```

The File Specification Parser — The FILESPEC function

If you need to parse a file name, consider using the FILESPEC built-in function. (Quercus REXX also has the PARSEFN function that does the same thing.) Here are examples using FILESPEC:

```
filename = 'c:\os2\apps\jigsaw.exe'
/* jigsaw puzzle - used for all of the following examples */
```

Parsing for drive letter

```
Drive = filespec('drive',filename) /* Drive = C: */
Drive = substr(Filespec('drive',filename),1,1)) /* Drive = C */
```

Parsing for directory/subdirectory name

```
Dirs = filespec('path',filename) /* Dirs = \os2\apps */
/* Must write your own sequence to parse any further */
/* For the above example */
parse value dirs with '\' first '\' second '\' /* first = os2 and second */
/* = apps */
```

Parsing for filename

```
fn = filespec('name',filename) /* returns jigsaw.exe */
/* Must write your own sequence to parse any further */
/* For the above example */
parse value fn with first '.' second /* First = jigsaw and second = exe */
```

For a portable sequence, use the following:

```
file_nm = 'c:\cmd.exe /* doesn't support subdirectories */
if pos(':',file_nm) > 0 then parse value file_nm with drive':\',
      base_nm '.' ftype
      else parse value file_nm with base_nm '.' ftype
```

REXX's "Change Directory (cd)" Command — The DIRECTORY Function

Here are examples of the DIRECTORY function that can be used to change the active directory and drive:

Return the current directory

```
say DIRECTORY() /* Maybe C:\OS2 */
```

Reset the current directory

```
say DIRECTORY('\temp') /* Returns C:\TEMP */
```

Resets the current directory and drive

```
say DIRECTORY('D:\SYSTEM')
/* Resets the active drive to D and the current directory to system */
```

DIRECTORY can simulate parts of the SETLOCAL/ENDLOCAL function. If you use DIRECTORY to save the active directory and drive to a symbol, later you can "restore" them with another DIRECTORY function using the symbol as an argument.

Customizing STARTUP.CMD

Although the START command was added back in OS/2 1.3 to eliminate the need for STARTUP.CMD (IBM 1990,3), the latter is still thriving in OS/2 2.1. Here is some uses of STARTUP.CMD found in the top directory. If a STARTUP.CMD is present, then consider having it do the following:

1. Automatically invoking the extend built-in function (REXX Utilities) DLL. Start a REXX procedure that contains the following:

```
call RxFuncAdd 'SysLoadFuncs', 'RexxUtil','SysCls'
```

Use the DETACH or START command to invoke it.

2. Automatically invoking a REXX procedure or an executable that initializes or customizes your REXX environment. Use DETACH or START to invoke it.
3. Have the Enhanced Editor on your desktop, for use at any time:

```
'start c:\os2\apps\epm.exe /i'
```

OS/2 REXX UNIQUE FEATURES: INTERMEDIATE (REXXUTIL)

Overview/Invoking Extended Functions: New with 2.0 were an additional 29 built-in external REXX functions. These are either called the extended built-in functions or the REXX utility functions. These functions are part of the REXXUTIL dynamic link library. (A Dynamic Link Library (DLL) is one means for multiple OS/2 processes to share resources. It is a set of functions stored in an executable files. Resident in the C:\OS2\DLL directory. Most of these functions are not complicated to use. However, some do require more than some casual knowledge of OS/2.) Note source for much of this code is included in the REXX samples subdirectory of the OS/2 Toolkit.

Making The REXXUtil DLL Accessible

Some new REXX programmers assume that these extended functions are automatically available to REXX procedures. This is not true. The dynamic link library must be first registered using the RxFuncAdd function dynamically links REXXUTIL.DLL at runtime. There appears to be no memory penalty in terms of registering functions — there are not loaded until a call to a function in the DLL is invoked. Here are some tips on doing this process:

1. You may want to add this to STARTUP.CMD so it is automatically done at OS/2 boot-time and it doesn't have to be done again.
2. Register the DLL with one of two approaches:

Register only one function

```
call RxFuncAdd 'SysSleep', 'RexxUtil', 'SysSleep'
/* Registers the function. */
/*     First argument       - Function name to register */
/*     Second argument - Name of DLL (extension not required) */
/*      Third argument - Name of the procedure in the DLL */
/* Now let's use the function - like any other built-in function invoked */
/* With call */
            call sysleep 10 /* terminal sleeps for 10 seconds */
```

Register all functions (SysLoadFuncs)

```
          call RxFuncAdd 'SysLoadFuncs', 'RexxUtil','SysLoadFuncs'
                    call sysloadfuncs
```

3. It is a good practice to use RxFuncQuery to see if the dynamic link library is already registered.

```
if rxFuncQuery('SysLoadFuncs') <> 0 then
/* 0 - already registered, 1 - not registered */
      call RxFuncAdd 'SysLoadFuncs', 'RexxUtil','SysLoadFuncs'
      else say 'REXXUtil already loaded'
```

4. Once registered, these functions are available to all processes (i.e. REXX procedures). So, if they are dropped, also called deregistering using the RxFuncDrop(function_name) to drop one extended function or call the SysDropFuncs to deregister all extended functions, they are dropped for all processes as well, Beware!

5. See the section on "External Functions" later in this chapter for more information on this topic.

6. Note these functions can either be invoked as functions or subroutines.

A Look At The External Functions

Table 3-6 lists the name of functions and generally what they do:

Table 3-6 REXX External Functions

Screen Operations	File Operations	Drive/ Directory Operations	Class/ Object Operations	General Operations
RxMessageBox	SysFileDelete	SysDriveInfo	SysCreateObject	SysDropFuncs
SysCls	SysFileTree	SysDriveMap	SysDeregisterObjectClass	SysIni
SysCurPos	SysFileSearch	SysMkDir	SysDestroyObject	SysOS2Ver
SysCurState	SysGetEA	SysRmDir	SysQueryClassList	SysSleep
SysGetKey	SysPutEA		SysRegisterObjectClass	SysWaitNamedPipes
SysGetMessage	SysSearchPath		SysSetObjectData	
SysTextScreenRead	SysSetIcon			
SysTextScreenSize	SysTempFileName			

Many of the extended functions simulate OS/2 commands. However, they use less overhead and better exception handling than an OS/2 command equivalent. The remainder of this section will examine these extended functions listed in Table 3-6.

Drive/Directory Operations

Drive Operations: Here is an example of what to do with SysDriveInfo (the Quercus equivalent DOSDISK gives additional information):

Create a Disk Usage Report

```
drive_info = SysDriveInfo('C:') /* Don't forget to register REXXUTIL.DLL */
/* Returns null string if unsuccessful */
parse value drive_info with drive_letter free_space used_space drive_name
drive = substr(drive_letter,1,1) /* gets rid of colon */
free = (free_space/1024)/1000||'M'
used = (used_space/1024)/1000||'M'

say '****************************************'
say '* Report on 'drive_name'              ****'
say '* drive letter free space      used space*'
say '* 'drive'        'free'           'used
say '****************************************'
Printed
****************************************
* Report on Joey                    ****
* drive letter    free space   used space*
* C              95.968M         207.24M
****************************************
```

SysDriveMap gives the current status and types of valid drives:

```
/* Lan Drive Status */
lan_drives = SysDriveMap('C:','REMOTE')
/* Returns a null string if unsuccessful processing */
/* First argument is starting search drive. */
/* Valid values for second drive (status/type) are (one of the following:) */
/*     Status (local and remote) - USED (default - drive in use), */
/*     FREE, and DETACHED (LAN drives only) */
/*     Type - LOCAL, REMOTE (LAN drives) */
Say 'LAN drives -- 'lan_drives /* Returns LAN drives - G: H: */
```

Directory Operations

Instead of using ADDRESS CMD "mkdir..." or "rmdir..." to create or delete directories, consider using SysMkDir and SysRmDir:

Create a Directory

```
ret_code = SysMkdir('c:\mytemp')  /* Creates the mytemp directory */
                                  /* Directory argument required */
                                  /* Ret_code may be 0 (worked) */
                                  /* 2-3 (invalid file specification) */
                                  /* 5 (access denied — directory may already */
                                  /* be created or in use) */
                                  /* 26 (unknown disk type */
                                  /* 108 (locked disk — can't write) */
                                  /* 87, 206 (miscellaneous error) */
```

Delete a Directory

```
ret_code = SysRmdir('c:\mytemp')  /* delete the mytemp directory */
                                  /* argument required */
                                  /* Samc return codes as SysMkDir */
```

File Operations

File operation's built-in functions simulate some of the capabilities of OS/2 commands. In addition, it provides a painless and safe way to modify or query the two INI files used to initialize and customize OS/2.

Query File Operations

This looks at built-in functions that do not change files but only gather information from them.

REXX's File Searcher

SysFileSearch is OS/2 REXX's equivalent of the FIND OS/2 system command. Unfortunately, it does not have rich pattern-matching capabilities as compared to UNIX's grep, egrep, fgrep commands. SysFileSearch is only limited to one file at a time.

Search for ADDRESS CMD in a REXX exec

```
Call SysFileSearch 'ADDRESS CMD', 'C:\SONG.CMD', 'address_find.', 'N'
/* First argument -  Search String */
/* Second argument - File to Search */
/* Third argument -  Symbol name. This is the stem name of a */
/*                   compound symbol "array" to hold the search listing. */
/* Fourth argument - Use one or both: C (Search for argument in */
/*                   the entered text case ), N (Display line number in */
/*                   with the search string.) Neither of these arguments */
/*                   are the default */
/* Stem_name.0 is the number of "lines" in the search list. */
/* Returns 0 (successful), 2-3 (error) */
do cnt = 1 to address_find.0 /* Display listing */
      say value('address_find'.cnt)
end

Output:
2 ADDRESS CMD "DIR" /* Found line starting with line number */
```

Create a Directory Listing Using REXX

SysFileTree is the file equivalent of SysDriveMap. It allows you to create your own directory listing using REXX. Table 3-7 may help you in coding the function by following these steps :

Table 3-7

Question	What to Code
1. What is the name of the symbol to hold the return code?	STEP 1: Enter — Code *name* = SysFileTree() name is the symbol name that you specify.
/* Return codes are 0 (successful) */ /* 2 (error — memory problems) */	
2. What is the file to search for?	Usually C:*.* — search all files. Wildcards (i.e. * and ?) supported. STEP 2: Change to: *name* = *SysFileTree('c:*.*')*

Table 3-7 Continued

Question	What to Code
3. What is the name of the symbol that will hold the output?	The second argument is the name of a compound symbol stem used to create an "array" to hold the directory listing. *Stem_name.0* is the number of "lines" in the output list. STEP 3: Change to: name = SysFileTree('c:*.*',*name*[2])
4. What is my "input" for the directory listing? a. Major type, search levels, report output	For <u>third</u> argument: Choose <u>one</u>: (Value in parentheses) Default —Files **and** Directories (B), Files (F), Directories (D), And also choose <u>one or more</u>: Recursive Directories (S) <u>(Report Formats)</u>, Time and date printed as one value (T), List file names only (O) STEP 4: Change to: name = SysFileTree('c:*.*',*name*[2], '*flags*')
b. Am I interested in searching for file attributes? If NO, invoke the function created as is.	If YES: There are five attributes: Archive, Directory, Hidden, Read-only, and System. These are either set or not. A template is specified in the above order with these flags: * (may be set or not), + (must be set), - (must not be set).

Table 3-7 Continued

Question	What to Code
	Examples: '+——' - Look for files with **only** the archived attribute enabled. '+****' - Look for files **with at least** the archived attribute enabled. STEP 5: Change to: name = SysFileTree('c:*.*',*name*[2], *'flags'*, *'template*[1]*'*)

Note that Archive, Directory, Hidden, Read-only, and System are stored in the File Allocation Table (FAT) or a part of the file (HPFS). They are either set (1) or not (0). Values include: Archive (if set, tells the backup program that the file has changed since the last backup), Directory (File is a directory), Hidden (Hidden file), Read-only (can't delete a file? See if this attribute is set — and thus stopping you), System (a system file — usually also hidden.)

Here are some examples:

Find all REXX procedures in the C drive

```
ret_code = SysFileTree('c:\*.cmd','rexx_execs','F')
```

Find all read-only REXX procedures in the C drive

```
ret_code = SysFileTree('c:\*.cmd',rexx_execs,'FD','***+*')
```

Print the directory listing for the above examples

```
do cnt = 1 to rexx_execs.0
      say value('rexx_execs'.cnt)
end
```

Output from first example

```
1/30/93     11:14a 4098  A— C:\CRY.CMD
2/10/92      3:22p   62  A— C:\TRY.CMD
```

Output from the second example

```
3/15/93        10:44p        9092 A—R- C:\A.CMD
```

SysGetEA retrieves an extended attribute of a file.

```
ftype=SysGetEA("C:\A.CMD", ".type". "TYPEINFO")
/* Returns file type — requires additional parsing */
/* The.type attribute */
/* is stored in the TYPEINFO REXX symbol and has a value similar to */
/* 5 ¢ < OS/2 Command file */
/* Return codes — 0 (successful). 1 (unsuccessful processing) */
```

The values for .type include: Text/Command Files (i.e., DOS Command File, OS/2 Command File, Plain Text), Source Files (i.e., Assembler Code, BASIC Code, C Code, COBOL Code, FORTRAN Code), Other (Bitmap, Binary Data, Dynamic Link Library, Executable, Icon, Metafile, PIF file, Printer-specific, Resource File). Other standard extended attributes are COMMENTS (notes about the file), HISTORY (who created the file and when), ICON (icon to be used with file), KEYPHRASES (keywords describing the type of file), and VERSION (version number). See the *OS/2 Programmer's Reference Vol. 1* (Chapter 5) for further information (S10G-6261).

Look for a File's Location

SysSearchPath will return both if a file exists and its location.

Find Path of REXXINIT.DLL

```
where_is_it = SysSearchPath('APATH','REXXINIT.DLL')
/* You can use environment names such as DPATH, and PATH or your own */
/* environment variable */
       say value(where_is_it)
/* OR say where_is_it */
end

Output:
C:\OS2\REXXINIT.DLL
/* Null string is returned if the file(s) is not found Non-zero return code — */
/* Unsuccessful processing (Perhaps invalid number of arguments) */
```

SysTempFileName returns a unique temporary file name that can be used for "quick and dirty" file operations (such as writing to a temporary file and then printing it out).

```
tname = SysTempFileName('C:\TRASH##.###','#')
/* Tname is the new temporary file name. Could be TRASH83.831 */
/* If a null string is returned, then a temporary file name could not be */
/* created */
/* First argument - is the template. Says that all files will be in the root */
/* directory and have a name of TRASHxx.yyy. xx and yy will be generated */
/* by the REXX interpreter. */
/* Second argument - the character (one only) to be used to specify the */
/* location of characters in the file name the REXX interpreter must generate */
```

File Modification Operations

These operations somehow change files.

SysFileTree can be used to change a file's attributes. Two cases are presented below:

```
Changes Read-only to Read-Write
ret_code = SysFileTree('C:\mytemp\*.*',changed,'S','***+*','***-*')
/* mytemp directory only. Fifth and Fourth arguments have similar templates. */
/*The fifth argument is the attribute transaction flags of * (no change), + (set) */
/* unset (-) */
```

Changes hidden files to visible.

```
ret_code = SysFileTree('C:\mytemp\*.*',changed,'S','**+**','**-**')
```

SysFileDelete allows you to delete one file at a time. Only the file name is needed as an argument. Non-zero return codes (between 2 and 206) indicate error. Some common errors are: 2-3 — file/path errors; 5/32 — file in use; 87/206 — Invalid Filenames.

```
ret_code = SysFileDelete("c:\temp\a.cmd")
```

SysPutEA writes an extended attribute to a file.

```
ret_code = SysPutEA('c:\temp\test.cmd',"TYPE",hex_string)
/* Where hex_string is the extended attribute string. */
```

Comment added

```
retcode = SysPutEA('c:\temp\test.cmd',FUDGE,'A comment!!!')
/* Created a new extended attribute called FUDGE */
```

Notes

Modifying extended attributes could bring unexpected results including file corruption and the inability to access the file. There is also no easy way in REXX to determine whether a file has extended attributes or not. The only method is to generate a directory listing with the /N parameter, then parse the listing. Next examine the extended attribute field to see it is used or not. An example of this can be found in the shareware utility EAPREP.CMD. There is third-party software that extends REXX's ability to deal with extended attributes. One example is EAREXX.ZIP.

SysIni directly manipulates and queries both system and application "INI" files. The standard OS/2 installation includes the following "INI" files listed in Table 3-8:

Table 3-8

Name/Location	What It Does
C:\OS2\MDOS\WINOS2\ATM.INI	Adobe Type Manager during MS-Windows sessions under OS/2.
C:\OS2\EPM.INI	Enhanced Editor customization file
C:\OS2\IMAGE.INI	Used during installation. Associated with monitor type. (OS/2 2.0)
C:\OS2\INSTALL.INI	Used during installation. Associated with monitor type. (OS/2 2.0)
C:\OS2\OS2.INI	Contains font filenames, localization values (such as date, time, money), application customization values, group names, components within groups, color preferences

Table 3-8 Continued

Name/Location	What It Does
C:\OS2\OS2SYS.INI	Contains print spool information and color schemes.

The remainder of this section will focus on modifying OS2.INI and OS2SYS.INI.

- When OS/2 creates the OS2 system files, it uses a utility called MAKEINI. MakeINI creates the INI files from "data" in two text files: PC:\OS2\INSTALL\INI.RC [2.0] or C:\OS2\INI.RC [2.1] (Creates OS2.INI) and C:\OS2\INSTALL\INISYS.RC [2.0] or C:\OS2\INISYS.RC [2.1] (Creates OS2SYS.INI). It may help to look at these RC files to learn more about the INI files it created.
- Use INI files to store values that will be accessible from any application — similar to environmental variables.

Here are some examples of things that can be done with the SYSINI command:

- The following was created by IBM and reproduced with the permission of IBM and Timothy F. Sipple's. It originally appeared in the OS/2 Frequently Asked Questions — one of the most downloaded files on CompuServe:

> To disable the automatic application restart feature, create a STARTUP.CMD file in the root directory of your OS/2 boot drive with the following REXX script:
>
> ```
> /* */
> call RxFuncadd 'SysLoadFuncs', 'RexxUtil', 'SysLoadFuncs'
> call SysLoadFuncs
> call 'SysIni 'USER', 'PM_Workplace:Restart', 'DELETE:'
> exit'
> ```
>
> or add the line SET RESTARTOBJECTS=STARTUPFOLDERS only to your CONFIG.SYS.

(Other values for RESTARTOBJECTS are YES, NO and REBOOTONLY. Yes, which is the default, will start everything that was running when OS/2 was shutdown. NO indicates don't start anything that was running when OS/2 was shutdown, REBOOTONLY (ONLY use with YES, NO, and STARTFOLDERONLY — start objects only after a reboot or starting the computer.)

See the section on "Invoking Extended Utilities" to understand the arguments for invoking REXXUtil.

Here are the arguments for SYSINI:

First argument: The name of the file to change. Valid values are the name of any valid INI file, USER (an alias for OS2.INI — the default), SYSTEM (OS2SYS.INI), BOTH (queries both files, modifies only OS2.INI)

Second argument: The name of the "application" or "category". In this case, PM_Workplace:Restart. ALL: (all categories) is a valid value.

Third argument: Delete all the subcategories with values, found under this category. Thus, SYSINI will not restart anything that was open. ALL: (all subcategories) is a valid value.

Returns: Null string (Successful processing — attribute deleted or retrieved), ERROR:, Other text (retrieved value).

- Creating/Deleting new Workplace Shell file association types and fonts. If successful the result is a null string.

Notes

1. Some changes will not be effective until the machine is rebooted.
2. You have to append a null (||x'oo') at the end of a SYSINI command being written out.

Creating a new Workplace Shell file association

```
fassoc = "Perl Code"
call RxFuncAdd 'SysIni','RexxUtil','SysIni'
SysIni('User','PMWP_Assoc_Type',fassoc,||'00')
/* Fourth argument - null value for type */
/* Workplace Shell file Association */
/* Also PM_ASSOC_Type for Presentation Manager file association */
```

Adding a new font file:

```
fname.1 = "JONES"
fname.2 = "JONES.PSF"
ffile.1 = "\OS2\DLL\JONES.FON"
```

```
ffile.2 = "\OS2\DLL\JONES.PSF"
call RxFuncAdd 'SysIni','RexxUtil','SysIni'
do cnt = 1 to 2
      SysIni('User','PM_Fonts',fname.cnt,ffile.cnt)
end
\
```

Deleting a Workplace Shell File Association

```
fassoc = "Perl Code"
call RxFuncAdd 'SysIni','RexxUtil','SysIni'
SysIni('User','PMWP_Assoc_Type',fassoc,'DELETE:')
```

Deleting Font File Values

```
fname.1 = "JONES"
fname.2 = "JONES.PSF
call RxFuncAdd 'SysIni', 'RexxUtil','SysIni'
do cnt = 1 to 2
      SysIni('User','PM_Fonts"',fname.cnt,'DELETE:')
end
```

Listed in Table 3-9 are some other useful types and values.

Table 3-9

2nd argument of SYSINI	3rd argument	4th argument
"EPM"	"EPMIniPath"	"\OS2\EPM.INI" (default) Change to new location.
"PM_National"	"iCountry"	"1" (Country Code 1 = USA)
"PM_National"	"iDate"	"0" (Date Format : 0 = Month/Day/Year, 1 = Day/Month/Year, 2 = Year/Month/Day)
"PM_National"	"iTime"	"0" (Time Format: 0 - 12 hour format 1 - 24 hour format)

Table 3-9 Continued

2nd argument of SYSINI	3rd argument	4th argument
"PM_National"	"iMeasurement"	"1" (Measurement System: 1 = English, 2 = Metric, 3 = Points, 4 = Pica)
PM_SPOOLER	"Queue"	"LPT1Q;" (Tells the default printer port)

Here are several other uses of SYSINI:

Getting a Value of a Sub-category

```
rvalue = SysIni('USER',"PM_National","iCountry") /* rvalue = 1 (USA) */
```

Getting all the Sub-category Values for a Category

```
ret_code = SysIni('USER','PM_National,'ALL:',aa)
/* Returns all the sub-categories of PM_National (such as ICountry and IDate) */
/* This is stored in a compound symbol array starting with aa.0 (number of */
/* categories). */
```

Getting the Sub-category Values for aLL Categories

```
ret_code = SysIni('USER',"ALL:",aa)
/* Returns all the sub-categories for all categories. This is stored in a */
/* compound symbol array starting with aa.0 (number of categories). */
```

See the REXX.TXT reference at the end for further information.

General Operations

This section reviews functions that didn't fit into the other categories. *SysDropFuncs* unloads the REXXUtil Dynamic Link Library. This may cause unpredictable results if another process is using REXXUtil at the same time — so use cautiously.

```
Call SysDropFuncs /* Returns 0 if successful */
```

SysOS2Ver returns the OS/2 version number. No argument is specified.

```
version = SysOS2Ver() /* version = 2.10 */
```

SysSleep is a controlled pause.

```
call SysSleep 20 /* Waits 20 seconds Returns null string if ok. */
```

Notes

SysSleep is useful if you want it to look like the computer is thinking (i.e., games); need to allow time for the user to read text on the screen or generally the need to slow down the procedure's processing.

SysWaitNamedPipe pauses a named pipe that was created by a non-REXX program (i.e., SysSleep using named pipes). A pipe allows two processes (programs) to exchange data. (Also called inter-process communication or IPC.) A **named pipe** can be accessed by other processes (even across networks). Here are how to use REXX functions to perform pipe operations.

```
Open a Stream   - Call stream '\\PIPE\pipe1','C','OPEN'
Close a Stream  - Call stream '\\PIPE\pipe1','C','CLOSE'
Read            - Call linein '\\PIPE\pipe1'
Write           - Call lineout '\\PIPE\pipe1', 'string'
```

Three other functions were supposed to have been created — SysMakeNamedPipe (create a named pipe), SysConnectNamedPipe (Get a named pipe ready for a connection to a client pipe), SysDisconnectNamedPipe (opposite of SysConnectNamed Pipe) — but were not done because it is hard to connect to a named pipe under REXX.

Screen/Keyboard Operations

REXX offers some primitive keyboard and screen operations. For more powerful functions, consider the RXWINDOW functions of Quercus OS/2 Personal REXX, Visual REXX from IBM, and Tritus SPF from Tritus, Inc. Here is an overview of what is included with the REXXUtil Dynamic Link Library.

RxMessageBox: creates a dialog box for a REXX application that is running under PMREXX (not the command-line). There is an exception to this. Starting the procedure as a Presentation Manager session, which invokes PMREXX by doing the following:

```
retcode = SysWaitNamedPipe("\PIPE\pipex",2)
/* TRAP: Thinking \PIPE is a directory name. */
/* Retcode — 0 (successful), 2 (non-existent pipename), 109 (broken pipe), */
/* 231 (Pipe timed out) */
/* First argument — Name of named pipe. */
/* Second argument — Number of microseconds. Also valid is -1 */
/* (keep waiting until the pipe is not in use.) */
```

Note that only a limited number of "standard" responses and you can't create your own.

```
START /PM CMD.EXE /C the_exec.cmd
/* /PM says run the Command interpreter (CMD.EXE) as a Presentation Manager session. */
/* /C says close the created session on completion */
/* the_exec.cmd is the REXX exec that has the RxMessageBox call */
```

Listed in Table 3-10 are the "standard choices", when to use them, and the return code if that key is pushed:

Table 3-10

Standard Choice (Keyset or Type of Dialog Box)	When to Use	Return code if Pushed.
One Choice Dialogs		
CANCEL	When an operation is never performed.	2 = Cancel Key pushed
- Use the hand, warning, or error Icon.		

Table 3-10 Continued

Standard Choice (Keyset or Type of Dialog Box)	When to Use	Return code if Pushed.
ENTER - Use the Information Icon	1. Provide a chance to read information. 2. Confirm an operation always performed.	8 = Enter key pressed
OK (default)	1. Provide a chance to read information.	1 = OK key pressed
- Use the Information or Exclamation Point Icons	2. Confirm an operation always performed.	
Multiple Choice Dialogs		
ABORTRETRYCANCEL - Use Exclamation, Error, Warning Icon.	1. Determine an action after an error has occurred.	2 = Cancel Key 3 = Abort Key 4 = Retry Key
ENTERCANCEL - Use Exclamation, Error, Warning Icon.	1. Confirm an operation that is nearly always performed.	2 = Cancel key pressed 8 = Enter key pressed (check)
OKCANCEL - Use Exclamation, Error, Warning Icon.	1. Confirm an operation that is nearly always performed.	1 = OK key pressed 2 = Cancel key pressed
RETRYCANCEL - Use Exclamation, Error, Warning Icon.	1. If an unsuccessful operation has occurred and you want to give the user to retry the operation or exit while the can.	2 = Cancel key pressed 4 = Retry key pressed
YESNO - Use Query or Question Mark Icon	1. For simple two-choice operations (such as exit).	6 = Yes key pressed 7 = No key pressed

Table 3-10 Continued

Standard Choice (Keyset or Type of Dialog Box)	When to Use	Return code if Pushed.
YESNOCANCEL - Use Query or Question Mark Icon	1. For three choice operations ("Delete the File — Yes, No-Cancel?")	

Here is some sample code:

Multiple Key Example

```
call RxFuncAdd 'SysLoadFuncs', 'RexxUtil', 'SysLoadFuncs' /* Load DLL */
call SysLoadFuncs
say "What is your Age?"
pull age
if age > 120 then do
        key_pressed = RxMessageBox("Are you sure this is correct?",,
       "Invalid Age","YesNoCancel", "Question")
/* First argument    - Dialog Box Text. Test for limits. */
/* Second argument   - Dialog Box Title. Overrides ERROR default */
/* Third argument,   - Keyset (listed above) */
/* Fourth argument   - Icon type displayed (NONE, HAND, */
/*                          QUESTION (question */
/*                          mark), EXCLAMATION (exclamation point) */
/*                          ASTERISK, INFORMATION, QUERY, */
/*                          WARNING, ERROR) */
select
       when key_pressed = 2 then signal can_r /* CANCEL - cancel routine */
        /* (not shown) */
       when key_pressed = 6 then signal yes_r /* YES - continue routine */
        /* (not shown) */
       when key_pressed = 7 then signal no_r /* NO - get new value routine */
        /* (not shown) */
otherwise
       say 'Unexpected key pressed. Return Code is ' key_pressed
       exit key_pressed
end
```

Figure 3-7 is an example of what the dialog box might look like:

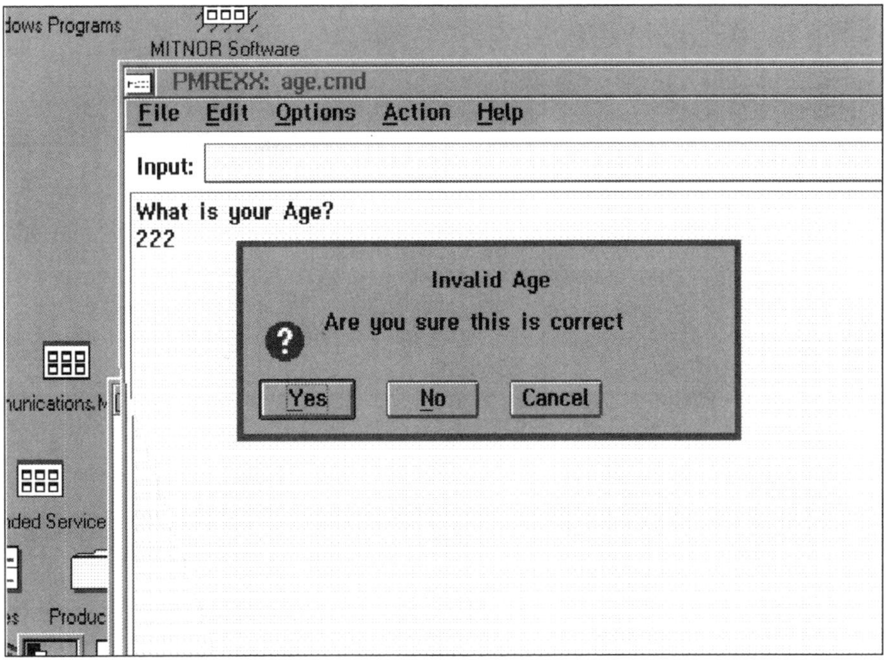

Figure 3-7 Invalid Age Dialog Box

Note that the user can either click on the desired button or enter just the first letter. The default button (YES) is highlighted.

SysCls: REXX's version of the CLS OS/2 command. It clears the screen with no required arguments. This command returns 0 if successful.

```
SysCls() OR call SysCls. /* Clears the screen */
```

SysCurPos: moves the cursor to a specified location on the screen or queries the current location. Use SysTextScreenSize if you are uncertain of the size of your screen.

Query the current location

```
/* Invoke RexxUtil DLL (not shown) */
row_col = SysCurPos()
say row_col /* Returns 24 0 (bottom left) */
```

Change the current location

```
call SysCurPos(24,80)        /* positions in the 24th row, 80th column */
                             /* right of the screen */
```

SysCurState: modifies the current cursor setting to either ON (show cursor) or OFF (hide cursor).

```
SysCurState('On') /* enables the cursor being shown */
```

SysGetKey: captures the next key pressed. The only argument has a value of either ECHO or NOECHO. Echo, the default, display the key pressed. NOECHO indicates don't display the key pressed.

```
key_pressed = SysGetKey() or SysGetKey('ECHO')
/* " " - space */
/* ? - F1-F10 */
```

SysGetMessage: similar to the standard Errortext REXX built-in function. Errortext returns the corresponding error text message for a specified REXX error number. SysGetMessage returns the error text message if it can find the error number in one of the message files in a known subdirectory.

Display all REXX error messages (like ERRORTEXT)

```
do cnt = 1 to 125
      msg.cnt = SysGetMessage(cnt,'REX.MSG')
/* First argument      - error number */
/* Second argument - error message library. Default is OSO001.MSG */
/*      (OS/2 system messages). Searches in DPATH subdirectories */
/*      plus the current and root directories */
/* Third-twelfth arguments - Values to be substituted in the error message */
/* Usually have to browse.MSG library to see where the values %1 to %9 */
/* are used. The messages are stored in compound symbol for later use */
      say cnt '--' msg.cnt
```

```
/* Displayed: 48 --?W%1 Failure in System Service%2 */
/* As mentioned earlier, %1 and %2 are substituted at the time the error */
/* message is processed */
end
```

SysTextScreenRead: will read characters at a specified screen location.

Read from Current Cursor Position

```
/* Invoke REXXUtil DLL (not shown) */
/* Cannot use symbols as argument values */
SysTextScreenRead(24,0,10) /* Reads from current position */
/* First and second arguments - specified row and column to read from */
/* If 0,0, then in starting location (top left) */
/* Third argument - the number of characters to read. The default is the end */
/* of the screen. A value of 80 is one line */
```

SysTextScreenSize: will return the number of rows and columns in the current screen. Also use this with SysCurPos which returns the current position.

Query Current Screen Size

```
/* Invoke REXXUtil DLL (not shown)*/
SysTextScreenSize()
/* Returns 25 (rows),80 (columns)*/
```

Object/Class Operations

Before reviewing REXXUtil functions, it is more than necessary to have a basic understanding of class and object operations. The following is a brief explanation — references to more complete treatments are included. Note that this is not for the casual REXX user, be forewarned! If you are not familiar with the basics of object-oriented programming, you may need to re-read the following section several times. You may also refer to chapter 7 which takes another look at object-oriented REXX.

What is a Class and an Object Anyway?

Underlying the Workplace Shell is another level of abstraction which uses object-oriented techniques. This evolving technology is called the **System Object Model** (SOM). It can be used with a number of programming languages including REXX some time in the near future. The Macintosh has a similar approach with the Apple Events Object Model (AEOM). Two good articles on that approach are Richard Clark's "Apple Event Object and You" in The May 92 issue of Develop (Apple's developer monthly journal) and "Better Apple Event Coding Through Objects." in the December 92 issue. Note that SOM-2, SOM's successor is already being developed.

So What is an Object?

There are two viewpoints: 1) The academic view which sees an object as a functional piece of code or program subset (which may or may not be GUI-based). It has two components: a description(s) of an item and some operations to perform on it. 2) The second is a marketing view which sees objects as only those things which are GUI-related. In the Workplace Shell, these would be unique entities such as folders, documents, applications, devices — things used everyday to perform work while under OS/2. This book will be using the second viewpoint as a simple analogy to explain how to use object-oriented programming under OS/2 REXX. This approach maybe revised in later editions. References are given later in this section that further explain the first view.

Each object belongs to a **class**. This class contains objects that are logically related (i.e., having similar properties). Each class defines set of methods to modify those properties and behaviors for specified objects. This is analogous to the REXXUtil functions.

What SOM offers is a tool that can create class libraries, sets of classes, that can be used with any of the supported languages. So, in the future, OS/2 REXX could use a class library created in COBOL. Each object is an instance (a case) of a class.

Here is an example of how class, object, property and method come together:

```
Class = Folder (unique entity)
       Object = Startup Folder (type [case] of folder)
       Property = No Delete (Don't delete ever)
       Method = Create Folder (Behavior)
```

This completes our overview of object-oriented programming. It by no means covers the richness or complexities of either SOM or object-oriented programming. For a more complete analysis, see the Berry and Reeves (92), or the Sessions and Coskum (92) references for further information on this topic.

What Classes and Objects can OS/2 REXX Manipulate?

Now that we are familiar with classes and objects, the next question usually asked is "What classes and objects can OS/2 REXX manipulate?" Note that there are three major classes that a REXX procedure may use: WPFolder (for folder objects), WPProgram (for program objects) and WPShadow (for shadow [copies of a folder or program] objects). For more information, look at the REXX.TXT file or Chapters 7 and 8 of the OS/2 2.1 Application Design Guide (S10G-6260). Table 3-11 should answer that question.

Table 3-11

Class	Object/ObjectID	Properties (attribute,value(s))
WPFolder	FOLDER OBJECTS can also be found in OS2.INI under the PM_Workplace: category. See the discussion on the SysIni function mentioned earlier for more information	Applies to **all** folder objects (CCVIEW, ICONFILE, MINWIN, and TEMPLATE also apply to all program objects)
	<MMP2_FOLDER>	MMPM/2 FOLDER
	<WP_CONFIG> System Setup such as Migrate Applications, Color, Fonts	1. What is my overall view format OPEN=*type* *type* = (choose one:) DETAIL (Item name, modified and creation date, and FAT attributes) ICON (folder/program name) TREE (folder/program name)
	<WP_DESKTOP> Workplace Shell Desktop such as Master Help Index, Information, Minimum Item Viewer Network, OS/2 System, Printer, Shredder, Templates	2. How will items/icons in my view be displayed? (Choose one attribute:) DETAILSVIEW=list ICONVIEW=list TREEVIEW=list

Table 3-11 Continued

Class	Object/ObjectID	Properties (attribute,value(s))
		List = one or more of the following separated by commas: FLOWED (column) or NON FLOWED (not in columns) **ICONVIEW attribute only:** NON-GRIDDED (Icon placement is random) NORMAL or MINI (icon size) or INVISIBLE (no icons) **TREEVIEW attribute only** LINES or NOLINES
	<WP_DRIVES> Disk Drives \OS2\BITMAP	3A. How can I use my own bitmap file stored in the directory as a folder background? BACKGROUND=file 3B. How can I use my own icon for a program or folder? ICONFILE=filename.ICO
	<WP_GAMES> Games such as Jigsaw and OS/2 Chess	4. Do I want to make this a work area folder? WORKAREA=YES
	<WP_INFO> Information such as Glossary, Tutorial, Command Reference, and REXX Information.	5. How do I want the folder/ program to behave when a minimize action is requested?

Table 3-11 Continued

Class	Object/ObjectID	Properties (attribute,value(s))
		MINWIN = list *list* = (choose one of the following:) DESKTOP (minimize to desktop) HIDE (hidden) VIEWER (put in minimized window viewer)
	<WP_NOWHERE> Hidden	6. Will the program/foler view be updated every time the item is opened? CCVIEW=YES/NO
	<WP_OS2SYS> Contains Command Prompts, Drives, Games, Productivity Tools, System Setup, and Startup. Also called OS/2 System folder.	7. Make the object into a template? TEMPLATE=YES/NO
	<WP_PROMPTS> Command (DOS, MS-Windows, and OS/2) Prompts	
	<WP_START> Startup. Place shadows of programs that you want to be started up after OS/2 is initially invoked.	
	<WP_TEMPS> Templates such as Bitmap, Data file. (Also can be found in OS2.INI in the PM_Workplace:Templates category.)	
	<WP_TOOLS> Applets such as Notepad, Calendar, Icon Editor, PM Terminal. Also called Productivity or Productivity Tools.	

Table 3-11 Continued

Class	Object/ObjectID	Properties (attribute,value(s))
	<WP_VIEWER> Minimized Item Viewer	
WPProgram	PROGRAM OBJECTS can also be found in OS2.INI under the PM_WorkPlace: category. See the discussion on the SysIni function mentioned earlier for more information. Only the major program objects are shown.	Applies to **all** program objects (Look above at the folder objects to learn about CCVIEW, ICONFILE, MINWIN, and TEMPLATE which also apply to **all** program objects.)
	<WP_CHESS> Chess Program	1. What is the basic information about the file? **A. Filename** EXENAME=*filename*.EXE/.COM **B. Hard-coded/ Substituted arguments** PARAMETERS=*values* Values may be explicitly included or symbolic variables that can be substituted at run-time **C. Associated directory** STARTUPDIR=pathname
	<WP_CLOCK> SystemClock	2. What are the DOS settings for the program? SET setting=value

Table 3-11 Continued

Class	Object/ObjectID	Properties (attribute,value(s))
		There are over 40 different DOS settings.* These can be found by bringing up a DOS window and selecting DOS Settings from the DOS Window menu. Possible (and current) values, and an explanation of the setting is provided.

*a) Hardware-related: HW_TIMER, MOUSE_EXCLUSIVE_ACCESS, PRINT_TIMEOUT, VIDEO_FASTPASTE, VIDEO_MODE_RESTRICTION, VIDEO_ONDEMAND_MEMORY, VIDEO_RETRACE_EMULATION, VIDEO_ROM_EMULATION, VIDEO_SWITCH_NOTIFICATION, VIDEO_WINDOW_REFRESH, VIDEO_8514A_,VGA_IOTRAP, IDLE_SECONDS, IDLE_SENSITIVITY, KBD_ALTHOME_BYPASS, KBD_BUFFER_EXTEND, KBD_RATE_LOCK, CCOM_HOLD, HW_NOSOUND, HW_ROM_TO_RAM, KBD_CTRL_BYPASS.

b) DOS-related: DOS_BACKGROUND_EXECUTION, DOS_BREAK, DOS_DEVICE, DOS_FCBS, DOS_FCBS_HELD, DOS_Files, DOS_HIGH, DOS_LASTDRIVE, DOS_RMSIZE, DOS_SHELL, DOS_STARTUP_DRIVE, DOS_UMB, DOS_VERSION.

c) Memory-related: DPMI_DOS_API, DPI_MEMORY_LIMIT, DPMI_NETWORK, BUFF_SIZE, EMS_FRAME_LOCATION, EMS_HIGH_OS_MAP_REGION, EMS_LOW_OS_MAP_REGION, EMS_MEMORY_LIMIT, XMS_HANDLES, MEM_INCLUDE_REGIONS, MEM_EXCLUDE_REGIONS.

Class	Object/ObjectID	Properties (attribute,value(s))
		Note that for multiple DOS_DEVICE statements, that a hex line feed (x'0A') is needed to separate each device.
	<WP_CLRPAL> Color Palette	3. What type of program is it? a. PROGTYPE = (Choose one of the following) FULLSCREEN (OS/2) PM (Presentation Manager)

Table 3-11 Continued

Class	Object/ObjectID	Properties (attribute,value(s))
		SEPARATEWIN (MS-Windows — virtual device such as for sharing devices)
		VDM (DOS full-screen)
		WIN (MS-Windows full-screen)
		WINDOWABLEVIO (OS/2 windowed)
		WINDOWEDVDM (DOS windowed)
		WINDOWEDWIN MS-Windows windowed)
	<WP_CMDREF> OS/2 Command Reference	4. Do I need to enable/disable any of the following settings?
		(All the following have a YES or NO value.)
		MAXIMIZED or MINIMIZED (on startup)
		NOAUTOCLOSE (when the program ends, close the window it resides in or not.)
		NOCOPY (Can someone copy this program? **If the value to this or any of the following attributes is YES, then the answer is NO.**)
		NODELETE (Can someone delete this program?)

Table 3-11 Continued

Class	Object/ObjectID	Properties (attribute,value(s))
		NODRAG (Can someone drag this program?)
		NOTVISIBLE (Will this program's icon be visible?)
		NOMOVE (Can someone move this program object?)
		NOPRINT (Can someone print this program object?)
		NORENAME (Can someone rename this object?)
		NOSHADOW (Can someone create a shadow of this program object?)
	<WP_CNTRY> Country Settings	5. What are some other items that can be set for a program?
		ASSOCFILTER=file(s) Can use wildcards and multiple file values (separated by commas). These are the series of files to be part of the association.
		ASSOCTYPE=type. See the discussion earlier in the chapter about types.
		HELPPANEL=number The default help screen for this program. (To create a HELP panel library, use the HELPLIBRARY=*file*.HLP attribute.)

Table 3-11 Continued

Class	Object/ObjectID	Properties (attribute,value(s))
		OBJECTID — how the object is known to OS/2. Examples of these are shown in the first column of this table such as<WP_TOOLS>. OPEN SETTINGS or DEFAULT Which view is shown when an object is created?
	<WP_DDINST> Device Drivers	
	<WP_DOS_DRV_A> DOS from Drive A	
	<WP_DOSFS> DOS Full Screen	
	<WP_DOSWIN> DOS Windowed	
	<WP_EPM> Enhanced Editor	
	<WP_FNTPAL> Font Palette	
	<WP_GLOSS> Glossary	
	<WP_INST> Selective Install	
	<WP_KEYB> Kcyboard Setting	
	<WP_KLDK> Klondike	

Table 3-11 Continued

Class	Object/ObjectID	Properties (attribute,value(s))
	<WP_MIGAPP> Migrate DOS/Windows/OS2 Applications	
	<WP_MINDEX> Master Index	
	<WP_MOUSE> Mouse Setting	
	<WP_OS2FS> OS/2 Full-Screen	
	<WP_OS2WIN> OS/2 Windowed	
	<WP_PMDDE> Dynamic Data Exchange	
	<WP_REXREF> REXX Reference/Tutorial	
	<WP_SCHPAL> Scheme Palette	
	WP_SHRED Shredder	
	<WP_SOUND> System Editor	
	<WP_SPOOL> Print Spool	
	<WP_SYSTEM> System Setting	
	<WP_TUTOR> Tutorial	

Table 3-11 Continued

Class	Object/ObjectID	Properties (attribute,value(s))
WPShadow		SHADOWID=*objectid* Where objectid is a valid OBJECTID value such as <WP_SPOOL> Note that NOSHADOW attribute described earlier in the table must be set to NO.

Why would you want to do this? The advantage is that the system, not you, automatically closes all associated open items (objects) and saves the last current view, when the folder is closed. Note that changes to one item (such as minimizing it affects all open items.) This can also be set by checking the appropriate check box in the Folder-Settings File window. The idea of a work area also reinforces the practice of having folders dedicated to a set of related tasks that may need to use several applications at once such as preparing a course on REXX. This differs in emphasis than a folder which stores related items.

How Can I Use OS/2 REXX to Manipulate these Objects?

With the understanding of what a class and an object are, and what classes and objects REXX can manipulate, then the question becomes: how can I manipulate these objects using REXX?" Please review the previous two subsections if this is unclear to you.

Note that the following will only work on OS/2 2.0 after installing the REXX20 patch or using OS/2 2.1 or later. This is because only those OS/2 releases include the REXXUtil functions of SysSetObjectData and SysDestroyObject. All of the following REXX functions are analogies to **methods** since they directly manipulate SOM objects and classes. Additional information on these functions can be found in the Workplace Shell API function call equivalents. Listed in the *OS/2 Technical Library Presentation Manager Programming Reference — Vol 2.* (S10G-6494)

Object Class Operations

In order to use a new object class, it must be registered. This is done with the *SysRegisterObjectClass*. This command is the equivalent of WinRegisterObject Class Workplace Shell API function call.

Registering the JAZZ class

```
ret_code = SysRegisterObjectClass("JAZZ","JAZZDLL")
/* Ret_code   - 0, (not registered), 1 (registered) */
/* First argument           - name of the new class */
/* Second argument   - name of DLL module that created the class
```

If this object includes a template, then it is placed in the Templates folder where users can copy it. To deregister a class, use the *SysDeregisterObjectClass*. This is the equivalent of the Workplace Shell API function of WinDeregisterObjectClass.

Deregister A Class

```
ret_code = SysDeregisterObjectClass('JAZZ')
/* First argument           Class name */
/* Ret_code   - 0, (not deregistered), 1 (deregistered) */
```

To retrieve and/or display all registered object classes, use *SysQueryClassList*. This is the equivalent of WinEnumObjectClasses, the Workplace Shell API function call.

Display all registered object classes

```
SysQueryClassList('class_list.')
/* First argument is the compound symbol name where the "array" of object */
/* classes is to be stored. Class_list.0's value is the number of "elements" */
/* (classes) in the "array." */
do cnt = 1 to class_list.0 /* Display the entire array */
       say class_list.cnt
end
Displayed: (partial listing)
WPCommandFile PMWP
WPPower WPCONFIG
```

Note that the Workplace Shell API function call WinReplaceObjectClass, which changes one registered object class to another, does not have a direct REXXUTIL function equivalent.

The remainder of this section will deal with where most of OS/2 REXX's object-oriented capabilities reside — objects.

Object Operations

To create an object, use SysCreateObject which is similar to the Workplace Shell API function of WinCreateObject.

Creating a folder

```
/**************************************************************************
/* Places the new folder on desktop. Look above for other ids */
/* Or the following code creates an instance of the WPFolder object class */
/**************************************************************************
       where_object = "<WP_DESKTOP>"
/**************************************************************************
/* ^ (caret) - Places text on another line at the point where the. */
/* caret appears. So Folder will appear on one line and Example below */
/* it. This is the text that will appear under the Folder icon. For greater */
/* than two lines, use the hexadecimal value for line feed (X'0A') instead */
/**************************************************************************/
       title="Folder^Example"
/**************************************************************************/
/* Define properties. Set the UNIQUE objectid (folder name) and the */
/* inability to drag the folder icon. Note that multiple properties are */
/* delimited by semi-colons. */
/**************************************************************************/
       vals='OBJECTID=<MY_FIRST_REXX_FOLDER>;NODRAG=YES'
/* Let's make the call and string together
ret_code = SysCreateObject(WPFolder,title,where_object,vals)
/**************************************************************************/
/* ret_code          0 (folder not created), 1 (folder created)
/* First argument    - Class name. In our examples will either be WPFolder */
/*       or WPProgram */
/* Second argument - Object title to appear under the icon (i.e. folder name) */
/* Third argument    - Where to place the object. See the previous */
/*       subsection for valid locations. Can be an objectid */
/*       or complete file specification*/
/* Fourth argument - Properties. In the form of argument equals value. These */
/*       are separated by semicolons. A list of the most common */
/*       properties for each class was shown in the previous */
/*       subsection */
```

```
/* Fifth argument - (Not shown) Exception handling capability that tells */
/*       REXX what to do if the OBJECTID is not unique. */
/*       Values are 'F' - (default - don't create a duplicate) */
/*      R (Replaces the old object with the new one.) */
/*      U (Updates the old object) */
/**************************************************************************/
```

Create a Program

```
/************************************************************************/
/* Program creates an instance of the Klondike program and places */
/* it on the desktop (could also go in a folder). */
/**************************************************************************/
       where_object = '<WP_DESKTOP>'
       title = 'Program^Example'
/************************************************************************/
/* Creates a windowable OS/2 session, prompts for arguments at */
/* runtime, specifies the Klondike executable/path name and the */
/* Klondike Object name */
/************************************************************************/
       vals='PROGTYPE=WINDOWABLEVIO;PARAMETERS=/?;,
EXENAME=C:\OS2\APPS\KLONDIKE.EXE;OBJECTID=<WP_KLDK2>'
/* Make the above one line*/
ret_code = SysCreateObject(WPProgram,title,where_object,vals)
```

Creating a DOS Session

```
where_object="<WP_NOWHERE>"
title="DOS^Example"
vals="EXENAME=C:\FIG.BAT;,
          PROGTYPE=VDM;
          SET DOS_FILE=40;"
action="OPEN=DEFAULT"
Call SysCreateObject 'WPProgram',title, where_object,vals,|replace
```

Creating a Shadow of a Program

```
/************************************************************************/
/* Creates a shadow of Klondike and places in Startup folder       */
/**************************************************************************/
       where_object ="<WP_Startup>"
       title = 'Shadow^Example'
       vals='SHADOW_ID=<WP_KLDK2>'
/* Let's make the call and string together */
ret_code = SysCreateObject(WPShadow,title,where_object,vals)
```

To delete an object, use the **SysDestroyObject,** the equivalent of the Workplace Shell API WinDestroyObject call.

Delete a program

```
SysDestroyObject("<WP_KLDK2>")
/* Deletes the Klondike shadow object created above. The complete file */
/* specification could also be used instead. */
```

To modify any of the properties of an object listed in the previous subsection, use *SysSetObjectData*. This is the equivalent of the Workplace Shell API function WinSetObjectData.

Modify a property

```
ret_code = SysSetObjectData("<My_Folder>","WORKAREA=YES")

/* First argument   - Object id or full file specification. Must exist */
/* Second argument  - A list of attribute=value delimited by semicolon */
/*           In our example, makes a folder into a work area */
/*     Using OPEN=DEFAULT will open an object */
```

Look at the REXX.TXT or *IBM OS/2 2.1 Application Design Guide* (S10G-6260-0) for further information.

OS/2 REXX UNIQUE FEATURES: ADVANCED FEATURES

The final sections of this chapter discuss how to combine the power of REXX with that of a programming language such as C. The assumption is an understanding of the basics of C (i.e., operators, data types, variable scope, header files). Note that the bulk of this information can be found in the header file REXXSAA.H for C coders or the REXXSAA.INC for Assembler programmers. These are part of the OS/2 Development Toolkit. These files along with REXX.LIB are needed to successfully interface a compiled program with OS/2 REXX. **Take the time to read through these files.**

Invoking REXX from a C Program (REXXSTART)

There may be a need for you to have C, or some other programming language to invoke the REXX interpreter at run-time. One reason would be to use REXX as an application macro or "glue" language such as the Enhanced Program Manager or PMGLOBE. Once invoked, a subcommand "environment" can be set up as well.

Note that the REXXStart function is defined in a header library called REXXSAA.H (for C) or REXXSAA.INC (for Assembler). This header library is part of the OS/2 Developer's Toolkit in the Headers subdirectory. Without either file, you will have to create your own REXXStart prototype. Fortunately, the Developer's Toolkit is included as part of the Professional Developer's Kit (PDK). So, early in your C program, you will need a line to include this header file. An example might be: (#include <rexxsaa.h>). You will also need the REXX.LIB for the LINK386 (link) operation.

Here are the elements of the C and REXX programs:

```
TEST.C                                          TEST.CMD

1. #define <rexxsaa.h>

2. int main ()
        {

3.      CHAR ret_area[500];

4.      SHORT sub_rc;

5.      LONG rexx_rc;

6.      RXSTRING argg;

7.      RXSTRING ret_str;

8.      UCHAR *hw = "Hello World";

9.MAKERXSTRING(arg,hw,strlen(hw));

10. MAKERXSTRING(ret_str,ret_area,sizeof(ret_area));

11. rexx_rc=REXXSTART(1,

        &argg,          Parse arg strr

        "TEST.CMD",     res_str = center(strr,12,'*')
                        /* Centers Hello World with, asterisks on both sides */
        0,

        NULL,

       RXSUBROUTINE,
```

```
        NULL,
         &sub_rc,
         &ret_str);    return res_str
12. DosFreeMem(ret_str.strptr)
13. exit
         }
```

To compile and link this program (TEST.C) using the IBM CSET/2 compiler use the following commands:

```
/* Invokes CSET/2 compiler and generates an object file without using */
/* the linker, (/c). */
icc /c test.c
link386 /PM-VIO test.obj,test.exe,,REXX,,
/* Creates a Presentation Manger application. Links the object file with */
/* the REXX.LIB library supplied with the OS/2 Programmer's Toolkit */
```

Our next discussion is on related areas: macrospaces, exit handlers, subroutines, and external functions in succeeding sections

Description Of Overall Process

Purpose: Takes a subroutine and returns it centered. Note the subroutine label is not needed. To do this execute the following:

1. The C Program must include the REXXSAA header file which is needed to use the REXXSTART function and the MakeRXString C macro. (Statement 1)
2. The main function is defined. Its purpose is to invoke the REXX interpreter via the REXXStart function. (Statements 2-13)

A. Various variables are defined:

- An array of 500 characters to hold the return string. (Statement 3.)
- A short integer to hold the return code from the REXX procedure (in this case, a subroutine called TEST.CMD — Statement 4.)
- A long integer to hold the REXX return code. (Statement 5.)

- RXSTRING is a structure defined in REXXSAA.H or REXXSAA.INC to hold the arguments (i.e., a variable-length REXX character (literal) string with mixed case) to be passed to the REXX subroutine. This is part of a created structure called RXSTRING. It includes two members: strlength (length of the string) and strptr (pointer to the string). RXSTRING can have one or more null values (i.e. a null string) or empty (no value). Note that the REXX string is converted to a C string (i.e., the string ends with a \0).

Here is the above as C code:

```
typedef struct {
       ULONG strlength; /* length of the string */
       PCH strptr; /* pointer to the string */
       } RXSTRING;
       typedef RXSTRING *PRXSTRING;
```

- Statement 6 defines the final version input string for the REXX subroutine.
- Statement 7 defines the result of the subroutine processing.
- Statement 8 defines the initial input string to be passed to the REXX subroutine.

B. REXXSAA.H includes the following useful C macros that can be used to manipulate RXSTRINGS:

- MAKERXSTRING (stru,str,len): Creates a RXSTRING. Stru points to a structure. Str points to the REXX character string to be used and len is the length of str.
- RXNULLSTRING(stru): Tells if a RXSTRING strptr value (i.e., the REXX string) is a null string. Returns TRUE (has no value) or FALSE (some value that is not null).
- RXSTRLEN(stru): Initializes or modifies the RXSTRING REXX string length.
- RXSTRPTR(stru): Initializes or modifies the RXSTRING REXX string value.
- RXVALIDSTRING(stru): Returns TRUE if the RXSTRING strptr value exists and has a length greater than zero. FALSE otherwise.
- RXZEROLENGTH(stru): Returns TRUE if the RXSTRING strptr exists but has a length of zero. (e.g. A REXX null string.)
- Statement 9 uses the MAKERXSTRING to create a RXSTRING structure using the REXX literal string of Hello World.
- Statement 10 does the same thing for the return (result) string.

C. Statement 11 is the most essential statement in the program. This calls the REXXStart function. Here is an overview of this function and the values selected for this program.

1. Here are the arguments of REXXStart:

- **Returns** 0 (worked), > 0 (REXX error)
- **First argument:** Number of arguments to be passed to the REXX procedure, function, or subroutine. May be 0 (RXSTRING strptr has no value.) or greater than 0. Use the REXX ARG function to check this value. In our example, we have only 1 argument ("Hello World")
- **Second argument:** The RXSTRING (REXX string) to be passed to the REXX procedure, function, or subroutine. In this example, this is argg — a RXSTRING structure that holds the value "Hello World".
- **Third argument:** The file name (really a pointer to a string having the file name as a value). It can be fully qualified with drive and directories/subdirectories. Any file extension may be used with .CMD as the default. This argument is required if the fourth argument has a null value. In our case, we are specifying TEST.CMD.
- **Fourth argument:** Allows user of an procedure stored in memory (**macrospace**). This allows for faster execution of heavily used REXX procedures but at the cost of taking away memory from other processes. To disable this feature, give this argument a value of 0 or NULL. (As done in the above example.) If this feature is used, you must supply an in-storage array name. This array contains two values.

The **first** element (i.e. [0]) is a RXSTRING strptr pointer. If a non-null value is supplied, this element points to a memory location of a copy of the entire REXX procedure. This is only needed if the REXXSTART function invokes a REXX procedure using the SOURCELINE (displays specified lines in a REXX procedure), otherwise it should be set to NULL.

The **second** element (i.e. [1]) is another RXSTRING strptr. If not null, this element points to a tokenized version of the REXX procedure. If it is NULL, a tokenized image will be produced. Also, this can be done by specifying as the first value of the second RexxStart argument being "//T." Note this tokenized version cannot be further manipulated by REXX, other than modifying the procedure.

1. If an procedure is not changed, a tokenized version needs to be only created once. Therefore, one may need a flow control structure to have two different REXXSTARTs depending if the tokenized image exists or not.
2. A created tokenized version is not portable to other platforms (such as if OS/2 was ported to a MIPS machine) or to a later version of the REXX interpreter. Unfortunately this limits tokenized images to short-term (i.e., the current session) use.

3. Forgetting to free the tokenized procedure from memory using the DosFreeMem(array[1]). (Array is the name used to hold the in-storage array.) This wastes memory that other processes could use.

4. Not realizing that by setting both of the in-storage array elements to 0, then the REXX interpreter tries to execute the program name specified in argument 3 of the REXXStart function if it exists in memory (macrospace).

See the section on Macrospace functions for further information on this argument.

- The **fifth** argument is the name of the default REXX ADDRESS environment. This is a character (literal) string. In our example, no default environment is supplied. This is usually used if the procedure is a macro to a specified application/environment. (Such as an editor or communications program.) Creating subcommands (and customized environments) is discussed later in the chapter.

- The **sixth** argument is the type of REXX procedure that is being executed. Valid values include: RXCOMMAND (a REXX application /utility procedure or an OS/2 system command(s)); RXFUNCTION (a REXX internal/external function); and RXSUBROUTINE (a REXX internal/external subroutine) — the value used in our example.

- The **seventh** argument is defining if an exit is specified using the RXSYSEXIT structure which has *sys_exit.name* (name of exit) and *sysexit_code* (value of the exit) as members. Exit values are discussed in the "System Exit Operations" section later in this chapter. In our example, we are not using an exit structure.

- The **eighth** argument is the address of the procedure's return code. If the return code is a number, then it is converted to an integer "data type". In our example, we supply the addresses of the variable &sub_rc.

- The **ninth** and last argument is the return (result) value passed back by a RETURN or EXIT clause in a REXX procedure. In our example, we supply the address of a RXSTRING structure called &ret_str.

D. Statement 12 frees the RXSTRING *ret_str* from memory. Statement 13 ends the processing of the C program. The right bracket marks the end of the main function definition (and the end of the program.)

System Exit Operations

The last section reviewed the REXXStart function which invokes the REXX interpreter from a compiled program. The **seventh** argument of REXXStart defines if a system exit is specified using the RXSYSEXIT structure which has *sys_exit.name* (name of exit) and *sysexit_code* (value of the exit) as members. This section presents an overview of System Exit Operations.

Why Use System Exits? (Overview of System Exits)

System Exit handlers allows the application to act as a host environment and perform a variety of activities such as queue operations, subcommand and external function handling. They are also part of the SAA standard. Figure 3-8 shows the various exits, sub-exits and functions used:

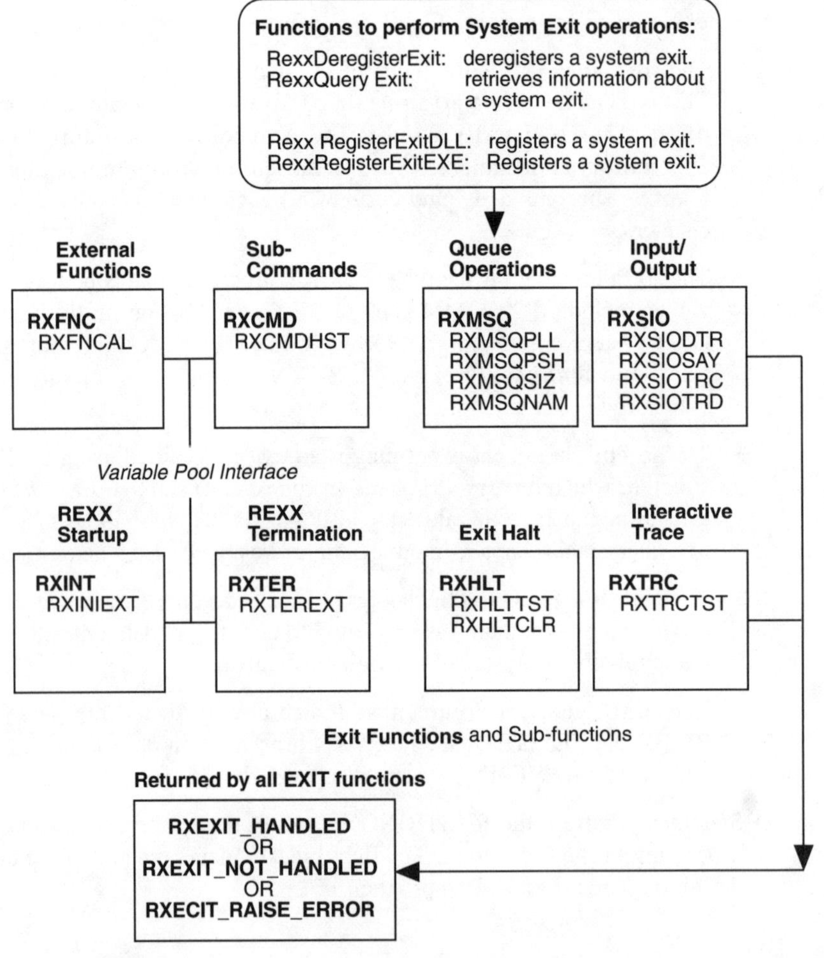

Figure 3-8 REXX System Exit Overview

Here is some information about System Exit operations:

1. Before the REXXStart function "turns" on the system exit features, an application must first do the following steps:

- Use the RexxQueryExit function to see if the exit "structure" currently exists.
- Create a system exit definition by creating a structure that contains as members an *ExitFunction* (defines the exit function), *ExitSubfunction* (defines one or more exit subfunctions) and *Parameters* (function/subfunction parameters). This would be followed by code further defining the behavior of the exit handler including return codes.
- Register the exit "structure" (also called **exit handler**) using the RexxRegisterExitExe (for executables) or RexxRegisterExitDLL (for dynamic link libraries). Here is a sample sequence:

Registering an Exit "Structure"

```
ret_code = RexxRegisterExitExe("Sample_App",&exit_def,&warea);

/* ret_code = Return code from register operation */
/* First argument    - name of exit handler (or exit "structure") */
/* Second argument - pointer to C structure that defines the exit handler */
/*     the components are listed in the previous point */
/* Third argument    - pointer to a work area array. The first element [0] */
/*     - is the global_workarea. The second element [1] is */
/*      set to NULL to make the work area re-entrant
```

- Create an RXSTRING that contains a structure similar to the following:

Create RXSTRING needed for REXXSTART

```
RSYSEXIT exitstr[2] /* Predefined RXSTRING for exit array used in REXXStart */
        /* It has two members: sysexit_name (name of exit) and */
        /* sysexit_code(value of exit) */
exitstr[0].sysexit_name = "Sample App" /* Name of exit "structure */
exitstr[0].sysexit_code=RXINI /* Initializes any other Exit functions used */
exitstr[1].sysedit_code = RXENDLIST /* Terminate exit function list */
```

- Invoke REXXStart (shown in the previous section) with the exit parameter enabled.

2. Other functions essential in performing exit "structure" operations are in Table 3-12.

Table 3-12

Function name	Purpose	Arguments
RexxDeregisterExit	Deregisters an exit "structure'	1) Name of exit "structure" (PSZ name)
		2) DLL function name (PSZ dll)
RexxQueryExit	Checks if an exit "structure" exists	1) Name of exit "structure" (PSZ name)
		2) DLL module name (PSZ dll)
		3) Exit structure flag (1 — exists or 0 —not) (ULONG flg)
		4) Workarea array (ULONG warea[2])
RexxRegisterExitDLL	Registers an exit structure that resides in a DLL.	1) Name of exit "structure" (PSZ name)
		2) Name of DLL (PSZ dll)
		3) Name of module in DLL (PSZ module)
		4) Workarea array (ULONG warea[2])
		5) Drop authority (Either RXEXIT_DROPPABLE OR RXEXIT_NONDROP — who can deregister DLL)

3. Once an exit structure is enabled and processed, it returns one of three possible values as shown in Table 3-13:

Table 3-13

Exit	Value	What it means
RXEXIT_HANDLED	0	Exit "structure" subfunction processed successfully and also completes processing the procedure. If appropriate, the subfunction argument list is updated.
RXEXIT_NOTHANDLED	1	Exit "structure" subfunction processed unsuccessfully. REXX processes the request as if the exit structure was not invoked and also completes processing the procedure. The subfunction argument list is not updated.
RX_RAISE_ERROR	-1	Exit "structure" subfunction processed unsuccessfully. The procedure is terminated with a REXX error — REX0048 "Failure in System Service".

4. Table 3-14 lists the built-in Exit structure functions, subfunctions, and argument lists:

Table 3-14

Function	Subfunction	Subfunction argument list
RXCMD — Invokes ADDRESS environment commands (subcommands)	RXCMDHST — Processes ADDRESS environment commands	1) RXCMD_FLAGS structure — exception conditions: structure members: a) rxcerr — ERROR condition. (Values of 0 — false, 1— true) b) rxcfail — FAILURE condition (Values of 0 — false, 1— true) 2) RXCMDHIST_PARM structure — Other arguments

Table 3-14 Continued

Function	Subfunction	Subfunction argument list
		structure members: a) rxcmd_address — pointer to a string with the ADDRESS environment name b) rxcmd_address1 — Length of the ADDRESS environment name c) rxcmd_dll — Pointer to a string with the DLL used to create the ADDRESS environment d) rxcmd_dll_len — Length of the ADDRESS environment name. e) rxcmd_command — The command to be passed to the ADDRESS environment. f) rxcmd_retc — Pointer to location that holds the return code (System variable RC's value)
RXFNC — invoke an external function.	RXFNCCAL — process an external function.	RXFNC_FLAGS structure — exception conditions: structure members: Values of 0 — false, 1—false a) rxcerr — ERROR condition. b) rxcffnfnd — Unknown function. c) rxffnsub — True if a subroutine. 2) RXFNCCAL_PARM structure — Other arguments

Table 3-14 Continued

Function	Subfunction	Subfunction argument list
		structure members: a) Pointer to RXFUNC_FLAGS structure. b) rxfnc_name — Pointer to a string that contains the external function name. c) rxfnc_namel — Length of the external function name. d) rxfnc_que — Pointer to the current queue name. e) rxfnc_quel — Length of the current queue name. f) rxfnc_argc — Number of arguments being passed to the external function. g) rxfnc_argv — Array of arguments being passed to the external function. h) rxfnc_retc — Return code from the external function
RXHLT — enables/ disables stopping after each REXX is processed.	RXHLTCLR — disables stopping after each REXX clause	RXHLT_FLAGS structure — exception handling clause is processed. structure member rxfhalt — 0 (false if halt did not take place), 1 (true if halt did take place).
	RXHLTTST	RXHLTFLAGS structure (look above)

Table 3-14 Continued

Function	Subfunction	Subfunction argument list
		RXHLTST_PARM structure structure member RXHLTFLAGS structure (and rxfhalt member)
RXINI — Determines what happens before the REXX interpreter is invoked. being used.	RXINIEXIT — Place before invoking the REXX procedure. Initializes any other system exit "structures"	None - Normally used to initialize variables in the Variable Pool Interface or turn on interactive trace.
RXMSQ — Perform external data queue operations.	RXSQNAM — Set/Modify the name of the external data queue.	RXMSQNAM_PARM structure — arguments for the RXSQNAM subfunction: structure member: rxmsq_name — An RXSTRING (string pointer) that points to the name of the external data queue.
	RXSQPLL — Retrieves (pulls) line from the external data queue.	RXMSQLL_PARM structure structure members rxmsq_retc — An RXSTRING that points to the line in the external data queue to be retrieved.
	RXSQPSH — Writes (Pushes) a line onto the external data queue.	RXMSQPSH_PARM structure structure members: 1) RXMSQ_FLAGS structure (with rxfmlifo — 0 ["First In First Out" push — false], 1 ["Last In First Out" push — true])

Table 3-14 Continued

Function	Subfunction	Subfunction argument list
		2) rxmsq_value (A RXSTRING that points to the line to be written).
	RXMSQSIZ — Number of lines in the external data queue	RXMSQSIZ_PARM structure — sets parameter for RXMSQSIZ.
		structure member: rxmsq_size — Number of lines in the external data queue.
RXSIO — Input/ Output operations	RXSIODTR — During an interactive debug session, read from the keyboard (standard input).	RXSIODTR_PARM structure —
		structure member: rxsiodtr_retc — An RXSTRING that points to the return code after reading the line from a terminal during an interactive debug session.
	RXSIOSAY — Output from a write to stdout (i.e., the screen using the SAY instruction). Instruction is symbolically interpreted before being written out.	RXSIOSAY_PARM structure — parameters for RXSIOSAY subfunction.
		Structure members rxsio_string — A RXSTRING structure that contains a pointer to the string to be written to the screen.

Table 3-14 Continued

Function	Subfunction	Subfunction argument list
	RXSIOTRC — During an interactive debug session, the trace output to write to the screen (standard error).	RXSIOTRC_PARM structure — supplies argument to the RXSIOTRC subfunction. structure member: rxsiotrc_string — An RXSTRING that points to the trace output to write to the screen.
	RXSIOTRD — Read from the keyboard (STDIN)	RXSIOTRD_PARM structure — supplies arguments for the RXSIOTRD subfunction. Structure member: rxsiotrd_retc — A RXSTRING that points to the return code (REXX System Variable RC) after reading from the keyboard.
RXTER — Invokes a termination exit structure.	RXTEREXIT — Invokes an exit structure after a procedure has completed processing.	No parameters. This can be to disable interactive trace or to read or write variables from the Variable Pool Interface.
RXTRC —Test if trace is enabled.	RXTRCTST — tests if trace is enabled. Traces for all clauses. Look at the next section for another way to do this.	RXTRC_FLAGS structure — to enable/disable TRACE.

Table 3-14 Continued

Function	Subfunction	Subfunction argument list
		Structure member: rxftrace (0 — TRACE disabled, 1 — TRACE enabled) RXTRCTST_PARM structure — supplies arguments for RXTRCTST subfunction. structure member RXSTRC_FLAGS structure and rxtrc_flags member.

5. The Variable Pool Interface relationship to System Exits is discussed in the section on the Variable Pool Interface later in this chapter.
6. Exits do exist under CMS and TSO but may have subtle differences.

Asynchronous Request Interface Functions (Trace and Halt)

In addition to system exit structures, another way to enable and disable halt and trace processing is by using one or more of the following three miscellaneous functions.

1. Using these functions result in faster processing than system exits because they are a one-time request to enable/disable halt or tracing rather than a request than affects all clauses (such as the RXTRC exit traces **EVERY** clause.)
2. Here are the three halt/trace functions:

	Enables	Disables
HALT condition	RexxSetHalt	NA
Interactive Trace (TRACE)	RexxSetTrace	RexxResetTrace

3. Note that all three functions have the same two arguments of process id and *thread id*, which are integer values.

Macrospace Operations

If the performance of a REXX procedure is a concern, then consider having it loaded into memory (macrospace). Once in the macrospace, a procedure (but usually a function) can be executed by other processes. For information on how to do this by setting the instorage argument use the REXXSTART function described earlier. The trade-off is that this takes away memory from other processes if the macrospace grows too big. Most of the following C functions manipulate the macrospace list of functions. Here is an overview of macrospace C functions:

1. First run *RexxQueryMacro* to see if a function is already loaded into macrospace:

```
ret_code = RexxQueryMacro("a.cmd",&poss)
/* First argument is a pointer to the function name. */
/* Second argument is the position of the function in the macrospace. Usually */
/* Initialized to 0. This is returned by the function if the function is found in */
/* the macrospace. */
/* A return code of 0 means the function was found in the macrospace */
/* A value of 2 means it was not */
if (rc > 0) {/*add new exec/function to macrospace... */}
```

2. If the procedure or function is not found, then use the *RexxAddMacro* to put (register) a function into the macrospace. RexxAddMacro can also be used to modify a function.

```
ret_code= RexxAddMacro("newfnc","aaa.cmd",RXMACRO_SEARCH_BEFORE)
/* Ret_code = 0 (macro added/changed), 1 (out of macrospace), 7 (invalid */
/* function location), 8 (invalid position argument) */
/* First argument -     name of function */
/* Second argument - name of function location (i.e. source file) Default */
/*       is a.CMD file */
/* Third argument       -       Position in list. RXMACRO_SEARCH_BEFORE (front */
/*       of list), RXMACRO_SEARCH_AFTER (end of list) */
```

3. Once a function is registered, you can do the following actions:

   a. Change the position of the function in the macrospace list:

```
ret_code = RexxReorderMacro("newfnc",RXMACRO_SEARCH_AFTER)
        /* ret_code = 0 (reordered), 2 (unknown function), */
        /* 8 (invalid position argument) */
        /* First argument is the name of the function to reorder */
        /* Second argument is the new position. (Same as RxAddMacro) */
```

   b. Eliminate a macro from the macrospace list:

```
ret_code = RexxDropMacro("newfnc) /*only argument is the function to remove */
/* ret_code = 0 (function dropped) 2 (unknown function) */
```

   Beware that because a macrospace is shared memory, dropping a function from macrospace may cause unpredictable problems if another process is using the dropped function at the same time.

4. The following functions perform these overall macrospace operations.

   a. Saving a function to an image (binary) file:

```
        ret_code = RexxSaveMacroSpace(1,oldfunc,"a.bin")
        /* Ret_code = 0 (function saved), 2 (unknown function), 3 (image file */
        /* needs extension), 5 (libfile is use) */
        /* First argument - Number of pointers of function names (i.e. number of */
        /*      functions to save). 0 means all loaded functions. */
        /* Second argument - Array of pointers of filenames to save (i.e. list of */
        /*      filenames to save) */
        /* Third argument      - Image (binary) file to save macrospace functions */
        /*      Unfortunately, this image will only work under */
        /*      the OS/2 version it was created under */
```

   Note that multiple image files can be loaded or saved.

   b. On startup (or the start of a C program), loads the REXX functions stored in one or more binary files back into macrospace:

```
ret_code = RexxLoadMacroSpace(0,0,"a.bin")
/* ret_code = 0 (loaded into macrospace), 1 (out of memory), */
/*      2 (unknown function), 4 (function already exists), */
/*      5 (image file in use), 6 (invalid image file format) */
/* First argument - Number of pointers to function names */
/*      (i.e. number of function names to load) */
/*      0 means load all functions.
/* Second argument - Array of pointers of function names to load */
/*     (i.e. list of function names) */
/* Third argument - Name of image (binary) file with an extension */
```

Note that multiple image files can be loaded:

```
c. retcode = RexxClearMacroSpace()
/* Retcode = 0 (all functions cleared from macrospace), 2 (no functions */
/* were found). No arguments are needed */
/* This should not be used too often because it clears functions from */
/* macro space even if they are being used by other processes!!! */
```

External Functions and Subcommands (Extending the REXX Language)

Using C or other programming languages provides two major ways to extend the REXX Language. Note that application programming interfaces exist for nearly all REXX interpreters/compilers but are not portable. However, there is a glimmer of hope. This topic will probably looked at during the second version of the REXX standard. Also at that time, an API for external programs to access REXX queues may be created external programs to REXX will remain a non-portable feature. The first of these are providing **external functions** which provide capabilities that are not included with REXX built-in functions. NOTE: Do not confuse this with REXX external functions — that is, functions written in REXX that reside in a file different than the "main" procedure. These are placed into libraries called **packages**. This results in faster execution time because the entire package resides in memory. The second approach is creating subcoms (subcommand environments) that can be accessed through the REXX ADDRESS instruction (discussed in Chapter 2).

Table 3-15 compares the two different methods:

Table 3-15

External Function	Subcommand
Interface to REXX	
Once registered can be invoked like any REXX function Best approach for a series of related commands that will be done entirely in REXX.	Invokes a series of commands through REXX ADDRESS instruction. Best approach for an entire application accessible through REXX.
How to Register/Deregister	
RexxRegisterFunctionExe RexxRegisterFunctionDll	RexxRegisterSubcomExe RexxRegisterSubcomDll
RexxDeregisterFunction	RexxDeregisterSubcom
How to Query	
RexxQueryFunction	RexxQuerySubcom
Interface to Exit	
RXFNC	RXCMD
Interface to RexxStart	
Yes	Yes

Subcommands

The following is an overview of subcommands:

1. Here is a suggested approach to creating a subcommand handler.

Step 1: Create a C program that will produce an executable or dynamic link library. This C program does the following:

a) includes REXXSAA.H

b) checks each the validity of each user-requested sub-command and performs the required action. This is done by creating a subcommand **handler**. This handler name that will be used to access the environment from REXX.

```
RexxSubcomHandler Handler_Name;
/* RexxSubComHandler is defined in REXXSAA.H */
```

Then define a structure with *handler_name*. The members are:

1. Command: A pointer to a RXSTRING that holds the subcommand.
2. Flag: An integer return code showing if the subcommand was successfully processed or not:

   RXSUB_ERROR (1 – Check if subcommand was entered correctly.)

   RXSUBCOM_FAILURE (-1 – Unknown subcommand or error)

   RXSUBCOM_OK (0 – Subcommand was successful.)
3. RetStr: Pointer to a RXSTRING that is the subcommand return command that is passed to REXX as the value of the special (system) variable RC.

```
In C format:
ULONG handler (
     PRXSTRING Command;
     PUSHORT Flag;
     PRXSTRING strptr;
)
```

c) The required action usually requires to place the data in a the REXX Variable Pool (shown in the next section.)

d) After querying to see if the subcommand environment already does not exist, then register the subcommand. This can be done one of two ways:

- Invoke from a REXX procedure (in quotes) as 'RXSUBCOM REGISTER car car car' or from a .CMD (batch) file or from the OS/2 command prompt.

  The first argument (car) is the name of the subcom environment (i.e., the subcom handler name). This will be used in ADDRESS instructions as the environment name.

  The second argument (car) is the name of the dynamic link library.

  The third argument (car) is the function within the dynamic link library that defines the subcom environment. Note that the dynamic link library may also contain the application or be separate of the application.

- Invoke from a C program:

  RexxRegisterSubComDLL function

  - The first three arguments are identical to those of RxSubcom Register. There are also two additional arguments: User Area (place to store subcommand information) and Drop Authority determines if only the current procedure can drop the subcommand environment. Values are RXSUBCOM_DROPPABLE (0 Default — any process can drop the subcommand environment.); and RXSUBCOM_NONDROP — (1 Only the process that registered the subcommand environment can drop it) to the RXSUBCOM REGISTER.

RexxRegisterSubComExe function

  - Has three arguments: the subcommand environment name, a pointer to the memory location of the subcommand handler, and the user area to store the subcommand registration information.

    Return values — 0 (SubCom registered), 10 (Subcom already exists), and 30 (SubCom not registered).

e) Then compile and link the program (with appropriate files such as a DEF file for a dynamic link library) with REXX.LIB.

Step #2 Invoke the Subcommands:

  - Through the REXX Address Command.
  - By invoking a REXX procedure using the REXXStart C function (shown earlier). If done, an environment (i.e. sub-command handler name (fifth argument) and a value of RXSUBROUTINE for the sixth argument are required. An example of doing this was shown in the earlier section on RexxStart.

- Through an exit handler (routine) that uses the RXCMD subfunction. This can be invoked with the RexxStart C function.

2. Once a subcommand environment is registered, then the following operations can be performed:

   - Query if a subcommand environment exists. This is especially useful to do, before creating a subcommand environment. To do this, use the RexxQuerySubcom C function or the RXSUBCOM QUERY command.

From a .CMD file or the Command line

```
        RXSUBCOM QUERY CAR CAR
        /* Queries to see if the CAR subcommand environment (first argument) */
        /* Associated with the CAR DLL (i.e. C:\OS2\DLL\CAR.DLL) exists */
```

From a C program

```
RxSubcomQuery("CAR","car_sub")
/* First argument is the subcommand environment name */
/* Second argument is the function in the dynamic link library that defines */
/* the subcommand handler */

/* The function returns three things: 1) an indicator flag with a value of 0 */
/* (subcommand not registered) and 1 (subcommand registered). 2) the */
/* subcommand registration information stored in the user area. And 3) a */
/* return code 0 (RXSUBCOM_OK - Subcommand registered), */
/* 30 (RXSUBCOM_NOTREG - Subcommand environment not registered) */
/* 1003 (RXSUBCOM_BADTYPE - Unknown registration type */)
```

   - Drop a subcommand environment. Doing this may cause problems if other processes are using the subcommand environment. Your process must also have the drop authority to do this:

From a .CMD file or the command prompt.

```
        RXSUBCOM DROP CAR CAR
        /* Deregisters the subcommand environment (handler) */
        /* Arguments are the same as RXSUBCOM QUERY */
```

From a C program

```
rc = DeRegisterSubcom("Car","Car")
/* rc = 0 (RXSUBCOM_OK -subcommand dropped), */
/* 30 (RXSUBCOM_NOTREG - subcommand not registered), */
/* 40 (RXSUBSUBCOM_NOCANDROP - don't have permission to */
/*       drop */
/* 1003 (RXSUBCOM_BADTYPE) - unknown subcommand registration */
/*      type */
```

- Users can also load a subcommand environment (handler) stored in a dynamic link library by entering RXSUBCOM LOAD.

From a .CMD file or the commands line.

```
RXSUBCOM LOAD CAR CAR
/* Loads the CAR environment (first argument) associates with the CAR */
/* dynamic link library (second argument) */
```

3. If a dynamic link library cannot be found, make sure that it is part of the LIBPATH (that is a pre-defined path OS searches for when a dynamic link library name is given). The default LIBPATH is the current directory, OS2\DLL, OS2\MDOS\WINOS2 (MS-Windows), and C:OS2\APPS\DLL (OS/2 Applications such as FaxPM and Chess. This can be found in your CONFIG.SYS file.)
4. Look in the OS/2 Programmer's Toolkit for an example of building a subcommand shell handler that uses REXX as a macro language. Keep the following in mind to do this:
   a. Create a routine that checks the data passed to it. (Using RXSUBCOM error conditions.)
   b. Usually perform some additional routine once the data matches one of the expected values.
   c. Make an OS/2 system call (if appropriate)
   d. Create a Shared Variable block to pass information back to REXX.
   e. Compile the program.
   f. Run the REXX procedure: First register the subcommand handler; then using the ADDRESS env 'env_command' for processing the appropriate subcommand statement.

Functions

The more common approach to extend the REXX language is to create a set of built-in functions using a programming language such as C. (Also called function libraries or function packages.) Here is an overview of this topic:

1. One future potential problem is there no standardized approach for REXX to interface with generic DLLs (that is non-REXX-ready DLLs.) The easiest approach (other than recoding the function to be REXX-ready) is to provide a startup function that defines all the external function (such as arguments, data types, defaults, return values, etc.). Creating a generic function will provide an already tested approach for future situations.

2. See the earlier discussion of invoking the REXXUtil function for a user viewpoint on invoking external functions.
3. If this is going to be a frequently used function package, you may want to have this added to STARTUP.CMD so it is registered automatically every time OS/2 start ups.
4. To create a function, do the following:
   a. Query as suggested below to see if the function exists.
   b. Have an include file to REXXSAA.H to make the required C functions accessible to your program.
   c. Also use a REXXFunctionHandler REXX_function — which declares your function as a REXX function. REXX_function is the name of your external function. RexxFunctionHandler usually defines a structure with five members:
      1) Name of the function (char *name)
      2) Number of arguments passed to the external function (ULONG argnumber).
      3) An array of argument values passed to the external function (RXSTRING argvals [].)
      4) The name of the REXX queue (if used). (CHAR *rxqueuenm)
      5) Any returned value (RXSTRING *ret_val). This is passed back to the REXX system (special) variable RESULT.
   d. Declare any structures that are used by your external function (such as access to the Variable Pool Interface.)
   e. Define your external function:

```
ULONG AddIt(CHAR *name, ULONG argnumber,RXSTRING argvals [], CHAR
           *rxqueuenm,
        RXSTRING *ret_val)
        MAKERXSTRING(ret_val,0); /* Sets default value */
      if (argnumber != 3) {
           return 1;
      }
     else {
        ret_val->strptr = argval[0] + argval[1]);
        /* Set to NULL if don't want a return value */
        ret_val->strlength = strlen(ret_val->strptr);
     }
      return 0;
      }
```

f. Compile and link the program (with any needed .DEF files for a dynamic link library and REXX.LIB) and then register the function by any of the following methods.

g Additional examples from Eric Giguère can be found on the anonymous ftpsite REXX_Waterloo.ca in pub/os2/vrexx/uxlechl/zip.

From a "C" Program

1. RexxRegisterFunctionDLL(*function_name,DLL_name,function name in DLL*) — *function* resides in a DLL

   Returns 0 (RxFunc_OK — function defined), 10 (RxFuncDefined — already exists), 20 (RxFuncNomem — Not enough memory to register function).

   Note that the SysLoadFuncs function that is part of the REXXUtil DLL is nothing more than a glorified version of this function.

2. RexxRegisterFunctionExe *(function name,location of function definition in EXE file)*

   Same return codes as RexxRegisterFunctionDLL plus 40 (RxFuncModNotFnd — Function definition not found in DLL. Check the .DEF and .C files that created the function.)

From a REXX Procedure

```
              call RxFuncAdd 'Addit', 'MyFuncs', 'AddIt'
/* Registers the function. */
/*     First argument       - Function name to register */
/*     Second argument - Name of DLL (extension not required) */
/*      Third argument     - Name of the procedure in the DLL */
/*      If captured, a return value is either 0 (function registered) or */
/*      1 (function not registered) */
```

h. An external function can be invoked one of the following ways:

   1. From a C program as specified as part of a REXXStart (shown earlier). If this is done, a value of RXFUNCTION for the sixth argument, and the ninth argument (the value of system [special] variable of RESULT) are required.

      – Through an exit handler (routine) that uses the RXFNC subfunction. This can be invoked with the RexxStart C function.

2. From a REXX procedure once the function is registered:

```
rc = Addit(1,2)        /* Within a REXX Procedure */
say Result             /* Returns 3*/
```

5. Once a function is registered and invoked, the following operations can be performed as well:

a. Deregister the function. Beware of doing this since other functions may be using the function at the time.

```
RexxDeregisterFunction('Addit')
 /* From a C program - Drops addit external function */
 /* Returns 0 (RXFunc_Ok - deregistered), */
 /* 30 (RxFunc_NotReg - function not found) */

or call RxFuncDrop('Addit')
/* From a REXX procedure. Returns 0 (dropped) or 1 (not dropped) */
```

b. Query the function to see if already exists.

```
ret_code = RxFunctionQuery('AddIt')
/* From a C program. ret_code = 0 (RxFuncOk - function exists) */
/* or 30 (RxFunc_NotReg - function does not exist) */

call RxFuncQuery('AddIt') /* From REXX */
/* Returns 0 (function exists), 1( function does not exist) */
```

6. Registering, deregistering, and querying functions are really adding, dropping, or reading lines from a function table (i.e., a database of function names and associated information).

Variable Pool Interface (RxVar)

The last section in this chapter deals with the glue used in C programs for functions, subroutines, and exit handlers to communicate with REXX procedures — the REXX Variable Pool Interface (VPI).

The REXX Variable Pool Interface is a SAA-defined feature that allows C programs (or other languages) to create, query, update, and delete the values of REXX variables. Note that VPI is mentioned in the forthcoming REXX standard. The following summarizes VPI operations:

Before Getting Started — Basic Concepts

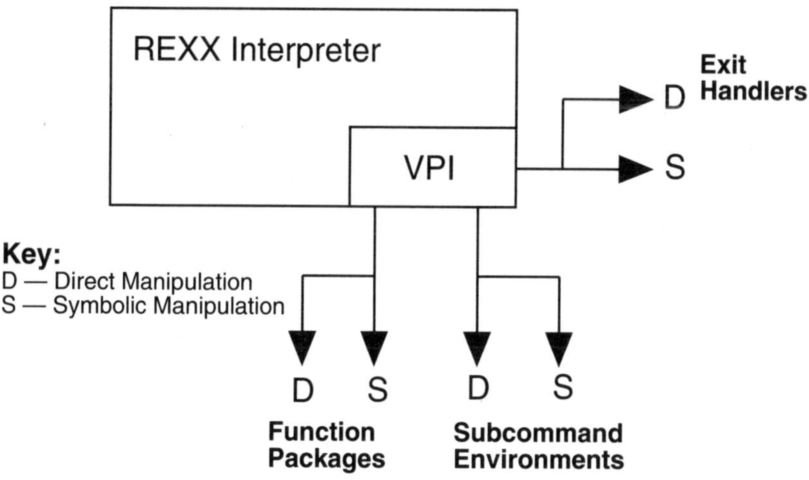

Figure 3-9 Variable Pool Interface

Figure 3-9 provides a logical (rather than actual) view of the Variable Pool Interface. It shows that there are two types of methods used to manipulate REXX variables (i.e., symbols with values):

Direct manipulation: Use this approach if the case conversion and symbolic substitution is not needed. Valid variables are: 1) simple symbols (names must be in uppercase and cannot begin with a number (0-9) or a period. and 2) Compound symbols (With any characters valid for the tail part (i.e., that following the stem).

Symbolic manipulation: The most flexible of the two approaches because: 1) case conversion and symbolic substitution is supported; and 2) Simple symbol and compound names can be in any case.

Step 1: Creating The Shared Variable Request Block

The foundation of all REXX VPI operations is creating one or more of Shared Variable Request Blocks (called SHVBlock). A **Shared Variable Request Block** is a C structure with the following members:

1) shvnext: Points either to NULL (no more SHVBlocks) or to the location of the SHVBlock. (struct shstr *shvnext)

2) shvname: An RXSTRING that points to the Rexx Variable (Symbol) to operate on. Default is the first REXX variable in the specified "set." The Current variable pointer will have this variable as its value. (RXSTRING shvname)

3) shvvalue: An RXSTRING that points to the value of the REXX variable (symbol) to be manipulated. (RXSTRING shvvalue)

4) shvnamelen: Length of REXX variable name (ULONG shvnamelen)

5) shvvaluelen: Length of the REXX value (if retrieved .ULONG shvvaluelen)

6) shvcode: The operation to perform on the REXX variable. The numbers in parentheses are the integer values to use in the C structure. (UCHAR shvcode)

   - RXSHV_DROPV (2 — direct) and RXSHV_SDRO (5 – symbolic): Clears a REXX variable and unassigns it.

   - RXSHV_EXIT: Specifies an exit handler to be used with an external function or system exit. The handler returns a result string accessed by the REXX system (special) variable named RESULT.

   - RXSHV_FETCH (1 – direct) and RXSHV_SYFET (4 – symbolic): Retrieve a REXX variable and its value. A compound symbol stem is an invalid value.

   - RXSHV_NEXTV (6): Changes the current variable pointer to the next REXX variable in the "set." There is no guarantee that these will be processed in a sequential order.

   - RXSHV_PRIV (7): Similar to RXSHV_FETCH but retrieves only limited information. The value of shvname is one of the following:

     - QUENAME: The active REXX data queue.

     - PARM: The number of arguments passed to the procedure as a character string.). You can also specify a specified argument such as PARM.n. (The number of arguments — same as the ARG(n) function.) n is an integer.

     - SOURCE: The output from PARSE SOURCE.

     - VERSION: The output from PARSE VERSION.

   - RXSHV_SET (0 — direct) and RXSHV_SYSET (3— symbolic): Assigns a REXX variable (symbol) a value.

7) shvret: The return code from the REXX variable operation: (Both the text and integer return code are given.) UCHAR (shvret)

- RXSHV_BADF (80 — Unknown/Invalid Shvblock [Shared Variable Request Block].)
- RXSHV_BADN (8 — Unknown/Invalid REXX Variable.)
- RXSHV_LVAR (2 — All the variables in the REXX Variable "set" have been processed. A RXSHV_NEXTV (retrieve next variable) cannot be successfully processed.)
- RXSHV_MEMFL (10 — Out of memory. Perhaps this is due to too many processes running or the shvname was null.)
- RXSHV_NEWV (1 — Requested a REXX variable that does not exist or have a value.)
- RXSHV_OK (0 —No errors.)
- RXSHV_TRUNC (4 — REXX Name/value truncated during a RXSHV_FETCH or RXSHV_SYSFET operation.)

Here are some additional notes about the Shared Variable Request Block:

1. The Variable Pool Interface is available if a RXCMD, RXFNC, RXINT, and RXTER exit handler is used.
2. The Variable Pool Interface is available if the Shared Variable Request Block contains a RXSHV_EXIT operation that accesses a RXCMD, RXFNC, RXHLT, RXSIO, and RXMSQ exit handlers. Several uses for this interaction include:
   - Initializing, changing, querying variables for an application, subcommand environment, or external function.
   - Checking why an application, subcommand environment or external function was HALTed.
   - Performing I/O operations on selected REXX variables.

Step 2: Performing The VPI Operation (The REXX Variable Pool Operation.)

Once you have the Shared Variable Request Block (shvblock) defined, then you must issue a RexxVariablePool function. Its only argument is the address of the shvblock.

Here is a code fragment as an example:

```
INT VPI_Ex (                      /* Generic function to drop REXX variables */
     PSZ varname                  /* Passed by invoking program */
     PSZ varvalue
   }
     SHVBLOCK vpi_block;          /* Initialize a vpi_block SHVBLOCK structure */
                                  /* Now set all the members of the structure */
     vpi_block.shvnext = NULL;    /* There is no other variables */
                                  /* Create the RXSTRING for shvname */
                                  /* and shvvalue       */
   MAKERXSTRING(vpi_block.shvname,varname, strlen(varname));
   MAKERXSTRING(vpi_block.shvvalue,varvalue, strlen(varvalue));
                                  /* Create length members of value and name */
   vpi_block.shvnamelen = strlen(varname);
   vpi_block.shvvaluelen = strlen(varvalue);
                                  /* Drop the REXX Variable */
   vpi_block.shvcode = RXSHV_SYDRO;
   vpi_nlock.shvret = 0;          /* Initialize the return code
    if (RexxVariablePool(&vpi_block) == RXSHV_BADN)
          return 1
                                  /* Drop the variable */
   }
)
```

REFERENCES

American National Standard for Information Systems 1992 *Programming Language REXX ANSI HTI B173.8-1991*

Andrew, Chris and James Taylor 1992 "Workplace Shell Programming Workshop" *OS/2 Developer Conference and Exposition* pp. 1-37

Berry, R.E. 1992 "The designer's model of the CUA Workplace" IBM Systems Journal 31(2) pp. 429-457

Berry, R.E. and C.J. Reeves 1992 "The Evolution of the Common User Access Workplace Model" IBM Systems Journal 31(2) pp. 414-428

Cowlishaw, M.F. 1990 *The REXX Language: A Practical Approach to Programming* 2nd ed. Englewood Cliffs, N.J.: Prentice-Hall

Command Technology Corporation 1991 *SPF/2 User's Guide & Reference Manual*

Dancy, Charles. 1990 "REXX In Charge" *Byte* August pp. 245-253

Giguère, Eric. 1992 *Frequently Asked Questions — REXX*. Text File

Giguère, Eric and Rob Veitch 1992 "Programming with Objects: A REXX-based approach" *Proceedings of the REXX Symposium for Developers and Users*. pp. 47-54 (See Chapter 1.)

German, Hallett 1992 *Command Language Cookbook for Mainframes, Minicomputers, and PCS*. New York: Van Nostrand Reinhold pp. 1-23, 71-142, 307-342,

IBM 1992 *IBM OS/2 2.1 Application Design Guide*, (S10G-6260-01)

IBM 1991 *IBM OS/2 Procedures Languages 2/REXX Reference* (S01F-0271-00)

IBM 1991 *IBM OS/2 Procedures Languages 2/REXX User's Guide* (S01F-0272-00)

IBM 1990 *IBM OS/2 Version 1.3 Technical Description and Performance Guide*

IBM 1992 *REXX.TXT* (Also called CRTOBJ.TXT. Part of REXX20.ZIP patch), Text File

IBM 1992 *System Application Architecture: Common Programming Interface REXX Level 2 Reference*. SC24-5549-01

Mansfield Software 1992 *KEDIT User's Guide 5.0*

Mansfield Software 1992 *KEDIT Reference Manual 5.0*

McGuire, Richard K. and Stephen G. Price 1992 "OS/2 Procedures Language 2/REXX. A Practical Approach to Programming and Adding REXX Power to Applications." *Proceedings of the REXX Symposium for Developers and Users*. pp. 217-230

McGuire, Richard K. 1992 "The IBM OS/2 and OS/400 REXX Interpreter" in the *REXX Handbook*, Gabriel Golberg & Philip H. Smith III (eds). New York: McGraw-Hill pp. 529-540, (See Chapter 1.)

Quercus Systems 1991 *Personal REXX User's Guide Version 3.0*

Quercus Systems 1992 *Personal REXX 3.0 for OS/2: Beta Test Notes — Beta version 3*

Quercus System 1992 *Personal REXX — OS/2 Addendum Version 3.0*

Quercus Systems 1991 *RexxTerm User's Guid*

Sessions, Roger and Nurcan Coskun "Object-Oriented Programming in OS/2" *IBM Personal System Develope*r Winter 1992

Sipples, Timothy 1992 *Frequently Asked Questions List: User Edition*. Text File

Tritus Inc. 1992 *Tritus SPF Version 1.2 Tritus SPF User's Guide*

Tritus Inc. 1992 *Tritus SPF Version 1.2 Tritus SPF Edit and Edit Macro Reference*

4

OS/2 REXX: IBM Extensions

Chapters 2 and 3 discussed at length the powerful capabilities of OS/2 REXX that can be used to build applications, front-ends, and utilities. This chapter looks at commercial and freeware IBM products that take advantage of OS/2 REXX but also extend its capabilities. This is done by showing how these tools can be used to build applications and also act as a means to communicate between processes (applications) and different computers (such as mainframes, workstations, or other PCs.)

Unfortunately, the products mentioned in this chapter are undergoing dramatic changes. All efforts were made by the author to keep as current as possible.

REXX procedures are used (but not always mentioned in the documentation) in almost all IBM OS/2 REXX products. This chapter will focus on some of the popular products that REXX can directly interface with. These can be divided into three areas: 1) Extended Services; 2) Other networking products; and 3) Visual REXX and IBM copyrighted freeware.

EXTENDED SERVICES

In 1987, IBM announced a separate product called OS/2 Extended Edition 1.0, OS/2 EE or EE. This included all of the capabilities of OS/2 Standard Edition 1.0, OS/2 SE or SE, plus Communications and Database Managers. Three updates to this product were created and distributed.

The product had limited success. One reason it had problems was that OEMs (such as Compaq and Olivetti) could only sell the Standard Edition and not the Extended Edition. This was unfortunate because REXX was originally available only under the Extended Edition starting with version 1.2 and was not added to the Standard Edition until 1.3. So many OS/2 users had a delayed introduction to the REXX language.

In 1991, OS/2.0 Extended Edition became Extended Services (or ES). This was available in two versions: IBM Extended Services with Database Server for OS/2 Version 1.0 (allows the computer to act as both a database client OR server) and IBM Extended Services for OS/2 Version 1.0. Extended Services was more than just a name change. The product no longer included a superset of Standard Edition but a separate and powerful product. More features were added. Communications Manager included APPN (Advanced Peer-to-Peer) Support, Netview remote operation support, and enhancements to the configuration and EHLLAPI (Emulator High Level Language Application Programming Interface) components. Database Manager included MS Window support, SQL (Structured Query Language) enhancements, and the Command Line Interface. Others (such as the LAN Requesters) became separate products. It also offered portability to other IBM platforms — being part of SAA (Standard Application Architecture).

In 1993, the product was renamed and enhanced again. Communications Manager became its own product called Communications Manager/2. Both products are planned to be available on other platforms (such as AIX, DOS, Windows, and Windows NT.) None of the features of the Communications and Database Manager contained in the Extended Services 1.0 are lost. (So everything presented in this chapter should remain unchanged in the new product.) Easier installation, simultaneous communications with mainframes, networked-based installations, automatic passing of status to a NetView Manager are the major enhancements.

Database Manager is also selling as its own product called OS/2 DB2/2. This is a 32-bit version of the Database Manager that includes better data retrieval from remote DB2 servers (remote unit of work or RUOW). The much desired capability of simultaneously having RUOW operations with multiple remote DB2 servers is a planned future enhancement. No plans have been announced when a 32-bit SQL Server from Microsoft will be available.

The result is a positive effort by IBM to make Database and Communications Manager widely available to those 1) not using IBM computers that may be also using other Network Operating Systems such as Netware. And 2) those on other operating systems that need enhanced database and communication services (whether accessing an OS/2 computer or not.)

Overview

Table 4-1 summarizes the major features of Extended Services:

Table 4-1 Major Features of Extended Services

Communications Manager	Database Manager
Application Programming Interfaces (such as in C)	Command Line Interface (CLI) - Dynamic SQL statement creation
- ACDI (Asynchronous Communications Device Interface)	- Interface to other Database Manager components
- APPC (Advanced Program-to-Program Communications)	
- Common Services	
- EHLLAPI (Emulator High-Level Language Application Programming Interface) Through languages such as C and REXX, a terminal session emulating a 3270 or 5250 can be created.	
- LU (Logical Unit) such as a 3270 emulator.	
- NETBIOS/IEEE 802.2 support.	
Programmable Configuration (A superset of REXX that customizes and automates the configuration process.)	
Server-Requester Programming Interface (SRPI)	
System Management (query information about SNA session)	
– X.25	

Table 4-1 Continued

Communications Manager	Database Manager
Interfaces to Various Protocols - ACDI - APPC - APPN - LU Support - SNA LAN Gateway - X.25	Database Application Remote Interface (Written in REXX, C, and other languages) - Allows an application to run a database operation on the same machine ("the client") which involves data retrieved from a central "server."
LAN Adapter and Protocol Support/ - NDIS (Network Device Interface Specification) - Token-Ring/Ethernet Support	Database Tools - Configuration (Perform global operations, change settings) - Directory (Database/ Workstation operations) - Recovery (Backup and recovery of databases)
Terminal Emulation/Keyboard Definition - 3101 - 3270 - 5250 - VT100 (DEC)	Distributed Database Connection Services/2 1.0 (separate product) (In 1993, Version 2 was announced and sold. The major enhancements included: a) being rewritten as a 32-bit application and b) it provides a LU6.2 link between an OS/2 client and a DB2 server. Thus avoiding the need of using CICS to do this.) - Single and multi-user versions are available. - Provides a means for client/server database operations. This can include using the CLI interface.
	MS-DOS and MS-Windows Application Enablers (**Server version only**) - Limited ability to access databases (run-time only)

Table 4-1 Continued

Communications Manager	Database Manager
	Query Manager - Create or update database/tables - Generate reports - Interface to Applications (through REXX, C, and other languages) Remote Data Services (**Server Version only**. Also needs Communications Manager.) - Provides access for one or more PCs (clients) to a central database (server) SQLQMF - Imports/exports data to/from a SQL/DS or DB2 database.

Table 4-1 stresses the following:

- Both Communications and Database Manager are highly configurable by either using REXX, built-in commands/windows, or a programming language such as C.
- Communications and Database Manager can work either as a standalone mode, or with other computers (whether mainframes, minicomputers, or personal computers.) It well supports the client/server concept.
- Both Communications and Database Manager are evolving products. 32-bit processing, continuing support of standards (such as SQL), and user-suggested enhancements will further fuel the success of these products.

DATABASE MANAGER

Before examining how to use REXX to interface with Database Manager, it may be useful to review some basic terms. Table 4-2 summarizes these important concepts:

Table 4-2 REXX Basic Terminology

Term	Meaning
Base Table	A table that contains data rather than be derived from another table (i.e. a view).
Catalog	A special set of tables maintaining information about various indexes, tables, and views. Sometimes called the system catalog or data dictionary,
Index	A pointer to one or more rows in a base table arranged in order by using a specified column(s). This results in faster access.
SQL	Structured Query Language (Pronounced either "see-kwel" or "ess-queue-ell.") is a standardized language (defined by ISO, ANSI, and SAA standards) that allows you to perform operations on **relational databases**. (A simplified definition is a collection of related data that is maintained in a two-dimensional table. This is sometimes called "a flat file" such as a phone listing.) SQL calls allow portability across the entire SAA line. Note that vendors often put in extensions to the SQL language. Under OS/2, SQL statements are created one of three ways: - Static. These are **embedded** in a programming language (such as C) that is then compiled. - Dynamic. These are created and executed at run-time. They may be embedded in a REXX, C, COBOL, FORTRAN, and other languages. - Interactive. A subset of Dynamic SQL which is entered at the keyboard by a user.
Table	A two dimensional array (i.e., columns and rows) that contains a set of related data retrieved from a database. A phone list is an example of a table.
Unit of Work	The basic element that Database Manager uses to guarantee that database integrity is maintained. It begins when a program or application connects to a database. And ends when a COMMIT (add transactions to the master database) or ROLLBACK (remove last changes made to the master database. A rollback (implied) will take place if there are any problems with the UNIT of work such as it being incomplete) or a DISCONNECT takes place. However, in between the start and end of a unit of work a series of COMMITs may be issued.

Table 4-2 Continued

Term	Meaning
Value	The data found in a table where a particular row and column cross.
View	A table(s) derived from another table with data arranged in a particular way. (Sometimes called a result table.)

The remainder of the chapter will look at the various ways REXX is used by Database Manager. These include the following:

- DARI (Database Application Remote Interface)
- DBM (Database Manager routines/Command Line interface): SQLDBS
- SQL statement creation and execution.
  - Embedded (Dynamic) SQL: SQLEXEC
  - Interpreted SQL (via DBM and Query Manager)
- Query Manager

* Callable Interface (DSQCIX, DSQSETUP)

- User Exits (such as backup)

Command Line/Database Manager Interface

By registering the SQLAR DLL, one can use the SQLDBS external function. This is done by placing the following line in a REXX procedure. (Place it in your STARTUP.CMD to be processed every time the computer is rebooted.):

```
ret_code = Rxfuncadd('SQLDBS','SQLAR','SQLDBS')
/* ret_code = 0 (registered) > 0 (not registered) */
```

Once successfully registered, then call the SQLDBS external function to process many of the Database Manager (DBM) commands.

Here is an example:

```
call SQLDBS 'START DATABASE MANAGER'
/* Needed to initially invoke Database Manager */
```

Here are some guidelines to follow when using this interface:

1. By using the Call instruction, a return code is placed in the REXX system (special) variable RESULT.0 means the DBM statement was successfully processed. Other values include -1 (out of memory), -2 (SQL statement successful processed), -3 — -8 (various SQL errors). Greater than 1 (Number of characters in an error message.)
2. Database Manager pre-defines several additional REXX system variables that are not part of Standard REXX: These are called **Host Variables** see the section on generating SQL statements.
3. Table 4-3 summarizes the major Database Manager (i.e. non-SQL) Commands that can be used with the call SQLDBS interface (i.e., call SQLDBS *'command'*.) Not shown are various commands associated with: 1) directory scans of catalogs (such as OPEN DATABASE DIRECTORY), 2) remote nodes operations (such as CATALOG NODE), 3) configuration files used in roll forward operations (such as GET DATABASE CONFIGURATION).

Table 4-3 Major Database Manager Commands Used with SQLDBS

Command Syntax	What It Does
Database Manager Operations	
START DATABASE MANAGER	Starts DBM. Needed before running any of the following commands:
STOP DATABASE MANAGER	Ends DBM if there are no active connections to the database.
Global Database Operations	
BACKUP DATABASE *dbn* (ALL or CHANGES) TO *drv* *dbn* = database name (to back up) *drv* = drive letter to place backup. ALL: Complete backup CHANGES: Incremental backup (default)	Performs a complete or total backup of *dbn* to drive *drv*.

Table 4-3 Continued

Command Syntax	What It Does
CATALOG DATABASE *dbn* (AS *al*) (ON *drv* <u>or</u> AT NODE *nd*) (WITH *cmt*) *al:* Optional alias for the database. *cmt:* Comment about the database *dbn:* Name of database to catalog. *drv:* Drive letter where database is located. *nd:* Name of node (on network) where the database is located.	Catalogs information about the database. This allows for a more efficient operation.
CHANGE DATABASE *dbn* COMMENT (ON *drv*) WITH *cmt* *cmt:* New comment. *dbn:* Database to change comment *drv:* Drive letter where database is located.	Changes the comment associated with the database dbn.
CREATE DATABASE *dbn* (ON *drv*) (WITH *cmt*) (COLLATE *col*) *col:* Sorting sequence (NONE, SYSTEM, USER) NONE: no sorting sequence SYSTEM: sorted by country sorting sequence. USER: Followed by up to a 256 character. (See SQLECSRX.CMD for valid values)	Creates a new database.
DROP DATABASE dbn *dbn:* Name of database to delete.	Deletes and uncatalogs a database.
RESTART DATABASE dbn *dbn:* Name of dataset to restart.	Restarts a database (such as after a fatal error.)

Table 4-3 Continued

Command Syntax	What It Does
RESTORE DATABASE dbn FROM drv[1] (TO drv[2]) (WITHOUT ROLLING FORWARD) *dbn:* Name of database to restore *drv[1]:* Drive where backup is located. *drv[2]:* (Optional) Drive where to restore the backup to. WITHOUT ROLLING FORWARD: (The database is rolled forward when meeting a specified database. However, all uncommitted transactions are not rolled forward.) Note: Once this command is issued, it is followed by : CONTINUE RESTORE STOP RESTORE	RESTORES database (such as after it is accidentally erased.)
ROLL FORWARD DATABASE dbn	After restoring a database, this rolls it forward to include any outstanding transactions that have taken place since the last backup (and were not part of the restored database.) Not shown are optional keywords (i.e., TO value that includes a date in a yy-mm-dd format and a time in a hh.mm.ss format.)
UNCATALOG DATABASE dbn (data dictionary). *dbn:* Name of database to be uncataloged.	Uncatalog dataset for catalog
Statistical Operations	
COLLECT (ALL <u>or</u> DATABASE <u>or</u> SYSTEM) STATUS (FOR DATABASE *dbn* or ON *drv*) USING *:stem*	Gather statistics about one or more databases on a particular drive.

Table 4-3 Continued

Command Syntax	What It Does
dbn: Database name. Information on other databases are not captured.	
drv: Drive letter. Captures information of all databases on the drive.	
stem: The stem of a compound symbol prefixed by a colon. "Array" elements include:	
stem.0 Number of elements sent back. 7 (for SYSTEM)	
stem.1 0 (SYSTEM status) -1 (database does not exist)	
stem.2 (Current time in seconds since 1/1/70)	
stem.4 Database product	
stem.6 Release number	
stem.8 (Time of current backup in seconds since 1/1/70)	
stem.10 (number of user connections to databases)	
stem.11 (Database alias)	
stem.12 (Database name)	
stem 14 (Drive)	
stem.15 (Node name)	
stem.16 (type of OS2 DBM)	

Table 4-3 Continued

Command Syntax	What It Does
ALL: All statistics (database, system, and user) should be captured.	
DATABASE: All statistics but user should be captured SYSTEM — Only system statistics are captured.	
FREE STATUS RESOURCES	Stops collecting statistics. Only required if the ALL keyword is not specified for COLLECT STATUS and GET DATABASE STATUS.
GET DATABASE STATUS USING :stem	Used after a COLLECT STATUS if wishing to save statistics about additional databases.
Stem "array" elements include: (These are not the same location as in the COLLECT STATUS array.)	
stem.0 (Number of elements returned — if successful, would be always 10)	
stem.1 (-1 [no info retrieved] > 0 [number of databases left to retrieve])	
stem.2 (Current backup in number of seconds since 1/1/70)	
stem.4 (Number of connections to the database)	
stem.5 (database alias)	
stem.6 (database name)	
stem.8 (database drive)	
stem.9 (node name)	

Table 4-3 Continued

Command Syntax	What It Does
stem.10 (type of OS2 DBM)	
GET USER STATUS FOR DATABASE *dbn* USING *:stem*	Useful if you want to check on all users that were/are connected since the database application was started.
dbn: Name of database to retrieve information on.	
stem: "Array" elements include: stem.0 (number of user status "packets")	(COLLECT STATUS must be issued before this command is used.)
X: "Packet" number	
stem.x.0 (Number of array elements. If successful is always 10)	
stem.x.1 (Number of transactions)	
stem.x.2 (Number of SQL calls)	
stem.x.3 (Number of SQL calls in last transaction)	
stem.x.4 (Time in seconds since start)	
stem.x.5 (Time in seconds since last connection)	
stem.x.6 (User name)	
stem.x.7 (Node name)	
stem.x.8 (Authority value - 01 (System Administrator), 02 (Database Administrator), 10 (SQL Connection)	

Table 4-3 Continued

Command Syntax	What It Does
stem.x.9 (Transaction Flag — C (modified database), R (read database), S(transaction begun)	
Miscellaneous Operations	
GET MESSAGE INTO *:symbol* (LINEWIDTH *wid*) *symbol:* REXX Symbol to hold the error message. *wid:* Width of each line .0 means no line breaks (continuous).	Note that any non-negative values of the system (special) REXX variable RESULT will also give the length of an error message.
INTERRUPT	Useful to stop a previous Database Manager operation. Also a way to provide controlled exception handling from a REXX procedure invoking Database Manager routines.
INSTALL SIGNAL HANDLER	Initializes use of a default exception handling routine for Ctrl-Break (interruption). You may have to create your routine if a more sophisticated exception handling sequence is required.
MIGRATE DATABASE *dbn* (PASSWORD *pw*) *dbn:* Name of database. *pw:* Password of database.	To migrate from Extended Edition databases to Extended Services.
START USING DATABASE dbn IN (SHARED or EXCLUSIVE) MODE (In DB2/2, this will be supplemented by the SQL statement — CONNECT TO dbn USING (SHARED or EXCLUSIVE) MODE) *dbn:* Database name	Connects an application (exec) to a database.

Table 4-3 Continued

Command Syntax	What It Does
EXCLUSIVE: Gives a user/ application sole use of a database.	
SHARED: The default of SHARING the database with other users.	
STOP USING DATABASE In DB2/2, this will be supplemented by the SQL statement — CONNECT RESET a database.	Disconnects an application (procedure) from a database

4. The following commands in Table 4-4 are not supported by the CALL SQLDBS interface or by other programming languages:

Table 4-4

Command	Not Supported by:
CHANGE SQLISL (SQL Isolation Level)	Other programming languages.
SQLGDREF (DEREFERENCE ADDRESS)	REXX (CALL SQLDBS)
SQLGADDR (GET ADDRESS)	REXX (CALL SQLDBS)
SQLFWNLS (GET CODE PAGE)	REXX (CALL SQLDBS)
REXX equivalent: GET DCS DIRECTORY ENTRY	Programming Language equivalent: SQKEGDGT (GET DCS DIRECTORY ENTRIES)
SQLEINT2 (INTERRUPT2)	REXX (CALL SQLDBS)

5. See the next section for an example of using these statements.

Running SQL programs

As mentioned in earlier sections, SQL is the standard language to perform database queries and produce reports. One of the capabilities of Database Manager is to execute SQL statements and produce a result table (i.e., an extract). Part of the process is creating an executable (i.e., machine-readable) version of the SQL statement. This is called preparing the SQL statement.

The process of *preparing* all the SQL statements for an application is called **binding** — i.e., producing a machine-readable application with executable SQL statements. It is a very efficient means to retrieve data. This is initially done when a database is created from REXX. Note that it is recommended to rebind an application after installing a new version to take advantage of hopefully an improved retrieval technique.

Under OS/2, SQL statements are created one of three ways:

- *Static*. These are **embedded** in a programming language (such as C) and then compiled. (But for this book, we will include interpreted language such as REXX.)
- *Dynamic*. These are created and executed at run-time. They may be embedded in a REXX, C, COBOL, FORTRAN, or other languages.
- *Interactive*. Similar to Dynamic SQL but keystroked by a user.

This chapter focuses on the last two approaches.

Basics

Here are some of the basic rules in preparing REXX to execute SQL statements:

1. You must register the SQLAR Dynamic Link Library in order to use REXX/SQL interface. Place the following statement in a STARTUP.CMD file to automatically do this when OS/2 is initially invoked, or type at the OS/2 command prompt:

```
ret_code = Rxfuncadd('SQLEXEC','SQLAR','SQLEXEC')
/* ret_code = 0 (registered) > 0 (not registered) */
```

2. Use any of the following approaches to execute SQL statements from REXX:

Embedded SQL (Static)

```
CALL SQLEXEC 'SQL_statement'
```

Where *SQL_statement* can only be:

CLOSE, COMMIT, DECLARE, DESCRIBE, EXECUTE, EXECUTE IMMEDIATE, FETCH, OPEN, PREPARE, ROLLBACK.

Use the following Dynamic SQL approach to process any SQL statement **not** listed above. Using this approach, statements are created at run-time.

Dynamic SQL

```
CALL SQLEXEC 'PREPARE....' /* Created SQL binding */
CALL SQLEXEC 'EXECUTE...' /* Then execute it */

CALL SQLEXEC 'EXECUTE IMMEDIATE...' /* OR DO IT IN 1 STEP! */
```

3. To continue an SQL statement on multiple lines: 1) Make sure the first word in quotes is SQL; 2) a comma is the last character on the line to be continued; and 3) the SQL statement on each line is in quotes. (This is not true for literal strings in standard REXX.)
4. Note any of the above SQL statements may contain REXX symbols or also called **host variables**.
   a. Note, host variables may have a name only 64 characters long (as opposed to 250 characters for symbol names under OS/2 REXX.)
   b. Host variables follow standard REXX symbol naming conventions with the following exception: Host variables may start and contain a period as part of the symbol name. (It does have the limitation of not ending the host variable name in a period.)
   c. Unless a value is quoted (such as a numeric value) it will be converted to a character string.
   d. Unlike other programming languages, host variables do not have to be initialized.
5. An important part of multi-user database operations is the means used to lock the data so only one user/application can update a database at a time and that both are working with the same database values. With SQL, this is determined by the **isolation** or **locking** level. REXX supports all three isolation levels:
   - Cursor Stability: **The default level.** Locks a specified row of an application until the next row is retrieved. No other application can modify (i.e., update) that row. However, all other rows can be manipulated, so the row's location in the database can still be changed. (Which may cause problems if you are not aware of it.) Another problem is the REXX application cannot access changes not yet committed to the master database by another application. In short, be aware of all the shortcomings of this approach if you select it.

- Repeatable Read: More powerful than cursor stability, while in affect, no other application can perform a row operation that would affect the location of the locked row. The REXX application with this isolation level can also operate on other rows. However, the REXX application still cannot access changes not yet committed to the master database by other application.
- Uncommitted Read: The approach to use when locking out other applications is less important than capturing those changes made by other applications that are not yet committed to the master database. (But only after the operation such as creating a table is performed.) This setting will not "lock out" other applications from manipulating a row as long as it is not a global operation (such as deleting a table.)

This is how REXX can be used to manipulate the isolation level:

a. Whenever a file is created or migrated, REXX uses one of three bound files, each supporting one of the various isolation levels. (Even though the file is compiled, it can still be browsed by an editor. Its contents is nothing more than a set of SQL statements that associate various cursor names (variables) with various statement names. (Note that a **cursor** is just a pointer to a row in a table [such as the current row.] Several cursors can be used at the same time.) The three files residing in the SQLLIB directory are: 1) SQLARXCS.BND (for the cursor stability isolation level); 2) SQLARXRR.BND (for the repeatable read isolation level); and 3) SQLARXUR.BND (for the uncommitted read isolation level).

b. Fortunately, you do not need to remember the name of the above bind files. To change the isolation level, simply issue one of the following three statements before accessing a database.

```
call SQLDBS 'CHANGE SQLISL TO CS' /* Cursor Stability */
call SQLDBS 'CHANGE SQLISL TO RR' /* Repeatable Read */
call SQLDBS 'CHANGE SQLISL TO UR' /* Uncommitted Read */
```

Since another REXX application may have changed the isolation level, it is good practice to always explicitly set the isolation level early in the REXX procedure.

For further information about isolation levels, please read the Guide to Database Manager (S04G-1013).

6. The following DBM statements in Table 4-5 can be used in SQL-oriented procedures:

Table 4-5 DBM Statements

Command with Syntax	What It Does
BIND *fn* TO DATABASE *dn* (USING *:stem*) (MESSAGES *loc*) *dn:* Name of database *fn:* A list file that contains the desired active bind files. Look at C:\SQLLIB\SQLUBIND.LST for an example. *stem:* REXX stem variable that contains the following array values: stem.0: Number of array elements specified. stem.1: Date format. (Values are def (default), usa, eur (europe), and iso. stem.2: Isolation level — CS, RR, UR (see explanation earlier in this section.) stem.3: Record blocking type ALL (If a cursor is not associated with any type of operation, then it is assigned a read-only status. Blocking takes place for read-only operations.)	Binds a file to a database.

Table 4-5 Continued

Command with Syntax	What It Does
NO (No blocking and special treatment of cursors not associated with any type of operation.) UNAMBIG (Similar to ALL but assigns a cursor not associated with any type of operation a modifiable status not read-only.) loc: Location of any messages. Valid values include: *filename* (Name of a file), LPTx (printer), NUL	
EXPORT sql FROM dbn TO fn OF type (USING :stem) MESSAGES loc *dbn:* Name of database. *fn:* Name of file to place the exported (converted file.) *loc:* Location of message file. Read the BIND command above for additional information. *sql:* A REXX symbol that has as a value a SQL statement. This statement (i.e. a SELECT) retrieves the specified data to be exported.	Converts a file from the OS/2 database format to an external format.

Table 4-5 Continued

Command with Syntax	What It Does
stem: A REXX stem with the following "array" values: stem.0 Elements in array stem.*n* The name of the nth column.	
type: DEL (Delimited file such as comma-delimited (the default delimiter type).)	
IXF (Exports the data and the table that created it. Recommended for exporting to IBM systems.)	
WSF (Format for 1-2-3)	
IMPORT TO dn FROM fn OF type (METHOD (L or N or P) USING :stem¹) (mode) INTO table (:stem²) MESSAGES loc	
dn: Name of the database to be created.	
fn: Name of the external database to be converted.	
loc: Location of error messages. See the description under the BIND command listed above.	
Method: (L [Location], N [Name], P [Position])	
mode: Is one of the following:	
CREATE: If the table does not already exist, and the IXF format was specified, then create it.	

Table 4-5 Continued

Command with Syntax	What It Does
INSERT: Adds data to a table regardless if it exists or not. INSERT_UPDATE: Similar to INSERT but additionally modifies data if a primary was specified (and the keys value is matched.) REPLACE: Delete existing data and add new table Table specification remains intact. REPLACE_CREATE: Identical to combining CREATE and REPLACE if the IXF format is specified. stem[1]: A stem with the following "array" elements: stem.0: Number of array elements. **LOCATION method** stem.1 (and all odd array elements) Starting column position. stem.2 (and all even array elements) Ending column position. **NAMES method** Stem.n (The name of the nth column.) **POSITION method** stem.1 (and all other non-zero array elements) Position of column.	

Table 4-5 Continued

Command with Syntax	What It Does
stem^2 : Another stem variable that has the following "array" elements: stem.0: Number of array elements. stem.n: Name of nth column.	
type: ASC (ASCII file but no delimiters) DEL (ASCII file but comma or some other delimiters) IXF (Format to use for other IBM platforms) WSF (1-2-3 format)	Convert a database to an OS/2 Database format.

7. Here are some other REXX compound arrays used during SQL and Database Manager operations:

   a. The most commonly used is the SQLCA array. Like the REXX system (special) variable RC, **these values will change when the next SQL or DBM statement is processed.** So, it suggested to copy this array to another REXX compound symbol. Array elements include:

      • SQLCA.SQLCODE: Return code from a SQL statement. These include (Note that positive values are warnings — the SQL statement will continue processing and negative values are errors — the SQL statement did not successfully complete processing.)

   0 (worked)
   513 (SQL statement will affect the entire table).
   -31, -32, -958, -968, -970, -78, -980, -982 (File problems)
   4943, -306, -307, -308, -310, -324, -4911, -4912
   (Host variable problems)
   4999 (Database Manager Error)
   -51, -954, -956 (Memory or disk space exceeded.)

All other errors (SQL syntax and miscellaneous errors)

1. To test for this variable, the following format is usually used:

```
IF (RESULT = 0 & SQLCA.SQLCODE = 0) then...
/* IF both variables are ok then.. */
```

2. The following values of the REXX system (special) variable RESULT are a consequence of what happened to SQLCA.SQLCODE:

   - 0: SQL statement processed. Look at SQLCA.SQLCODE to figure if the SQL statement was successfully processed.
   - -2: SQLCA.SQLCODE has a 0 value.
   - -3: SQLCA.SQLCODE has a non-zero (error) return code.
   - -6: Cannot create SQLCA compound array. Check your available memory.
   - -8: Cannot retrieve SQLCA.SQLCODE value.
   - -9: The value of SQLCA.SQLCODE was longer than the 5 characters allowed. The extra characters were not saved.

SQLCA.SQLERRD.1 -.6 Additional error information. .3: Rows changed after an operation (such as delete), 5: Rows changed or deleted.

SQLCA.SQLERRML: Length of a SQL error message. Ranges between 0-70. (SQLCA.SQLERRMC.)

1. The following values of the REXX system (special) variable RESULT are related to SQLCA.SQLERRML

   - -11: SQLCA.SQLERRML: Cannot be retrieved.
   - -12: SQLCA.SQLERRML had a value longer than the 2 characters allowed. The extra characters were dropped.

SQLCA.SQLERRMC: One or more values that correspond to a REXX error message.

The following values of the REXX system (special) variable RESULT are related to SQLCA.SQLERRMC

- -11: SQLCA.SQLERRMC cannot be retrieved.
- -12: SQLCA.SQLERRMC has a value longer than the 70 characters allowed. The extra characters were dropped.

SQLCA.SQLERRP: An 8 character code that identifies the product (SQL) and the component where the error occurred.

SQLCA.SQLSTATE: A 5 character return code about the last SQL statement.

SQLCA.SQLWARN.0 -.10 Blank if no warnings, W (otherwise)

b. Other REXX compound symbol includes:

SQLDA: Used in such SQL statements as DESCRIBE, EXECUTE, FETCH, OPEN, and PREPARE. Elements include Data Type (.SQLTYPE), Value (.SQL-DATA), and Column Name (. SQLNAME).

SQLOPT: Used with the BIND statement.

SQL_DIR_ENTRY: Used with the Distributed Database Connection Services/2.

SQLENINFO: Information about Nodes.

SQLESYSTAT and SQLEDBSTAT: Used with the COLLECT DATABASE STATUS (SQLESYSTAT/SQLEDBSTAT), or GET NEXT DATABASE STATUS (SQLEDBSTAT)

SQLEURSTAT: Used with COLLECT USER STATUS

SQLDCOL: Used with IMPORT/EXPORT

SQL_AUTHORIZATIONS: Used with GET ADMINISTRATIVE AUTHORIZATION.

SQL Overview

Unfortunately, space allows only a brief look at the powerful Structured Query Language (SQL). The following are some of the major SQL concepts:

a. SQL statements currently support the following data types:

CHAR: A character string up to 254 characters.

DATE: Contains year month and day. It is output to a 10 byte format such as EUR [European — dd.mm.yyyy], ISO [yyyy-mm-dd], USA [mm/dd/yyyy].

DECIMAL: A decimal number that can be positive or negative. Values range from -10 31+1 — 10 31+1.

FLOATING POINT: For large positive or negative decimal numbers (including zero).

INTEGER: For large numbers (between -2 billion and 2 billion).

LONG VARCHAR: Variable-length character string up to 32,700 characters. Can be used in a limited number of SQL statements (such as SELECT.)

SMALLINT: For small numbers (between -32,768 and 32,767.)

TIME: Time format (such as EUR [European — hh.mm.ss], ISO [International Standard: hh.mm.ss], JIS [Japanese Standard — hh:mm:ss], USA [hh:mm AM or PM])

TIMESTAMP: A 26 byte string that contains DATE and TIME plus time (i.e., the seconds in decimal values. The entire format is yyyy-mm-dd hh.mm.ss.zzzzzz. With zzzzzz being seconds as decimal values.)

VARCHAR: Variable-length character string up-to-4000 characters. Can be used in a limited number of SQL statements (such as SELECT.)

b. Special (System) variables: CURRENT DATE, CURRENT TIME, CURRENT TIMESTAMP, USER. There will probably be a CURRENT SERVER special variable in the DB2/2 version.

c. The following are some of the current built-in functions: FLOAT: Returns *arg* as a floating point argument; and INTEGER — Returns *arg* as an integer value.

Applies to entire COLUMN or unique values in a COLUMN (with the DISTINCT keyword.)

AVG(col) or AVG(DISTINCT col): Average of col [column-name].

COUNT(*) or COUNT(DISTINCT col): COUNT(*) gives the total number of rows. COUNT(DISTINCT col) gives the total number of values.

MAX(col)/ MIN(col) OR MAX(DISTINCT col)/ MIN(DISTINCT col): Gives the highest (MAX) or lowest (MIN) value of a column.

SUM(col) or SUM(DISTINCT col): Gives the total for a column.

Functions that only work on one VALUE. (Also called SCALAR FUNCTIONS.)

(The following new scalar functions will probably be the DB2/2 version: DECIMAL(arg,n^1,n^2) — Returns arg as a decimal. N^1 is the number of digits to the left of the decimals point desired, N^2 is to the right of the decimal point.);

Conversion/Date and Time Functions

CHAR(arg,fmt): Converts a date or time value to a character string. arg — date or time value. fmt — date/time format (i.e., EUR, ISO, JIS, USA).

DATE(arg): Converts a value to a character string in a date format.

DAY(arg), HOUR(arg), MICROSECOND(arg) MINUTE(arg), MONTH(arg), SECOND(arg) YEAR(arg): Returns the function_name part of an *arg* string — i.e., DAY (1-31), HOUR (0-24), MICROSECOND (0-999999), MINUTE (0-59), MONTH (1-12), SECOND (0-59), YEAR (1-9999).

DAYS(arg): Converts a date into an integer format — such as for date comparisons.

TIME(arg): Return a time value from arg.

TIMESTAMP(arg) or TIMESTAMP(arg^1,arg^2): Returns a timestamp value from one or two strings (arg^1 — date part, arg^2 — time part).

String Operations (Similar to REXX)

LENGTH(arg): Gives the length (i.e., total number of characters in *arg*.)

SUBSTR(arg, bp,len): Extracts part of the arg string starting in *bp* for a length of *len* characters.

TRANSLATE(arg, conversion_list, character_list, pad_chars): Identical to REXX TRANSLATE function. Converts the string *arg*. Changes characters found in the *character_list* to the corresponding values in the *conversion_list*. The string may also be padded with the pad_chars if no *conversion_list* character exists.

c. The following are some common SQL statements

Database Operations

Adds the transactions to the master database.

COMMIT WORK

Negates the latest transactions to the master database.

ROLLBACK WORK
Table Operations

Add a column or primary index.

ALTER TABLE *tbn*
ADD *col type*
PRIMARY *colname*

tbn: table name, *col:* name of column to be added, *type* = data type (see the list shown earlier in the chapter.) *Colname* = name of column that is to be the primary key.

Creates or modifies comments about a table, view or column.

COMMENT ON TABLE *name* IS *'comment'*
or COMMENT ON COLUMN *$name^1$.$name^2$*

name: name of table or view, *comment:* description about column/table/view that is up to 254 characters, *name*[1] (table or view name), *name*[2] (column name). Note that name[1] and name[2] are separated by a period.

Creates an index for a table.

CREATE (UNIQUE) INDEX *idx* ON *tbn* (*col* ASC or DESC)

idx: name of index, *tbn:* table name, *UNIQUE:* no other row can have the value of an index.

Creates a table

CREATE TABLE tbn
col^n $type^n$ (PRIMARY KEY (colname)

tbn: table name, $col^n/type^n$: One or more columns and corresponding data types. Each column/type pair may also include one of the following values. (FOR BIT DATA — allows columns to be seen as binary data. This is especially useful for exporting to other platforms. NOT NULL — sees null values as invalid. And NOT NULL PRIMARY KEY.) Note, the list of column names/data types should be enclosed in parentheses.

Creates a view

CREATE VIEW *vnm* (*column list*) AS *sql-select*

vnm: name of the view to create, column list: list of column names to be included in the view, sql-select: A SQL SELECT query (such as a SELECT ALL).

Creates/ Prepares a cursor

DECLARE *cn* CURSOR FOR *sn* or sql-select

cn: Use values c1-c50, sn: s1-100. Identifies a SELECT statement. The actual SELECT statement can also be used.

Note the BIND files described earlier are nothing more than a series of DECLARE CURSOR statements. This statement is usually followed by an OPEN CURSOR cn statement to prepare the cursor for retrieving a row.

Delete/Insert rows

DELETE FROM *nm* WHERE *cond*

nm: Name of table or view, cond: usually in the format "column =, >, or <, values". Can also use the clause WHERE CURRENT OF *cn* where *n* is the cursor number 1-50 defined earlier in a DECLARE CURSOR statement.

INSERT INTO *nm* (*column list*) VALUES (*value list*)

nm: table or view name, *column list:* list of column names, *value list:* list of values to be inserted into the row.

Deletes an index, table or a view.

DROP INDEX *nm* or TABLE *nm* or VIEW *nm*

nm: Name of index, table or view to be deleted.

Retrieves a row.

FETCH *cn* INTO *:sym*

cn: The cursor name with n being 1-50. *sym:* Name of one or more symbols to place the retrieved row into.

Grant privileges to a table/Locks a table

GRANT priv ON TABLE nm TO id

priv = ALL or ONE of the following (ALTER: Add column/index, CONTROL: ability to change other's privileges, DELETE: Delete a row, INDEX: create an index, INSERT: insert rows, SELECT: use SELECT or EXPORT statements, UPDATE: update table), *nm:* name of table or view, *id* = id of person being granted privilege. PUBLIC gives it to all users.

LOCK TABLE tn IN mode MODE

tn: table name to lock, mode — Has one of two values — EXCLUSIVE (no one else can read the dataset.) SHARED (other users can only read the database).

Exception handling

WHENEVER NOTFOUND or SQLERROR or SQLWARNING *action.*

action: One of the following: CONTINUE, GOTO :REXX_label
REXX_label is the label in a REXX procedure.

Updating the database

UPDATE nm SET col = value^1 WHERE value^2

nm: Name of table or view to be updated, col: a non-derived column name, value^1: May be NULL or actual/calculated value, value^2: Is either a) a search condition (i.e., col = value), or b) CURRENT OF c^n With n: 1-50.

Creating a result table

SELECT ALL * FROM nm
Selects all values from table/view *nm.*

```
SELECT (column-list) /* Actual or derived (using functions) columns */
   FROM nm           /* Table/view name */
   WHERE col         /* Matches rows where col = value */
   GROUP BY col      /* Groups table by value (If a [HAVING condition]
                        statement is used */
```

Kong (1991) presents an example of building an interactive REXX SQL parser.

Example

The following brief, but documented example is meant to show some of the things you can deal with the SQL-REXX connection. Unfortunately, space does not allow us to add many of the real-world extensions such as indices. This basic skeleton should be sufficient to get you up and running. Note it works well with PMREXX (highly recommended) or from the OS/2 command prompt.

An OS/2 SQL Example

```
/* REXX */
init_dll:
        rc = Rxfuncadd('SQLDBS', 'SQLAR','SQLDBS')
                say rc
        rc = Rxfuncadd('SQLEXEC,'SQLAR,'SQLEXEC')
                say rc
        call sqldbs 'START DATABASE MANAGER'
                if ( result <> 0) then say RESULT
                if (sqlca.sqlcode <> 0 ) then say 'Start DBM' sqlca.sqlcode
        call sqldbs 'CREATE DATABASE BOOK1 ON C'
                if ( result <> 0) then say RESULT
                if (sqlca.sqlcode <> 0 ) then say 'Create DB' sqlca.sqlcode
        call sqldbs 'START USING DATABASE BOOK1 IN SHARED MODE'
                if ( result <> 0) then say RESULT
                if (sqlca.sqlcode <> 0 ) then say 'Start DB' sqlca.sqlcode

create_tb:
        cm1a = 'create table test'
        cm1b = '(ID SMALLINT NOT NULL'
        cm1c = ' NAME CHAR(25) NOT NULL'
        cm1d = ' PCMOD CHAR(25) NOT NULL'
        cm1e = ' MEM CHAR(10)    '
        cm1f = ' OS CHAR(10) NOT NULL'
```

```
        cm1g = 'PRIMARY KEY(ID))'
        cm1 = cm1a||cm1b||','||cm1c||','||cm1d||','||cm1e||','||cm1f||','||cm1g
        call sqlexec 'execute immediate :cmd1'
                if ( result <> 0) then say RESULT
                if (sqlca.sqlcode <> 0 ) then do
                        say 'Create Table' sqlca.sqlcode
                        say 'Create Table' sqlca.sqlstate
        end

insert_tb:
        cmd2 = 'insert into text'
                'values('2','Martha Smith','AST 486','5MB',OS2')'
        call sqlexec 'execute immediate :cmd2'
                if ( result <> 0) then say RESULT
                if (sqlca.sqlcode <> 0 ) then do
                        say 'Insert Rows' sqlca.sqlcode
                        say 'Insert Rows' sqlca.sqlstate
        end

del_tb:
        cmd4 = 'drop table test'
        call sqlexec 'execute immediate :cmd4'
                if ( result <> 0) then say RESULT
                if (sqlca.sqlcode <> 0 ) then say 'Drop Table' sqlca.sqlcode

del_db:
        call sqldbs 'stop using database'
                if ( result <> 0) then say RESULT
                if (sqlca.sqlcode <> 0 ) then say 'Stop Db' sqlca.sqlcode

        call sqldbs 'stop database manager'
                if ( result <> 0) then say RESULT
                if (sqlca.sqlcode <> 0 ) then say 'Stop DBM' sqlca.sqlcode
```

What is happening:

1. /* REXX */ — identifies the .CMD as a REXX file */
2. init_dll — Does all of the initial housekeeping working:
   a. Registers the SQLAR DLL (Dynamic Link Library) needed to use the SQLDBS and SQLEXEC interface. This also can be placed in a STARTUP.CMD so it is processed immediately on OS/2 invocation. (**Rxfuncadd...**)

b. Starts the Database Manager. This is also needed before beginning to use any Database Manager routines (**START DATABASE MANAGER**). If you have not logged in yet, look at the LOGON icon under the User Profile Management group. If this is a standalone PC, you can use the USERID account which has a password of PASSWORD.

   After each statement is processed, the REXX system (special) and the SQL-CODE variables are examined for non-zero with an error message being returned (with a description of the statement). (**if result...if sqlca.sqlcode**)

c. A database called book1 is created on drive C. (**CREATE DATABASE**.)

d. The exec is connected to the database in a shared mode.

3. create_tb — Creates a table.

   a. Creates several REXX symbols that are concatenated together. The table created is a simplified PC asset database. Each record has a unique key called id. Other fields are PC user's name, model name, memory, and operating system. See the description listed earlier in this chapter.

   b. EXECUTE IMMEDIATE dynamically creates, prepares, and executes the SQL statements. Note it cannot be used with all statements such as SELECT. Note the host command symbol is prefixed by a colon. Unfortunately, since not all sql-codes are listed, one must rely on the sqlstate for additional information. (The on-line error messages includes a fairly complete list of sqlstates and proposed actions.) (**Execute immediate :cmd1**)

4. insert_tb — inserts one row into a table.

5. del_tb — deletes the table from the database.

   a. Deletes the table from the database.

   b. Stops the database connection and performs a COMMIT of transactions to the master database.

   c. Stops the entire database manager (not implicitly done!) unless another application is still using it.

Query Manager

Another approach to performing database operations is to use the QUERY MANAGER. Query Manager can be processed using a full-screen application. However, a program (written in C) / REXX exec can invoke a customized version of the full-screen Query Manager application. Here is an overview of using this latter approach (also called the Query Manager Callable Interface):

1. The following initialization tasks must be performed before using the Query Manager Callable Interface: (Note these can be placed in STARTUP.CMD so they are processed every time OS/2 is invoked.)

```
ret_code = Rxfuncadd('DSQCIX','DSQCIX','DSQCIX')
/* Registers Query Manager DLL */
ret_code = Rxfuncadd('DSQSETUP,DSQCIX','DSQSETUP')
/* Registers the DSQSETUP */
call DSQSETUP
/* This initializes all of the return code and error-handling variables */
/* OR just have one line with the following: DSQRGSTR */
call DSQCIX ' START', 'DSQMODE=INTERACTIVE', 'DSQCMD = A'

/* Invokes Query Manager */
```

Note, the following are keywords that can be used with the START command:

- 'DSQSCMD = name': The name of an OS/2 batch (.CMD file. Do not specify the .CMD extension.) The default is the QRWEXECZ.CMD (pronunciation is left as an exercise for the reader.)

  This does the following:

  a. Turns off displaying any commands

  b. Defines the drive and path for the batch file.

  c. Switches to the C: drive (or the value of the QRWWDR environment variable).

  d. Goes to the SQLLIB directory

  e. Invokes QUERY Manager using Callable Interface (QUERYMGR/DSQDSPLY:IMMEDIATE)

     Up-to-nine other options may also be entered. (such as /DATABASE:name, /DSQSMODE: [INTERACTIVE or BATCH (the default)], /RUNPROC: name (REXX exec) — these correspond to the START keywords listed here.)

  f. Exits the batch file after restoring the drive and path settings before the batch file is invoked.

     DSQSDBNM = name': A one to eight character name of the database to be queried.

- 'DSQSMODE = mode': The mode of the Query Manager process — either BATCH [the default] or INTERACTIVE. Note that not all Query Manager commands will work in BATCH mode. These are listed later in this section.

- 'DSQSRUN=name': Name of REXX procedure to execute.

2. The Callable Interface supports the following Query Manager commands: (to invoke any of them, use the syntax CALL DSQCIX 'command','keyword^1=value^1', 'keyword^2=value^2...')

Table 4-6

Syntax/Type	What It Does
Global Operations	
'BEGIN WINDOW' *Query Manager commands* 'END WINDOW'	Creates a Query Manager window. Usually followed by one of the other and concludes with a END WINDOW
'BEGIN WORK'	Starts one unit of work until a COMMIT, ROLLBACK or database disconnect takes place. IMPORTS and EXPORTS are not allowed during this time.
'CANCEL WORK'	Ends current unit of work but no transactions are written to the master database.
'END WORK'	Makes a COMMIT of all transactions since the unit of work began to the master database. This is implied if Query Manager is terminated.
'START arguments'	Starts Query Manager. See later in this section for an explanation.
'EXIT'	Ends Query Manager
Query/Table Operations	
'CONVERT QUERY *name*' *name:* query name.	Assigns a SQL Query to a global symbol.
'DEFINE TABLE *name*' *name:* name of table to create or modify.	Defines a new or existing table (INTERACTIVE mode only). Also COMMITS transactions when issued.

Table 4-6 Continued

Syntax/Type	What It Does
DISPLAY *item* itemname' *item* = one of the following: FORM MENU PANEL PROC (Procedure) QUERY *itemname:* A 27 character name describing the Query Manager.	Create/Modify the definition of various Query Manger objects. (Interactive Mode Only). Results in a COMMIT if a unit of work is active.
'EDIT TABLE *name* MODE = (ADD or CHANGE)' *name:* Table name	Adds or Modifies (depending on MODE) one or more records to a table.
'ERASE item *itemname* CONFIRM = (YES [display confirm message] or NO' [don't display message such as in BATCH MODE])' *itemname* = one of the following: FORM MENU PANEL PROC (PROCEDURE) QUERY TABLE	Deletes a Query Manager object with an optional confirmation message.
'EXPORT TABLE name[1] TO name[2] (CONFIRM = [YES or NO], DATAFORMAT = DEL, IXF, or WSF)' DATAFORMAT = One of the following: DEL (character-delimited such as a comma), IXF (IBM Database Format),	Copies data from a table/view into an external file in a specified format.

Table 4-6 Continued

Syntax/Type	What It Does
WSF (1-2-3 Format) Name[1] = table/view name Name[2] = external file name YES (Confirmation message before replacing a file.)	
'GET type (var[1] = var[2])' *type* = CURRENT, GLOBAL (see later in this section), LOCAL *var[1]* = REXX symbol that will contain the value of the Query Manager variable. *var[2]* = the Query Manager variable or numeric/character string.	Retrieves a Query Manager variable and its value. Then assigns it to a REXX symbol.
'IMPORT TABLE name[1] FROM name[2](CONFIRM = [YES or NO], DATAFORMAT = [DEL,IXF,WSF], REPLACE= [YES or NO)' *name[1]:* table name to create/modify *name[2]:* external file name CONFIRM: YES (confirms that you wish to delete an existing file.) DATAFORMAT: See description under EXPORT. REPLACE: NO (Adds on to an existing table), YES (overrides an existing table if the same name is specified.	Copies data from an external file in a specified file to a table.

Table 4-6 Continued

Syntax/Type	What It Does
'LIST menuname (keyword = value)' Menuname is one of the following: FORM, FORMS, MAIN (main panel), MENU, MENUS, PANEL, PANELS, PROC (Procedures), PROCS, QUERIES, QUERY, TABLE, TABLES keyword=value: (For QUERY/QUERIES only) TYPE= RETURN — If enabled, displays the Exit Queries screen which can the pass the query result to the REXX exec.	Displays a Query Manager menu
'MESSAGE (DISPLAY=CANCEL)' OR 'MESSAGE (TEXT = 'text', DISPLAY = [IMMED or ONLY])' CANCEL: Stops any unshown messages from being displayed. IMMED: Displays message before the next screen is shown ONLY: Displays the message on the next screen.	Displays a message on or before the next screen.
'PRINT item itemname' OR 'PRINT REPORT (FORM, keyword= value)'	

Table 4-6 Continued

Syntax/Type	What It Does
item = one of the following: FORM, MENU, PANEL, PROC, QUERY	
itemname = Name of item *keyword* = value (One or more of the following separated by commas) CONFIRM = YES (default) or NO: Sends a confirmation message if you are going to replace an existing report listed stored in a file. (Use with FILE keyword) DATETIME = YES (the default) or NO: determines if the date or time is printed at the end of each page in the listing. FILE = name. Puts the report listing in a file instead of being printed. FORM = name (formatted report definition) LENGTH = 1-999 (default 66). The maximum number of lines per page a report listing is allowed. In choosing this value, also include lines for date/time values, and various headings.	Prints a QUERY MANAGER item OR Prints a listing about a QUERY generated by a run QUERY command.

Table 4-6 Continued

Syntax/Type	What It Does
PAGENO = YES (the default) or No. Determines if a page number appears in the top right-hand corner of each page in the report listing.	
PRINTER = alias (default is PRINTER)	
PRINTTYPE = NORMAL or COMPRESSED. (describes font size).	
WIDTH = 22-999 (Default is usually 80 or 132). The maximum number of characters a report listing can have on a line	
'RESET item'	Starts a new definition for an item.
item: is one of the following: FORM, MENU, PANEL, PROC, QUERY	Closes a unit of work and causes a COMMIT of transactions to the master database. Do not run in BATCH mode.
'RUN item name (keyword = value)'	Executes a Query or a Query Manager item.
item = one of the following: MENU, PANEL, PROC, QUERY	
name = name of the item	
keyword = value (Separate keywords by commas.)	
FORM = name: For QUERY only. Uses a formatted report form.	

Table 4-6 Continued

Syntax/Type	What It Does
INTERACT = [NO or YES (default)]: For QUERY only. If YES, then displays a copy of the report listing on the screen.	
MODE = [ADD or CHANGE] For PANEL only. Determines if the table has new rows added or existing rows modifying.	
REPORT = [NO or YES (the default)] If YES, then displays a copy of the report listing on the screen.	
'SAVE DATA AS name (keyword=value)'	Saves a query as a table in a database.
name: Name of table to save the query in.	
Use one or more of the following keywords enclosed in parentheses and separated by commas.	
COMMENT = 'text': Adds up to a 55 character comment to a table.	
CONFIRM = [NO or YES (the default)]: Confirms that you want to override an existing table with the new table.	
REPLACE [NO or YES (the default)]: YES (overrides an existing table), NO (adds at the end of an existing table)	

Table 4-6 Continued

Syntax/Type	What It Does
'SET type (var^1 = var^2)' *type* = CURRENT, GLOBAL (see later in this section), LOCAL var^1 = the Query Manager variable. var^2 = REXX symbol that will contain the value of the Query Manager variable. Or a character/ numeric string	Assigns the value of a REXX symbol to a Query Manager variable.

3. Query Manager uses the following environment variables (initialized in CONFIG.SYS).

   QWRDR: The drive where Query Manager resides. Used by the default Query Manager invocation file — QRWEXECZ.CMD.

   QRWINST: The directory where the Database Manager and Query Manager resides. Usually has a value of C:\SQLLIB.

4. Table 4-7 are a list of the variables that are returned by various Query Manager commands. These can be captured using the Query Manager GET command.

Table 4-7 Variables Returned by Various Query Manager Commands

Variable/Values	QM Command	What It Does
DSQAFORM	DISPLAY LIST RESET	Form name edited (if DISPLAY FORM)
DSQAMENU	DISPLAY LIST RESET	Menu name edited (if DISPLAY MENU)

Table 4-7 Continued

Variable/Values	QM Command	What It Does
DSQAQNAM	DISPLAY LIST QUERY LIST QUERIES RESET	Name of object edited.
DSQAPANL	DISPLAY LIST RESET	Panel name edited (if DISPLAY PANEL)
DSQAPROC	DISPLAY LIST RESET	Procedure name edited (if DISPLAY PROC)
DSQAQTYP	DISPLAY LIST QUERY LIST QUERIES RESET	SQL or PQ (Prompt) — Type of Query.
DSQATABL= name	DEFINE TABLE	Name of table/view last accessed. (1-27 characters)
DSQATTYP	DEFINE TABLE	T (Table) or V (View) depending what was accessed.
DSQCL001 = length	CONVERT QUERY	Length of DSQCQ001 such as 00033.
DSQCQ001 = string	CONVERT QUERY	SQL statement to be converted.
DSQCQCNT	CONVERT QUERY	Number of SQL queries converted to variables. Values are 000 or 001.
DSQCQLNG = 1 (SQL), 3 (PROMPT)	CONVERT QUERY	The type of query.
DSQCQTYP = 1-8 character string	CONVERT QUERY	SQL statement to be converted.

Table 4-7 Continued

Variable/Values	QM Command	What It Does
DSQEFORM	LIST RUN	Form name edited (if DISPLAY FORM)
DSQEMENU	LIST RUN	Menu name edited (if DISPLAY MENU)
DSQEPANL	LIST RUN	Panel name edited (if DISPLAY PANEL)
DSQEPROC	LIST RUN	Procedure name edited (if DISPLAY PROC)
DSQEQTYP	LIST RUN	SQL or PQ (Prompt) of last query successfully executed.

5. Each Query Manager command returns the following:

   DSQ_MESSAGE_ID: Query Manager error message number. Ranges from QRW0001N - QRW2688W. These are listed in the Database Manager Messages (stored in C:\SQLLIB\BOOK\DBMSG.INF) which can be found in the Database Manager group on the Desktop.

   DSQ_REASON_CODE: Reason Code giving additional information.

   0 DSQ_COMMAND_SUCCESS (Successfully processed)

   15-130 Various errors.

   DSQ_RETURN_CODE: Return Code

   0 DSQ_SUCCESS (Successfully processed)

   4 DSQ_WARNING (Successfully processed with at least one warning)

   8 DSQ_FAILURE (Syntax error. Query failed.)

   16 DSQ_SEVERE (Such as requesting a panel in batch mode)

6. Query Manager REXX execs cannot contain the following SQL statements:

   BACKUP DATABASE

   CATALOG (such as CATALOG APPN NODE, CATALOG DATABASE, and CATALOG DCS DATABASE),

CHANGE DATABASE COMMENT

CHANGE SQLISL

GET CONFIGURATION

INVOKED STORED PROCEDURE

LIST (DATABASE, DCS, NODE) DIRECTORY

REORGCHK

(RESET, RESTART, RESTORE, ROLLFORWARD) DATABASE

STOP DATABASE MANAGER

UNCATALOG and UPDATE

Database Application Remote Interface (DARI)

DARI or ARI supports the model of distributed computing by executing a REXX procedure that resides on a remote server along with the database. This procedure may access the database one or more times. Using this approach may greatly improve the efficiency of your processing by reducing network traffic. This is especially good for database extracts or 'canned' SQL database (such as capturing transaction data on a daily basis.)

In order to do this, there must be two REXX procedures:

a. **client procedure:**

   – Allocates the SQLDBS and SQLEXEC Dynamic Link Library.

   – START USING DATABASE (Makes a connection to a database.)

   – Invokes the SERVER exec using the DARI interface:

   CALL SQLDBS INVOKE a.cmd USING rexxsym;

   a.cmd: Name of server exec or dynamic link library

   USING: Optional keyword. *rexxsym* is a REXX symbol. This is stored in the compound symbol SQLCHAR.DATA.

   INPUT STRUCTURE: Optional keyword. The name of the REXX compound symbol (prefixed by a colon) that passes data to the server command. This "array" includes:

   SQLD (Number of array elements)

   number = number for each data item.

   number.SQLTYPE (SQL data type such as CHAR. Complete list was shown earlier.)

number.SQLLEN (length of SQLDATA)

number.SQLDATA (data)

number.SQLIND (null values allowed)

number.SQLNAME (column name)

SQLRIDA is the default name of this structure. (And may be specified as the INPUT STRUCTURE keyword value.)

OUTPUT STRUCTURE: Optional keyword. The name of the REXX compound symbol (prefixed with a colon) that will hold data passed back by the server procedure. It contains the same "array" elements listed above under INPUT STRUCTURE. SQLRODA is the default name of this structure (and may be specified as the OUTPUT STRUCTURE keyword value).

- STOP USING DATABASE (disconnect from database).

b. server.cmd

- SQL statements. One of them passes the data to the output descriptor. Another is a COMMIT of database transactions to the master database on the server.

User Exits

Another way to customize the OS/2 environment is by creating **user exits**. User exits are REXX procedures that perform a backup or restore the database archive or restore log files, (these log files are stored as S0000000.LOG through S9999999.LOG in the SQLOGDIR and SQL00001\SQLOGDIR subdirectories) non-text files that have information about past transactions using non-standard devices.

1. The key statement in user exits is one of the following:

```
BACKUP d: db1 a.rsp db1-700000000 1 /* backups a database */

d: - Drive to backup to, db1 - database name/alias, a.rsp - File that
contains files to backup, db1-700000000 - backup (i.e. tape) label.
      1 - first backup call, 2 - second or more backup call.

      RESTORE c: db1 a.c:\sql00001 1 /* restores a database */

c:- Drive to restore to, db1 - database name/alias, a.rsp - File that
```

```
contains files to restore, c:\sql00001 - subdirectory to restore to
1 - first restore call, 2 - second or more restore call.

ARCHIVE g: db1 c:\sqlogdir c:S00000001.LOG  /* backups a log file */
RETRIEVE g: db1 c:\sqlogdir c:S00000001.LOG /* restores a log file */

c:- Database drive, db1 - database name/alias, c:\sqlogdir - Log
file directory, c:S00000001.LOG -Log file to restore
```

2. Most user exits allow the above arguments to be passed from the command line.
3. If a complete installation of Database Manager was done on your computer, then you can find 4 REXX procedures in the SQLLIB directory that are unsupported samples from IBM of user exits:
   - SQLUEXIT.EX1:Uses Sytron's Systos Plus program to backup or restore a database.
   - SQLUEXIT.EX2: Uses Mountain Corporation's FileSafe program to backup or restore a database.
   - SQLUEXIT.EX3: Uses Maynard Corporation's MaynStream program to backup or restore a database.
   - SQLUEXIT.EX4: Uses the XCOPY, PKUNZIP2 (compression) commands to do backup.
4. Some of these examples use the XCOPY command which returns the following values: 0 (worked), 1 (invalid files), 2 (Ctrl-Break pressed), and 4-5 (miscellaneous errors).
5. User Exits (i.e., the DBM commands BACKUP DATABASE and RESTORE DATABASE) give the following return codes:

   0 worked successfully

   4 temporary unsuccessful (will try again for ARCHIVE/RETRIEVE)

   8 Program needs your help (i.e. no tape in the tape drive)

   12 Hardware Error (Contact your peripheral manufacturer.)

   20 Check arguments passed at the command line or by the BACKUP/RESTORE command.

   16,24,28,32 Miscellaneous errors

6. User Exits can be written in other programming languages such as C. See Bezviner and Lawrence (1992, 119-120).

INTERFACING REXX WITH COMMUNICATIONS MANAGER

Listed early in the chapter was an overview of the components of Communications Manager. This section shows some of the means that REXX can be used as a communications macro language. These means should still be valid in the forthcoming unbundled version of Communications Manager.

Using REXX to Control Host Sessions. (Getting Started)

EHLLAPI stands for "Emulator High-Level Language Application Program Interface." It is one way (there are third-party alternatives) that a user can control either a 3270 (i.e., terminals connected to IBM mainframes) or 5250 (i.e., terminals connected to a System/3x or AS/400 computer) session. Sessions can also be run in a DOS window on an OS/2 computer. Additional documentation can be found in a file called RXHLLAPI.DOC in the C:\cmlib directory. This is not installed by default and can be found in a compressed ("ZIP") file called GRP_0584.ZIP. It also includes two fully documented examples.

1. To begin a terminal session with a host, the following is necessary:

   a. First, a hardware connection to the host and the Communications Manager components to support such a connection. (This is beyond the scope of this book. Fortunately, IBM includes much documentation with the Extended Services product on this topic.)

   b. The installation of the 3270/5250 emulation and the EHLLAPI Dynamic Link Library (SAAHLAPI.DLL) placed in the C:\CMLIB\DLL directory.

   c. Registering the dynamic link library:

```
ret_code = Rxfuncadd('HLLAPI','SAAHLAPI','HLLAPISRV')
/* ret_code = 0 (registered) > 0 (not registered) */
```

   d. Connecting to a mainframe/ minicomputer host:

```
session_id = 'G'                          /* A one character letter */
                                          /* This is used by all later */
                                          /* hllapi calls */
ret_code = hllapi('Connect',session_id)   /* Connect to host */
      if rc > 0 then do
            say 'No connection took place. RC =' rc
            signal quit
end
```

2. Note you must explicitly disconnect the session at its conclusion — **this is not done for you.** The standard approach is after receiving an error is to go a SIGNAL routine such as the following:

```
quit:
    Say 'Disconnecting the session..'
    ret_code = hllapi('disconnect')
    if ret_code = 0 then say 'Successfully disconnected'
      else say 'Disconnection unsuccessful'
    hllapi('reset_system') /* reset back to the defaults */
    return
```

3. In Table 4-8 are some other commands that may be useful:

Table 4-8 Additional Useful Commands

Command/Syntax	What It does
General Operations	
ret_code = hllapi ('**Pause**', '20', 'A#')	Pauses the screen for a particular session for a specified number of half seconds. Useful if waiting for a screen refresh or update.
First argument: command name	
Second argument: Number of half seconds to wait	
Third argument: The Session id (Used in the connect command shown above.) immediately followed by a '#'	

Table 4-8 Continued

Command/Syntax	What It does
Ret_code = 0 (screen paused) 9 (error) 26 (Pause ended. host screen updated)	
ret_code = hllapi('**Query_Sessions**') Returns: A 12 byte result string: - 1 byte = session id - 8 byte = session name (if available) - 1 byte = H (host) or P (personal computer) - 2 byte (space size of a session)	Information about each current session.
ret_code = hllapi('**Receive_file**', "C:\test.txt 'hag1.test.txt(abc)' / ahh ASCII ") first argument: command name second argument: RECEIVE.EXE arguments. In our example (TSO), this includes a) the file on the PC to save the host file (C:\test.txt), b) the file on the host computer to transfer ('hag1.test.txt(abc) — partitioned dataset), c) the password (/ahh), d) ASCII to convert the file to ASCII so it is readable on the PC.)	Receives a file(s) from a host. (Uses RECEIVE.EXE). If the file does not exist, then supplying DCB (Data control blocks) attributes may be necessary.
ret_code = hllapi('**Send_file**', "C:\test.txt,'hag1.test.txt(abc')/ ahh" First argument: command name	Sends (Using SEND.EXE) a file from a PC to a host computer.

Table 4-8 Continued

Command/Syntax	What It does
Second argument: SEND.EXE argument. In our example (TSO), this includes a) the file on the PC to copy to the host file (C:\test.txt); b) the file on the host computer to transfer ('hag1.test.txt(abc) — partitioned dataset); and c) the password (/ahh).	
ret_code = hllapi ('**Set_session_parms**', *values*)	Override session defaults. Usually issued before connecting to a host.
First argument: command name Second argument: One or more attributes. These include: CONPHYS (connect to physical session), NOQUIET (Show SEND/RECEIVE messages) or QUIET (default — Do not show SEND/RECEIVE messages.) SRCHALL (default — searches entire presentation space) or SRCHFROM (Search only from a specified position.) SRCHBKWD (Searches presentation space backwards.) or SRCHFRWD (default — Searches presentation space forwards)	

Table 4-8 Continued

Command/Syntax	What It does
TIMEOUT = 0 CTRL-BREAK cannot be sent if the host connection appears dead. Other values = TIMEOUT = 2 (Send CTRL-Break after 1 minute), 4 (2 minutes), 6 (3 minutes)	
Ret_code = 0 (worked correctly) 2 (check arguments)	
Key Operations	
Ret_code = hllapi ('**Get_key**',session)	Retrieves the next key or combination of keys pressed.
First argument: command file	
Second argument: session id.	
Ret_code: Null (No host connection) A 1-6 character string. (This may be b, or @ @rb — cntrl b.) Note that @ is the default character for ESCAPE. It can be changed with the Set_session_parms using the ESC=attribute.)	
ret_code = hllapi('**Sendkey**','@ra')	Sends a key or key combination to a host session. Up to 255 keys can be sent at once!
first argument: command name	
second argument: Key sequence to send (including escape characters)	

Table 4-8 Continued

Command/Syntax	What It does
In our example sends Ctrl A. ret_code = 0 (operation successful) 1 (no host connection) 4-6 (miscellaneous errors)	
String Operations	
ret_code_hllapi ('**Copy_PS**')	Copies the entire Presentation Space.
ret_code = '' (didn't work or wasn't connected)	
ret_code = hllapi ('**COPY_PS_to_str**', position,length)	Captures the Presentation Space (the host session).
length = length of string to capture.	
position = Starting position to begin capture.	
ret_code = '' (didn't work or wasn't connected) the string.	
ret_code = hllapi ('**Copy_str_to_PS**', 'copy_string', position)	Copy a specified string to the Presentation Space (host session)
First argument: command name	
Second argument: String to copy to the Presentation Space. ret_code = 0 (string copied to Presentation Space) 1,2,5 (Invalid string)	
ret_code = hllapi ('**Query_cursor_pos**')	Obtains the current cursor position for a host session.

Table 4-8 Continued

Command/Syntax	What It does
ret_code = 0 (not worked or no host session) cursor position	
ret_code ('**Search_PS**', 'search_string', position)	Searches the Presentation Space for a specified string.
First argument: command name	
Second argument: String to search for.	
Third argument: Starting position. Usually not needed if the default session attribute of SRCHALL is not overwritten.	
Window Operations	
ret_code = hllapi ('**Get_window_status**', session)	Gives the status of a window
First argument: command name	
Second argument: session id. (Single letter character.)	
ret_code = '' (Didn't work or no host session) 0008 (Visible) 0010 (Not Visible) 0080 (Active Window) 0100 (Not Active Window)	
ret_code = hllapi ('**Query_window_coord**', session)	Coordinates of the host session window.

Table 4-8 Continued

Command/Syntax	What It does
First argument command name Second argument: session id. (Single letter character.) Ret_code: '' (Didn't work or no host session) Left Bottom Right Top (coordinates of the window)	

Interfacing REXX with the Communications Manager Programmable Configuration

This topic will not be of interest to the majority of OS/2 users so it's fine to "sneak ahead" to the section on Visual REXX. However, System Administrators who are responsible for heterogeneous computers using Communications Manager will be interested in the following. Each PC unfortunately, needs its own configuration maintained (although the default configuration installed at installation time may be satisfactory). With OS/2 Extended Edition, this can be done by a superset of the REXX language. (You may see more than a passing resemblance to TSO's Job Control Language — JCL.)

Getting Started

Here is an overview of the basics in this area:

1. The default configuration file is either ACSCFG.CFG (generic configuration) or ACSCFGcn.CFG where cn is the country code such as US or UK. This file is nearly completely readable by a text editor. Additional files are usually associated with a configuration. These are: C:\IBMCOM\PROTOCOL.INI (Network Interface Card Configuration — a science in itself!) and various files for the APPN protocol which reside in the C:\CMLIB\APPN directory). These will not be discussed any further in this chapter.
2. The configuration generation file follows the rules of any other REXX exec:
   - An up-to-eight character name separated by a period and followed by .CMD extension.
   - A comment must begin in column one of line one.

- Usually not a lot of the REXX language is used. The following statements may be needed:
  - ARG (to parse command-line arguments)
  - CALL/SIGNAL (exception handling)
  - Comments for documentation.
  - Flow Control Structure (IF, DO, SELECT — looping and (conditional testing)
  - Labels (easier to read)
  - SAY (view symbol values/ return code values.
- A comma will continue a statement across multiple lines.

3. Most Programmable Configuration statements are in the format:

   ret_code = (command,arguments)

   command: Programmable Configuration command

   arguments: 1-20 arguments delimited by commas. Note that arguments containing invalid REXX characters such asterisk and colon should be placed in quotation marks. Also unlike REXX, an argument may have the format of keyword EQ (meaning equals) value such as STATE EQ NY.

   ret_code = 0 (command worked), > 0 (some error)

4. The following is a typical skeleton of a Programmable Configuration REXX procedure:

```
ret_code = JOB(BEGIN,3270)
     /* Unique 1-8 character job name that is also used to create the */
     /* log file, in this case 3270.LG. Note that this overrides the default */
     /* job name of BATCH */

ret_code = FILE(ADD,newf,LOCAL,MODEL EQ ACSCFGUS)
     /* Creates a new configuration file [with the name being the value of the */
     /* second argument. The third argument specifies if the PC is */
     /* local or remote. The last argument specifies the configuration file */
     /* to be used as a template] */

ret_code = value1(ADD,keyword EQ value2)
     /* Creates a new “record” and adds the values of the “fields” */
     /* for the record. Value1 is the type of configuration (i.e.  */
     /* 3270SNA, APPN, GATEWAY, MACHINE, SNA. X25,5250) */
      OR
```

```
ret_code value1(PUT, keyword EQ value2)
     /* Places new values for the "fields" in the "record." */
Other Programmable Configuration Statements...

ret_code = FILE(VERIFY,3270)
     /* Checks the configuration file */

ret_code = JOB(END)
     /* Configuration Job ends */
say 'End of Rexx procedure'
```

5. Other useful programmable configuration commands are:

```
ret_code = FILE(LIST,,'SYM.') — List configuration files
/* Second argument — The current path (default) */
/* Third argument — A REXX stem for creating a compound symbol 'array' that */
/* will hold the file list */.

ret_code = FILE(OPEN,3270,RO)
/* Second argument — configuration name */
/* Third argument — operation — RO (Read-only) or RW (Read/Write — the */
/* default) */
```

Conversion

For those with configuration files created using earlier releases of OS/2, a conversion utility is supplied.

C:\CMLIB\RCBUPG.CMD: Creates a REXX Programmable Configuration file. Take a look at this 1600 line file. It provides lots of examples of REXX techniques including: file operations, string conversion, string parsing, and more.

```
RCBUPG file1 file2 file3

/* file1 — File to convert */
/* file2 — REXX procedure to create */
/* file3 — Optional — Configuration file that will serve as a template */
```

There is also a conversion utility for those who want to create their own instructions for generating an input file. These instructions are placed in a file called the profile. The profile is nothing more than a list of user-specified aliases for programmable configuration commands and arguments.

C:\CMLIB\RCBREN.CMD: Creates a REXX Programmable Configuration file using a user profile. Once again, it is worth looking at this 300-line REXX file for techniques used.

```
RCBREN file1 file2

/* file1 – REXX procedure to create */
/* file2 – User profile file. Default extension is .PRO. File has lines like the */
/* following: RENAME "alias", "real_name" */
/* file3 – Optional – Configuration file that will serve as a template */
```

RCBREN also create an output file with the same file name as the new REXX procedure followed by a $ and an extension of .CMD. (So FUNGUS.CMD has an output file of FUNGUS$.CMD.)

CPICOMM

You can use the ADDRESS Command to send selected APPN (Advanced Peer-to-Peer Networking) between an IBM host and an OS/2 PC. This is done using the SAA CPICOMM environment. Use the following steps to do this:

1. Make sure that CPICREXX.EXE is installed in the C:\CMLIB\APPN directory and the CPICREXX.DLL is installed in the C:\CMLIB\DLL directory.
2. Run the CPICREXX.EXE program to create CPICOMM environment. The following text is then issued:

```
Communications Manager Register CPI-C Subenvironment
CPICOMM CPI-C/REXX environment registered successfully.
```

3. You may then issue any appropriate commands:

   ADDRESS CPICOMM *'command'*

INTERFACING REXX WITH OTHER IBM PRODUCTS

IBM has also included REXX interfaces in other separate OS/2 based-products that they distribute. These are divided into two areas: 1) networked-based products; and 2) programming products. Examples of both of these are discussed below. Future editions of this book will attempt to expand in this area.

LAN Management Utilities/2

LAN Management Utilities/2 (Usually called LMU/2.) is a collection of tools to allow system administrators to collect data about Novell and LAN Manager nodes. These can be stored in a Database Manager database. It also has an "alert " (with pager capability) to notify the system administrator that an application/node is unavailable. Many other useful utilities are also included with this product. The following is an overview of the various ways REXX is used in this product: (This is not a tutorial on LMU/2.)

1. Many of the .CMD files used by LMU/2 are written in REXX. These include:

   LMUGETCF: Copies information in an OS/2 Communication Manager configuration file to the server.

   LMUINST: Installs LMU/2

   LMUPAGE: Front-end to LMUPAGER which pages a system administrator.

   LMUSRVFL: Processes change log (changes in reporting info since the last report was created.)

   TBACONV: Converts Alerts from LMU/2 Version 1 to Version 2.

2. A useful place to look for additional information about LMU/2 is the CompuServe forum. This includes frequently asked questions about LMU/2, LMU/2 patches, and code samples on how to interface with LMU/2. Once in CompuServe, enter GO LMU2.

3. If your STARTUP.CMD is written in REXX, then you may want to add the following:

```
'CALL c:\LMU2\LMUSTART.CMD'
/* Starts LMU/2 - created after LMUCUST is invoked */
/* If this file is deleted, rerun LMUCUST */

' START LMUCLI.EXE'
/* client LMUCLI initializes the client machine (in LMU's terms a managed */
/* host) So the server (in LMU's terms, the managing host) can issue the */
/* powerful LMUCMD command */

OR 'START LMUSRV.EXE' /* server */
/* LMUSRV - updates the Database Manager database and initializes the */
/* The server so it can issue commands to a client node. It also allows */
/* specification of those alerts that will require system administrator */
/* notification */

/* Additional START and DETACH statements for other LMU/2 services */
....
/* These commands can also be placed in the LMUSTART.CMD */
```

4. Three examples of using REXX to query an LMU database in Database Manager format are provided with the product. These are LMUCOMPN.CMD, LMUDISKU.CMD, and LMUTABLE.CMD.

5. This product includes a utility called LMUREXX. It will capture information about a client node and pass it to a REXX procedure.

   a. To invoke LMUREXX, to use LMU2REXX, make sure that LMU2RX.DLL is an appropriate DLL directory as specified by the LIBPATH command in the CONFIG.SYS file. (i.e. C:\OS2\DLL.)

      Place the following in your STARTUP.CMD file:

```
ret_code = Rxfuncadd('IMU2RX','IMU2RX','LMU2REXX')
```

   b. Then you may issue CALL IMU2RX in a REXX procedure to invoke LMU2REXX.

   c. If RESULT of the CALL IMU2RX command equals 0, then your REXX procedure may access the values of any of the following symbols in Table 4-9:

Table 4-9

Symbol name	What it contains
LMU_boot_drive	What hard drive the client node boots from.
LMU_machine_name	Computer name or network address
LMU_managing_system	The server associated with this LMU client.
LMU_nw_network_id	Novell network number
LMU_nw_node	Novell network node address

6. Another way that REXX can be used to interface with LMU/2 is the DBMTO DB2.CMD file. This will convert a Database Manager table to a DB2 database and transfer it to a server. In reality, DBMTODB2 a front-end to the IXFUTIL executable. It exists as C:\LMU\DBMTODB2.SMP. Always make a copy before modifying this file.

This command typically defines the result table and then runs IXFUTIL to create the database.

(Sample — "IXFUTIL 'DBNAME: dbn TABLE: stem.i SOURCE: OS/2'")

Note that only the first letter of the above keyword is required.

dbn: Name of Database Manager database to be created source: Either HOST or OS/2 depending which way the conversion is taking place.

table (name of LMU/2 table). Values are compound symbol array.

Also may be needed are the host file name and data control block parameters.

7. REXX procedures are also commonly used to check for viruses with a sequence similar to the following:

```
' FCHECK C:|' /* substitute your favorite virus-checker here*/
       if RC <> 0 /* virus detected. */.
'C: \ VIRALERT'
/* LMU command to send a 'virus-detected' alert to the "fault manager" server */
/* A fault-manager must be specified in the LMU.INI AND the proper software */
/* MUST be running */
```

8. A REXX procedure can be used to generate alerts. A sample exec AUERX01.CMD is included. This includes a RxFuncAdd to the AUERXGA.DLL dynamic link library and then a statement similar to the following:

```
ret_string = AUEREXGA ( '21', 'Ayy', 'Bad FORMAT')

/* ret_string - GOOD (worked ok) or BAD (didn't work. An additional */
/*     error message */
/* First argument - Error message ranging from 21 to 102. 21 is software */
/* Second argument - Eight character REXX application name */
/* Third argument - Error message of no more than 44 characters. */
```

Network Transport Services/2

Network Transport Service/2 (hereafter called NTS/2) is a means for providing scheduled unattended installations of OS/2 2.x and other OS/2 products from a **code server** (that is a PC containing the images of the diskettes) to a "client" (or **code receiver**). This process is called **CID** (Configuration Installation Distribution Services). IBM plans to offer this capability using a variety of network protocols (such as NETBIOS, TCP/IP, SNA, etc.). Other OS/2 products will also support this in time. Part of this process may include **distributed REXX processing**. That is the code receiver node running REXX code residing on the code server. As more computers become networked together, the trend of distributed REXX processing should continue and perhaps will become the norm. In time, perhaps standards may exist in this area.

The following is an overview of some of the ways that REXX interfaces with the NTS/2 product.

1. The latest information about NTS/2 can be found on CompuServe in the OS/2 Developers 2 Forum. (GO OS2DF2). These include news items about NTS/2, and the latest network configuration files.
2. Part of the NTS/2 components are REXX procedures. These include the following:

Component	What it does
GETBOOT.CMD	Unpacks the necessary files to run SETBOOT.EXE command which reboots the client (sometimes necessary to initialize certain changes).
GETREXX.CMD	Unpacks REXX files on the code server in the DLL subdirectory. These files are needed for the code receiver to run REXX from the code server.

3. Once the images are created, the next step is usually creating REXX procedure (called **LCU** [LAN CID Utility] **command files**) that are used to install selected OS/2 products including OS/2 2.1. Fortunately, there is a well-documented sample procedure named CASSKEL.CMD can be found in the SAMPLES directory of the NTS/2 floppy. You can use this file as a model and copy it to the appropriate directory (usually \CID\CLIENT).

   The file contains the following parts:

   Variable definition section:

   - Defines values of global variables: *Bootdrive* (default is c:), *configsys* (CONFIG.SYS path. Uses bootdrive to create this value) and *exepath* (Path of install programs).
   - Other variables are initialized.
   - Invoke various external functions stored in CASAGENT DLL

     Define the compound symbol "array." (such as x.1.*symname* with *symname* defining the unique array element.)

a. *Product number:* With a symbol name of x.number.*name* (*Name* is a unique name that is usually the same as the image subdirectory.)

NOTE: **number** is the unique array number and used for all array elements.)

b. *Product name* (With a symbol name of x.*number*.name)

c. *State* (With a symbol name of x.*number*.statevar.) Is the concatenation of CAS_ and the product name. This value is an environment variable that keeps track of installs during a reboot.

d. *Installation command string* (With a symbol name of x.*number*.instpro.) This is a lengthy concatenated string that includes the following :

   1. The installation program.
   2. /B: followed by the bootdrive path. (All / parameters may be in upper or lowercase.)
   3. /L1: followed by the installation log path. Additional log files (i.e., L2 and L3 are allowed).
   4. /R: The last parameter with no value if you wish to use the default response file. Else the name of the response file.
   5. /S: followed by the path of the images. This path may be on a code server.

   Note that particular OS/2 installations may have additional parameters.

e. The response file's path (With a symbol name of x.*number*.rspdir.) Blank means the default response file is used.

f. The default response file name. (With a symbol name of x.number.*default*.)

Installation Section

1. Retrieves the OVERALL_STATE symbol. If 0, go through a select loop.
2. Checks if being installed from floppy diskettes or from the hard drive.
3. Does a run install and checks the return code (i.e., *IF RunInstall (x.name) == BAD_RC then exit*. With name being the product name). This backs the CONFIG.SYS, AUTOEXEC.BAT, and STARTUP.CMD before proceeding to do the install.
4. Checks if the software needs a reboot. Then reboots it. The OVERALL_STATE = 1 after reboot.

   Subroutine definition/External function Invocation. Not meant to be defined by users. But well-worth taking a look at.

Table 4-10 is a list of subroutine/external functions used in this section.

Table 4-10 Subroutine/External Functions

Function/Subroutine	What It Does
BootDriveIsDiskette: no arguments	Function: Invokes the external function (IsBootDriveRemovable). Returns YES if booted from floppy drive and increases by 1 the value of OVERALL_STATE. Else returns NO.
BootDriveIsFixedDisk: no arguments	Function: Invokes the external function (IsBootDriveRemovable). Returns YES if booted from hard drive and increases by 1 the value of OVERALL_STATE. Else returns NO.
CheckBoot: no arguments	Subroutine: Reboots the machine else increases by 1 the value of OVERALL_STATE.
GetEnvironmentVars	Function: Captures current value of OVERALL_STATE else sets to 0.
LogMessage (Message Number, product name, message, logfile)	External function usually used for logging installation messages.
PreserveStartupCmd	Subroutine: renames current Startup.CMD.
Reboot: no arguments	Subroutine: Reboots machine. Uses the AskRemoveDiskIfFloppy external function (tells user to remove a floppy disk before rebooting).
RebootandGotoState argument: state (a whole number)	Subroutine: Changes values of state_var. Uses SaveStates and Reboot subroutines.
RunInstall: Arguments: number — Usually the value of x.number.name.	Function: Installs image, logs messages.
state: Whole number. The new value of OVERALL_STATE	Returns GOOD_RC (worked) or BAD_RC (failed)

Table 4-10 Continued

Function/Subroutine	What It Does
SaveStates	Subroutine: Tries to put the value of the various statevar symbols into CONFIG.SYS.
SetEnvironmentVar	Function: Sets the value of REMOTE_INSTALL_STATE to 0 for unattended installs (or the value of the statevar symbol).
SetState	Subroutine: Resets statevar to a desired value. Uses the external function PutStateVar.

4. The other major use of REXX with the LMU/2 product is in helping to create command files (such as described in the above point.) This is done with the aid of the CASPREP.EXE utility.

   a. The syntax of the CASPREP utility is

      CASPREP *key out skel*

      key: List of file that contains nothing other than labels (such as :vars) and statements with the syntax keyword= value (such as bootdrive=c:)

      out: Name of output command file to be created.

      skel: Name of REXX skeleton file to be used

      Returns 0 (worked) or 1 (failed)

   b. CASPREP is usually invoked from a REXX procedure.

      1. Usually checks if all files used by CASPREP exist. (Such as using STREAM('QUERY EXISTS')).

      2. Invokes CASPREP with its own command processor (i.e., using the OS/2 CMD command).

      3. Provide for exception handling if the installation file fails.

Interfacing REXX with the Enhanced Editor (EPM)

Included with OS/2 in the "Productivity" folder is a treasure of a program called Enhanced Program Editor (EPM). This editor is also available on some other IBM platforms as well. The following are some of the characteristics of EPM:

- EPM is a *programming editor*. For C, Pascal, and REXX (if enabled), the editor will automatically indent appropriate statements and "type in" the remaining part of a flow control structure (such as an END for a DO structure). The editor "knows" which set of statements to include based on the extension of the file.
- EPM is a *configurable editor*. Nearly all of the elements of EPM can be easily changed by adding the appropriate command to the various profile/setup files EPM can also be modified by compiling programs (or macros) written in the E language (of which a healthy number of examples are available).
- EPM is an *environment*. The idea is similar to some UNIX-based editors which is used for a variety of activities including mail reading. Some of EPM's capabilities include: 1) file transfer to a host computer using the Extended Services's ALM-COPY command; 2) edit a host computer files on your PC; 3) Ability to run Workframe from EPM; 4) spell checking and thesaurus; 5) sorting capability; 6) run OS/2 within EPM (though scrolling is 'jerky'); and 7) interface to many low-level DOS calls and much more.

  EPM is *portable*. E language editors exist for AIX and DOS.

The following is an overview of the major points of interfacing REXX with EPM.

1. EPM uses the environment variable EPMPATH to "know" which directories to search when looking for compiled E macros.
2. EPM uses files with the following extensions:

Extension	What it is used for
E	Uncompiled source of EPM Macros written in the E language.
ERX	REXX procedures combined with a subset of EPM's E language.
EX	Compiled EPM Macro.

3. If installed from the Professional Developer's Kit, EPM is also installed with over 50 source (.E) files. (This is also available from all "standard" OS/2 BBSes plus anonymous ftp sites, in addition to CompuServe. These will be in the compressed files E_MACROS.ZIP and SAMPMACS.ZIP. (In total nine files are supplied but not all are pertinent to everyone.)

Two files of interest are:

CALLREXX.E (Uses the REXXSAA interface to invoke the REXX interpreter. This is described in detail in Chapter 3.)

REXKEYS.E (the logic behind REXX syntax checking and command typing.)

4. Also included are a good many REXX (.erx) macros. These include:

   MOUSE.ERX: Uses REXX to control mouse movement while in EPM.

   TICTAC.ERX: How to play Tic Tac Toe using REXX and EPM.

5. Why was the E language used for EPM macros instead of REXX? The major reason appears to be speed. However, enhanced REXX support is expected to happen in the future. Table 4-9 is a comparison:

Table 4-11

E	REXX
Compiled language: Enter ETPM *source compile*	Interpreted Language: Enter REXX *procedure_name* or just the procedure name.
source: macro name (.E extension optional) *compile:* Optional argument naming compiled macro. EX Extension is optional.	No message will appear if there are no errors and no writing to the screen was done.
From the OS/2 command prompt: A message will appear: The 'E' Language Translator for OS/2 Version 5.51 © Copyright IBM Corporation 1986, 1989,1990,1991 compiling. Else with an error it will say: *error message* filename=*xx.e* line=*line_num* col=*col_num*	

Table 4-11 Continued

E	REXX
This is usually followed by a LINK or RELINK (if EPM is already active). UNLINK unloads the compiled macro from memory.	
Runs only in EPM and EPM add-on products on SAA platforms only.	Runs as an interpreter, compiler and a variety of applications on many platforms.
Variables are local by default. UNIVERSAL statement makes them global	Variables are global unless a PROCEDURE instruction is used in a subroutine
No variable lookup at run-time	Variable lookup at run-time
Uninitialized Variables have no values	Uninitialized variables have a default value of the variable name in upper case.
No continuation punctuation needed — automatically detected.	Comma required as a continuation parameter.
Comments are one of three formats: a) Prefixed by semicolon b) /*...*/ (may be nested) c) On the same line as a statement. Prefixed by two dashes.	Comments are in the format: /*..*/ (May be anywhere and be nested)
Flow control structures: - Similar IF but uses ELSE IF - Has LOOP-ENDLOOP (same as DO-WHILE)	Flow control Structures: Uses ELSE IF

Table 4-11 Continued

E	REXX
- Has FOR AND Complex Do - Has Nearly all other DO, IF, SELECT combinations that REXX does plus LEAVE and ITERATE	

6. Here is an overview of REXX EPM macros .ERX:

   a. Look at the file EPMHELP.QHL for additional information about using EPM. The same information can be found by selecting "Quick reference" under the HELP menu.

   b. To invoke an ERX macro do the following sequence:

      1. Invoke EPM by double-clicking on the Enhanced Editor icon found in the Productivity folder (which is in turn part of the "OS System" area).

      2. Once the EPM window appears, enter RX *macro_name* or EPMREXX macroname on the command line.

      3. A REXX macro name is searched in the PATH and EPMATH directories.

      4. The macro is then processed.

   c. Here is what usually found in EPM:

      1. EPM commands which are in single quotes.

      2. REXX statements:

         a. assignment statements

         b. parse arg (parse arguments)

         c. Capturing epm variable values into REXX symbols using the extract */epmvar1 (/epmvar2)*...epm^n includes the following: (note some are in compound symbols)

         autosave (number of changes since last save),

         col (current column position), line (current row position) — useful in doing line operations [such as C (change) or l (find)]

         cursorx, cursory (cursor x/y position in a window)

         filename (name of currently edited file)

getline.1 (value of the specified line)

last.1 (number of lines in a file)

modify (text changed — 0 or 1)

mousex, mousey (Current row, column mouse position)

userstring (temporary holding area)

windowheight, windowwidth (height/width of window)

windowx, windowy (space between edge of window and edge of the screen)

d. The following is a list of some of the external EPM functions available for your use:

```
call etkdeletetext, |1                     /* deletes line at |1*/
call etkinserttext 'insert_text' line      /* Insert text at current or */
                                           /* specified line */
call etkprocessededitkey 'action'          /* Test keys for various edit
                                              actions (i.e. BEGIN_LINE,
                                              CENTER, TOP) */
call etkreplacetext 'replace_text', |1     /* Replace text at current */
                                           /* line */
call etksetfilefield 'epmvar', 'value'
/* Modifies value of EPM variable. This includes cursorx/y, */
/* mousexy, last windowheight/width, windowx/y */
```

7. A special EPM is PROFILE.ERX (make sure PROFILE ON was issued and saved), usually includes the following:

   initializing global variables with the UNIVERSAL statement (usually with the format UNIVERSAL *var value* all in single quotes. With var being an EPM global variable and *value* being its value.)

   Some EPM commands that set overall editor settings (i.e., EXPAND ON.)

Visual REXX (Producing Full-Screen REXX Applications)

IBM has released a new category of software called Employee-Written Software (abbreviated as EWS.) These are copyrighted internally-written and used software that is released "as is" (i.e., without support and upgrades). Some of these software packages use or support REXX. The four most popular REXX EWS features are:

- PMGLOBE: A program that was written by Mike Cowlishaw (creator of REXX) that allows you to simulate what the earth looks at varying locations and times during the day. This program may be customized using specialized REXX procedures (ending with a .PMG macro). PMGLOBE can be invoked at the OS/2 prompt as PMGLOBE2 macro *macroname*. Two sample macro files are included.
- GOPHER: Another program by Mike Cowlishaw that allows you to set-up a server that can be used to access text, graphic files and much more!
- RXD: A full-screen REXX Debugger. Enter RXD *execname* to use this product. Created by Patrick Mueller.
- VREXX: Until IBM comes out with their object-oriented REXX (discussed in Chapter 7) and the two commercial products come out, (Hockware and Watcom have announced OS/2 Visual REXX products. Both are now available, addresses listed in Appendix F) Visual REXX is the copyrighted freeware answer to Visual Basic. Well, at least it tries to be. Created by Richard Lam.

Visual REXX was internally created by IBM to demo other products. It was immediately adopted by OS/2 REXX users as a tool for application development. Most have asked that it be included in future releases of OS/2. This appears to be highly unlikely but if enough people lobby for it…A second complaint is that the source IS NOT included, so user-generated modifications cannot be created. Because of this, the future of this product is uncertain. The last user gripe is a desire to further include customization capabilities.

Here is an overview of Visual REXX (VREXX):

1. Documentation included with the VREXX2.ZIP file is available in .TXT (ASCII Format) or .INF (Use the VIEW command)
2. To invoke Visual REXX, you must first register the VREXX DLL:

```
call RxFuncAdd 'VINIT', 'VREXX', 'VINIT'
      call VINIT /* Initializes Visual REXX */
      if RESULT = 'ERROR' then signal err_rot /* error routine not shown */
      call VEXIT
```

3. The following REXX components are used:
   a. Various VREXX built-in function return compound variables. The .0 elements is usually the number of elements in the array.
   b. CALL/SIGNAL for exception handling
   c. Flow control structures
   d. Comments and labels

4. Here are some keypoints to know about Visual REXX:

   a. Most of the window controls (i.e. boxes) usually include a button value as the *last* argument. This value is one of the following:

      1 (OK); 2 (CANCEL); 3 (OK and CANCEL); 4 (YES); 5 (NO); or 6 (YES and NO). [The value in parentheses are the buttons that will be generated. If a button is pressed (such as OK), the VREXX function that created that control will return that value (i.e. 'OK')].

   b. Most window controls require a compound symbol array to specify text, control height, control width, etc. If any user selection is made (such as a line in a List Box), then it is captured in the symbol *stem*.vstring.

   c. If invoked as a function, it may be necessary to capture the return code to avoid an error.

   d. In addition to the functions shown below, VREXX supports these additional types of functions:

```
ret-code = VInit()
```

- Graphics: VARC (draws a semi or complete circle), VDRAW (draws other objects).
- Window Customization: VRESIZE (Changes window size and location), VSETTITLE (Changes Window's title).
- Additional Controls: VCHECKBOX (Check box — good for multiple selections), VDIALOGPOS (Moves Window Position), VMULTBOX (Multiple Input), VRADIOBOX (Selects one item).

5. Some users have reported that Visual REXX will abnormally exit and then will no longer run Visual REXX procedures. Others say this also happens if you kill a session. At a minimum, do include exception handling sequences in your Visual REXX procedures. Some of these problems may be fixed in a future release.

6. Rather than dwelling over the syntax of the more popular 24 VREXX built-in functions, Figures 4-1 and 4-2 are two documented sample VREXX programs:

Various Controls

```
/* EX1.CMD */
/* Purpose — To show you some of the ways that you can */
/*      show the same information */
/* Let's initialize VREXX */

init_it:
        call RxFuncAdd 'VInit', 'VREXX', 'VINIT'
        ret_code = VInit()

versions:
/* Gets versions of VREXX and OS/2 REXX. Used in all of the examples */
        vr_ver = VGetVersion()     /* VREXX Version */
        parse version with orexx   /* OS2 Version */

method1:
/* displays as message box */
       ln.0 = 3
       ln.1 = 'REXX Version —-' orexx
       ln.2 = 'VREXX Version —-' vr_ver
       call VMsgBox 'Example #1 — Version INFO', ln.1

method2:
/* Displays in a table which could then be selected */

f.rows = 2          /* Number of Rows in the table */
f.cols = 2          /* Number of Columns in the table */
f.label.1 = 'Product'       /* Column labels */
f.label.2 = ' Version'
f.width.1 = 20      /* column widths */
f.width.2 = 20
f.1.1 = 'OS2 REXX'  /* Our first column of data */
f.1.2 = orexx
f.2.1 = 'VREXX'     /* Our second column of data */
f..2.2 = vr_ver
pressed = VTableBox('Versions in a Table',f,1,50,3,3)

method3:
/* Choose from List Box then display version in a Message Box */
       vbox.0 = 2     /* Number of items in the array */
       vbox.1 = 'REX'       /* List box selections */
       vbox.2 = 'OS2 REXX'
```

Figure 4.1

```
pressed = VListBox('Please choose a product', vbox, 35, 10,3)
       a.0 = 2
vbox.vstring = 'OS2 REXX' then do /* IF OS2 REXX chosen */
       a.1 = 'Product - OS/2 REXX'
       a.2 = orexx
end
else do        /* IF VREXX chosen */
       a.1 = 'Product - VREXX'
       a.2 = vr_ver
end
ret_code= VMsgBox( 'Version/Product', a,3)
BYEBYE:
       call VExit
```

Figure 4.1 Continued

Explanation:

init_it: module

a. Program documentation

b. Registers VREXX dynamic link library and initializes the VREXX environment as explained earlier in this section.

versions module:

a. Retrieves the version of VREXX using the VGetVersion function.

Returns *1.0*

b. Retrieves the version of OS/2 REXX. Returns *4.00 08 July 1992*

method1 module — Message Box

a. First create the ln compound symbol array. ln.0 — holds the number of elements in the array, ln.1-.2 Message Box text and symbol value.

b. MsgBox :

— Return Value — Button pressed (i.e. OK)

— First argument — Title of the window

— Second argument — Compound symbol

— Third argument — Button value (1-6 described above)

method2 module — Table Box

a. The bulk of this module is defining the compound symbol array elements. These include:

Table descriptors :

.cols Number of columns (1-10)

.label.n Column labels (n = 1-10)

.rows Number of rows

.width.n Width of columns (n= 1-10)

.x.y Table data (x— row number, y — column number [1-10])

b. Creating the table: (VTableBox)

Return value — Button pressed (i.e. OK)

—.vstring (has user selection in table)

first argument — Table title (1-80 columns)

second argument — compound variable stem name

third argument — Default row in table

fourth argument — table width

fifth argument — table height

sixth argument — Button created (1-6 described above)

method3 module — List Box and Message Box

a. A compound symbol array of list box values.

b. ListBox

return value — Button value (i.e. OK)
User selection (.vstring)

First argument — List Box title

Second argument — Compound array name

Third argument — List Box width

Fourth argument — List Box height

Fifth argument — Button created (1-6 described above)

c. Based on the user selection (in.vstring), the message box values are set and the message box is created.

BYEBYE module

a. closes VREXX environment

Enhanced Rename

```
/* EX2.CMD */
/* Purpose - To show how to use VREXX to enhance a file renaming */
/* Let's initialize VREXX */
init_it:
      call RxFuncAdd 'VInit','VREXX','VINIT'
      ret_code= VInit()

intro_win:
/* Introductory Window */
      w.left = 10
      w.right = 30
      w.top = 70
      w.bottom = 30
      wid = VOpenWindow('Example #2','BLUE',w)
ret_code = VForeColor(wid,'RED')          /* Change color */
ret_code = VSetFont(wid,'HELVB',12)       /* Change Font and size */
      wtext.1 = " Enhanced Rename... "  /* Window Text */
      wtext.2 = "An example using VREXX"
      h=900
      do cnt = 1 to 2
      ret_code = VSay(wid,20,h,wtext.cnt)
       /* Write Window Text */
      h = h-100
      end
msg_box:
/* Message Box keeps screen up so user can read it */
      ms.0 = 2
      ms.1 = "Using a Message Box means the window will"
      ms.2 = "stay on the screen until the user can read it!"
ret_code = VMsgBox('Keeping Window on the Screen', ms, 1)
ret_code = VCloseWindow(wid) /* Close Window */

rename_file:
/* Get file to rename */
```

Figure 4.2

```
ret_code = VFileBox('Which File to Rename?','*.*',flist)
if ret_code = 'OK' then from1 = flist.vstring
       u.0 = 1
       u.1 = 'Please enter the new name'
ret_code = VInputBox('New Name',u,30,1)
if ret_code == "OK" then to1 = u.vstring
       address cmd 'rename' from1 to1
       rrc = rc
       if rrc = 0 then do
       rmsg.0 = 1
       rmsg.1 = 'RENAME SUCCESSFUL!'
       ret_code = VMsgBox('Rename OK',rmsg,1)
       end
       else do
       rmsg.0 = 1
       rmsg.1 = 'RENAME FAILED!'
       ret_code = VMsgBox('RENAME FAILED',rmsg,1)
       end
BYEBYE:
call VExit
```

Figure 4.2 Continued

Explanation

init_it: module

a. Program documentation

b. Registers VREXX dynamic link library and initializes the VREXX environment as explained earlier in this section.

intro_win module

a. Defines the compound symbol array. Each value (.left, .right, .top, .bottom is the percentage on the screen [0-100])

b. Opens the Window (VOpenWindow)

Return value — Unique id of the window.

First argument — Title of the window.

Second argument — Color (such as BLUE,RED).

Third argument — Compound symbol name.

c. Change the foreground color (VForeColor)

Return value — None
First argument — window id (from VOpenWindow)
Second argument — Color changed (i.e., BLUE, WHITE, RED)

d. Change the Font and Size (VSetFont)

Return value — None
First argument — window id (from VOpenWindow)
Second argument — Name of Font (such as SYSTEM [default], COR [Courier], HELV [Helvetica], TIME [Times Roman].
Third argument — Font Size (>= 1)

e. Define the compound symbol used for the window text.

f. Write the text in the window (VSAY)

Return value — none
First argument — window id (from VOpenWindow)
Second/third arguments — X/Y coordinates (0-1000)
Fourth argument — Window Text (usually processed as part of a DO loop that iterates each compound symbol array element).

msg_box module

a. Displays a message box to keep the window on the screen until the reader can read it.

rename_file module

a. Gets the name of the file by showing the standard file selection box.

VFileBox (Standard file selection box)
Return String — Button pressed (OK/CANCEL)
First argument — Title of file selection box.
Second argument — File selection (Wild card characters can be used.)
Third argument — Compound array name.vstring holds the file name selected to be renamed.

b. If the OK key is pushed, then display an input box which has the new name of the file.

c. Rename the file (OS/2 command). Checks the return code and display the appropriate message box.

BYEBYE module

a. Closes VREXX environment

REFERENCES

Amundsen, Larry and Richard Hoffman 1992 " Advanced Considerations for Database Manager" *OS/2 Developer* 4(3) pp. 103-109

Amundsen, Larry and Richard Hoffman 1992 "Passing Blocks of Data Using ARI" *OS/2 Developer* 2(3) pp. 98-103

Bezviner, Dawn E. and Richard Lawrence 1992 "User Exits: Using Nonstandard Devices with DBM" *OS/2 Developer* 4(3) pp. 110-120

Giguére, Eric 1992 *Frequently Asked Questions — REXX*. Text File

IBM 1991 *Database Manager Messages* (DBMSG.INF file)

IBM 1992 *Enhanced Editor (EPM) User's Guide*

IBM 1992 *Enhanced Editor — Quick Reference*, EPMHELP.QHL text file

IBM 1992 *EPM Editor Technical Reference Manual*

IBM 1991 *Extended Service Command Reference* (ESCMDREF.INF file)

IBM 1991 *Extended Services for OS/2: Communications Manager Additional Functions: Installation Guide and Reference* G96F-8312

IBM 1991 *Extended Services for OS/2: Communications Manager User's Guide* S04G-1015

IBM 1991 *Extended Services for OS/2: Database Manager Programming Guide and Reference. Volume 1. Common Programming Info* S04G-1022

IBM 1991 *Extended Services for OS/2: Database Manager Programming Guide and Reference. Volume 2 Client/Server Programming Information* S04G-1022 (focuses on DARI)

IBM 1991 *Extended Services for OS/2: Database Manager Programming Guide and Reference. Volume 3 Programming Reference* S04G-1022 (command reference),

IBM 1991 *Extended Services for OS/2: Database Manager Programming Guide and Reference. Volume 4 Host Language Information* S04G-1022 (focuses on REXX interface to DBM)

IBM 1991 *Extended Services for OS/2: Database Manager Programming Guide and Reference. Volume 5 Appendices* S04G-1022 (focuses on Import/ Export)

IBM 1991 *Extended Services for OS/2: Guide to Database Manager* S04G-1013

IBM 1991 *Extended Services for OS/2: Programmable Configuration Reference* S04G-1003

IBM 1991 *Extended Services for OS/2: Query Manager: Programming Guide and References* S04G-1022

IBM 1991 *Extended Services for OS/2: Structured Query Language (SQL) Reference* S04G-1012

IBM 1992 *IBM Network Transport Services/2 LAN Adapter and Protocol Support Configuration Guide* A3S11MST

IBM 1992 *Network Transport Services/2 Messages and Problem Determination Guide* A3S13MST

IBM 1993 *Introducing: IBM Database 2 OS/2 Field Television Network* January 26 (Text file)

IBM 1992 *LAN Management Utilities User's Guide* SC30-3555

IBM 1992 *OS/2 REXX EHLLAPI Programming Reference and User's Guide* (RXHLLAPI.DOC text file)

IBM 1992 *Redirected Installation and Configuration Guide* A3S12MST

Kong, Jerry Y. 1991 "The Bounty of OS/2 EE REXX" *Enterprise Systems Journal* 8(9) September pp. 112-115, 129

Lam, Richard B. Lam 1992 *VREXX — Visual REXX for Presentation Manager Version 1.0*

Proffit, Brian 1992 "The Enhanced Editor" *OS/2 Developer* 4(3) pp. 32-33

Thompson, Keith M. 1992 "IBM's LAN Utilities Solve Problems Remotely" *PC Magazine* March 17 pp. 44

5

OS/2 REXX: A Third-Party Interpreter

In previous chapters we looked at an overview of standard REXX, saw how IBM implemented a standard REXX interpreter under OS/2, and provided a summary of the powerful and unique extensions available for OS/2 REXX. Chapter 5 examines the only available third-party OS/2 REXX interpreter — Personal REXX for OS/2 by Quercus Systems. It is more than highly likely that others will shortly follow. This product is being sold as a replacement (not a supplement) to OS/2 REXX. Although the chapter will discuss how you can combine some elements of both products.

This chapter has two goals:

- To provide an understanding of the differences and similarities between the IBM and Quercus REXX interpreters. This includes comparison charts and benchmarks; and
- To review the unique features of Personal REXX and how to take advantage of them.

All examples ran using OS/2 2.1 and Personal REXX 3.0, which was released shortly before this writing.

THE HISTORY OF PERSONAL REXX

- 1985: Mansfield Software started selling *Personal REXX for DOS and KEDIT* — an XEDIT "clone" for DOS. Also discussed in Chapter 6.
- 1988: Quercus Systems released *REXXTERM* — a asynchronous communications package that interfaces with REXX. REXXTERM was released for both DOS and OS/2.

- December 1988: Mansfield released *Personal REXX 2.0* which offered faster performance, smaller memory requirements, and full compliance with REXX language version 3.5 — as documented in the first edition of Cowlishaw's The REXX Language. Several patches were issued in 1989 and 1990.
- October 1989: Mansfield released *Personal REXX 2.0 for OS/2*. Also Command Technology Corporation (CTC) developed a beta of an OS/2 REXX product, around this time. This product was not released and the team that created it left to form Tritus Inc., creators of Tritus SPF. This product, released in 1993, includes documented REXX support.
- 1991: One year after the availability of REXX language version 4.00, Quercus (which had taken over the development and distribution of Personal REXX) released *Personal REXX 3.0 for DOS* which was REXX language version 4.0 compliant, and less memory-hungry.
- 1992: Quercus issued *Personal REXX 3.0 for Windows*. This product offered most of the functions/capabilities found in the DOS product. However, it also included a full-screen programming environment (similar to OS/2's PMREXX) and the capability of using REXX to develop full-screen Windows-aware applications. This functionality is similar to RxMessageBox and Visual REXX available for OS/2.
- 1993: *Personal REXX 3.0 for OS/2* was released. Personal REXX 3.0 for OS/2 specifically takes advantage of the operating system's features. A version for Windows NT was also released.

A COMPARISON OF OS/2 REXX INTERPRETERS

Is the bundled REXX interpreter adequate for my needs? Or should I purchase Quercus' Personal REXX? This section will provide you with the information needed to begin answering these questions.

Implementation Limits

Eventually, a REXX procedure will exceed one or more implementation limits. The user will be notified by the various REXX error messages. Quercus REXX will tell you the specific implementation limit value exceeded, IBM OS/2 does not.

Table 5-1 is a list of known implementation limits

Table 5-1

Limit	Standard REXX	SAA REXX	IBM OS/2 REXX	Quercus OS/2 REXX
Program Length	Not specified	Not specified	Based on memory	Also based on memory — Up to 64K
Clause length	Not specified	250 characters	Based on memory	10,000 characters
Symbol name length	No less than 50 characters	250 characters	250 characters	250 characters
Symbol value length	Not specified The REXX ANSI standard will suggest a minimum of 250.	Not specified	Based on memory	Based on memory — no more than 32K.
Literal string length	No less than 100 characters	No less than 100 characters	No more than 250 characters	No more than 250 characters
Nesting structures	No less than 100	No less than 100	100	100
I/O streams opened at once	None specified	None specified	15	50
CALL arguments	None specified	No less than 20	20	250

Table 5-2 is a comparison of the files used: (Equivalent files may have similar uses but it may not be relevant to compare file sizes).

Table 5-2

IBM	Quercus
REXX interpreters	
CMD.EXE — 87K PMREXX.EXE — 54K	PREXX30.EXE — 26K
Dynamic Link Libraries	
REXXAPI.DLL — 33K	REXXAPI.DLL — 21K
REXX.DLL — 243K PREXXA.DLL — 207K	REXX.DLL — 18K
REXXINIT.DLL — 1K	
PMREXX.DLL — 15K	
	PRXCMD.DLL — 82K PRXQUEUE (stack operations) — 17K
REXXUTIL.DLL — 31K	QREXXLIB.DLL (REXXLIB) — 136K
VREXX.DLL (Visual REXX not bundled with OS/2) — 52K	RXWIN30.DLL (RXWindow) — 31K

Comparison of REXX Statements

Standard REXX: Personal REXX supports all the features of REXX language version 4.0 as outlined in Cowlishaw's *The Rexx Language (second edition)*. This means a high degree of compatibility exists between the IBM and Quercus OS/2 REXX interpreters. The Quercus product also supports CMS extensions not supported by SAA or the IBM REXX interpreters and functions found in their DOS and Windows products.

Similarities

Here is a list of the major similarities:

1. REXX procedures end with a .CMD extension for both interpreters. Also, the first line of the procedure must be a comment that has to start in the first column.

Usually the comment will contain the word REXX) that has to start in the first column.

2. Both interpreters support the statements and functions part of REXX Language Version 4.0
3. Both interpreters support ADDRESS CMD *'OS/2 command'*

Differences

The differences between the two products, in terms of "Standard REXX", are small and rather subtle. Differences include:

1. Parse PULL for IBM REXX (OS/2 1.3 **not** 2.x) gives a ? prompt while Quercus does not. Thus, an information message is always needed to tell the user to input text.
2. Personal REXX automatically supports REXX procedures being processed as an OS/2 system command. For IBM REXX procedures, this is done with the OS/2 CALL (not the REXX CALL) command.
3. Personal REXX supports some obsolete REXX 3.5 features such as DATE('C') and DATE('J'), and PARSE EXTERNAL. *Do not use these features unless absolutely necessary — they may go away in a future release.* TRACE S is not one of the obsolete features supported.
4. IBM REXX processing automatically displays OS/2 commands as they are processed using the PREXX30 command, Personal REXX does not.
5. Quercus error messages will display the implementation limit exceeded, IBM's does not and currently has no plans to do so.
6. There are two major areas of differences: File I/O and TRACE:

   a. FILE I/O

   - Personal REXX uses separate read and write pointers for CHARIN, CHAROUT, LINEIN, LINEOUT. IBM REXX uses one pointer for both read/write operations.
   - Personal REXX's CHARS function returns the actual number of unread characters in a file. IBM REXX will return 1 if there are unread characters in a file.
   - The STREAM function is nearly identical for both interpreters with this difference: Personal REXX does "smart mode" setting for the STREAM OPEN (i.e., read-only for LINEIN/ CHARIN/CHARS/LINES, read-write if CHAROUT, LINEOUT), IBM REXX does not.

b. TRACE

- Both interpreters support the RXTRACE environment variable. However, the values are different. For IBM REXX, the only values are ON, enable interactive tracing, and OFF. For Personal REXX, valid values are the desired TRACE values with a default of TRACE N.
- Personal REXX supports the non-portable $, such as TRACE $N which traces a procedure and sends the output to a printer. The CMS TRACE ! value command (i.e., TRACE R) which enables/disables processing operating system commands.

7. PARSE VERSION yields different output from both interpreters:

```
IBM OS/2 REXX produces:

      Language            Version      Implementation Date
      REXXSAA             4.00         08 July 1992

Quercus OS/2 Personal Rexx produces:

      Language            Version      Implementation Date
      REXX /Personal      4.00         8 Feb 1993
```

"OS/2 REXX" Similarities

Although it is not part of Personal REXX, the interpreter will work with the following:

- PMREXX
- REXXUTIL (provided the functions are registered as suggested in Chapter 3, and includes the RxFunc functions).
- RXSUBCOM (command) and RXQUEUE (function and command).
- The non-standard OS/2 REXX functions that are not part of REXXUTIL: BEEP, DIRECTORY, ENDLOCAL, FILESPEC, and SETLOCAL.
- Environment variable operations with the VALUE function.
- Database and Communications Manager and the other extensions, such as Visual REXX, shown in Chapter 4.

All of these elements are described in detail in Chapters 3 and 4. Therefore, all of the examples presented in those chapters will also work.

Differences

There are not as many differences as one might think:

1. Only IBM supports the Double-byte character set. So, Personal REXX does not support OPTIONS EXMODE/ETMODE and DBCSs functions.
2. The other difference is in how both interpreters store procedures. IBM REXX will tokenize a procedure and store it in an extended attribute. This will result in faster processing the next time the procedure is processed. The disadvantages of this approach include the following: the extended attribute is not portable to any other operating system and a 64K limit exists for the extended attribute. Personal REXX, if using the format PREXX30/o procedure_name, does not use extended attributes. Rather, it appends the object code at the end of the procedure. This results in less memory being used and faster execution speed. Personal REXX is also portable to the Personal REXX DOS product if the /o16 invocation flag is used.
3. Personal REXX supports the RXFLAGS OS/2 environment variable. The value of this environment variable is an invocation option discussed later in the chapter.

Functions

Basics

The following summarizes the differences between built-in functions in "standard REXX" and Personal REXX.

1. Personal REXX DATE function supports the obsolete C and J arguments.
2. I/O functions: All functions use different pointers for read and write operations — IBM OS/2 REXX only uses one pointer.
    - CHARS: Returns the actual number of unread characters unless a device or the keyboard (standard input) stream is used. (Then only a value of one is allowed to indicate 1 or more unread characters in the stream).
    - LINES: Can only return 1 to indicate that there are unread lines in a stream. Cowlishaw specifies the actual number.
    - LINEIN: Can only read in one line at a time. *Line_number* (second) argument ignored. And, *number_of_lines* (third argument) cannot have a value larger than 1.
    - LINEOUT: The *line_number* (third argument) can only have a value of 1 (start of file) and is usually omitted. Cowlishaw specifies any valid line number as a value.

- The STREAM function is nearly identical for both interpreters with this difference: Personal REXX does smart mode setting for the STREAM OPEN (i.e., read-only for LINEIN/CHARIN/CHARS/LINES read-write if CHAROUT, LINEOUT), IBM REXX does not.

3. TRACE function supports the $ and ? prefix. See the previous section for examples.

Benchmarks

In choosing an interpreter, it may help the user to compare benchmarks on typical daily operations. These tests were performed on a 486/33 MHz computer with 8MB of RAM running OS/2 2.1 beta (FAT) under OS/2 full-screen mode using FAT file format. The benchmarks are presented "as is" without weighting for:

- the interpreter's implementation of the command language;
- the interpreter's ability to take advantage of the OS/2 operating system;
- measurement error; and
- file buffering, which has a major effect on file operating speed

As an additional item of comparison, benchmarks are also included for OS/2 Perl and batch languages. The standard disclaimer applies here —"your mileage may vary if performing these tests yourself." So without any further hesitation, see Table 5-3 for the benchmarks.

Table 5-3

Action	IBM OS/2 2.1 REXX	Quercus Personal REXX for OS/2 3.0*	OS/2 Batch 2.1	OS/2 Perl 4.019****
Read 10 80 character records	< 1 second	< 1 second	5 seconds***	< 1 second
Read 100 80 character records	1 second	< 1 seconds	5 seconds***	< 1 second
Read 1000 80 character records	6 seconds	2 seconds	5 seconds***	<1 second

Table 5-3 Continued

Action	IBM OS/2 2.1 REXX	Quercus Personal REXX for OS/2 3.0*	OS/2 Batch 2.1	OS/2 Perl 4.019****
Write 10 80 character records	< 1 second	< 1 second	5 seconds	< 1 second
Write 100 80 character records	< 1 second	< 1 second	8 seconds	< 1 second
Write 1000 80 character records	4 seconds	4 seconds	35 seconds	1 second
Print 10 80 character records	< 1 second	< 1 second	6 seconds	< 1 second
Print 100 80 character records	2 seconds	2 seconds	8 seconds	2 seconds**
Print 1000 80 character records	17 seconds	17 seconds	29 seconds	17 seconds**
Concatenate String 1000 times	2 seconds	4 seconds	Not Applicable	4 seconds
Create a 1000 element array	1 second	1 second	Not Applicable	1 second

Notes

*There are many things that Quercus REXX will run faster than IBM REXX such as REXXUTIL or Visual REXX. For example, using the /O option when invoking the interpreter or running the procedure in macrospace will produce faster execution times. This option was not used during the above benchmarks will produce faster execution times. A C program can be used to execute a "IBM" REXX procedure in macrospace.

**Both an OS/2 and DOS Perl interpreter was tested. Amazingly, MS-DOS Perl printed 100 records in 1 second and 1000 records in 15 seconds — faster than the OS/2 version! Should you be using Perl instead of REXX? This is discussed in Chapter 7.

***There is no READ command for OS/2 batch language. This was done using a FIND command for the last record in the file.

****A copy of OS/2 Perl 4.036 (the latest version) was obtained but not used for these benchmarks.

Additional Notes:

1. REXX I/O was done with LINEIN/LINEOUT not EXECIO.
2. Regular arrays were used in Perl.
3. The concatenation test consisted of concatenating the variable b to a variable containing the entire counter sequence 1000 times.
4. The array test consisted of looping 1000 times and assigning the array element the value of the counter variable.
5. Only REXX and Perl passed all of the tests.

Table 5-4 is a ranking in descending order. Assigning 1 to first place, 2 to second, and so on. Note that NA was assigned a rank of 3.

Table 5-4

Command Language	Rank — Quercus and IBM only (out of 2)	Rank — All Command Languages (out of 4)
Perl	-----	1.09
Quercus Personal REXX	1.07	1.18
IBM REXX	1.18	1.45
OS/2 Batch	-----	2.36

What Can We Conclude From All This?

1. *There are better alternatives than using OS/2 batch language* for anything besides "quick and dirty" coding. REXX, being bundled with OS/2, is an attractive and portable choice.

2. *The gap between Perl and REXX execution speed appears to be decreasing.* When I ran the same tests (on a much slower MS-DOS computer) for the *Command Language Cookbook*, Perl programs ran overall faster than REXX (Personal REXX 2.0D). This gap appears to have been nearly eliminated with the arrival of Personal REXX 3.0. IBM REXX also did as well or nearly as well as the Quercus and Perl interpreters on most tests.

3. *If you are an intermediate to advanced REXX user, then you should seriously consider purchase of the Quercus product.* With its "plug compatibility" with IBM REXX utilities and products, and a rich function library — it is an attractive choice. (This is called REXXLIB and discussed later in this chapter). Quercus includes a good REXX tutorial with many samples that may be invaluable to a new REXX programmer. However, for beginning to intermediate users, the IBM REXX interpreter is adequate.

QUERCUS EXTENSION: BASICS

This section deals with the extensions to OS/2 (and usually MS-DOS) that Personal REXX offers. This includes invocation options, various REXX statements, samples, online help, and REXXLIB (a function library).

Invoking Personal REXX

The following are the unique features of invoking Personal REXX under OS/2. Review chapter 3 for further information on invoking using part or all of the procedure name, creating an icon to run in foreground, and running a procedure in background.

1. If you wish to always use any of the flags listed below when Personal REXX is invoked, then set the RXFLAGS OS/2 environment variable with that flag.

2. The following is the format to explicitly invoke the Personal REXX interpreter (PREXX30) from the OS/2 command prompt.

    - PREXX30 *flags procedure_name arguments*

    - *flags* include the following:

- */O:* object code created. Use /O16 to create DOS-compatible (16-bit) object code.
- */S:* Keeps the procedure in memory during execution. This is the default (unless the procedure contains object code). /NS is the opposite.
- */TR setting*. The setting is a TRACE prefix (i.e. ? or =) followed by a TRACE setting.
- *procedure_name:* Name of the procedure which usually ends with a .CMD extension.
- *arguments:* One or more arguments for the REXX procedure named *procedure_name*.

3. The following are the major reasons for explicitly invoking REXX (i.e., with the PREXX30) instead of implicitly doing this (i.e., just entering part or all of the command name).
   a. The ability to use the PREXX30 flags listed above.
   b. For production procedures, PREXX30 will not display to the screen the various OS/2 commands used. (For either debugging or developing REXX procedures, displaying these commands to the screen may be invaluable).
   c. Allows you to invoke a procedure as a system command without using the OS/2 CALL system command. This is more of annoyance than an advantage.
   d. You can also use another extension for *procedure_name*. This can be useful if you have a series of REXX extensions (usually from another operating system) that have a different extension. (Thus saving you from major renaming operations).

Unique Statements

Personal REXX provides some additional statements/commands that are mostly derived from CMS counterparts. EXECIO, GLOBALV, and LISTFILE can also be invoked as an external environment with a sequence similar to the following:

```
Rxfuncadd('prxcmd','prxcmd', 'prxcmd') /* register function */
address prxcmd 'execio, globalv, or listfile command'
```

I see this as a more complicated approach (although it may yield faster performance) and so it is not presented above. Note that these three commands have far more options than shown.

These include the following:

1. **EXECIO** is an alternative. It is a non-REXX standard that is portable after some minor modifications to CMS, DOS, and TSO input/output mechanism. Return codes include 0 (successful), 2 (unexpected end-of-file during a read), 24 (Invalid EXECIO syntax), 28 (unable to open file to read from/write to), 36 (miscellaneous read/write error). EXECIO and LISTFILE can use files using either the FAT or HPFS (high-performance file system) formats. The following are two simple examples using the EXECIO command:

Write to file

```
/* Build array to hold simple self-executing REXX procedure */
Line. =
Line.1 = '/* REXX */'
Line.2 = "say 'hello world' "
'execio 2 diskw 'c:\prexx30\a.cmd (stem line. finis'
/* Above writes 2 lines to a.cmd using the compound array line. */
```

Read from a file

```
/* Read from the same file. Place in a compound array */
'execio 2 diskr c:\prexx30\a.cmd (finis stem line.'
do cnt = 1 to 2
      say "Line number" cnt ':' line.cnt
end
```

2. **GLOBALV** creates global variables, which is CMS's equivalent of environment variables. That is to say, variables whose values exist after the procedure that created it finishes processing. They can then be accessed/modified by other REXX procedures. Return codes include 0 (worked successfully) and > 0 (minor to major errors). Here is an example using two procedures:

```
/* Note the procedures can be invoked either implicitly or explicitly */
```

A.CMD (Create Global Variable)

```
/* REXX*/
'globalv select ex1' /* Places global variables in ex1 group */
'globalv set aa 25'  /* Assigns the aa global variable a value of 25 */
'globalv list aa'    /* Lists value of aa */
                     /* Displays */
```

```
      /* SELECTED TABLE IS: EX1 */
      /*       =25 */
```

S.CMD (Second procedure that accesses/deletes global variable)

```
/* REXX */
'globalv select ex1' /* get right group */
'globalv get aa'     /* Retrieve global variable aa with its value of 25. */
say aa               /* 25 is displayed to the screen */
'globalv purge'      /* erase all global variables */
'globalv list aa'    /* Shows that aa is not defined. */
```

3. **LISTFILE** is a CMS utility that is an enhanced equivalent to the OS/2 DIR command and the REXXUTIL SYSFILETREE function. Return codes include 0 (worked successfully), 24 (Invalid LISTFILE syntax), 36 (miscellaneous file error). The following are two examples of the LISTFILE command:

```
'LISTFILE *.* (today header' /* Displays all files created/modified today */
/* Displays something like the following */
```

Name	Ext	Size	Date	Time
A	CMD	43	3/28/93	10:11:56

```
'LISTFILE *.* (SORTD EXT NAME STEM SORTLIST.'
          /* sort in descending (SORTD) order by name and extension */
          /* Place the result in the compound array named sortlist. */
do i = 1 to sortlist.0 /* sortlist.0 has count */
     say sortlist.i
end       /* Output similar to the previous example but with no header */
```

4. **MAKEBUF** and **DROPBUF** are CMS extensions that can be used under DOS and OS/2. MAKEBUF (creates a buffer and buffer pointers for stack operations) and DROPBUF *bufno* deletes buffers numbered *bufno* from stack operations. If *bufno* is not specified, the last buffer created is deleted. They operate on **buffers** which are user-allocated partitions of the stack. Typical return codes are 0 (worked successfully) and 255 (minor to major error). Here is an example of using both:

```
"MAKEBUF"              /* Creates buffer. An optional queue name */
                       /* can be specified */
bufno = rc             /* Buffer number assigned to buffno */
queue "element #1"     /* Write three lines to stack */
queue "element #2"
queue "element #3"
say "Number of elements in the data queue" queued()
                       /* Display number of lines in the stack */
  n = queued()         /* "Freeze" this number */
  do i = 1 to n        /* Display buffer contents */
    pull a
  end
"DROPBUF" bufno        /* Delete buffer */
```

5. The last statements are also used in stack operations: **STACKGET** which retrieves lines from a stack which is usually piped to another procedure or redirected to a file and **STACKPUT** which places lines on a stack such as output from an OS/2 system command. This is not available on other REXX interpreters. An optional queue name is also allowed. Here is a typical use:

```
'dir *.dll'|stackput     /* Takes the output from the DIR command and places */
                         /* it in a stack. The default order is FIFO (first in first out) */
                         /* which can also be specified with the /F parameter or */
                         /* use the /L (last in first out) flag i.e. stackput /L. */

'stackget> a.txt'        /* Redirects output to a file named a.txt. Also popular is */
                         /* piping the output to an application or procedure i.e. */
                         /* 'stackget|a.cmd' If you do not want all the lines from a */
                         /* stack, then consider using the /Mnumber flag to specify */
                         /* the maximum number of lines that you wish to capture */

/* Note: both STACKPUT and STACKGET support an optional queue name */
/* argument */

type 'a.txt'             /* displays directory listing to the screen. Can also be */
                         /* further parsed by a procedure. */
```

On-line Help and Examples

One attractive feature of Personal REXX is the wealth of "extras" that are included with the product. These include information utilities, on-line help and many examples.

These include the following:

1. **RXINFO** tells you information about a procedure that has object attached (i.e., invoked with the /o option). This command also is available under the DOS version of Personal REXX.

```
rxinfo a.cmd

RXINFO Error 171: File 'a.cmd' has no appended REXX object code.
/* Error message if procedure was processed without the /o option. */

OR
```

File	a.cmd
Object code format	22
REXX Version	3.02
Object code flags	03
Object code size	14
Number of literals	3
Size of literals	43
Number of symbols	3
Size of symbols	6
Label table size	0
Number of instructions	3
Instruction table size	39

2. On-line documentation is provided. **REXXLIB.INF**, information about the REXXLIB utility functions and **RXWINDOW.INF**, information about the RXWINDOW full-screen window functions can be accessed by using the VIEW command (i.e., VIEW REXXLIB.INF).

3. The **SAMPLES** directory has 37 examples of what you can do with Personal REXX. Table 5-5 list them:

Table 5-5

REXX Command	Example
ANOTE.CMD	Uses extended attributes to add a description to a file.
ASC2PS.CMD	Converts ASCII to Postscript. An input and output file must also be specified.
DELBLANK.CMD	Deletes blank lines from a procedure. This may help with an procedure's performance. An input and output file must also be specified.
EALIST.CMD	Displays extended attributes for a file.
ENVED.CMD	Modifies environment variables. Uses RXWINDOW.
FINDEA.CMD	Finds all the files with extended attributes in a specified directory.
NOSOURCE.CMD	Strips object code from a REXX procedure. An input and output file must also be specified.
REXXIFY.CMD	Converts a .CMD/.BAT file to a REXX procedure. An input and output file must also be specified.
REXXTRY.CMD	Self-contained REXX environment described in Chapter 3. This version uses less code (29 lines).
REGREP.CMD	Performs a file search using UNIX "regular expressions" (i.e. characters used in pattern matching). File and pattern arguments are also required.
SERVER.CMD	Shows an example of named pipes.
TRYRXWIN.CMD	Examples of RXWindow functions.

4. Two other sample procedures worth looking at are:

INSTALPR.CMD	The Personal REXX installation program that was written in...REXX! It shows some good examples of RXWINDOW functions.
INSTEST.CMD	Used after the installation to see if Personal REXX was installed. Shows examples of: registering the various dynamic link libraries; example of using RXQUEUE command; example of using GLOBALV and LISTFILE commands.

5. The OS/2 Personal REXX product does not include the **HELP** and **LEARN** directories found with the DOS and OS/2 products. LEARN includes all of the examples found in Chapter 5 of the *Personal REXX User's Guide*. The chapter is brief, but is a fine REXX tutorial. HELP includes text files describing the REXX syntax. See Chapter 3 for equivalent files provided by IBM and shareware vendors for OS/2.

REXXLIB — Personal REXX Function Library

REXXLIB is a major feature of Personal REXX. It is recommended even if you are using the IBM OS/2 REXX interpreter. With over 150 functions, many compatible with Personal REXX on other platforms, this can greatly enhance your REXX processing capability. Table 5-6 gives an overview of the these functions.

Table 5-6

Screen/Keyboard	Miscellaneous	Directory/Volume Operations
CHARSIZE	DATECONV	DOSBOOTDRIVE
CURSOR	DELAY	DOSCD
CURSORTYPE	DOSENV	DOSCHDIR
INKEY	DOSENVLIST	DOSCOMMANDFIND
SCRBLINK	DOSENVSIZE	DOSISDEV
SCRBORDER	DOSKILLPROCESS	DOSISDIR
SCRCLEAR	DOSMAXPATH	DOSMAKEDIR
SCROLLDOWN	DOSPATHFIND	DOSMKDIR
SCROLLLEFT	DOSPID	DOSRENAME
SCROLLRIGHT	DOSPIDLIST	DOSRMDIR
SCROLLUP	DOSPRIORITY	DOSRENAME
SCRPUT	DOSPROCINFO	DOSRMDIR
SCRREAD	LOWER	DOSVOLUME

Table 5-6 Continued

Screen/Keyboard	Miscellaneous	Directory/Volume Operations
SCRSIZE	SOUND	
SCRWRITE	UPPER	
SHIFTSTATE		
STRINGIN		
TYPEMATIC		

Invoking REXXLIB Functions

Before using any of the REXXLIB functions, you must first register the dynamic link libraries one of the following ways:

Register all functions

```
ret_code = rxfuncadd('rexxlibregister','qrexxlib','rexxlibregister')
ret_code = rexxlibregister()
ret_code = function_name or
call function_name
```

Register a particular function

```
rxfuncadd('pcmodel','qrexxlib','lib_pcmodel')
/* Third argument always starts lib_ prefix */
call pcmodel or ret_code = pcmodel()
```

Deregister all functions

```
ret_code = rexxlibderegister()
```

Getting Help on REXXLIB

Information on help and sample programs generally available for OS/2 Personal REXX is provided earlier in this chapter. Here is a review of the available help on REXXLIB:

- Either CompuServe (Go Quercus) or the Quercus BBS (408-867-7488) are filled with many documented procedures using REXXLIB functions.

- Enter VIEW REXXLIB.INF to look at an on-line reference to REXXLIB. The main advantages of this approach are: the immediacy of on-line help; and search and index capabilities.
- The PREXX30 and PREXX30\SAMPLES directories have many REXXLIB examples. See Table 5-7 for some examples.

Table 5-7

ANOTE.CMD	Annotates a note to an extended attributes using REXXLIB (i.e., dosenv, dosdel, and dosdir) and REXXUTIL functions (i.e., sysgetea, sysputea)
ASC2PS.CMD	Converts an ASCII file to PostScript. using REXXLIB functions (dosisdir, dosisfile)
ASCII.CMD	Builds an ASCII chart but also a good example of most of the REXXLIB screen functions (cursor, scrput, scrsize, scrwrite).
CMPDIR	Compares the dates/times of files in two directories. Uses the REXXLIB functions doscd, dosdir, dosdirpos, dosdrive, dosisdir, parsefn, upper.
EALIST	Lists the extended attributes of a file. Uses dosealist and doseasize REXXLIB functions.
INSTEST.CMD	Used to test if Personal REXX was installed correctly. Of interest are: an example of registering the REXXLIB DLL (using the rexxlibregister function); and an example of how to query if a dynamic link library is already registered.

4. Table 5-8 is a complete list of sample procedure names by REXXLIB functions. It may help when looking for examples of particular REXXLIB functions.

Table 5-8

arraysort	TREED
cursor	ASCII, LSDIR, TREED2
doschdir	TRAVERSE, TREED2
doscd	CMPDIR, COPYEX, FINDEA, LSDIR, RXGREP, SYNCH, TREED, TREED2, UPDIR
UPDIR	
dosdel	ANOTE, DELCH, LOWER, PATHEDIT, SYNCH, UNIQUE, WORDFIND
dosdir	ANOTE, CMPDIR, COPYEX, DO, FINDEA, LSDIR, MODMAP, RXGREP, SYNCH, TRAVERSE, TREED, TREED2, UPDIR
dosdirpos	CMPDIR, FINDEA, LSDIR, RXGREP, SYNCH, TRAVERSE, UPDIR
dosdrive	CMPDIR, COPYEX, DELCH, FINDEA, LSDIR, REXXIFY, RXGREP, TREED, TREED2, UPDIR
dosealist	EALIST
doseasize	EALIST, FINDEA
dosenv	ANOTE, ENVED
dosenvlist	ENVED
dosfname	NOSOURCE, SYNCH
dosisdir	ASC2PS, CMPDIR, COPYEX, HEXBROWS, SYNCH, UPDIR
dosisfile	ASC2PS
filecrc	DELCH
filesearch	RXGREP

Table 5-8 Continued

inkey	TRYRXWIN
lower	ENVED, LOWER, PATHEDIT
nmpipe_connect nmpipe_disconnect nmpipe_read nmpipe_write	SERVER
parsefn	CMPDIR, COPYEX, DELCH, FINDEA, LSDIR, NOSOURCE, REXXIFY, RXGREP, SYNCH, TREED2, UPDIR
pcvideomode	ENVED
scrput	ASCII, LSDIR, TREED2
scrread	TREED2
scrsize	ASCII, ENVED, NOSOURCE, XMORE
scrwrite	ASCII, ENVED
upper	CMPDIR, COPYEX, DO, FINDEA, REXXIFY, RXGREP, TREED2, TRYRXWIN, UPDIR, UPPER, WORDFIND

The remainder of this section will look at some of the more interesting functions.

REXX-Oriented Functions

Personal REXX adds many useful functions that extend the REXX language, especially for compound symbols. Here are two examples that show these capabilities:

"Array" functions

```
      /* Register the dynamic link library as described earlier */
ret_code = rfuncadd('rexxlibregister','qrexxlib','lib_rexxlibregister')
call rexxlibregister
```

```
        /* Build the "from" (source) "array" */
a.0 = 4
        /* Elements a.0 and b.0 are needed for these functions to work. */
        /* Both show the number of elements in the array. */
a.1 = 88
a.2 = 'Charles'
a.3 = ' p' /* leading blank */
a.4 = 'damsel'
b.0 = 1

/* Let's copy all of "array" a to "array" b. All of the following functions */
/* generally return either 0 (failed) or 1(worked). Not shown are the third */
/* (the element in the "from array" to start copying from. Default is */
/* the first element), fourth (The element of position in the "to array" to */
/* copy into. Default is the first [start of the array] position, and fifth (Number */
/* of elements to copy. The default is all of the elements after the "from array */
/* element" specified in the third argument) arguments. */
call arraycopy 'a.','b.'
call arraydelete 'a.', 1,2
/* The above call deletes two elements (third argument ) starting with */
/* with element one (second argument. i.e. the first and second elements) */
/* in "array" a (the first argument). */
do cnt = 1 to 4 /* Let's confirm this happened... */
        say a.cnt b.cnt
/* displays a.1 = p, a.2 = damsel, a.3 = A.3 and a.4 = A.4 */
/* displays b.1 = 88, b.2 = Charles. b.3 = p, b.4 = damsel */
end
call arrayinsert 'b.',a.',1,1,2
/* Now let's put the elements back in array a. To do this, specify that */
/* you want to copy from "array" b (the first argument) to "array" a (the */
/* second argument). Specifically, you want to copy from the "first */
/* element" in "array" b (The default value and also the third argument). */
/* to the "first element" in "array" a (the default value and the fourth */
/* argument). Only two array elements (the fifth argument) are being copied */
do cnt = 1 to 4
        say a.cnt b.cnt
/* Displays that a.1-a.4 and b.1-b.4 have the values of Charles, p, damsel, 88 */
end

call arraysort 'b',1,,1,,'D'
/* Now let's sort the b "array" (the first argument) starting in the first array */
/* element (the second argument) and the starting character of that element */
/* (the fourth argument). The sort will be a descending (the sixth argument) */
/* character (the seventh argument is not shown. Values are C [character and */
/* the default] or N [numeric] ) Also not specified are the second (number of */
```

```
/* "array" elements to sort) and fifth (sort field length with a default value of */
/* 100) arguments. */
do cnt = 1 to 4
        /* displays a.1 = damsel, a.2 = 88, a.3 = Charles, a.4 = p */
        /* displays b.1 = damsel, b.2 = Charles, b.3 = 88, b.4 = p */
        /* POTENTIAL TRAP: This modifies your existing array */
        /* Sort a copy of the array if you don't want it permanently sorted */
         say a.cnt b.cnt
end
```

Compound Symbol Operations

If the tail (e.g. catnip in a .catnip) is non-numeric than consider using the "cv" functions presented below:

Compound symbol functions

```
ret_code = rxfuncadd('rexxlibregister','qrexxlib','lib_rexxlibregister')
call rexxlibregister   /* Register dynamic link library */
                       /* Initialize the array with non-numeric tails */
a.0 = 4
a.fungus = 88
a.winter = 'Charles'
a.clinton = ' p'
a.1 = 'damsel'
b.0 = 1
c.0 = 1
d.0 = 1
call cvcopy 'a.','b.'
                       /* Copy the entire array from a to b. */
say b.fungus b.winter b.clinton b.1
                       /* Returns 88 Charles p damsel */
call cvwrite 'a.txt', b /* Writes the entire compound "array" to the file a.txt */
                       /* Not shown is the CVTAILS function which can */
                       /* save parts of a compound array based on the */
                       /* values of the tail. */
call cvread 'a.txt', c /* Reads the entire compound "array" from a.txt */
say b.fungus b.winter b.clinton b.1 /* Returns 88 Charles p damsel */
call cvsearch 'b.','d.','^Charles'
/* Searches the compound array for elements with a value starting with */
/* the string "Charles." ^ is a regular expression (special characters used */
/* to match character and numeric patterns) that means "start of an element" */
/* UNIX and perl users will already be familiar with these. */
```

```
/* Other regular expressions include:         */
/*      $ - end of an element   */
/*      [a-z] - matches lowercase only       */
/*      [A-Z] - matches upper case only       */
/*      [0-9] or :d - matches numeric digits only     */
/*      :a - matches any letter in any case    */
/*      . - matches all characters except newline.   */
/*      \ - Use to allow special characters or operators as a string       */
/*      such as \/\ (matches on /)     */
say d.0 d.1 d.2 /* Returns 1 WINTER D.2 - winter has a value of Charles    */
```

Macrospace Functions

Chapter 3 discussed how to use C programs to load REXX functions into macrospace for faster execution. Here is an example of doing this using REXX:

```
ret_code = rxfuncadd('rexxlibregister','qrexxlib','lib_rexxlibregister')
call rexxlibregister /* Register dynamic link library */
call macroclear /* Removes all procedures from macrospace. Use */
       /* MACRODROP */
       /* (not shown) to drop specific functions */
       /* All functions generally return 1 (worked) or 0 (failed) */
call macroadd 'bb','a.cmd','B'
       /* Loads a REXX procedure into macrospace. Function name */
       /* is bb */
       /* (first argument) which comes from the a.cmd file */
       /* (second argument). The last argument specifies if */
       /* the REXX procedure is to be searched before ('B') or after ('A') */
       /* any registered functions. This may help performance */
       say result
call macroquery 'bb'
       say result /* Returns B (searched before registered functions) */
call macroreorder 'bb', 'A' /* Changes the 'B' setting to 'A' */
       say result
       d.0 = 1
       d.1 = 'bb'
call macrosave 'c.cmd','d.' /* Saves the functions specified in the d */
       /* compound array (second argument) */
       /* to c.cmd (first argument) */
       say result
call macroclear       /* Clears any loaded procedures from macrospace */
       say result
call macroload 'c.cmd', 'd.' /* Loads the saved procedures */
```

DOS and OS/2 Information Functions

The following procedure shows some of the information functions available for REXXLIB.

```
ret_code = rxfuncadd('rexxlibregister','qrexxlib','lib_rexxlibregister')
call rexxlibregister /* Register dynamic link library */
        /* Note: for all functions that return compound symbol arrays, The */
        /* first (.0 ) element has a value of the number of total array elements */
ret_code = doscd('d:')
        /* DOSCD - gives the current directory. Could return a value of \ */

ret_code = dosapptype('c:\os2\cmd.exe')
         /* DOSAPPTYPE - Returns a three-part string. such as 2 0 1 */
        /* that tells what type a.EXE or.COM file is */
        /* First part - 0 (unknown), 1 (full-screen OS/2), 2 (Presentation */
        /* Manager text window), 3 (Presentation Manager), 16 (Dynamic */
        /* Link Library), 32 (DOS program */
        /*      */
        /* Second part - 0 (works under MS-DOS), 1 (doesn't work under */
        /* OS/2) */
        /* Third part - 0 (not a 32-bit executable), 1(is a 32-bit executable) */

ret_code = dosdisk('T','d:') /* Has a value of 190863360 */
        /* DOSDISK - gives information about a disk */
        /* First argument - information flag - F (free bytes on disk) */
        /* T (total number of bytes on disk), U (used bytes on disk) */
        /* Second argument - disk drive */

ret_code = dosealist('c:\os2\cmd.exe','a.','b.','c.')
        /* DOSEALIST - retrieves information about extended attributes */
        /* of a file. First argument (file name), second argument (compound */
        /* variable that holds the extended attribute names), third argument */
        /* (compound variable that holds the extended attribute values) */
        /* fourth argument (compound variable that holds additional */
        /* extended attribute information). Returns -1 (no EAs in a file) */
        /* >= 1 (actual number of Extended attributes) */

ret_code = doseasize('c:\os2\cmd.exe')
        /* DOSEASIZE - size of extended attributes in a file(first argument ) */
        /* Returns -1 (no extended attributes), > 1 (size of extended attributes) */

ret_code = dosenv('path')
        /* DOSENV - Returns the value of an environment variable (only */
        /* argument). If 'path' is selected, may return a value of c:\;c:\os2.. */
```

```
ret_code = dosenvsize()
        /* DOSENVSIZE - Returns the total environment size and free
        space. Both of these are in bytes. A sample value may be 1194 31 */

ret_code = dosenvlist('r.')
        /* DOSENVLIST - Lists all current OS/2 environment variables. */
        /* Only argument is the compound symbol to contain the list of */
        /* environment variables. Usually returns a value greater than 1 */
        /* (number of environment variables) */
        /* Typical value - WP_OBJHANDLE USER_INI SYSTEM_INI... */

ret_code = dosisdev('d:') /* Has a value of 0 */
        /* DOSISDEV - Tells if an argument is a device */
        /* (such as COM1) and returns 1 if true else returns 0 */

ret_code = dosisdir('c:\') /* Has a value of 1 */
        /* DOSISDIR - Tells if an argument is a directory */
        /* Returns 1 if true else returns 0 */

ret_code = dosisfile('d:') /* Has a value of 0 */
        /* DOSISFILE - Tells if an argument is a file */
        /* Returns 1 if true else returns 0 */

ret_code = dosispipe('d:\') /* Has a value of 0 */
        /* DOSISPIPE- Tells if an argument is a named pipe */
        /* Returns 1 if true else returns 0 */

ret_code = dospid()
        /* DOSPID - Returns a process id. Such as 7. */

ret_code = dossessiontype()
        /* DOSSESSIONTYPE - Returns the session type. 0 (full-screen) */
        /* 2 (virtual window), 3 (Presentation Manager), 4 (detached session) */

ret_code = rexxlibver()
         /* REXXLIBVER - Returns version of REXXLIB. Sample value of 1.1 */

ret_code = shiftstate('C',1) /* Has a value of 0 */
        /* SHIFTSTATE - Returns the current setting of the "lock keys" */
        /* First argument - key type of C (capslock), N (numlock), */
        /* and S (scroll lock). Second argument 0 (shift key enabled) */
        /* or 1 (shift key disabled). Returns shift state */
```

DOS and OS/2 "Action" Functions

Here are some of the functions that perform some action under DOS or OS/2:

```
ret_code = rxfuncadd('rexxlibregister','qrexxlib','lib_rexxlibregister')
call rexxlibregister /* Register dynamic link library */
ret_code = doschdir('c:\')
        /* DOSCHDIR - Changes the current directory/drive to the specified */
        /* argument. Returns either 0 (change failed) or 1 (change made). */

ret_code = dosdrive()
ret_code = dosdrive('d:')
        /* DOSDRIVE - Has two functions. Without an argument, returns the */
        /* current drive. With an argument, changes the current drive to the */
        /* specified drive. */

ret_code = upper('lower_case')
        /* UPPER - Converts the argument to upper case. In the above */
        /* example returns LOWER_CASE */

ret_code = lower('UPPER_CASE')
        /* LOWER - Converts the argument to lower case. In the above */
        /* example returns upper_case */
```

RXWINDOW (FULL-SCREEN WINDOW CAPABILITIES)

One of the earliest full-screen REXX interfaces to the PC was RXWINDOW function package, available first in Personal REXX for DOS. You may not be aware of it, but you have already been introduced to the capabilities of this software — a Personal REXX procedure using RXWINDOW was used to install the product on your PC! Table 5-9 lists the major functions of RXWINDOW.

Table 5-9

Window Attributes	Overall Operations	Input/Output Operations
W_ATTR	W_CLEAR	W_GET
W_BORDER	W_CLOSE	W_KEYS
W_FIELD	W_HIDE	W_PUT
W_UNFIELD	W_MOVE	W_READ
	W_OPEN	W_SCRPUT
	W_SIZE	W_SCRREAD
	W_UNHIDE	W_SCRWRITE

The 18 functions are divided into three areas. One group sets the overall characteristics of the window (such as color). Another performs all non-input/output window operations (such as opening or closing a window). The last group either writes text to a window or reads text entered in a window. These calls are 100% compatible with the RXWINDOW functions for Personal REXX for DOS. RXWINDOW is not included in Personal REXX for Windows. Unfortunately, the down side is that RXWindow screens look more "DOS-like" than "OS/2-like" such as Visual REXX or RxMessageBox in REXXUtil. However, many users will be attracted to this product because of its portability and good support.

Registering the RXWINDOW Dynamic Link Library

As with all dynamic link libraries, the RXWindow DLL must first be registered. Use the following sequence to do this:

```
if rxfuncquery('w_register') <> 0 then do /* check if already registered */
      ret_code = rxfuncadd('w_register','rxwin30','rxwindow')
      call w_register /* functions may also be registered separately */
      end
```

To deregister RXWINDOW, use the following:

```
call w_deregister
      /* Deregisters function library. May cause problems if other processes */
      /* are still using it */
      /* May also use Rxfuncdrop function showed in chapter 3. */
```

Information on help and sample programs generally available for OS/2 Personal REXX is discussed earlier in this chapter. Here is a review of the available help on REXXLIB:

Getting Help on RXWindow

- Either CompuServe (Go Quercus) or the Quercus BBS (408-867-7488) are filled with many documented procedures using RXWINDOW functions.
- Enter VIEW RXWINDOW.INF to look at an on-line reference to RXWINDOW. The main advantages of this approach are: the immediacy of on-line help; and search and index capabilities.
- The PREXX30 and PREXX30\SAMPLES directories have many RXWINDOW examples. See Table 5-10 for samples:

Table 5-10

Name	What it does
ENVED.CMD	Changes OS/2 environment variables.
INSTALPR.CMD	Installs Personal REXX. Uses the following RXWINDOW functions: W_CLOSE, W_GET, W_OPEN, W_SCRREAD, W_SCRWRITE. Shows example of registers each function separately.
LOADRXWN.CMD	Example of registering RXWINDOW DLL. Similar to above example.
MENUS.CMD	Uses RXWindow to do GUI-like pull-down menus. (Looks more like DOS than OS/2). Uses the following RXWINDOW functions: W_ATTR, W_BORDER, W_CLOSE, W_OPEN, W_PUT.
TRYRXWIN	Like REXXTRY, it allows you to try nearly all RXWINDOW functions in a non-harmful environment. On-line help is included.

Sample Program

```
Build a window
call rxfuncadd "w_register","RXWIN30","rxwindow"
call w_register
      /* Register the RXWINDOW function library */
  call w_open 10,10,10,40,74
      /* W_OPEN - Open the window. First argument (starting row) */
      /* second argument (starting column), third argument (number */
      /* of rows in window), fourth argument (number of columns in */
      /* window), color (light green foreground [10] + red background */
      /* [64] = 74) */

  wh = result
      /* Window handle from w_open. Used by all other */
      /* functions */

  call w_border wh,2,0,2,0
      /* W_BORDER - Creates border for the window. Values */
      /* for all arguments are 0 (no border), 1 (single line), */
      /* 2 (double line - default), Arguments in order are: */
      /* top, right, bottom, left. First line appears in the border */

  call w_scrwrite wh,1,15,"A sample screen"
      /* W_SCRWRITE - Writes specified text (fourth argument) */
      /* in the specified window (first argument) in the first row */
      /* (second argument) and the 15th column (third argument) */
      /* Additional arguments (such as pad characters and color) */
      /* are not shown. */

  call w_attr wh,4,1,40,25
      /* W_ATTR - Sets color for a specified window (first argument) */
      /* in a specified row (second argument) and column (third */
      /* argument) for up to 40 characters (fourth argument). Last */
      /* argument is light blue foreground (9) and blue background */
      /* (16) = 25 */

  call w_scrwrite wh,4,15,"Use of w_attr"
      /* Writes a second line of text */

  call w_put wh,6,1,"What is your quest?",,44
      /* W_PUT - W_SCRWRITE is the preferred method */
      /* Arguments - first (window handle), second (window row) */
      /* third (window column), fourth (string), seventh (12 [light */
```

```
       /* red foreground] + 32 [green background] = 44) */

call w_field wh,"quest",7,1,30,36
       /* Creates a field (for input) within a window. Arguments */
       /* - first (window handle), second (field name. Must */
       /* be in quotes)., third (row of field), fourth (column of field) */
       /* fifth (length of field), sixth (4 [dark red foreground] + 32 */
       /* [green background] = 36 ) */

call w_read wh,"quest",'F'
       /* Reads input in field. Use with W_KEYS to additionally */
       /* control key movement. Arguments - first (window */
       /* handle), second (field name), third (either N [normal - */
       /* Either ENTER or ESC is active], or F [also uses function */
       /* keys] */

call delay 10
       /* hold screen on window for 10 seconds */
say quest
       /* print user input */
call w_close wh
       /* close window */
```

This produces a screen similar to the following:

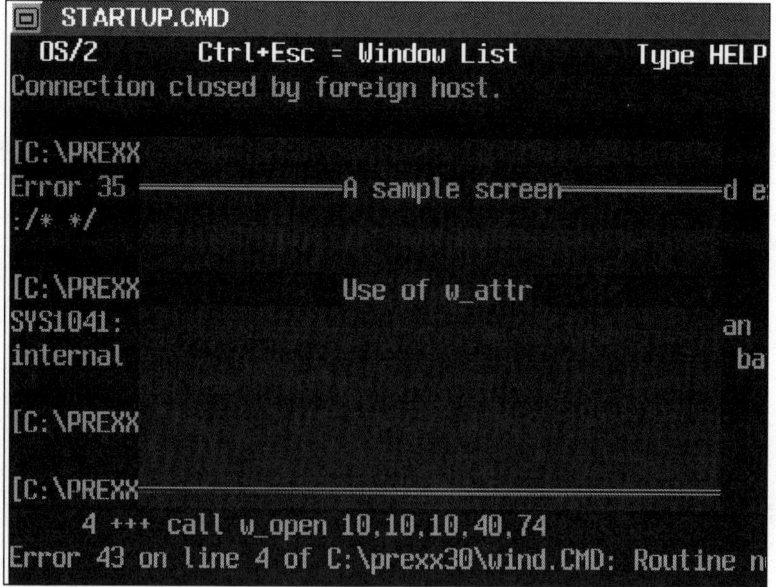

Figure 5-1 RXWINDOW Sample Screen

Additional Information

Here is some additional information on RXWINDOW:

- Memory availability is important when creating windows. Keep this in mind when problems occur.
- When coding and you get error message 984 (argument not numeric), check if you are missing a comma.
- Up-to-20 windows can be open at the same time, if memory is adequate.
- Use w_size(*window_handle*) returns the window and height of a window. This may be used in creating another window.
- Only w_... functions should be used for writing from a screen/reading input from a screen. Other methods may cause unexpected results (such as overwriting to a screen).

REFERENCES

Daney, Charles 1993 Various Letters
Mansfield Software 1989 Mansfield Software Group News
Quercus System 1992 Personal REXX OS/2 Addendum 3.0
Quercus Systems 1991 Personal REXX User's Guide Version 3.0
Quercus Systems 1993 REXXLIB.INF text file
Quercus Systems 1993 RXWINDOW.INF text file

6

OS/2 REXX: Third-Party Shareware and Commercial Extensions

Chapter 6 continues looking at third-party products. This includes a variety of third-party non-interpreter products such as editors (and edit macros written using both REXX and built-in editor languages), communication packages, and programming tools. Note that these are not just small companies supplying commercial and shareware REXX support but also "established" companies such as Borland and Lotus. Expect third-party OS/2 REXX products to continue to arrive in healthy numbers in future years. This is similar to the trend on the Amiga where AREXX (bundled with AmigaDos since 2.0) has become the application macro (or glue) language supported by hundreds of Amiga software programs. Additional shareware products are mentioned in the Appendices.

INTERFACING REXX WITH THIRD-PARTY EDITORS

All third-party REXX-enabled editors are derived from their mainframe cousins — XEDIT. XEDIT was available on CMS and one of the reasons that REXX surpassed EXEC2 in popularity on the CMS platform. ISPF which was first available on TSO and originally comprised of user-built "macros" with clists was another mainframe cousin. ISPF stands for Interactive System Productivity Facility. Originally called SPF — Structured Program Facility. All of these environments support some form of edit macros or subcommands. In other words, it supports a new or customized version of an existing command written with a combination of REXX and built-in editor commands. Examples of special edit macros include the startup macro, initial macro, or profile macro or profile. These macros are processed when the third-party editor starts up. Like everything in REXX, you are only limited by your imagination in what you can make an edit macro do.

A Brief Look at History

The history of MS-DOS, OS/2, and third-party REXX-enabled editors goes back to 1985 when KEDIT for MS-DOS was first distributed by Mansfield Software Group, Inc. In 1989, KEDIT was at version 3.0 and Command Technology Corporation (CTC) had SPF/PC 2.0 for both DOS and OS/2 2.0. By 1993, KEDIT had released version 5.0 with major improvements and support for Windows NT. Also in 1993, CTC SPF 3.0 was released. A new company Tritus, Inc., had released version 1.2 of Tritus SPF, a short time after version 2.0 supported ISPF-like full-screen dialogs. In 1993 a freeware XEDIT-like editor named THE (The Hessling Editor) became available on OS/2, DOS, and soon UNIX. All three offered REXX support.

A Comparison of Features

While this book does not endorse any specific product, Table 6-1 may aid in your selection.

Table 6-1

Feature	KEDIT (Mansfield)	THE (Mark Hessling)	SPF/PC (CTC)	Tritus SPF (Tritus)
Overall *(file operations)*				
Binary files	YES	NO	YES	YES
Extended Attributes	YES — protected if SET EAPRESERVE ON is issued.	No explicit support	No explicit support	No explicit support
File line length (width)	32000 (default 512)	16960 (default 2048)	32000 (default 80)	32000 (default 250)
File length size	Limited by memory or up-to-100 files simultaneously!	Limited by memory. A 200K file took a while to do operations.	Limited by memory. Up -to-2 files simultaneously.	256MB (OS/2). Up-to-2 files simultaneously.
HPFS support	YES	YES	Not specified	Not specified.
Interface to Operating System	YES — DOS command	YES — DOS command	YES — on command line. Enter OS2 *os2_command.*	YES — on command line. Enter OS2 *os2_command.*
Number of files opened at once.	100	Not specified	Not specified. At least two	8

Table 6-1 Continued

Feature	KEDIT (Mansfield)	THE (Mark Hessling)	SPF/PC (CTC)	Tritus SPF (Tritus)
Operating systems	DOS, OS/2, MS-Windows aware	DOS, OS/2, UNIX	DOS, OS/2	DOS/OS/2
Text files	Yes	Yes	Yes	Yes
Line operations				
Delete	Deletes line(s) — DELETE command.	Deletes line(s) — DELETE command.	Delete line(s) — D or DD line commands	Delete line(s) — D or DD line commands.
Insert	Insert lines — F2 key, CINSERT, INPUT	Insert lines — ADD command	Insert lines — I line command.	Insert lines — I line command.
Move	Move lines — MOVE command	Move lines — MOVE command	Move lines — M or MM line command.	Move lines — M or MM line command.
Search	CLOCATE, FIND commands	LOCATE command	FIND edit command.	FIND edit command
Sort	SORT command. Limited by memory.	None	SORT edit command. Unspecified file limit	SORT edit command. Unspecified file limit
Undo	UNDO command — can go back specified levels.	CANCEL command — ALL changes to a file are lost (or since last SAVE	CANCEL command — ALL changes to a file are lost (or since last SAVE command.)	CANCEL command — ALL changes to a file are lost (or since last SAVE command.)
Macro Operations				
Editor Commands Supported	Yes using the MACRO command	Yes using the MACRO command	Yes using the ISREDIT/ISPEXEC environment	Yes using the ISREDIT/ ISPEXEC environment
Full-screen dialogs	Limited support	No support	No support	In future release 2.0
Interfaces to REXX.	Yes, can use Personal or IBM OS/2 REXX.	Yes can use IBM OS/2 REXX. Uses the ADDRESS THE command.	Yes, can use IBM OS/2 REXX.	Yes, can use IBM OS/2 REXX.

Table 6-1 Continued

Feature	KEDIT (Mansfield)	THE (Mark Hessling)	SPF/PC (CTC)	Tritus SPF (Tritus)
Length of Macro line	250 characters a line (KEDIT or REXX macro).	Not specified	Not specified	Not specified
Macro extension	.KEX (single macro) or .KML (macro library — multiple macros)	.CMD	.SPF, .REX	.SPF
Maximum size of macro	500 lines long (KEDIT macro) Limited by memory (REXX macro)	Not specified	32K	Not specified
Startup macros supported commands into	Yes. Just put all appropriate commands into PROFILE.KEX. This file is automatically processed on KEDIT's startup.	Yes, put all appropriate IMACRO field PROFILE.THE. This file is automatically processed on KEDIT's startup.	Yes, put the name of a macro in the Initial MACRO field of the EDIT panel or enter IMACRO *macroname* at the COMMAND line.	Yes, put the name of a macro in the Initial MACRO field of the EDIT panel or enter IMACRO *macroname* at the COMMAND line.

Using KEDIT

This section takes a look at the essentials for getting started with KEDIT. Then we will focus on the KEDIT edit macro capabilities. Listed below are the major features of KEDIT:

- Mouse support
- LAN Support (not specified if supported under OS/2).
- Over 120 Edit commands
- Over 110 Edit customizable settings
- REXX-like KEXX edit macro language supporting 19 instructions and nearly 100 built-in functions
- On-line help
- Nearly 30 sample macros

[All KEDIT screens reproduced in this chapter are done with the permission of the Mansfield Software Group, Inc.]

Invoking KEDIT

You can use any of the following formats from the OS/2 prompt to invoke KEDIT or create an icon to invoke KEDIT as discussed in Chapter 3:

No Filename

```
KEDIT /* No filename specified */
What file do you want to edit?
       /* enter filename */
       /* Brought into editor */
```

Filename specified

```
KEDIT filename
       /* Filename may include full specification (directory/drive) */
       /* Wild cards are not supported */
```

Directory list

```
KEDIT DIR
       /* Directory listing of the current directory */
KEDIT DIR C:\
       /* Directory listing of all files in the C directory */
KEDIT DIR C:\*.CMD C:\KEDIT\SAMPLES\*.KEX
       /* Display all .CMD files in the C:\ directory and all the .KEX files */
       /* in the KEDIT samples directory. Different drives can be specified */
       /* as well. */
```

KEDIT with options

```
       /* Can be used with DIR and filename */
KEDIT a.a (NOMOUSE NOPROFILE
       /* Use of multiple options. NOMOUSE disables mouse menu */
       /* NOPROFILE disables profile (PROFILE.KEX) settings */
```

Once in KEDIT, the directory output looks similar to the following:

```
c: beep     .cmd    57    3-20-93    22:51    \

c:caseword.kex   1365    5-31-92    5:00    \kedit\samples
```

This output includes in order: the filename (with drive letter), file size, file modification date, file modification time, and the directory (subdirectory). You may then select one or more files to edit. If the mouse features are enabled (i.e., a **set mousebar** on was issued), you can select from the bottom menu the desired way to sort the directory list from the bottom menu.

Options may be entered one of two ways:

1. In a CONFIG.SYS file — SET KEDIT=option (e.g. SET KEDIT=NOMOUSE NOPROFILE). Affects all KEDIT sessions until the computer is shutdown or a SET KEDIT= [clears KEDIT settings] is issued.
2. Specified when KEDIT is invoked. (i.e. KEDIT a.a. (NO MOUSE NOPROFILE. This option affects only the current KEDIT session.)

Table 6-2 is a list of some of the options that can be specified.

Table 6-2

Option	What it Does	Settings (including Default)
DEFPROFILE	Overrides the default profile file name of PROFILE.KEX	Profile specification (may include drive and path)
LOCK	Locks file so other programs/users can't edit it.	None. Just the option name of LOCK is needed.
MACROPATH PATH	Determine search path for KEXX macros (MACROPATH) or files (PATH).	OFF (search only the current and KEDIT directories), *environment_var_name* — name of environment variable with search path.
NEW	Assumes that the file does not exist (even if it does) and creates a new file.	None. Just the option name of NEW is needed.
NOLOCK	Does not lock a file.	None. Just the option name of NOLOCK is needed.

Table 6-2 Continued

Option	What it Does	Settings (including Default)
NOMOUSE	Disables the mouse features of KEDIT.	None. Just the option name of NOMOUSE is needed.
PREXX20	Uses Personal REXX instead of IBM OS/2 REXX. Personal REXX must be loaded before KEDIT to do this.	None. Just the option name of PREXX30 is needed.
PROFDEBUG	Executes the profile in debug (trace) mode. Useful for solving those tricky profile problems.	None. Just the option name of PROFDEBUG is needed.
WIDTH	Changes the width (i.e., maximum line length)	Default is 512. Can range from 255 to 4095.

Refer to the discussion later in this chapter on KEDIT profile macros for other ways to customize KEDIT editing sessions on initialization.

Leaving KEDIT

Use any of the following approaches to quit KEDIT:

1. From the ====> (command) line:

   Enter *qquit /* Cancels changes */ or quit /** if no changes were made */

2. From menubar, select [Quit] option (far right).

Getting Help on KEDIT

The following are tips on getting help for using KEDIT:

1. Mansfield Software maintains a bulletin board at 203-429-3784. (Baud rates 300-9600 are supported. Communication protocols are 8-N-1.) or check the PCVENA CompuServe Forum. Both have many examples of macros and other files KEDIT related (such as patches).
2. KEDIT includes a healthy-sized on-line help manual. It is accessible a variety of ways:

From the OS/2 Prompt

```
KHELP or KHELP keyword (such as KHELP REXX)
```

Within KEDIT

```
      /* Pressing the F1 key or the HELP mouse menu option */

KHELP or HELP /* General help */

KHELP keyword or HELP kcyword
```

This command uses the file KREF50.HLP. KEDIT.HLP which also contains additional information.

3. Nearly 30 sample macro files are included with EDIT:

COLORFUN.KEX	4 edit sessions in many different colors.
DIRMAC.KML	Directory operations
EXTRTEST.KEX	EXTRACT command options
MISC.KML	Miscellaneous options
MYMACROS.KML	Sample macros
PROFILEA.KEX, PROFILEB.KEX	Sample profile macros
VMPROF.KEX	A VMS style profile for KEDIT
WC.KEX	Word count in a file.

Basic KEDIT Operations

To better understand how to simulate an edit command via an edit macro, one must have a basic understanding of how the KEDIT editor works. The following summarizes basic KEDIT operations:

The Basic KEDIT Screen

The following are some examples of the basic KEDIT screen.

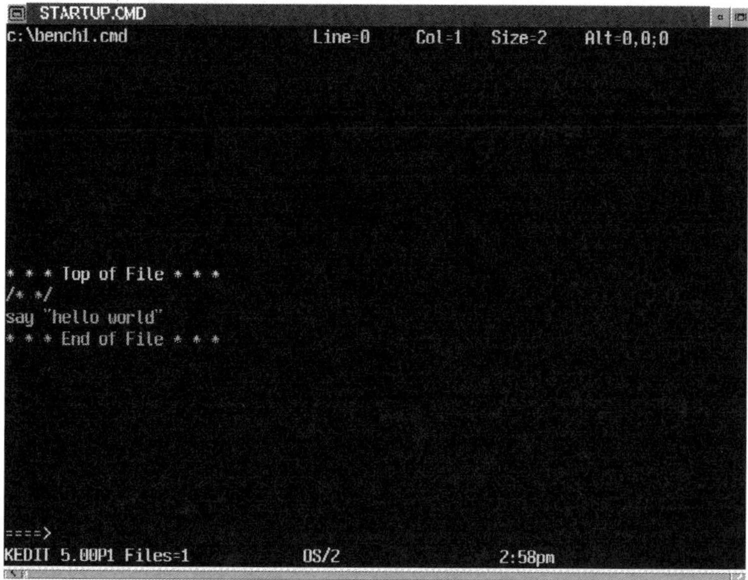

Figure 6-1 Existing File

Note that the bottom line then quickly changes to something like:

```
KEDIT 5.00P1 Files=1 OS/2   9.25pm
```

```
STARTUP.CMD
c:\kedit\a.cmd                    Line=0     Col=1   Size=0    Alt=0,0;0
New file...

* * * Top of File * * *
* * * End of File * * *

====>
KEDIT 5.00P1 Files=1              OS/2                2:59pm
```

Figure 6-2 New File

With MouseBar and ScrollBar enabled

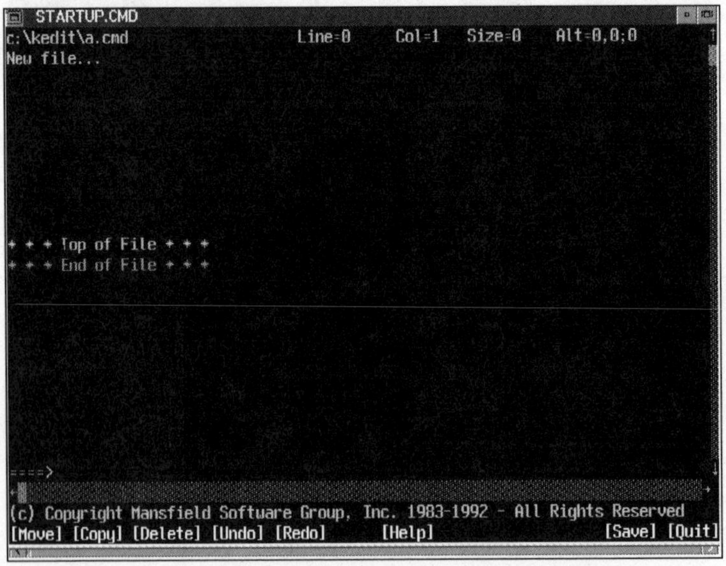

```
STARTUP.CMD
c:\kedit\a.cmd                    Line=0     Col=1   Size=0    Alt=0,0;0
New file...

* * * Top of File * * *
* * * End of File * * *

====>
(c) Copyright Mansfield Software Group, Inc. 1983-1992 - All Rights Reserved
[Move] [Copy] [Delete] [Undo] [Redo]      [Help]              [Save] [Quit]
```

Figure 6-3 KEDIT Screen with MouseBar/ScrollBar enabled

What are some of the components of these screens?

1. The top line is the **ID line**:

c:\bench1.cmd	Line =0	Col=1	Size=6	Alt=0,0;0
^	^	^	^	^
Filename (fileid)	Current line position	Current column position	Number of lines in file	0 changes since last save, 0 changes since last autosave, 0 levels of changes can be restored by UNDO.

2. The second top line is the **message line**. All warning, error and information messages are listed on this line. The screens above included the following example of a message line:

```
New file...
```

3. The next major portion of the screen is the file area:

```
* * * Top of File * * * – Top of file marker            -|
/* */                 | OS/2 REXX procedure              -|File area
say "hello world"     | OS/2 REXX procedure              -|
* * * End of File * * * – bottom of file marker         -|
```

Not shown above is the current line which is highlighted in a rectangular area. The current line is the first line in the REXX procedure.

4. =====> marks the location of the **command line.** This is where all KEDIT commands (including macro invocation) are entered. The Home key will place the cursor on the command line.

5. The last, but far from least important line is the status line. The screens above included two examples:

```
c) Copyright Mansfield Software Group. Inc. 1983-1992 - All Rights Reserved
                                  OR
KEDIT 5.00P1 Files=1  OS/2   9.25pm
```

The lists above show the copyright/version information, operating system, and current time.

6. If set scroll bar on and set mousebar on are issued (such as in PROFILE.KEX) then, a mousebar (really a mouse-activated menu) and scrollbar appears.

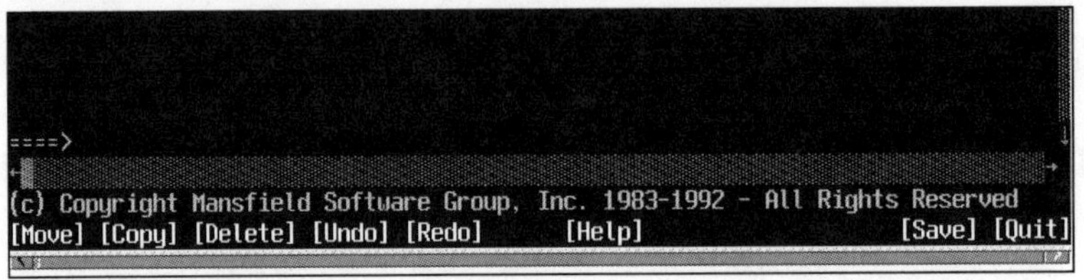

Figure 6-4 KEDIT Scrollbar

You may then use your mouse to select the appropriate action.

Line Operations

Not shown in using the prefix area (an area to the left or right of the text) where various line commands can be entered. These commands could be used instead of the above approach. The following summarizes KEDIT line editing operations.

1. Basic cursor operations:

   a. Use the arrow (up and down) keys to move the cursor up or down a line.

   b. Use PgUp and PgDn to scroll down or up in a file.

   c. Use Ctrl-PgUp and Ctrl-PgDn to scroll to the top or the bottom the file.

   d. Use F7 to move to the start of the current line and the End key to move to the end of the current line.

   e. Here are what other function keys do:

      F1 (help), F2 (insert), F3 (quit), F4 (tab), F5 (makes the cursor line the current line), F6 (Redisplay last line entered on the command line. Same thing as the ? command), F7 (places the cursor in the first column of the current line), F9 (Same as the = command. Reexecutes the last command.)

2. To **insert line(s)** press the F2 key as many times as needed:

Before

```
* * * Top of File * * *
* * * End of File * * *

Press F2 twice to enter two lines:
```

After

```
* * * Top of File * * *

* * * End of File * * *
/* Also can used the INPUT edit command at the command line*/
```

3. To **delete line(s)** use one of two methods:

```
a. line approach
```

Before

```
 * * Top of File * * *
Delete this line — Make sure the cursor is at this line.
Line will still be there
* * * End of File * * *

Press Alt-D
```

After

```
* * * Top of File * * *
Line will still be there
* * * End of File * * *

b. block approach.
```

Before

```
 * * Top of File * * *
Delete this line
Delete this line
* * * End of File * * *

Press Alt-L to mark the start of the block and Alt-L to mark the end of the block.
(Use the cursor [arrow keys] keys if needed to do this.) The text is then highlight-
ed. Then press Alt-G to delete the block.
```

After

```
* * * Top of File * * *
* * * End of File * * *
```

4. To **copy line(s)** use the following approach:

```
b. block approach.
                              Before

* * * Top of File * * *
Line 1
Line 2
Line 3
* * * End of File * * *

Press Alt-L to mark the start of the block and Alt-L to mark the end of the block.
(Use the cursor [arrow keys] keys if needed to do this.) The text is then highlight-
ed. Then press Alt-C at the location where you want the block copied to.

                              After

* * * Top of File * * *
Line 1
Line 2
Line 3
Line 1
Line 2
* * * End of File * * *
```

5. To **change a line of text**, use the following approach:

```
Press the Home key to get to the ==> (command) line.

enter c/from_string/to_string/ line1 line2

              or

change from_string/to_string/ line1 line2
     line 1 - Number of lines down
     line 2 - number of matches on a line to change.
e.g. change /business/profit/ * *
- changes all matches of a string from current position to the bottom of
the file

c/business/profit/all *
- changes all matches of a string in the file regardless of the current
position.

c/business/profit/
changes one match on the current line.
```

6. Use the LOCATE command to search for text:

```
Press the Home key to get to the ===> (command) line.
```

enter locate */string/* <u>or</u> */string*
— string matching is insensitive. Text is highlighted when found.

e.g. locate /profit/ <u>or</u> /profit

Macro Overview

To define a macro:

One-line macro

```
define aa 'status'     /* Defines the aa as an alias for the status command. */
                       /* Just enter aa on the command line to invoke. */
```

Multiple line macro

```
define aa 'status';'help rexx;'locate /KEDIT'

                        Multiple line macro in a.KEX file

macro aa /* invokes aa.kex */
[contains the lines:
      'status'
      'help rexx'
      'locate /KEDIT' ]
                                  OR
define aa.kex /* loads aa.kex into memory for faster execution */
```

Macro Libraries

These approaches are satisfactory for most macros. But, suppose you have many macros that must be stored and loaded at the same time. What do you do then? The solution is to use macro libraries. These are stored in a .KML file.

Macro Library Setup (EX1.KML)

```
:stu ——————————- Start of macro #1
'status'
:hlp ——————————— Start of macro #2
'help rexx'
:lct ———————————-Start of macro #3
'locate /KEDIT'

define ex1.kml /* load into memory */
       /* Then just enter stu, hlp, or lct at the command (===>) line */
```

Profile (Startup) Macros

A special type of KEDIT macro is called a profile macro. This macro is processed when KEDIT is initially invoked. Its major use is to customize the KEDIT environment. This can be done to the point where other users may not be able to use it or understand how it is set up! The default profile name is PROFILE.KEX, but you may enter KEDIT *edit_file* or PROFILE *new_prof* where *new_prof* is the named of alternative profile file. Use NOPROFILE to disable the profile from being processed.

The following example should give you an idea on some of the things that you can do with a profile macro:

```
/* PROFILE.KEX */
/* NOTE: The word set is optional */
'set scrollbar on'   /* Turn on a scrollbar for a mouse */
'set mousebar on'    /* Turn on a menubar */
'set color cmdline red on blue' /* Changes color of command line. Other */
                     /* areas to change are block (highlighted block) */
                     /* curline (current line), filearea (file area), mousebar */
                     /* msgline (message line) scrollbar, statarea (status area) */
'set synonym hrexx help rexx' /* builds an alias for help rexx named hrexx */
'set autosave 10'
/* Overrides the default an automatically saves your file after */
/* ten changes are made */
'set backup keep' /* Creates an automatic backup. The default is not to do this */
' set beep on 262 250'
/* Beep on error messages at 262 Hertz for 250 milliseconds */
'set border light green'   /* default is set border 0 — keeps the invocation color */
'set eapreserve critical'  /* Keeps extended attributes if they were set as */
                           /* critical. */
'set keyboard enhanced'    /* Other value on keyboard type is standard */
```

```
'set mouse on nohide'      /* Enables mouse and makes it visible at all times */
'set scale on'             /* Displays column number */
'set wordwrap on'          /* default off */
```

Don't forget to look in the SAMPLES subdirectory for the following sample macros:

PROFILEA.KEX	Sample profile macro
PROFILEB.KEX	More complicated version of PROFILEA.KEX. Shows examples of setting keyboard key definitions.
VMPROF.KEX	Creates a simulated XEDIT environment using KEDIT.
XPROFILE.KEX	Creates a customized menubar.

Also look at the section below on the extract statement for other ideas.

Macro Components

KEDIT edit macros are comprised of up-to-500 lines of KEXX statements. KEDIT macros cannot be used in the prefix area. Each line is a maximum of 250 characters. Statement cannot be continued on multiple lines. But, multiple statements can be on one line. **KEXX** is a subset of the REXX Version 4.00 language.

Here is an overview of the KEXX language:

1. KEXX supports the KEXX comment (*) as well as the REXX comment (/*..*/) statements.
2. REXX and KEXX symbols have identical syntax rules, especially on quoting numbers, compound symbols, operators, and literal strings. There are apparently no maximum KEXX symbol name or value length limits. Numbers can only be a maximum of nine digits long and supports only integer math.
3. KEDIT edit are placed in quotes and passed to the KEDIT "master environment". KEXX statements are not placed in quotes.
4. KEXX does not support the following "standard REXX components"

   The / (Divide) and the ¬ (not equals) operators.

   These instructions: ADDRESS, CALL ON/OFF... (rest of CALL supported), NUMERIC, OPTIONS, PROCEDURE EXPOSE (rest of PROCEDURE supported), PUSH, QUEUE, SELECT, SIGNAL, TRACE VALUE (rest of TRACE supported).

These functions: ADDRESS, B2X, CHARIN, CHAROUT, CHARS, CONDITION, DIGITS, ERRORTEXT, FORM, FORMAT, FUZZ, LINEIN LINEOUT, LINES, QUEUED, RANDOM, SOURCELINE, SYMBOL, TRACE, TRUNC, VALUE, X2B.

5. The following KEXX components offer slightly different results than their REXX counterparts:

   - PARSE SOURCE returns **OS/2 COMMAND a.kex**
   - PARSE VERSION returns **KEXX 5.00 31 May 1992**

   The DATE function supports the obsolete J (Julian) argument (just like Personal REXX).

   The second argument is not supported for C2D, D2C, D2X, X2D. Many of functions (also including C2X and X2C) can return smaller values than their REXX counterparts.

   The DATATYPE KEXX function does not support the B (binary), S (symbol), W (whole number), and X (hexadecimal) arguments.

   TRACE + (enables interactive tracing), - (disables interactive tracing)

6. The KEXX language has the following extensions of the REXX language:

   - These functions: *beep*(frequency,time in milliseconds) — beeps the speaker [identical to the REXXUTIL function described in Chapter 3], *dosenv*('env_var') — returns the value of an OS/2 environment variable [Similar to VALUE(OS2ENVIRONMENT) described in Chapter 3.] and *upper*(string) — converts a string to uppercase.
   - Over forty additional Boolean functions (1 if true, 0 if false) are supported. These are useful for condition testing (i.e. IF statements).

See Table 6-3 for some examples.

Table 6-3

Function	What it tests
ALT()	If file has had any modifications since the last SAVE.
BUTTON1() and BUTTON2()	If mouse button 1 or 2 had been pressed.
COMMAND()	If the cursor on the command line.
CURRENT()	If the cursor is on the current line.
EOF()	If the cursor is at the end of the file.
FILELINE()	If the cursor is not on the command line.
INBLOCK()	If the cursor is in a block (such as a copy).
SCROLLOCK()	If scroll lock is active.
SHIFT()	If shift key is active.
TOF()	If the cursor is at the top of the file.

7. The following KEDIT commands are particularly useful to KEXX edit macros:

   Query *keyword* will display the current value of a SET KEDIT, not OS/2 setting. Keywords are discussed in the profile section. Here is an example after the above profile is processed:

```
'query autosave'     /* Returns autosave 10 */
'query backup'       /* Returns backup keep */
'query beep'         /* Returns beep on 262 250 */
'query border'       /* Returns border bright green */
'query color'        /* Returns all color settings (26 lines) */
                     /* including color cmdline bright red on blue */
'query eapreserve'   /* Returns eapreserve critical */
'query keyboard'     /* Returns keyboard enhanced */
'query mouse'        /* Returns mouse on nohide right 500 100 */
                     /* right (right-handed mouse), 500 milliseconds */
                     /* (double click speed), 100 milliseconds */
```

```
                       /* scroll times */
'query mousebar'       /* Returns mousebar on */
'query scrollbar'      /* Returns scrollbar on both — both (both scrollbars) */
'query scale'          /* Returns scroll on m+1 (one above middle of */
                       /* screen) */
'query synonym'        /* Returns synonym on */
'query wordwrap'       /* Returns wordwrap on */
```

This KEDIT SET value can also be placed in a KEXX compound symbol using the **Extract** command. One of two formats are used:

Explicit

```
extract /mouse/
```

Implicit (useful for profiles)

```
if mouse.1() = 'ON' then do /* Turn on features if there is a mouse */
      'set mousebar on'
      'set scrollbar on'
end
```

Table 6-4 are other compound array "elements" that may be useful in KEXX macros:

Table 6-4

autosave.1	autosave number (setting)
backup.1	backup setting
beep.1	ON or OFF
border.1	border color
color.3	block color
color.6	cmdline color
color.9	curline color

Table 6-4 Continued

color.12	filearea color
color.13	highlight color
color.14	idline color
color.15	mousebar color
color.16	msgline color
color.20	scrollbar color
debugging.1	ON or OFF
eapreserve.1	eapreserve setting
macro.1	NOT SUPPORTED. use parse source instead.
mousebar.1	ON or OFF
opsys.1	Operating system name (OS/2)
opsys.2	Operating system version (2.10)
rexxversion.1	REXX interpreter: Returns REXX interpreter (such as REXXSAA or Personal REXX)
rexxversion.2	The version number (such as 2.1)
scrollbar.1	ON or OFF
shiftstate.1	ON or OFF
time.1	Date in local format
time.2	Time in hh:mm format
time.3	Date in mm-dd-yy format
time.4	Time in hh:mm.ss.ff

Table 6-4

version.2	KEDIT version number (e.g. 5.0)
version.3	KEDIT revision level and release date (such as P1 May 31 1992)
width.1	Width setting (default 512)
wordwrap.1	ON or OFF

SOS *command* processes cursor and edit operations. The following are some of the valid values of *command:*

ABORT: quits all opened files without saving.

ADDLINE: adds a blank line.

CURRENT: moves cursor to the current line.

EXECUTE: processes command on command line.

SAVE: saves the cursor position.

Three Sample Macros

Three sample macros are presented:

Example 1: Creating a dialog box

```
'dialog   /Put a value here/Title/Sample Dialog Box/EDITFIELD/a.txt'
          /* This looks more complicated than it actually is: */
          /* 'Put a value here' - The text above the edit */
          /* (field (user input) */
          /*   area */
          /* 'Title...Sample Dialog Box' - The title of the dialog box */
          /* EDITFIELD - sends that an edit field will be provided */
          /* This means that the OK and CANCEL buttons will be provided */
          /* a.txt - the default value of the edit field */
          /* Other keywords not shown above - OK or OKCANCEL or YESNO */
          /* or YESNOCANCEL - types of buttons allowed in the dialog box */
say dialog.1    /* lists user input placed into the edit field. Could then be */
                /* used for conditional testing for further edit operations */
say dialog.2    /* Lists the value of the key pressed to exit the dialog box */
                /* Such as OK, CANCEL, YES, or NO */
```

Figure 6-5 is what the dialog box looks like (with the cursor at the edit field):

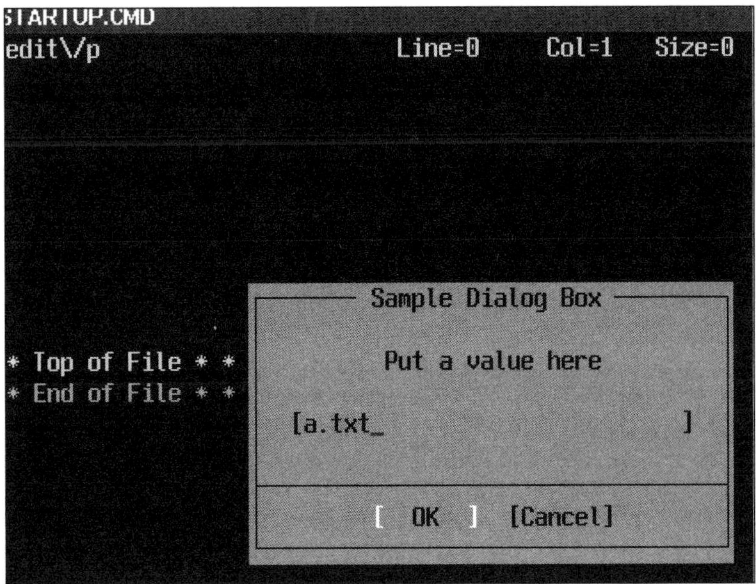

Figure 6-5 KEDIT Sample Dialog Box

Example 2: Deleting a selected range of lines

```
          /* If macro named ex2 entering macro ex2.kex 2 4 */
          /* would delete lines 2 through 4 */
arg line1 line2
          /* Assumes valid input for line1 and line2 */
          /* Line 1 - first line in range to delete */
     'cursor file' line1
          /* Moves the cursor to the specified line */
          /* Regardless where the current line is now */
          /* Note that KEXX variable is not in quotes */
     'sos makecurr'
          /* Then make this the current line */
     if cursor.3() = line1 then do
          /* If the specified line to delete is the current line... */
          lines = line2-line1 + 1
          /* Set the number of lines to delete */
          'delete' lines
          /* delete these lines */
     end
```

Example 3: Finding lines with a string, then changing them

```
say 'File' fname.1() 'has' size.1() 'lines'
      /* Implied extract returns something like File b has 10 lines */
cursor file' 1 1
      /* Moves the cursor to the first line and column */
'sos makecurr'
      /* Makes this the current line */
'change /windows/OS2/ * */
      /* Change all occurrences of windows (first *) on all lines (second *) */
      /* to OS2 */
```

Debugging Macros

Use the following techniques when resolving macros:

1. Use the PROFDEBUG invocation option when debugging those tricky profile problems.

```
KEDIT (PROFDEBUG
```

2. Instead of using the KEXX SAY command, use DMSG *message* to place a message in the debugging window — provided that SET DEBUGGING was previously issued.

3. To turn on debugging, use any of the following approaches:

   From the command line, issue SET DEBUGGING ON 15 I. This opens the debugging window and traces the macro in intermediate mode. The debugging window will be 15 lines long. (The default is 10 lines. SET is optional.)

   Then issue the DEBUG *macros*, with **macro** being the macroname.

   OR

   issue DEBUG /I *macro*

   Use a KEXX TRACE statement. This is identical to the REXX statement and its output discussed in Chapter 2. Unlike standard REXX (which supports the TRACE ? toggle), TRACE + enables interactive tracing and TRACE - disables it.

   OR

   Enter a DEBUG START *macro* to trace an in-memory macro and DEBUG STOP *macro* to disable tracing.

4. SET DEBUGGING OFF entered at the command line disables debugging.
5. Use the QUERY and EXTRACT commands to determine the current KEDIT settings.
6. See the REXX debugging section in Chapter 2 for an explanation and a sample of TRACE/DEBUG output.

Should I Use REXX Instead of KEXX?

Consider using REXX instead of KEXX when any of the following are a concern:

- You have sufficient memory to run both KEDIT and REXX.
- Fast execution speed is a concern.
- You need to develop a large macro.
- You need some REXX capability that is not available in KEXX.

Notes

1. If a *KEDIT SET REXXIO OFF* is issued, all input and output operations are handled by the REXX interpreter instead of KEDIT. This option may overwrite part of the KEDIT screen and is generally not recommended.
2. If a *SET KEDIT=PREXX20* OS/2 command is issued, KEDIT will use the Personal REXX instead of the OS/2 REXX interpreter.

Using THE — A Freeware XEDIT Editor

As I began writing this chapter, several products were or about to be distributed. One of these was THE (The Hessling Editor named after its creator Mark Hessling of Griffith University in Australia.) This editor is distributed with copyrighted source and uses the Curses screen interface. As part of the GNU software license, the software can be freely distributed and used with some versions currently available for DOS, UNIX, and MS-Windows. One thing that will strike KEDIT users is the similarity between the two products. This is true to the extent that much of the above information on KEDIT applies to THE with slight modification.

Invoking THE

To invoke THE, use any of the following formats from the OS/2 prompt: (Or, create an icon to invoke THE as discussed in Chapter 3.)

No Filename and Options

```
THE
/* Generates a directory listing similar to the one shown in a later exam-
ple. */.
```

No Options

```
THE a.txt /* Invoke THE with one or more files and no invocation options */
```

With options

```
THE -p a.prf -a 88 -w 2000 a.txt
        /* NOTE THAT OPTIONS MUST ALWAYS BE ENTERED IN */
        /* LOWERCASE */
        /* -p (Uses a profile instead of the default PROFILE.THE.) */
        /* -a (The command line arguments being passed to the profile) */
        /* - w (Maximum line width)
```

Directory listing

```
THE c:\os2
[Displays a directory listing similar to the following:
```

....(dir)	0	28-Jan-93 18:14	.
....(dir)	0	28-Jan-93 18:14	..
.a..	5655	9-Dec-92 21:43	ANSI.EXE

Press Alt X to edit a file or display a subdirectory.]

Invoking THE invokes one of the following screens:

A New File

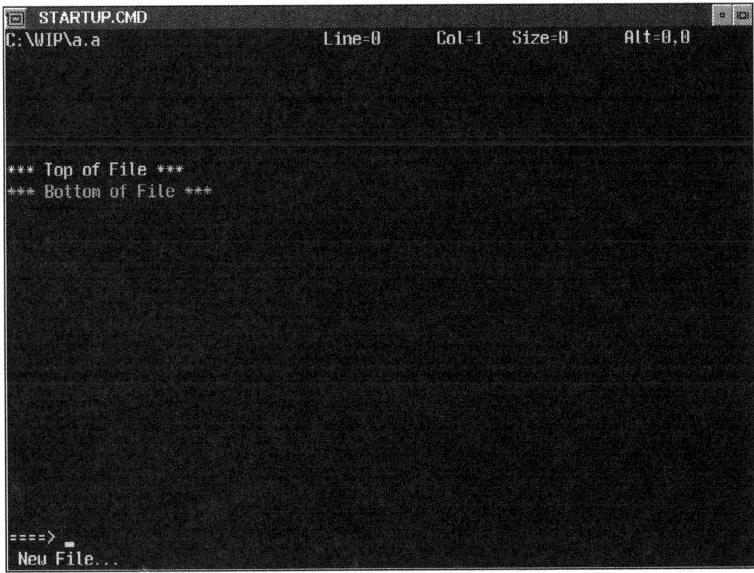

Figure 6-6 THE General Screen (new file)

An Existing File

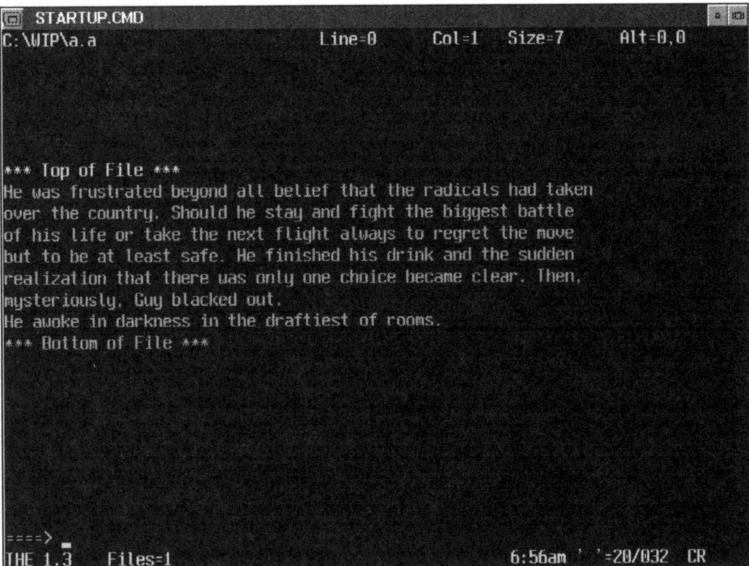

Figure 6-7 THE General Screen (existing file)

You can also use the following OS/2 environment variables:

MACROPATH: The search directory for THE to look for a macro file.

THE: The search path for the profile macro. The default is PROFILE.THE, which resides in the same directory or subdirectory as the THE executable.

THE_HELP: The search path for help file. The default is THE.HLP which resides in the same directory or subdirectory as the THE executable.

Interfacing THE with REXX

THE can directly use REXX edit macros. These are invoked by the macro *macroname* with *macroname* being the name of the REXX edit macro. Here are some tips for interfacing the two environments:

1. To issue a THE edit command within a REXX procedure, use the following format:

```
     address the 'extract /size/'
          /* Get the number of lines in a file */
          /* Note the ADDRESS THE interface to process edit commands */
OR
     'extract /size/'
          /* Address the is not required */
     say size.1
          /* Returns the number of lines in a file */
     say printer.1()
          /* Fails because implied extracts are not supported */
```

2. Note that in 1.3 and later implied extracts are supported.

3. Note that in-memory macros are not supported.

4. New in 1.1 is the capability to direct where REXX output goes. The syntax for this is the following:

```
address the 'set rexxoutput file' or address the 'rexxout display 500'

/* Note: SET is not needed and rexxoutput can be abbreviated to rexxout */
/* Output can be sent to an opened file if the FILE keyword is used. */
/* Or go to the screen (with scrolling) if the DISPLAY keyword is used. An */
/* number of lines may also be displayed. The default is to DISPLAY 1000 */
/* lines. The current setting can be found in the rexxoutput.1 EXTRACT array */
/* rexxoutput.2 has the value of display (if used) */
```

5. Use the REXX TRACE facility (described in Chapter 2) to debug REXX edit macros.

Using CTC's SPF/2

SPF/2 is a commercial ISPF-inspired editor that works under DOS and OS/2. Of particular interest is the capability to issue ISPF edit macros using OS/2 REXX. With the recent competition from Tritus Inc., it is likely that CTC will continue to enhance the product at a healthy rate.

Invoking SPF/2

Prior to version 3.0, you had to manually create an icon to invoke SPF/2. This process is discussed in Chapter 3. In version 3.0, this icon can be automatically created for you during installation. Use any of these approaches to invoke SPF/2 from the OS/2 prompt:

Into edit mode

```
spf2 a.txt
/* The location of the SPF2 executable should be added to your PATH */
/* statement during installation. Going to the actual directory. (SPF2 before */
/* version 3.0, SPFPC30 in version 3.0) */
```

With options

```
spf2 a.txt /Imacro.spf /Pkex.prf
       /* I — initial edit macro (with REXX statements) */
       /* Determines which edit profile to use. The default is to use */
       /* xxx.prf where xxx is the file name. Profiles include */
       /* information such as maximum file length, data format, count */
       /* 0.7 can be used to display/change a profile. */
       /* There are at least 20 profiles included with the product */

       /* Other options include /B (browse only), /K macro (processes */
       /* keyboard macro named macro), /T (trace of profile) */
```

With "jump" capability

```
spf2 =2 or spf2/2 or spf2 -2 /* all drop you in the edit entry screen. */
```

Exit SPF/2

```
Enter =x and any command ==> prompt. OR keep pressing F3 to exit.
```

There are many different menu options that space unfortunately does not allow us to discuss. These are 0 (SPF/2 parameters), 1 (browse), 3 (Utilities such as move, copy search), 4 (foreground to run various programs via a SPF panel), 6 (Execute a DOS command, C (Changes from the last release), T (Tutorial).

Once entering any of the above commands, the following screens appear:

[All screens are reproduced with the permission of Command Technology Corporation.]

EDIT ENTRY PANEL

```
SPF/PC(2)——————————————-Edit - Entry Panel ————————————V3.0
COMMAND ====>

Project File:
DRIVE ====>C
PATH ====>\spfpc30
PATH ====>
PATH ====>
NAME ====>a.prf
       (Blank or pattern for file selection list)

SYSTEM CUR DIR: C:\SPFPC30
SYSTEM FILE SPECIFICATION:
====>

PROFILE ====>
       (Blank defaults to file extension)

MAX RECL====> (1- 32000, new profile default = 80 )
IMACRO ====>
XMACRO ====>
```

EDIT SCREEN

```
EDIT C:\SPF\A.PRF———————————————————————COLUMNS 001 072
COMMAND ====>  SCROLL ====>CSR
****** *********************TOP OF DATA ******************************
000001 backup on
****** *********************BOTTOM OF DATA*****************************
```

The **Edit Entry Panel (Screen)** allows the user additional customization before editing a file. This includes: path and name (including blank or wildcards); profile name; maximum line length; an initial (startup or imacro) macro; and an exit macro (or xmacro). Note that the menu option selected (2) and the version of the product (3.0) also appear on the top line of screen.

The **Edit Panel (Screen)** displays the data in a file with a top and bottom of data text provided. Any edit primary commands can be entered in the command line ====>. Commands effecting one or more lines can be entered in columns 1-6 — also called the **line number area**. A scrolling amount may also be specified.

Getting Help About SPF/2

Pressing F1 at any panel will provide context-sensitive help about a panel. You may then explore further information about a topic.

Entering *SPF2/T* at the OS/2 prompt or =*T* on the command line ====> will place you at the start of the SPF/2 tutorial. You may then select information about a particular SPF menu option (such as 2 — EDIT) or select I for the tutorial Index.

Entering *SPF2/C* at the OS/2 prompt or =C on the command line will place you at the start of the changes tutorial which discusses recent enhancements to the SPF/2 product (i.e., topics include DOS and OS/2 compatibility, and XMACRO Edit Macro).

Additional information can be found in README.DOC including undocumented features, and MACROS.DOC (information about PDF edit macros in version 2.x) or REXX.DOC (information about PDF edit macros and a REXX reference in version 3.x) in the SPF2 (2.x) or SPFPC30 (3.x) subdirectory.

Nearly twenty-five documented edit macros are also provided. See the edit macro section later in this chapter for further information.

Basic Edit Operations

Here is a summary of the basic edit operations:

1. Here are some commonly used PC keys for edit operations:

   a. *PageUp* (scrolls up) and *PageDown* (scrolls down)

   b. *Ctrl-Page Up* (scrolls to the top of the file) and *Ctrl-Page Down* (scrolls to the bottom of the file) or enter M (on the command line) and then press *Page Up* or *Page Down* to do the same thing.

   c. Use the *arrow keys* to move up, down, left or right in either the line number or data areas.

   d. Each function key has a meaning: F1 (HELP — enters help menus) F2 (SPLIT — enters split screen), F3 (END — exit current screen), F5 (RFIND — "repeat find" a string in a file), F6 (RCHANGE — "repeat change" a string in a file), F7 (UP — scrolls up), F8 (DOWN— scrolls down), F10 (LEFT — scrolls left), F11 (RIGHT — scrolls right)

2. To *insert a line*, enter an I or i anywhere in the line number area:

Before

```
****** **********************TOP OF DATA****************************
I00001
****** **********************BOTTOM OF DATA*************************
```

After

```
****** **********************TOP OF DATA****************************
000001
...... <—- New Line
****** **********************BOTTOM OF DATA*************************
```

Then enter text and press Enter to make the line permanent, and you may then insert the next line. Just pressing Enter will "lose" the inserted line.

3. To *delete a line(s)*, use any of the following approaches:

   a. Entering **d** or **D** in the line number area will delete the specified line.

   b. Entering **DD** or **dd** in the line number area once at the start of the lines to delete and then at the end of the lines will delete them.

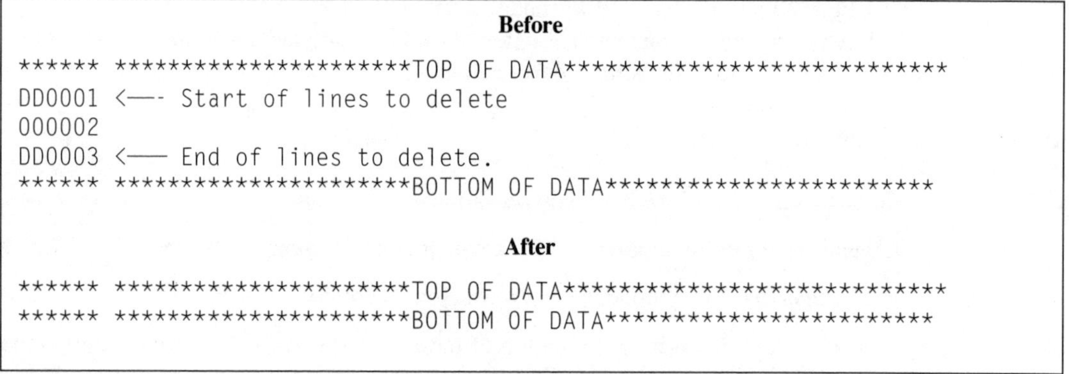

Before

```
****** **********************TOP OF DATA****************************
DD0001 <—- Start of lines to delete
000002
DD0003 <—— End of lines to delete.
****** **********************BOTTOM OF DATA************************
```

After

```
****** **********************TOP OF DATA****************************
****** **********************BOTTOM OF DATA************************
```

   c. Entering the **DELETE** command at the command line.

   For example: DELETE ALL NX to delete all lines. (Any excluded lines (i.e., to exclude a specified line, enter a X in the line number area) are saved.)

4. To perform *copy* operations, use any of the following approaches:

   a. Enter C in the line number area (the source line) and a B (before — the target line) or A (after) will copy a line.

   b. Enter CC in the line number area (the source lines) and a B (before — the target line) or A (after) will copy a line.

Before

```
****** *********************TOP OF DATA***************************
CC0001 1<—- Start of lines to copy
000002 2
CC0003 3 <—— End of lines to copy.
000004 4
****** *********************BOTTOM OF DATA************************
```

After

```
****** *********************TOP OF DATA***************************
000001 1
000002 2
000003 3
000004 4
000005 1<—- Start of copied lines.
000006 2
000007 3 <—— End of copied lines..
****** *********************BOTTOM OF DATA************************
```

   c. Entering on the command line COPY filename (such as c:\autoexec.bat) and an A (after) or B (before) on the desired line number will copy an entire file into the currently opened file.

   d. CUT (and CC commands in the line number area to mark the lines to cut) and PASTE commands (and A or B commands in the line number area to mark the target area) can also be used.

5. To *change the text* in a file, enter the CHANGE command on the command line.

   Here are some examples:

Change the next match

```
/* Quotes are optional if there are no embedded blanks or special characters */

change 'remote' 'demote' next OR change 'remote' 'demote'
```

Change all matches

```
change 'remote' 'demote' all
```

Change all matches in selected columns

```
change 'remote' 'demote' 1 10 all
```

   Once the line is changed, a ===CHG> will appear in the line number area for the specified line.

6. Use the *FIND command to find* matching text in a file.

Find next match

```
FIND 'remote' or FIND 'remote' NEXT
```

Find first match in a file

```
FIND 'remote' FIRST /* LAST keyword also available */
```

Find all matches in a file

```
FIND 'remote' ALL /* Press F5 to see additional matches */
```

The line number of the line with the matched line is highlighted.

Interfacing REXX With SPF/2: Using Edit Macros

SPF/2 supports the creation and execution of **edit macros**. An edit macro is a program written using SPF/2 commands. These macros are used to perform some specified edit task (usually repetitively) or to replace a built-in edit command. Edit macros either end with .SPF (SPF/2 and REXX commands only). There are three types of macros:

a. initial macros: Macros that are processed before an edited file is opened.

b. edit macros: Edit macros that can be processed within an open edited file.

c. exit macros: Macros that are processed before saving a file.

The mainframe version supported two additional types of macros:

- Program macros: Macros written in APL2, Assembler, C, COBOL, Fortran, PASCAL, and PL/I. This allows faster executionk, and various enhanced capabilities.
- Recover macros: These are edit macros that restore an edit macro after an edit session is unexpectedly aborted.

Invoking Macros

Use any of the following approaches to invoke an edit macro:

1. Enter the appropriate macro name in the imacro ====> (initial macro) or xmacro ====> (exit macro) fields of the Edit- Entry panel.
2. Once in edit, enter any of the following from the command (====>) line:
   - IMACRO *macroname:* Makes *macroname* the initial macro the next time a file with the same extension as the currently edited file is opened. This information is stored in the edit profile.
   - XMACRO *macroname:* Makes *macroname* the exit macro the next time a file with the same extension as the currently edited file is opened. This information is stored in the edit profile.

     Entering the name of edit macro without the extension — such as A for A.SPF accompanied by any parameters in the command line will also execute an edit macro.

   Note: Entering IMACRO NONE or XMACRO NONE will erase any currently defined IMACRO or XMACRO value for that particular file extension.

Macro Components

Note that in Version 3.0 and later, the first line of a macro skeleton must be a comment starting in column 1. The following is a typical macro skeleton:

Macro skeleton

```
/* All SPF2 statements must in be in quotes to avoid being viewed as a REXX */
/* instruction. */
1. /* */ – Required

2a. 'ISREDIT MACRO()'
arg val1 val2... /* lets REXX do the parsing */

                                OR

2b. 'ISREDIT MACRO (case, name)'
       /* Receives two parameters */

                                OR
2c. 'ISREDIT MACRO'
       /* No parameters */

3. Various parameter checking. For example:
       if val1 = '' then exit /* Checks if blank */

4. Then issue a series of edit macro (SPF/2) statements. These are:
'ISPEXEC command '
       /* Such things as displaying an error message or setting/retrieving */
       /* function keys and other values. */

                                OR

'ISREDIT command'

5. exit /* Exit the macro with an optional value */
```

Edit Macro Concepts

1. Macros can have an alias:

   Either enter *DEFINE* a *alias b* at the edit command line or in a macro '*ISREDIT define* a *alias b*: This command will define "a" as an alias for the macro b.spf.

2. Any line in a file can be defined with a character label, starting with a period followed by 1-8 characters composed of any valid letter. There are some pre-defined built-in macros.

   .ZF or .ZFIRST: first line in a file

   .ZL or .ZLAST: last line in a file

   .ZCSR: The current line that the cursor is pointing to.

Labels are used by commands such as CHANGE, COPY, CURSOR, DELETE, FIND, LINE_AFTER, LINE_BEFORE, LOCATE, MOVE, PROCESS, REPLACE, RESET, or SORT.

To assign a label in a macro, the following syntax is used:

```
'ISREDIT LABEL.ZCSR =.AAA' /* Label keyword on left */
```

To assign a label name to a REXX symbol, use the following syntax:

```
'ISREDIT (VAL1) = LABEL.AAA' /* Label keyword on the right */
```

2. There are three types of assignment statements. As we have seen above, a keyword may be placed on either side of an assignment statement:

   a. Command = Value/Setting

      Example — 'ISREDIT SCAN = ON' [setting = ON or OFF] and 'ISREDIT IMACRO = TT' [value = name of edit macro]

      Under SPF/2, the equal sign is usually optional for this type of assignment statement.

   b. (Symbol) = Command

      Example — 'ISREDIT (scanset) = SCAN'

      /* Assigns to the REXX symbol scanset the current SCAN setting */

   c. (Symbol1, Symbol2) =Command

      Example — 'ISREDIT (fcol,lcol) = DISPLAY_COLS'

      /* Assigns to the REXX symbols fcol and lcol the settings of */

      /* DISPLAY_COLS */

      Other commands using this format are AUTOSAVE, BOUNDS, CHANGE_COUNTS, CURSOR, DISPLAY_LINES, EXCLUDE_COUNTS, FIND_COUNTS, FLOW_COUNTS, HEX, LABEL, NUMBER, SEEK_COUNTS, and TABS.

3. To debug macros

   - Issue SAY instructions to see a) which line a label is pointing to (if any), b) the value of a variable, c) how far you got in a macro, and d) the return code of an edit macro statement (RC).

- Or use the REXX Trace facility as described in Chapter 2 or PMREXX as described in Chapter 3 to aid in debugging the REXX procedure.
- Use the MONITOR macro shown a little later on.

4. You may want your initial macros to do the following:
   a. Set various mode setting (i.e., CAPS, HEX, NULL).
   b. Retrieve SPF/2 variables setting (i.e., VGET).
   c. Determine the initial cursor setting.
   d. Execute any nested macros.
   e. Define any macro aliases.
5. You may want your exit macros to do the following:
   a. Save any SPF/2 variable settings (i.e., VPUT).
   b. Save the various mode settings.
   c. Save the current cursor setting.
6. Any edit macro can use REXX to provide any of the following:
   a. exception handling
   b. flow control instruction (including conditional testing and looping)
   c. labels
   d. parsing and string handling
   e. mathematical operations
   f. input/output operations
   g. execution of "foreign" (such as OS/2 or another application) commands

Sample Edit Macros

Here are three examples of edit macros. These are slightly modified versions of those appearing in my first book, TSO/E *Clists*!

Number of lines in a file

```
/* */
'ISREDIT MACRO'
'ISREDIT (FIRST) = LINENUM.ZF'
       /* Set REXX symbol to number of first line */
'ISREDIT (LAST) = LINENUM.ZL'
       /* Set REXX symbol to the value of the last line */
DIFF = LAST - FIRST + 1
       /* Now find line number and print it */
Say 'Number of lines in a file is' DIFF /* OR */
ZEDSMSG = 'Lines =' DIFF
       /* Short message. This may be up to 24 characters enclosed in single */
       /*     quotes. This appears in the far right side of the */
       /*     first line (i.e. where columns 001 072 appears) */
ZEDLMSG = 'Lines are' DIFF /* Not required*/
       /* Long Message. This may be up to 78 characters enclosed in single */
       /*     quotes. Displayed on the third line of a panel */
       /*     (i.e. the blank line under the command line). Can be */
       /*    seen if the user presses the F1 (help key) */

'ISPEXEC SETMSG MSG(ISRZ000)'
       /* Display short message using a pre-determined message id */
'ISPEXEC VPUT DIFF'
       /* Places in the edit profile so can be remembered the next time */
       /* the file is open. To retrieve put a 'ISPEXEC VGET DIFF' in the */
       /* macro. System variables include ZPFxx -where xx is the function */
       /* key number*/
```

Find a string and delete a line

```
/* */
'isredit macro'
'isredit number off'
'isredit find "a string" all'
       /* find the string 'a string' */
'isredit (fc,lc) = find_counts'
       /* capture number of matches — fc */
counts = strip(fc,,0)
       /* strip the leading zeros */
cnts = 1
do while cnt <= counts
       /* Do until all matched lines are processed */
       'isredit find "a string" '
       /* Find each match */
       rcc = rc
```

```
       if rcc = 0 then do
       /* If found then label and delete line */
       'isredit label.zcsr =.aaa'
       /* Assigns a label to the matched line */
       'isredit delete .aaa.aaa'
       /* Then delete the line */
       cnt = cnt + 1
       /* Increment counter */
       end
       if rcc = 4 then cnt = counts + 1 /* For those weird cases when the */
        /* the macro is still searching when it shouldn't */
end
       'isredit end'
       /* End the edit macro and save the file */
       cnt = cnt - 1
       /* Adjust counter */
       say 'A string found' cnt 'times'
       /* Display count */
       exit
```

Monitor macro

```
/* */
isredit macro'
lblset:
       'isredit (zc) = linenum.zcsr'
       'isredit (zf) = linenum.zfirst'
       'isredit (zl) = linenum.zlast'
       say '   LABEL SETTINGS'
       say '.ZCSR (Current position)       ' zc
       say '.ZFIRST (First line)    ' zf
       say '.ZLAST (Last line)      ' zl

dcbset:
       'isredit (bs)        = blksize'
       'isredit (dn)        = dataset'
       'isredit (dw)        = data_width'
       'isredit (ll)        = lrecl'
       'isredit (dc) = data_changed'
       say '   FILE CHARACTERISTICS'
       say ' Block Size     '      bs
       say ' File Name      '      dn
       say ' File Width     '      dw
       say ' File logical record size            ll
       say ' File changed?   ' dc
```

```
modeset:
       'isredit (ca) = caps'
       'isredit (h1,h2)     = hex'
       'isredit (a1,a2)     = autosave'
       say ' MODE SETTINGS'
       say ' Caps mode       ' ca
       say ' Hex mode        '      h1 h2
       say ' Autosave mod    '      a1 a2

othset:
       'isredit (fc,lc)     = display_cols'
       'isredit (fl,sl)     = display_lines'
       'isredit (al,ac)     = cursor'
       say '.  OTHER SETTINGS'
       say ' Columns on screen      ' fc '-' lc
       say ' Lines on screen ' fl '-' sl
       say ' Cursor position' al ',' ac

Displayed:
       LABEL SETTINGS
.ZCSR (Current position)    000000
.ZFIRST (First line) 000001
.ZLAST (Last line)   000013
       FILE CHARACTERISTICS
Block size     000080
File Name      C:\SPF2\A.A
File Width     080
File logical record size    080
File changed   NO
       MODE SETTINGS
Caps Mode      OFF
Hex Mode       OFF
Autosave Mode ON NOPROMPT
       OTHER SETTINGS
Columns on screen    001 - 072
Lines on screen      000001 - 000013
Cursor position      000001, 000
```

Using Tritus SPF

1993 brought the production release (1.2) of Tritus SPF. Features of Tritus SPF 1.2.5 which was just released:

- Edit macro optimization.
- Nested edit macro capability.
- CUT/PASTE Support.

The forthcoming release promised the capability of building full-screen applications. It is similar to CTC SPF/2 with subtle differences. (Please read the section on SPF/2 for a broader understanding.) This chapter will focus on the unique features of this product.

[All screens are reproduced with the permission of Tritus Inc.]

Invoking Tritus SPF (TSPF)

Tritus SPF (TSPF for short) resides in the TSPF12 subdirectory by default. At the OS/2 prompt use any of the following approaches to invoke TSPF: (You can also create an icon to invoke TSPF as discussed in Chapter 3.)

```
                          No filename or options
TSPF2

/* Drops you at the TSPF primary menu */
                              With filename
TSPF2 FF.SPF
/* Drops you in the edit screen for FF.SPF */

                            Using jump option
TSPF2 2. or TSPF2 =2
/* Drops you in the edit entry panel */

                              With options
TSPF /p_default.epr /iff.spf c:\tspf12\a.a
/* Overrides the default profile (being _ext.EPR with ext being the extension */
/* of the edited file) and specifies an initial macro of ff.spf. */
                                EXIT TSPF
Enter =X at the command line of each screen or Press F3 as many times as needed to
exit TSPF.
```

/? will list all of the invocation options.

The following screens are then displayed:

EDIT ENTRY PANEL

```
---------------------- Edit - Entry Panel ----------------------
COMMAND        ====>

Project File:
DRIVE          ====>C
PATH           ====>tspf12 ====>   ====>
FILENAME       ====>*        (Blank filename.ext for all files)
EXTENSION      ====>prf

Current directory C:\TSPF12
OS/2 FILENAME:
====>

PROFILE NAME   ====>         (Blank defaults to file extension)

MAXIMUM LRECL  ====> (1- 32000, New profile default = 250 )
INITIAL MACRO  ====> EXIT MACRO ====>
----------------------------------------------------------------
TSPF             512K .2... 02/15
----------------------------------------------------------------
```

EDIT SCREEN

```
EDIT C:\TSPF12\A.PRF-----------------COLUMNS 00001 00072
COMMAND ====>  SCROLL ====>CSR
****** ********************TOP OF DATA *****************************
000001 backup on
****** ********************BOTTOM OF DATA***************************
----------------------------------------------------------------
SPF              512K .4...  02/15
----------------------------------------------------------------
```

Getting On-line Help on Tritus SPF

You can get Tritus SPF in the following areas:

1. Until the release of 2.0 becomes available, there is no online tutorial available.
2. Look at the .DOC files and the C(hanges) option of Tritus SPF for further information (such as undocumented and recent features).

3. There are several examples of REXX edit macros included. These examples end with either a .REX or .SPF extension. An example is COUNSTR.REX which counts all matches of a string.
4. The file TSPANEL12.PDS has examples of panel definitions and REXX procedures used to run them. See below for further information on accessing this file.
5. Entering TSPF2/? to list the invocation options.

Here is additional information about Tritus SPF:

1. TSPF can use the values of OS/2 environment variables. These include:

Environment variable	What it does
TSPFPATH	Location of TSPF executable
TSPFOPT	Invocation options

2. TSPF includes some useful utilities:

TPDS ? — lists options TPDS tpanel12.pds /l Or do this under foreground (Option 4 on the primary menu)	TSPF supports partitioned data sets — that is a dataset that is comprised of multiple members (which are sequential files). This is a mainframe carryover. Two PDS are included with the product: TPANEL12.PDS (the panels, messages, and REXX procedures used by TSPF) and TFONTS12.PDS (TSPF Fonts).
TSPFDUMP	Formats a dump file
MEMTEST	DOS program to check memory. Related DOS utilities include EMS, XMS, and MAPMEM.
TPANRLDC	Removes the box graphics from text files. Enter TPANRLDC to find out further information.

3. The main (primary) menu includes the following options:

   0 (Parameters such as 0.3.7 keyboard rate), 1 (Browse), 2 (Edit), 3 (Utilities. This will be greatly enhanced in 2.0), 4 (foreground such as invoking a compiler or listing the members of a .PDS file.) 5 (system info — such as PC type), 6 (command — enter OS/2 command), V (view — a variant of browse), and X (exit).

4. Here are some commonly used PC keys for edit operations:

   a. *PageUp* (scrolls up) and *PageDown* (scrolls down)

   b. *Ctrl-Page Up* (scrolls to the top of the file) and *Ctrl-Page Down* (scrolls to the bottom of the file) or enter M (on the command line) and then press Page Up or Page Down to do the same thing.

   c. Use the *arrow keys* to move up, down, left or right in either the line number or data areas.

   d. Each function key has a meaning: F1 (HELP — enters help menus) F2 (SPLIT — enters split screen), F3 (END — exit current screen), F5 (RFIND — "repeat find" a string in a file), F6 (RCHANGE — "repeat change" a string in a file), F7 (UP — scrolls up), F8 (DOWN — scrolls down), F10 (LEFT — scrolls left), F11 (RIGHT — scrolls right)

Interfacing REXX with TSPF

See the section on CTC's SPF/2 for further information on editing macros.

Here is some additional information on interfacing REXX with TSPF:

1. The following extensions are used by TSPF

.Extension	How used
.PAN	PDF Panel definition
.PRX	Program to run PDF panel (REXX and ISPEXEC).
.REX	Edit macro with REXX and TSPF statements (ISREDIT and ISPEXEC).
.SPF	Edit macro with REXX and TSPF statements (ISREDIT and ISPEXEC).

2. Note that .REX and .SPF programs have a 32K size limit.
3. TSPF may yield strange results when used with Personal REXX. (Personal REXX must have REXX.DLL removed to work correctly and TSPF requires this file.)
4. TSPF supports nearly identical ISREDIT and ISPEXEC statements discussed in the earlier section on SPF/2. To use such statements, use the following format in your .REX and .SPF files:

```
'ISREDIT command '
'ISPEXEC command '
```

5. A discussion on REXX procedures processing panels is not included since this interface will radically change in the forthcoming 2.0 release.
6. TSPF supports the BUILTIN command, such as BUILTIN COPY. This allows you to replace the COPY (or any edit command) with your own customized version of this command (i.e., COPY.SPF).
7. To invoke edit macros, use any of the following approaches:
   a. Enter the appropriate macro name in the initial macro ====> or exit macro ====> fields of the Edit - Entry panel.
   b. Once in edit, enter any of the following from the command (====>) line:

      IMACRO *macroname:* Makes *macroname* the initial macro the next time a file with the same extension as the currently edited file is opened. This information is stored in the edit profile.

      XMACRO *macroname:* Makes *macroname* the exit macro the next time a file with the same extension as the currently edited file is opened. This information is stored in the edit profile. **This is not supported in 1.2.**

      Entering the name of edit macro without the extension (such as A for A.SPF) accompanied by any parameters in the command line will also execute an edit macro.

      Note: Entering IMACRO NONE or XMACRO NONE will erase any currently defined IMACRO or XMACRO value for that particular file extension.

Sample Macros

All of the macros that were created for the SPF/2 example were run under TSPF. The following changes were made in order to make the work under TSPF:

1. First example: Counting number of lines in a file — NO CHANGES.
2. Second example: Find a string and delete a line:
   a. Use 'isredit seq off' instead of 'isredit num off' before the first FIND statement else the FIND command (and the rest of the macro) will not work correctly.
3. Third example — lists edit macro/file settings:
   a. Eliminate all statements with AUTOSAVE. This is apparently not supported in this release.
   b. HEX settings are stored in only one variable:

```
'isredit (hl) = hex'
....
'say 'Hex mode        ' hl
```

This displays the following : note this is the same file used with SPF/2 but with different results!

```
                                            LABEL SETTINGS
.ZCSR (Current position)                    000000
.ZFIRST (First line)                        000001
.ZLAST (Last line0                          000013
                                            FILE CHARACTERISTICS
Block size                                  00400
File Name                                   C:\SPF2\A.A
File Width                                  00250
File logical record size                    00250
File changed                                NO
                                            MODE SETTINGS
Caps Mode                                   OFF
Hex Mode                                    OFF
Autosave Mode                               ON NOPROMPT
                                            OTHER SETTINGS
Columns on screen                           00000 -00000
Lines on screen                             00000000 - 00000000
Cursor position                             00000000, 00000
```

INTERFACING REXX WITH THIRD-PARTY PROGRAMMING UTILITIES AND LANGUAGES.

Various OS/2 commercial and shareware developers have built some interesting interfaces and extensions to the REXX language. These vendors include well-known companies like Borland, Lotus, and Watcom.

Using REXX with Lotus Tech Pack

In 1991 Lotus released a copyrighted freeware OS/2 1-2-3 "add-in" named Lotus 1-2-3 for OS/2 Release 1.1 Tech Pack. This package (with C source code and a generous number of REXX examples included), among other things, allows OS/2 users to create new functions and macros using REXX procedures. This product was released on an "as is" basis and may not be supported in the future. Lotus resources are instead being placed in developing a "macro (i.e., command) language" that will be used across the entire Lotus line of products that should be out in 1994. (However, the latest release of AMIpro for OS/2 now supports REXX.) This section assumes that you are familiar with 1-2-3 for OS/2.

Using REXX procedures allows for:

- Better string handling capabilities
- Better access to OS/2 operations (through the REXXUTIL external functions).
- Potential portable macros and functions. If Lotus adds REXX support to MS-DOS and MS-Windows. Lotus, are you listening?

Invoking the Lotus Tech Pack/Tech Pack Overview

Tables 6-6, and 6-7 are the REXX components of the Tech Pack:

REXX 1-2-3 Functions

```
@REXX("procedure log",arglæargn)
@REXXD("procedure log",arg1,argn) — used for recalculations
Examples:
REXXABRV.CMD — Tests if word is an abbreviation in a range.
REXXARGS.CMD — Returns number of arguments.
REXXDISK.CMD — Returns free disk space.
REXXMATH.CMD — Performs arithmetic operation.
```

Table 6-6 REXX 1-2-3 Functions

REXX 1-2-3 Macros

```
{REXXV "procedure log",value1..valuen} – Value(s)
{REXXR "procedure log",range1..range2} – Range
{REXXRV "procedure log",range1..rangen,value} – Range and Value

External Functions that can be used by REXX 1-2-3 Macros:
Display123Error("error message") – Displays error in a window
Get123Cell(range, sheet, column, row) – Retrieves cell value
Set123Cell(range, sheet, column, row) – Assigns cell value
Examples:
REXXADD.CMD  – Increments value to each cell in a range. Uses REXXRV.
REXXEMSG.CMD – Displays specified text as an error message. Uses REXXRV.
REXXPRSE.CMD – Parses a column into a range of cells. Uses REXXRV
```

Table 6-7 REXX 1-2-3 Macros

Table 6-8 are also files that may be of interest:

Table 6-8

CHAP3.TXT	Describes the REXX components of the Tech Pack.
REXXLINK.C, REXXLINK.DEF, REXXLINK.MAK, REXXLINK.MAP, REXXLINK.OBJ	Source files needed to create the REXXLINK.DLL (You also need REXXSAA.H from the DEVELOPER'S TOOLKIT installed. See Chapter 3 for more information on this header file.)
REXXLINK.DLL	The dynamic link library that contains all of the above functions and macros.
REXXLINK.WG2	Sample spreadsheet using these above macros and functions.

To use any of the functions and macros, first register the dynamic link library within 1-2-3.

```
                              Load REXXLINK
{library-attach rexxlink} — Command stored as a macro.
                              Unload REXXLINK
{library-detach rexxlink}
```

REXX 1-2-3 Functions

Here is an overview of the functions:

1. All functions return these codes:

   -3 Unknown REXX procedure

   -4 User interruption of the REXX procedure processing.

   -5 Out of memory, disk space

2. These functions are not supported a) double byte characters, b) data length (buffer overrun) and numeric precision checking, and c) full checking of return codes from other functions.

@REXX

Purpose: Call a REXX procedure using a 1-2-3 function

Arguments: First argument (in quotes). The name of the REXX procedure. It must reside in a PATH or the current directory. A path may be specified (any extension can be used.) An optional log file may be specified to store the result of REXX output operations (i.e., SAY and TRACE). This is the only way to perform output operations (but at the price of slowing down overall performance.)

Second-... arguments: Up-to-20 arguments may be passed to be used by the REXX procedure. These are separated by commas. An argument can be a range of cells. These are accessed within the REXX procedure as compound symbol array elements (e.g. RANGE3.1, RANGE3.2, etc.) The .0 element (such as RANGE3.0) has the number of cells in a range and the stem such as RANGE1 holds the values of the entire range.

Example: @REXX("REXXPROC.CMD LOG.LOG",name,age)

Tips/Traps

1. Returned strings may include 1-2-3 cell justification prefixes (i.e., " or ^)
2. Data will be unexpectedly truncated if a number is used in a procedure that is larger than 32-integers — has no decimal value or 64-bits (floating — has a decimal value).
3. A REXX or REXXD function can call any other 1-2-3 function.
4. Use a macro (listed below) if you wish to manipulate a cell(s). Use REXX or REXXD if you wish to retrieve information about a cell(s).

@REXXD

Purpose: Call a REXX procedure using a 1-2-3 function during recalculation operations. (i.e., is always dirty).

Arguments: Same as @REXX

Example: @REXXD("REXXPROC.CMD LOG.LOG",name,age)

See the four sample REXX procedures for further information: REXXABRV.CMD, REXXARGS.CMD, REXXDISK.CMD, and REXXMATH.CMD.

REXX 1-2-3 Macros

Another powerful capability is the ability to create 1-2-3 macros that are using REXX procedures. The following is an overview of doing this:

1. There are three 1-2-3 macros that do this:

{REXXR}

Purpose: Allows a REXX procedure to be invoked a macro, specifying the arrange of cells to manipulate.

Arguments: First argument (in quotes). The name of the REXX procedure. It must reside in a PATH or the current directory. A path may be specified (any extension can be used). An optional log file may be specified to store the result of REXX output operations (i.e., SAY and TRACE). This is the only way to perform output operations (but at the price of slowing down overall performance.)

Second-third arguments. 1 or 2 arguments may be passed to be used by the REXX procedure. These are separated by commas. An argument is a range of cells. These are accessed within the REXX procedure as compound symbol array elements (e.g. RANGE3.1, RANGE3.2, etc.) The .0 element (such as RANGE3.0) has the number of cells in a range and the stem such as RANGE1 holds the values of the entire range.

Example: {REXXR "REXXPROC.CMD LOG.LOG",RANGE1}

Tips/Traps

1. Use any of these macros if you wish to manipulate a cell(s). Use the REXX or REXXD functions to retrieve information about a cell(s).

{REXXRV}

Purpose: Allows a REXX procedure to be invoked a macro, specifying the arrange of cells to manipulate and an optional value.

Arguments: First and second arguments. Look at the explanation under {REXXR}

Third argument is a value. This is either a string, number, or type (such as NA or ERR).

Example: {REXXRV "REXXPROC.CMD LOG.LOG",RANGE1,VALUE1}

{REXXV}

Purpose: Allows a REXX procedure to be invoked a macro, specifying the values to change.

Arguments: First argument. Look at the explanation under {REXXR}.

Second and third argument is a value. This is either a string, number, or type (such as NA or ERR). The third argument is optional.

Example: {REXXV "REXXPROC.CMD LOG.LOG",VALUE1,VALUE2}

2. Any of the macros ({REXXV}, {REXXR}, {REXXRV}) may include the following 1-2-3 external functions in the REXX procedure being invoked:

CALL DISPLAY123ERROR "This is an error message"

Purpose: Displays a specified 123 Error Message in a Dialog Box.

CALL GET123CELL"RANGE1", sheet, column, row, "NA"

Purpose: Retrieves the value of a cell at the specified worksheet, column, and row.

Arguments include range of cell (first — the stem name), worksheet (second), column and row (third and fourth) and type (fifth. Values include: EMPTY [empty cell], ERR [error in cell. Seen by 1-2-3 as an empty cell], NA [error in cell. Seen by 1-2-3 as an empty cell], NUMBER [Either an integer (has no decimal) or floating value (has a decimal.]

CALL SET123CELL"RANGE1", sheet, column, row, "NA",value1

Purpose: Assigns a value to a cell at the specified worksheet, column, and row.

Arguments are identical to GET123CELL and also includes a sixth argument that sets a new cell value. (So value1 in the above example would have been assigned a value in an earlier REXX assignment clause.)

Returns: 0 (unchanged value), 1 (value changed)

Tips and Traps

1. An extension of SET123CELL is SET123RANGE. Its arguments are identical to SET123CELL but you can specify as many additional value/type pairs as needed.

   CALL SET123RANGE "RANGE1", sheet, column, row, "NA",value1,NA,value2

   Since this function does not appear in the documentation but does appear in the examples and C source, it is unclear if this function is recommended for use or not.

2. If a function gives a return code of 40, it is due to a syntax error.

Using REXX with Borland's ObjectVision

1992 was both a good and a bad year for ObjectVision. In June, ObjectVision 2.0 for OS/2 was released. The product originally came out on MS-Windows. Among other things, it offered REXX support for OS/2, and an interface to OS/2 Database Manager. See Seltzer (1992). A cautiously positive review came out in September of that year (Crenshaw 1992). That same month, complimentary copies of ObjectVision were given out to all attendees of the OS/2 Developer Conference in New York. As late as November 30 of that year, Borland was discussing future releases. ObjectVision 3.0 was to go into beta at the end of 1992 and was to be bundled with a third-party report writer. Features included ties to other languages and the ability to develop custom objects. 4.0 was to have a dBASE-compatible code generator (Moser 1992b).

Shortly thereafter, Borland in a major organization move, either let go or reassigned the ObjectVision staff to concentrate on its major business of databases (Moser 1992c). The future of the product is uncertain, but support continues to exist. However, Borland will soon offer migration tools to other Borland products (like Paradox).

What is ObjectVision?

ObjectVision is a visual application tool (i.e. you visually create the application — a kind of visual flow chart) that can be used for prototyping, and "quick and dirty" applications. Unfortunately, ObjectVision applications are not portable. Perhaps in time some of the Visual REXX products will include these capabilities. The major advantages of the product are the following:

1) Changes can be made without compiling.
2) Compatibility with the Windows product. However, REXX applications cannot be used with the Windows product.
3) "Smart" Forms can include graphics. Rules can be built to determine the relationship between the various fields on a form, including automatic updating when a related field is modified.
4) Network and external database support for products such as Paradox, dBASE.
5) Free runtime license.

The Vocabulary of ObjectVision

Part of the learning curve for ObjectVision is understanding the vocabulary needed for developing applications. Here are the major terms used:

- Application: An .OVD file that contains a stack (which in turn contains one or more forms).
- Field: Where data is inputted or displayed. Fields can hold one or more values.
- Form: The major component of an ObjectVision application. This is similar to the idea of paper forms.
- Object: Something that appears in a form. Can be a field, text, or table (i.e., a multi-valued field). Objects can have different attributes such as color, size, font, etc.
- Stack: A collection of forms in an application (.OVD file)
- Tree: A graphic view of the appropriate processing that will take place when a change takes place on an object.

Getting Help about ObjectVision

Here are some places that you find information and ideas about ObjectVision:

1. Borland has a TechFax service that includes information about ObjectVision and other Borland products. Call 800-822-4269. Look at information about ObjectVision under programming languages.

2. Borland also has an electronic bulletin board that operates at 2400 baud only. It can be reached by calling 408-439-9096.

3. Borland has a healthy amount of information on various paid on-line services. These include BIX (Enter JOIN BORLAND), CompuServe (enter GO BORLAND), and GEnie (Enter BORLAND).

4. An on-line context-sensitive help is provided.

5. Two third-party books exist on ObjectVision. They are:

   Allen G. Taylor 1992 *OBJECTVISION 2.0 DEVELOPERS GUIDE*, Bantam Electronic Publishing

   Arnold & Edith Shulman/Robert Marion Jr. 1992 *OBJECTVISION 2 SELF-TEACHING GUIDE*, John Wiley & Sons, Inc.

6. Here is a sample of the files available on CompuServe: (Note that far more files deal with the MS-Windows version than the OS/2 version.)

On OSUSER LIB4

REXXOV.ZIP/Bin Bytes: 3033, 22-Aug-92

Description: Two simple ObjectVision applications demonstrating the ObjectVision REXX hooks. SEEK.OVD is a simple clone of the OS/2 Seek and Scan applet. ADDTYPE.OVD adds new associated types to the system and displays the currently defined associated types. Neither of these are particularly sophisticated, but they show some of the things you can do with the REXX support.

ON BORLAND LIB6

AUTO2.ZIP/Bin Bytes: 7449, 13-Nov-92

Description: This application demonstrates three things. How to auto-number an invoice, a table column, safe guard against storing extra items in the detail link and how to delete an item.

AUTONM.ZIP/Bin Bytes: 8948, 09-Dec-91

Description: Demonstrates how to autonumber OV table objects. This is a modified version of ORDER.OVD — one of the demo apps included with ObjectVision 2.0.

CALNDR.ZIP/Bin Bytes: 21193, 10-Mar-92

Description: CALNDR.ZIP is a sample calendar application created with ObjectVision version 2.0. It calculates the correct location, and day for each day of the year from Jan-1-1899 to 2000. It compensates for 31 and 30 day months, as well as leap year. It also demonstrates the use of the @EXECUTE function in OVLOOPS.DLL

DEMOS1.ZIP/Bin Bytes: 7680, 13-Apr-92

Description: This file contains four sample ObjectVision 2.0 apps that demonstrate one-to-many relationships, secondary lookups, linked comboboxes, same buttons on many forms, string and variable concatenation and more.

GUIDE.ZIP/Bin Bytes: 885, 18-Jan-92

Description: ObjectVision version 2.0, demonstration of how to alter guided completion.

LOCATE.ZIP/Bin Bytes: 2734, 18-Jan-92

Description: ObjectVision version 2.0 locate example. Demonstrates how to locate using one or two locate fields.

OVDTRE.ZIP/Bin Bytes: 70102,10-Mar-92

Description: Utilities for ObjectVision version 2.0. OVDTREE2.EXE, OVDLINK.EXE, AND OVDFIELD.EXE. Used to extract tree, link, and field information from OVD files. These can be used to print and view for quick reference.

OVDUTL.ZIP/Bin Bytes: 45049, 20-Nov-92

Description: Utility for correcting OVD files that report inconsistent data.

OBJVUT.ZIP/Bin Bytes: 7855 12-Apr-93

Description: Text file listing all known (91) Public Domain and Shareware Object Vision products found on BBSes in the USA, organized by type, with release date and short description.

RTINST.ZIP/Bin Bytes: 39050, 23-Oct-92

Description: OV 2.0: This file contains a sample single disk install for ObjectVision Developers. With this file, you just need to modify two forms with information specific to your application, and copy the appropriate files to your floppy disk. This program will copy your files to a destination drive, create a group, and place an icon in your group.

UNPAK.ZIP/Bin Bytes: 18644, 08-Feb-93

Description: Manually install ObjectVision 2.x. This file contains instructions for installing ObjectVision 2.x manually. Also includes Borland's UNPAK.EXE.

UPLOAD.ZIP/Bin Bytes: 2266, 13-Nov-92

Description: Whenever an ObjectVision Technician asks you to upload your application you must complete the standard ObjectVision download README.TXT file, rename it OVREADME.TXT and include it in your.ZIP file. Completing this form will save us time by giving us a detailed description of your ObjectVision problem and a profile of your system configuration.

WFIELD.ZIP/Bin Bytes: 3963, 26-Mar-92

This file demonstrates the use of the @WHILEFIELD function found in the OVLOOPS.DLL. It is much easier to use than the @WHILELOOP function.

3LINKS.ZIP/Bin Bytes: 12930, 21-Sep-92

Description: This zip file contains a sample ObjectVision application that demonstrates the technique of connecting multiple databases to the same fields or columns.

12MDOC.ASC/Asc Bytes: 7907, 07-Sep-92

Description: This text file covers step by step, how to create a one to many application. It details the steps needed, and not the underlying theory, of how to create these applications. It is written for the novice and/or intermediate user of ObjectVision who is just starting to learn advanced linking techniques.

Invoking ObjectVision

ObjectVision can be invoked one of the following ways:

Icon Approach

1. Double click on the ObjectVision icon.
2. The Icon View of ObjectVision appears. Double click on the ObjectVision Icon. The other icon is ObjectVision Demos, well worth a look…but not at this moment.
3. The ObjectVision Window should then appear.

OS/2 Prompt Approach

1. At the OS prompt, enter *cd\vision*. This places you in the ObjectVision subdirectory.
2. Once in the vision subdirectory, type *vision*.
3. The ObjectVision window should then appear.

Interfacing REXX with ObjectVision

Before discussing how to interface REXX to ObjectVision, a brief discussion of "Why use REXX? " is in order.

REXX offers the following enhancements to ObjectVision:

1. Better string handling and file operations.

2. A random number generator.
3. Better flow control and exception handling capabilities. ObjectVision has no looping structure.
4. The ability to have local variables. ObjectVision's variables are all global in scope.
5. Better ties to OS/2 through the REXXUTIL external function library.
6. Faster execution speed than ObjectVision.
7. Subroutine capability. ObjectVision has none.

ObjectVision does offer some advantages over REXX:

1. A 150 @ functions, similar to those found in spreadsheets such as 1-2-3 and Quattro, as opposed to over 60 in Standard REXX and over 30 additional functions in the REXXUTIL external function library. ObjectVision functions are stronger than REXX in the areas of: mathematical functions; Financial functions; Linking (external file/database) operations; and menu operations.
2. ObjectVision, with its reliance on visual programming, offers a more "modern" and arguably more intuitive approach to programming than REXX.

The major interface ObjectVision has with REXX is the ability to register REXX procedures as external functions. In turn, these procedures may contain other ObjectVision functions. The ObjectVision application is stored in a file with an .OVD extension. The REXX procedures may use any extension (but usually use the .OVR extension). A comment is **not** required starting in the first column and the first line for REXX procedures used in ObjectVision functions.

The following is an overview of interfacing REXX with ObjectVision:

1. To use an ObjectVision function in a REXX procedure, enclose it in single quotes:

   '@CLEARALL'

Notes

1. The REXX rules about using double quotes within single quotes or enclosing single quotes within a pair of single quotes applies to ObjectVision functions used within REXX procedures.
2. To send a multi-line command to ObjectVision via the REXX ADDRESS instruction, make sure that each ObjectVision line is enclosed within brackets (i.e. [ ]). Note that the REXX continuation character (comma) is not needed in this case.

3. On invoking ObjectVision, it becomes the default external REXX (i.e., ADDRESS) environment. If you issue an explicit or implied ADDRESS command that changes to another ADDRESS environment, issue an ADDRESS vision '*ObjectVision command*' to restore ObjectVision as the current environment.

2. REXX ObjectVision procedures should contain at least one of the following ObjectVision external REXX functions:

```
GETOVVALUE("fieldname")
    /* Gets the value of an ObjectVision field fieldname in a form and */
    /* assigns it to a REXX symbol) */

PUTTOVVALUE("fieldname"value",1)
    /* Assigns a value (explicit or derived using REXX symbols) */
    /* To the ObjectVision field fieldname in a form. A 1 is needed */
    /* only is you want a field value be seen as a string */
```

Notes

1. These are external REXX functions and do not need to be in quotes.

2. Either the function or subroutine format is acceptable:

```
Task1 = GETOVVALUE("Field2")
    /* Function. Result placed in TASK1 */
      OR
CALL GETOVVALUE "Field2"
    /* Subroutine. Result placed in RESULT */
```

3. A fieldname can also be a column. (Really the current row in a table of columns.)

3. To make a REXX procedure recognized as an ObjectVision function, it must first be registered. This must be done using the @REXXRegister ObjectVision function:

```
'@REXXREGISTER('@RIGHTX',2,"This is a sample function ", 'RIGHTX.OVR',0)'

    /* First argument - alias name for ObjectVision (i.e. the ObjectVision */
    /*        function name). It must start with a @, is */
    /* 1-254 characters, and must not be an already */
    /* function name*/

    /* Second argument - Number of expected arguments for the function */
    /*        Somehow, ObjectVision does the automatic */
    /*        from REXX to Objectvision "data types." */

    /* Third argument - Help text when pasting this ObjectVision into */
    /* an ObjectVision expression. Only needed if */
    /* the second argument has a value greater than */
    /* zero. */

    /* Fourth argument - The name of the REXX procedure associated */
    /* with this function. Usually resides in the VISION directory and has an */
    /*.OVR extension. A full path specification is allowed. */

    /* Fifth argument - The type of function. 0 (modifies values) or */
    /*        1 (performs an action [event] ) */
```

Notes

1. If a REXX function is going to be used every time that you access ObjectVision. Then it should be placed in the REXX procedure:

   REGISTER.OVR. This will register all desired REXX ObjectVision functions if invoked by the @REXXREGISTERALL ObjectVision function.

   To create @REXXREGISTERALL for new applications, read the instructions or the on-line help "Registering any REXX function." The essence is a @REXXREGISTER that has @REXXRESISTERALL as its first argument and REGISTER.OVR as the fourth argument. All other arguments are 0 or blank.

2. @REXXREGISTERALL registers these REXX ObjectVision functions:

   EXECUTE: Executes an OS/2 command. An Event function.

   RAND: Returns a random number between 0 and 1. A Value function.

   WHILEFIELD: Loops and writes value to field.

   WHILELOOP: Loops and performs action.

4. In debugging REXX procedures, you can use a full-screen window called the REXX Transcript window. This is similar to using PMREXX. Also, any output/input from a REXX procedure also goes into this window. Unfortunately, this window is not available for the run-time version. This can be enabled several ways:

   a. Using a REXX input (such as PULL), output (such as SAY), or debugging (such as TRACE) instruction.

   b. It is automatically brought up when a REXX error occurs.

   c. If you select the REXX Transcript property under the Forms Tool.

   The window that is brought up is similar to PMREXX (discussed in Chapter 3). The Trace output is the same as the standard REXX TRACE output discussed in Chapter 2 (including interactive tracing).

Converting from REXX to C — REXXTACY

One of the most frequently asked questions about OS/2 REXX is "is there a REXX compiler available for OS/2?" The answer is "not yet." Although IBM is rumored to be working on it. The best available solution for the moment is REXXTACY. REXXTACY is a REXX to C copyrighted freeware, converter on DOS and OS/2 and maybe someday on UNIX. It will eventually become shareware or a commercial package. The C code produced can be made to look at REXX code. Within its limitations, it works satisfactory.

The code produced will be Microsoft C compatible which should work, with some modification, with most OS/2 C and C++ compilers.

[All screens are reproduced with the permission of Ruddock and Associates Inc.]

Invoking REXXTACY

To invoke REXXTACY from the DOS and OS/2 command prompt, do the following:

Invoking with filename

```
REXXTACY a.cmd
/* Converts a REXX procedure from a.cmd to a.c. If there are no errors, */
/* it returns to the DOS or OS/2 prompt. Else any errors are displayed */
```

Listing Invocation options

```
REXXTACY -h or REXXTACY -?
/* Displays all the invocation options for REXXTACY */
```

Invocation with options

```
REXXTACY -o a.cmd
/* Attempts to optimize the REXX program */
/* Other useful options provide debugging information -p (parser info. For */
/* advanced users only. ) -z (optimizer info). Only one hyphen is needed */
/* when supplying multiple invocation options. Options b, u, g provide */
/* additional debugging information. */
```

Once invoked, the following text appears on a screen:

```
REXXTACY 2.0 - (C) 1992 Ruddock and Associates. All rights reserved.
```

Looking for Additional Help

REXXTACY includes some text files to get you up and running.

- README.TXT: Information about each file in the basic package and how to print out the documentation.
- RXCDOC20.XXX: Print out the user's guide in various formats. (The extension indicates the format.) These are TEXT (.TXT), LaserJet (.LJ), TEX (.DVI), and PostScript (.PS)

REXX Conversion Tips

1. The following REXX instructions should work without problems:

   All clause types (see Chapter 2) and all symbol types.

   Instructions: ARG, CALL (except CALL ON/OFF), DO, EXIT, NOP, PARSE (except PARSE SOURCE), PROCEDURE, PULL, RETURN, SAY, SELECT.

   Functions: The following are explicitly supported. Others may work as well: LENGTH, LINEIN (only filename [not devices] argument supported), LINES (only filename [not devices]).

2. The following is not yet supported by REXXTACY:

   ADDRESS (Other than the CMD environment for OS/2 which executes any passed commands in a child environment. This means that OS/2 environment changes passed by the child will not be recognized by the master environment. Changing directories also works in a similar way) DROP, INTERPRET, ITERATE, LEAVE, NUMERIC OPTIONS, PARSE SOURCE, PUSH, QUEUE, SIGNAL, TRACE.

   Hex and binary strings.

Interfacing REXX with SourceLink

Earlier sections in the chapter showed examples of REXX as a macro language to aid in editing files. Combined with SourceLink, REXX provides a means to generate and modify programs and thus becomes a critical piece of the software development process.

What is SourceLink?

Mueller and Rath (1992) call SourceLink a Source Code Processor. It offers the following capabilities for both new and experienced programmers:

- A one-stop environment to create, modify, and analyze your C, C++, and Assembler programs.
- A dramatic reduction in the time to write a program with the use of clip library of code sequences, and using existing code.
- An invaluable program analysis tool with such items as the call tree and other reports.
- HyperLink capability that means you are only a click away from accessing a function definition, application documentation, or a specific file.
- A good editor that allows you to have open up-to-22 files simultaneously!
- WorkFrame/2 support.
- File operation utilities (such as copy, delete).

Invoking SourceLink

Enter SLSTART *name_of_file_to* list or click on the SourceStart icon if you are using SourceLink with WorkFrame/2. This will reduce multiple instances of SourceLink being created when multiple files are opened. Make SLSTART the default editor for WorkFrame/2.

[All screens are reproduced with the permission of SourceLine Software, Inc.]

To invoke Sourcelink do either of the following:

1. Click on the SourceLink group icon on the desktop.
2. Click on the SourceLink32 icon.
3. The SourceLink32 window should then shortly appear.

OR

1. From the OS prompt, enter *CD\SLINK32* to make this the current directory. You may have installed SourceLink into a different directory. Use that name instead.
2. Type *SLINK2*
3. The SourceLink32 window should appear.

Notes

1. To exit SourceLink. Press *Control X* or Click on the *Exit SourceLink* option under the File Menu.
2. The following environment variables are used by SourceLink:
   - BOOKSHELF: appends SOURCELINK directory to look for VIEW (.INF) files.
   - HELP: appends SOURCELINK directory to look for help files.
   - PATH: Adds SOURCELINK directory to look for SOURCELINK executable.
   - SL_BACKUP2: Search path for backup files. (Default C:\SLINK2\BACKUP.)
   - SL_SLINK2: Search path for SOURCELINK (DEFAULT C:\SLINK2)
   - SL_TEMP2: Search path for work files.(Default C:\SLINK2\TEMP.)

Getting Help on SourceLink

Look in the following places for information about SourceLink:

1. README.NOW has additional information about the product.
2. The example files used in the tutorial found in the SourceLink technical manual can be located in the C:\SLINK2\SAMPLE directory or in the appropriate directory and drive.
3. Sample REXX macros can be found in the C:\SLINK2\MACRO directory or in the appropriate directory and drive.

4. On-line Help can be accessed in a variety of ways:

   a. Clicking on the *Help* menu option. You can then access the appropriate help item. These include the following:

      - Help Table of Contents
      - Help Index
      - Help Window (to use with Microsoft QuickHelp or any other desired application to use for help.)
      - View Help (to look at other .INF files)

   b. Pressing the Help button or F1 for context-sensitive help within a window.

5. SOURCELINK now has a CompuServe forum. Enter GO OS2AVEN, and select area number 3.

Interfacing REXX with SourceLink

To process a REXX macro while in SourceLink, use any of the following three approaches:

a. Click on the *Macro* menu item on the Main menu. Click on *Run Macro File*. The following window then appears:

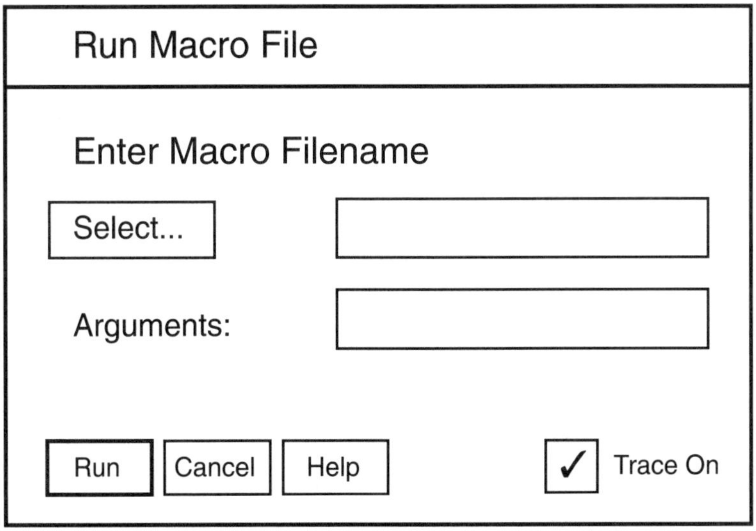

Run Macro File

Enter Macro Filename

Select...

Arguments:

Run Cancel Help ✓ Trace On

Figure 6-8 SourceLink run Macro File

Enter the name of the SourceLink macro that you wish to run with any accompanying arguments. The check box allows trace to be turned on or off.

b. SourceLink allows you to define up-to-16 macros. Once defined, select *User Defined Macros* under the Macro menu. A secondary menu listing the available macros are then displayed. Click on the desired macro which is then processed.

c. Another option is running the SourceLink macro in another window that is similar to PMREXX. In SourceLink terminology, this is called the Interactive Macro Window. To do this, select *Interactive Macro Window* under the Macro menu. A window similar to Figure 6-9 appears:

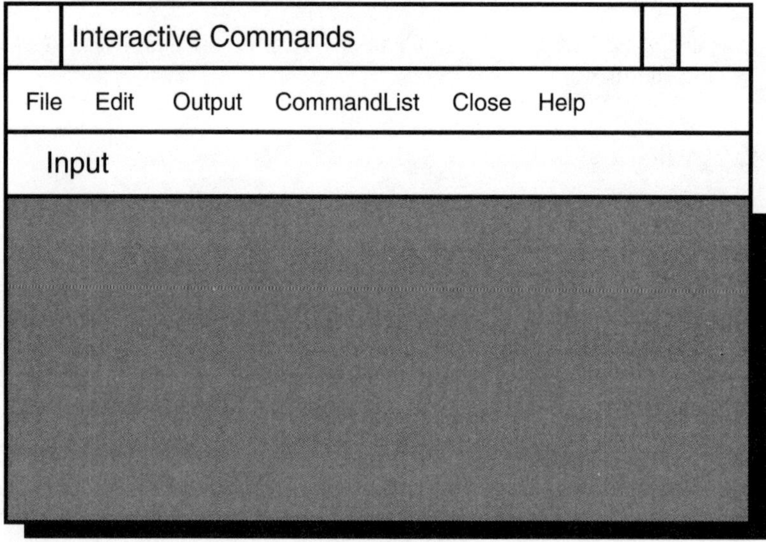

Figure 6-9 SourceLink Interactive Macro Window

Menu options include the following:

- File (Run Macro File, Trace On, Trace Last, Trace Next)
- Edit (Cut, Copy, Paste, Delete)
- Output (Clear Output, Copy to Clip File)
- CommandList (Operations on commands associated with the interactive macro window. These include: open command window, load list, and save list)
- Close (no other options).

- Help (Identical to what was described above.)

Notes

1. Unless you process the REXX macro using an interactive macro window, all output goes to a file named C:\SLINK2\TEMP\SL_*dnn*.OUT, or, whatever directory the OS/2 environment variable SL_TEMP2 points to *d* — day of the week. *nn* -is a unique number identifying the file.
2. Then select *Ref* on the main menu and then *Macro Output* to view any macro output.
3. A good practice is to select *Clear Macro Output* under the *Macro* menu option to have an empty output file every time.
4. To add a macro to the menu, select *Define Menu Item* under the *Macro* menu. Click on the *Add* button. Supply the necessary menu text (legend), macro file, arguments, and associated key sequence (such as Alt 1.), and enable/disable notify on macro completion. Alt 1 is also referred to as the accelerator keys.
5. Entering an = will re-execute the last instruction in the interactive macro window. The trace last menu option does the same thing.
6. You can specify your own startup and exit (or close) macro. To do this, select the *Options* menu and then *Setup*. You may then select the appropriate macros and any necessary arguments for the startup and exit macros

Building SourceLink REXX Macros

Keep the following points in mind when building SourceLink REXX macros:

1. SourceLink REXX macros use standard OS/2 REXX instructions. They must also have a comment starting in the first column of the first line. These files generally use the .CMD or .REX extensions.
2. SourceLink supplies over 100 built-in commands that can be used in SOURCELINK REXX Macros. These are called S_ commands.
   a. The S_Commands do the following types of operations: keyboard simulation, file operations, edit operations, clip operations, information operations, and window operations.
   b. Use quotes for arguments to a S_ command if they are not to be evaluated by the REXX interpreter.
   c. If a HPFS file name is used in a macro, place it in double quotes.

d. You can use the REXX command TRACE to debug a macro. This is discussed in Chapter 2.

e. The REXX special (system) symbol RC contains the value of the last S_ or REXX command processed. This should be saved if you are planning to use this later in the macro — because RC is reset after each REXX or S_ is processed.

3. Table 6-9 shows examples found in the C:\SLINK2\MACROS subdirectory, or the appropriate subdirectory and drive. A description also appears in the README.NOW text file.

Table 6-9

CHGDB.REX	Changes the link database. An example of the S_LISTBOX and S_PROMPT commands.
CHGDIR.REX	Changes the current directory. An example of the S_LISTBOX and S_PROMPT commands.
GREPFIND.REX	Search for a pattern in a file(s).
REST_ENV.REX	Retrieves the environment: current cursor location, edit mode and other information about a file. Example of S_DOES_FILE_EXIST command. This may used as part of the startup macro.
SAVE_ENV.REX	Saves the environment: All files that were opened at the time of closing and current cursor location, edit mode plus other information about a file. This may used as part of the exit (closing) macro.
SHUTDOWN.REX	A potential exit (closing) macro.
SMARTC.REX	Generates a C template which can be used to easily create a C program.
STARTUP.REX	A potential startup macro.

Sample Macros

Show SourceLink Info

```
/* SHOW.REX - Shows some of the information you can retrieve that may */
/* be useful for debugging */
S_GET_CURR_FILENAME 'cf'
S_GET_CURR_SL_DIR   'cfd'
S_GET_DISK_SPACE    'cds'
S_GET_CURSOR_POS    'ccp'
S_GET_ENV_INFO      'PATH cpt'
S_GET_FILE_INFO     'c:\autoexec.bat cfi'
S_GET_NUM_SL_FILES  'nsf'
say    'Current file                    '      cf
say    'Current Source Link Directory   '      cfd
say    'Disk space                      '      cds
say    'Current cursor position         '      ccp
say    'Current path                    '      cpt
say    'Info on autoexec.bat            '      cfi
say    'Number of open files            '      nsf
```

Displayed

```
Current file                     c:\slink2\macros\show.rex
Current Source Link Directory    c:\slink2\macros
Disk space                       -168092912 /* free */
Current cursor position          126
Current path                     C:\SPF2;C:\OS2;C:\....
Info on autoexec.bat             Size: 0000217 Date: 02/20/93 13:55:02
Number of open files             1
```

Delete file front-end

```
/* */
S_PROMPT 'File to Delete?,' fd
       /* Creates a dialog box with OK and CANCEL buttons */
S_DOES_FILE_EXIST fd fe
       /* Put result of file exist (TRUE or FALSE) in fe */
if fe = 'TRUE' then do
              /* If it exists.. */
       address cmd 'del' fd
              /* then delete it */
       if rc = 0 then say 'file' fd 'deleted'
              /* let the user know what happened.. */
              else say 'file' fd 'not deleted'
       end
       else say 'file' fd 'not found'
```

USING REXX WITH COMMUNICATION PROGRAMS

In Chapter 4, we saw how REXX enhanced Communications Manager in accessing host, minicomputers, and other PCs. In this last section, we will look at two asynchronous (i.e., dial-up) programs that use REXX as a macro language in performing communications.

Table 6-10 is a comparison of features for the two products:

Table 6-10

Feature	Quercus System's REXXTERM	Oberon Software's TE/2
Baud Rate Supported	300-57600	110-57600
Protocols Supported	ASCII CompuServe B, Kermit, Xmodem, Xmodem 1K, Ymodem, Ymodem-G, Zmodem	ASCII CompuServe B+, Xmodem, Xmodem 1K, Ymodem, Ymodem-G, Zmodem
Terminal Emulations Supported	ANSI, DEC VT52, DEC VT100, DEC VT220 (Subset),	ANSI, ANSI-TE2, DEC VT100, IBM 3101
Com (Serial) ports supported	1-8	1-8
Keyboard Macros	Most keys can be redefined.	All 48 function keys
Dialing entries	No limit	1-200
Scripting language	REXXTERM Scripting language	TE/2 Script language
Interface to REXX	Yes	Yes

Interfacing REXX with TE/2

TE/2 was first available as a "production" shareware release in 1990 and has generally become one of the more popular OS/2 communications packages. A shareware version allows you to "try before you buy."

Installing TE/2

With release 1.2.3 and later, TE/2 uses an installation program named TE2SETUP.CMD. What is interesting about this program is that it is a lengthy REXX procedure that uses a good many of the capabilities of standard and OS/2 REXX such as the REXXUTIL external function library. It is worth a look if you are considering your own installation script using REXX.

Invoking TE/2

To invoke TE/2, use either of the following approaches:

1. From the Workplace Shell:
   a. Click on the Oberon Software "window" icon.
   b. Then click on the TE/2 icon.
   c. The TE/2 logo should appear (including any error messages) and then the "terminal mode" screen. This screen will also list session status and common key combinations.
2. From the OS/2 prompt:
   a. Type CD \TE2.
   b. Type TE2.
   c. The TE/2 logo should appear (including any error messages) and then the terminal mode" screen should appear. This screen will also list session status and common key combinations.

Notes

1. To set default settings for TE/2, add them to the text file TE2.INI. An example is a baud rate, terminal emulation, initialization and termination strings (i.e., the Hayes AT commands), or screen colors.

```
; A sample TE2.INI
INCLUDE COLOR.INI
;Can nest INI files. (with no stated limit). This allows you to modularize
;various INI components. Returns to processing the next line in TE2.INI
:on completion. Most commonly used for modem initialization files
baud 4800
;changes the baud rate from the default of 2400
emulate vt100
;terminal emulation. Changes from the default of ANSI_TE2 (enhanced ANSI).
```

2. TE2.INI rules:
   a. Each line must end with a semicolon.
   b. Blank lines are allowed.
   c. A line beginning with a semicolon is viewed as a comment.
   d. Text may be entered in any case.
3. Rather than manually adding color values to TE2.INI, you can use the utility TE2COLOR. Enter TE2COLOR *INIfile* to change the current default settings.

Getting Help on TE/2

Here are some tips on looking for information about TE/2:

1. The on-line text (.DOC files) has current information about TE2. SCRIPT.DOC has information about the REXX-TE/2 interface.
2. TE/2 support is available on many of the major electronic services including tech support on GEnie in the IBM PC roundtable (615), category 30, topic 25 and maintains a BBS at 507-388-1154.

Interfacing TE/2 with REXX

Note the following rules when interfacing REXX with TE/2:

1. TE/2 REXX procedures must begin with a comment starting in column 1, line 1. Use the RC special (system) variable and the REXX TRACE facility to debug TE/2 REXX procedures, (see Chapter 2).
2. TE/2 REXX procedures usually end with a .SCR extension. To invoke, use any of the following approaches by:

a. Supplying it at invocation time: TE2 -m A.SCR.

b. Assigning it to a macro key. The value would be !call A.SCR.

c. Entering Alt / once in terminal mode, the Command prompt then appears. Enter the REXX procedure name including the full path.

3. The REXX rules about using double quotes within single quotes or enclosing single quotes within a pair of single quotes applies to TE/2 statements used within REXX procedures.

4. TE/2 script statements are placed in quotes within a REXX procedure. On invoking TE/2, it is the default external REXX (i.e., ADDRESS) environment. If you issue an explicit or implied ADDRESS command that changes to another ADDRESS environment, issue an ADDRESS te2 '*TE/2 command*' to restore TE/2 as the current environment.

5. TE/2 includes local and global variables. Local variables are not accessible to a TE/2 REXX procedure but nearly eighty global variables are. The appropriate way to retrieve the global variable depends on the "data type" of the global variable. This is explicitly listed in the TE/2 script language reference. It is either STRING or INTEGER.

For STRING global variables:	For INTEGER global variables:
/* */	/* */
'streval(modeminitstring)'	'itoa(baud,10)'
/* modem initialization string */	/* baud rate. Section argument is */
	/* radix of the value */
is = rc /* rc holds the value */	if rc = 2400...

Interfacing REXX with REXXTERM

Since 1988, REXXTERM has been available for both DOS and OS/2. Because it is developed by the same company (Quercus Systems) that sells Personal REXX for DOS, Windows, and OS/2, REXXTERM has strong REXX ties.

[All screens are reproduced with the permission of Quercus Systems.]

Invoking REXXTERM

Use the following approaches to invoke REXXTERM:

From the OS/2 prompt

1. Go into the directory or subdirectory where REXXTERM resides. (i.e., CD C:\REXXTERM. REXXTERM can be copied to any directory).
2. Enter RXT2
   a. There are various options that can be specified as well.

      /n — n is COM (serial) port to use.

      /N (no profile)

      /AM (use a monochrome display)

   b. You may wish to use the following OS/2 environment variables:

      SET RXTFLAGS = /*options*. Where *options* is one of the above invocation options.

      SET RXTPATH = directory. Directory is the location of the REXXTERM executable.

   c. After the switches, a new profile and profile arguments can also be supplied (such as modem initialization and exit strings.) A profile is similar to the TE2.INI file (The default file is PROFILE.RXT.)

From an icon.

1. Create an icon as outlined in Chapter 3.
2. Click on the icon.
3. The REXXTERM information screen appears followed by the terminal screen.

Notes

1. REXXTERM commands (such as SET REXX) can be entered from the menu (Alt-Q), the various Alt "speed" keys (Press Alt-H for a list.), and pressing the insert key to bring up the command line.
2. Pressing Alt-X or selecting EXIT from the menu will exit you from REXXTERM.
3. The REXXTERM information screen appears followed by the terminal screen. See Figure 6-8.

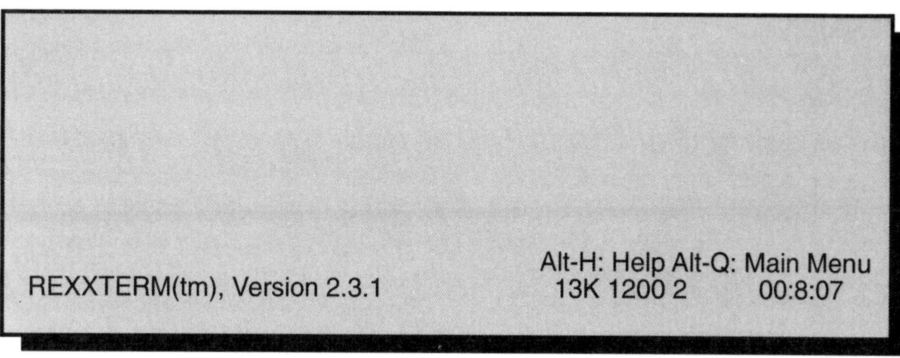

Figure 6-10 REXXTERM General Window

Getting Help on REXXTERM

Consider looking at the following places for further information about REXXTERM:

1. Either CompuServe (Go Quercus) or the Quercus BBS (408-867-7488) are filled with many documented procedures using REXXTERM functions.

   The following is a sample of the files on CompuServe (look in Library 11 under PCVENA).

   - RXTERM.ZIP: Description of REXXTERM
   - UNCTRL.ZIP: Strips VT100 (Escape) codes from a text capture file.

2. There are a variety of text files included with the disk. These include:

   - CONTENTS.DOC: What's on the disk.
   - README.DOC: Generally undocumented and new features.
   - README.OS/2: OS/2 undocumented and new features.
   - WHATSNEW.23: New features in the 2.3 release.

3. Alt-H will list which "speed keys" you can use in REXXTERM.

Interfacing REXX with REXXTERM

Here are some guidelines in creating REXXTERM REXX procedures:

1. REXXTERM is compatible with Personal REXX 3.0 (including RXWINDOW functions), Personal REXX 2.0, and IBM OS/2 REXX interpreters. That is the default invocation order. It can be changed within REXXTERM by entering the command SET REXX PREXX (3.0) or PREXX20 (2.0) or REXXSAA (IBM OS/2 REXX. If using the IBM interpreter, you must use the PREXXFCN.DLL dynamic link library. This allows REXXTERM REXX procedures only but not "regular" IBM OS/2 REXX to use Personal REXX "extended" functions. Enter PREXXDEF to automatically register the dynamic link library.

2. REXXTERM REXX procedures must begin with a comment starting in column 1, line 1. Use the RC special (system) variable and the REXX TRACE facility to debug REXXTERM REXX procedures (see Chapter 2).

3. You can use any of the editors mentioned earlier in the chapter to edit files while in REXXTERM, by selecting External Editor under the Utilities Menu. The default is KEDIT. To change this, enter the command SET EDITOR *name_of_executable*.

4. REXXTERM REXX procedures usually end with a .RXT extension. This is the default but others can be used. To invoke, use any of the following approaches:

   a. Supplying it at invocation time as a profile.

   b. When creating a dialing entry, supplying a "procedure" that will be mostly used to help automate the logon process and possibly the entire session.

   c. Entering the name of the .RXT file at the command line.

5. The REXX rules about using double quotes within single quotes or enclosing single quotes within a pair of single quotes applies to Quercus statements used within REXX procedures.

6. Quercus script statements are placed in quotes within a REXX procedure. On invoking REXXTERM, it is the default external REXX (i.e., ADDRESS) environment. If you issue an explicit or implied ADDRESS command that changes to another ADDRESS environment, issue an ADDRESS REXXTERM *'REXXTERM command'* to restore REXXTERM as the current environment.

7. REXXTERM includes the following sample procedures in Table 6-11:

Table 6-11

A_TO_DIR.REX DIR_TO_A.REX	Convert a REXXTERM directory to/from an ASCII format.
COLOR.RXT	Uses RXWINDOW functions to allow users to change colors of REXXTERM screens.
HOST.RXT	To create your own bulletin board (host).
LEARN.RXT	LEARN will first "learn" the necessary keystrokes (but not function and cursor keys) and input to perform part of a session (such as logon and logoff). It then converts these keystrokes and input into a ready-to-run REXX procedure, which will probably need some customization. Or also enabled by pressing ALT-L (toggle — start/stop recording).
REXFMTDIR.REX	Converts a REXXTERM 2.2 directory format to 2.3.
\EXAMPLES	Examples of logon REXX procedures.
BIX.RXT, BIXAUTO. RXT, BIXDNLD.RXT	Scripts to automate logon and downloading of files to BIX online service.
CISAUTO.RXT, CISAUTO2.RXT COMPUSRV.RXT	Scripts to automate logon and downloading files/mail to the CompuServe on-line service
MODEMREG.RXT	Shows a Hayes-compatible modem registers.
PROFILE.RXT	A sample PROFILE procedure. This example initializes the modem, sets an area code, and enables the capture buffer.
SETDIR.RXT UMENDEMO.RXT	Useful if you have multiple dialing directories and wish to display one. Example of REXXVSET used to pass the value of a REXX symbol to a user-generated (using the UMENU command). A related item is UMENDEMO.RXT which is an example of a user-generated menu.

Table 6-11 Continued

VT100KEY.RXT, VT100S1.RXT, VT100SIM.RXT	Set up VT100 for a 3270 and other types of sessions.
WELLAUTO.REX	Automate access to the WELL on-line service.

8. Note that using REXX output instructions (such as SAY) will overwrite the REXXTERM screen.
9. Use the following in REXX LOGON procedures:
   a. 'BREAK' Sends a break signal.
   b. 'CLOSE *port*.' Under OS/2, this is the way to close a port while still in REXXTERM.
   c. 'HANGUP' Ends session.
   d. 'MATCH *text*': The key part of a logon script. The text from the "host" to match on before performing and action. MATCHX will allow you to match up-to-20 multiple strings!
   e. 'SEND *text\r*' Sends text followed by a carriage return (\r) or line feed (\l).
   f. 'SET TIMEOUT *nsec*.' Say how long you will wait to recognize an input string (such as Password:) from a "host" Nsec is number of seconds.
   g. 'WAIT *nsec*.' How many seconds to delay before performing the next action.
10. In addition to commands, REXXTERM also supports some 24 built-in functions that are well-documented in LEARN.RXT. One function that is extremely useful is READSTR which reads data up-to-1024 characters up or to a matched string and assigns it to a REXX symbol, READSTRX does the same thing except for multiple strings which are assigned to a REXX compound symbol array.

```
val = readstr('\r')
/* Assigns the last 1024 characters up to the carriage return(/r) to the REXX */
/* symbol val */
```

11. As we discussed earlier regarding KEDIT and THE, you can use the EXTRACT and QUERY command to capture an editor setting. REXXTERM supports similar commands to retrieve the values of any SET command (except ATTR) plus some others including: CAPTURE (capture file), CARRIER (ON or OFF — state of modem), CWD (current directory), HANDLE (Name or handle), RC (Return code of last REXXTERM command), VERSION (of REXXTERM).

Here is an example:

Use of extract

```
/* */
'extract /capture/'
'extract /carrier/'
'extract /cwd/'
'extract /handle/'
'extract /rc/'
'extract /timer/'
'extract '/version/'
'extract /rexx/'
'extract /baud/'
say 'Capture file' capture.1
say 'Carrier status' carrier.1
if carrier.1 = 'OFF' then say 'example of using IF'
say 'Current directory' cwd.1
say ' OS/2 handle' handle.1
say 'Last return code' rc.1
say 'Elapsed time of session' timer.1
say 'Rexxterm version' version.1
say ' Which REXX interpreter' rexx.1
say 'Baud rate' baud.1
```

Displayed

```
Capture file
Carrier Status OFF
example of using IF
Current directory C:\REXXTERM
OS2 handle 3
Last return code 0
Elapsed time of session 23
REXXTERM version 2.3..1
Which REXX interpreter REXXSAA
baud rate 1200
```

REFERENCES

Borland International 1992 *ObjectVision for OS/2 Version 2.0 User's Guide*, pp. 241-252

Command Technology Corporation 1991 *MACROS.DOC text file*

Command Technology Corporation 1991 *SPF/2 2.0 User's Guide & Reference Manual*

Command Technology Corporation 1993 *SPF/2 3.0 User's Guide & Reference Manual*

Command Technology Corporation 1991 *MACROS.DOC text file*

Crenshaw, Jack W. 1992 *Windows Tech Journal 1(8)* pp. 59-66

Daney, Charles " REXXTERM" in *The REXX Handbook*, Gabriel Goldberg & Philip H. Smith III (eds.), New York: McGraw-Hill pp. 463-473

Garvey, Kathleen. 1992 "Application Development with ObjectVision Pro 2.1"

The Connection 7(1) pp. 16, 63,77

German, Hallett 1990 *TSO/E CLISTS: Basics, Applications, and Advanced Techniques.* pp. 390-411

Green, Anthony T. Green 1992 *REXXTACY: The REXX to C Translator*

Hall, Carroll Ray 1992 "ObjectVision 2.0 — An Ideal Rapid Development Tool for Business Applications" *Borland Language Express* (Includes separate section on OS/2 version.)

Lotus Corporation 1991 *OS/2 Lotus 1-2-3 Tech Pack. CHAPTER3.TXT* electronic text file

Mansfield Software 1992 *KEDIT Reference Version 5.0* Mansfield Software

Mansfield Software 1992 *KEDIT User's Guide Version 5.0* Mansfield Software

Moser, Karen D. 1992a "Borland readies report writer for ObjectVision 3.0" *PC Week* November 30 p.79

Moser, Karen D. 1992b "Borland to unveil new ObjectVision, other programming tools." 9(33) August 17 p. 10

Moser, Karen D. 1992c "Layoffs and reorganization cloud future of Borland's Brief and ObjectVision" 9(51) December 21 p.33

Mueller Bill and Ina Roth. 1992 "SourceLink: A Source Code Processor" *OS/2 Developer* Fall pp. 30-35

Mueller Bill 1992 "SourceLink" *OS/2 Developer Conference & Exposition*

Oberon Software 1992 *TE/2 User's Manual*

Oberon Software 1991 *TE/2 Script Language Reference*

Oberon Software 1993 *TE/2 User's Manual—Revisions and Addenda Version 1.23*

Quercus Systems1991 REXXTERM User's Guide Version 2.3

Seltzer, Larry J. "REXX extensions boost ObjectVision for OS/2." *PC Week 9(26)* June 29th pp. 77-78

SourceLine Software 1992 *SourceLink: Technical Manual Version*

Tritus Inc. 1993 *Tritus SPF Version 1.2 Tritus SPF Edit and Edit Macro Reference*

Tritus Inc. 1993 *Tritus SPF Version 1.2 Tritus SPF User's Guide*

7

OS/2 REXX: Other Concerns

Chapter 7 is our final look at OS/2 REXX. This chapter examines the more general REXX concerns that were not appropriate for previous chapters. This includes one possible approach to REXX application development, portable REXX concerns, REXX style, and the future of OS/2 REXX.

APPLICATION DEVELOPMENT USING REXX

The following is one approach that can be applied for REXX application development. It is used throughout my previous book, the *Command Language Cookbook*, and applies not only to REXX but any command language. The version used in this book has been modified for OS/2 and is listed in Figure 7-1. Note the sequence:

1. Determine the type of application and appropriate command language.
2. Review the components generally used with the application type.
3. Examine the commands in the selected command language that correspond in the particular command language component. (Shown only for REXX in Chapter 2.)
4. Learn more about the command.
5. Determine if you need to use any shareware or third party software to enhance your application.
6. And then, create your program.

All this is completed before a single line in the program is created. The result is that you are up to one-third done with the application, having avoided some common traps and dead-ends. Using this approach diagrammed in Figure 7-1, you'll never have to say "I don't know how to start coding my application."

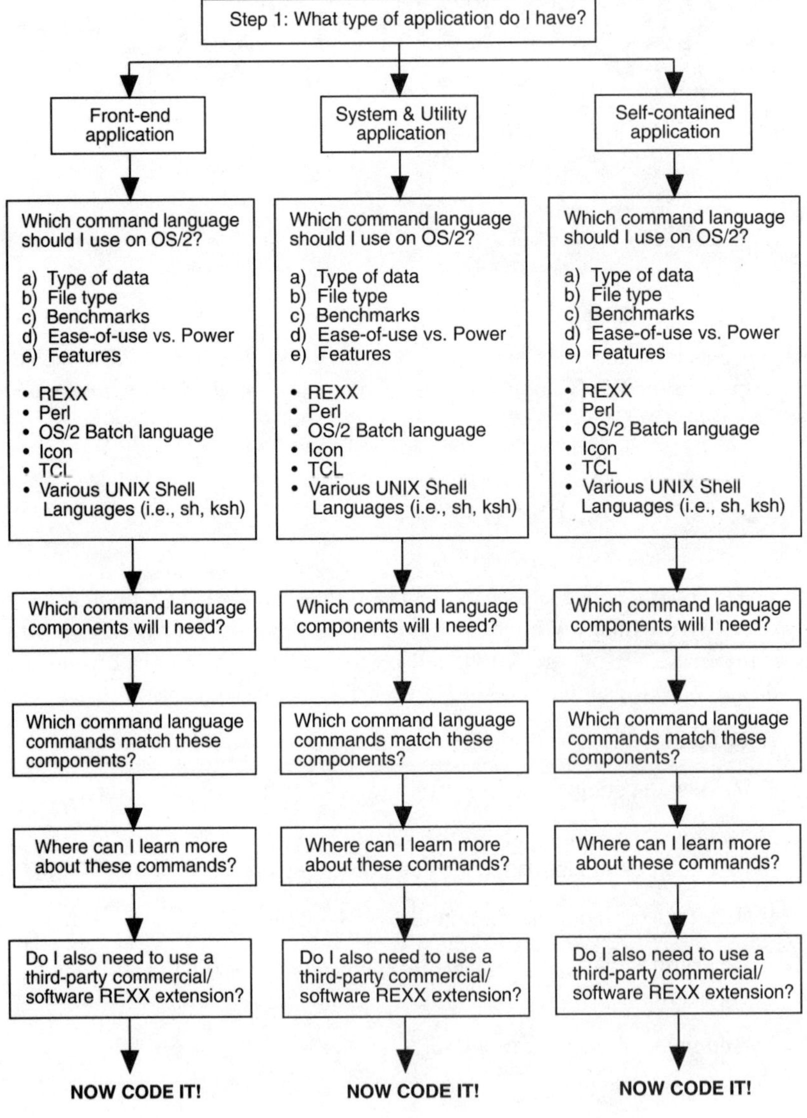

Figure 7-1 Application Development Strategy

The following sections will look at five crucial questions that are part of this approach:

1. What are the major types of command language applications?
2. Which command language should I choose?
3. What are the major components of command languages?
4. Should I use a programming language instead?
5. When should I consider third-party commercial and shareware REXX extensions?

What are the Major Types of Command Language Applications?

There are three distinct types of command language applications.

- *Front-end (or housekeeping) applications:* This type of application uses a command language to interact with a programming language by either providing input or receiving output to them. REXX with ObjectVision and OS/2 Lotus Tech Pack is an example of this.
- *System and Utility applications:* This is similar to the front-end application but emphasizes on performing system operating tasks, such as compressing files. The same applies to general purpose utilities that can be used as an internal/external REXX subprocedure or function instead of interacting with a programming language.
- *Self-contained applications:* These are applications that are usually created by the computer/information center staff for end-users of all levels. They often contain full-screen capabilities such as Visual REXX.

Table 7-1 provides additional information about these types of applications:

Table 7-1 Types of Command Language (REXX) Applications

Type of application	Function
Front-end	1) Provide input to or receive output from other applications and programs. 2) Sometimes performs "housekeeping" tasks. (Such as allocations, deletions.) 3) A special type of front-end application is startup/login programs.

Table 7-1 Continued

Type of application	Function
System and utility	1) Similar to front-end applications but performing system and utility operations. 2) Performs system operation tasks such as archiving or recovering files. 3) Also includes general-purpose utilities that can be used as a function/ subprocedure in the "main" command language program. (Such as a function that returns the modification date of a file.)

In the section "What are the major components of command languages?" we will return to looking at these application types.

Which Command Language Should I Use?

No two people use the same strategy in choosing a command language for an application. Some view command languages as a means to an end, so any command language is appropriate. Others are only familiar with one command language, or perhaps their site only uses one command language. So they'll use a command language for every application whether or not it is a "good fit." But there is another group that view command languages as a "tool" and choosing the right "tool" for the "best fit" does matter. However, looking for objective information for doing this is hard to find. At best, comparisons are made of two or three command languages. My second book, *Command Language Cookbook*, was created in the spirit of creating such an effort. **It assumes that the more you know about an application before your create it, the easier it is to find the right "tool."** This section summarizes the major information from the text.

Here are some recommended factors in choosing a command language:

1) Operating System/Environment

The operating system or environment that you use does largely (but not solely) determine which command language to use. Because OS/2 can easily run either DOS, MS-Windows or OS/2 command language applications, OS/2 users have a healthy number of command language interpreters available. But, obviously, only OS/2 command language interpreters, such as REXX take full advantage of the OS/2 operating system. Here is a summary of the major command languages:

- **Batch language** is ideal for operating system operations involving symbolic substitution and repetitive operations. Its lack of major programming features (such as flow control structures), makes it a limited choice for DOS and OS/2 users.
- **DCL** (Digital Command Language) is similar to batch language by it is well suited to one operating system — VMS. However, it has limited programming features. Third-party DOS and UNIX versions are also available.
- **Icon** is a general-purpose command language especially good for manipulating text. There are two books on Icon and it has its own Usenet newsgroup (comp.lang.icon). It is available for the Atari, Amiga, CMS, DOS, Macintosh, OS/2, TSO, UNIX, and VMS.
- **Perl** (practical extraction and report language) is a popular command language for system management, text file generation, and report generation. It is available for the Atari, Amiga, Macintosh, MS-DOS, MS-Windows, OS/2, VMS, and UNIX. It has its own Usenet newsgroup (comp.lang.perl).
- **Python** is a general-purpose command language ideal for prototyping. It is available on DOS, UNIX, and Macintosh. It has its own mailing list. The documentation and features are now stabilized.
- **REXX** has already been discussed throughout the book. Note that REXX's precursors **CLIST** and **EXEC2** do have MS-DOS versions. It has its own Usenet new group (comp.lang.rexx.)
- **TCL** (Tool Command Language) is an embedded general-purpose command language. TCL interpreters are available for Macintosh, MS-DOS, OS/2, and UNIX. It has its own Usenet news group (comp.lang.tcl). A book on this language will soon be forthcoming.
- **Various UNIX shells** such as sh (Bourne), csh (C-shell), and ksh (Korn) have been ported to non-UNIX platforms like the Amiga, Atari, Macintosh, MS-DOS, and OS/2. A possible trend is the standardization and popularization of the POSIX interpreter (POSIX 1003.2) which is based on the Korn shell.

2) Type of Data/Files

Another major consideration in choosing a command language is the type of data and files the proposed application will use. Figure 7-2 provides a flow diagram for choosing a command language based on these factors:

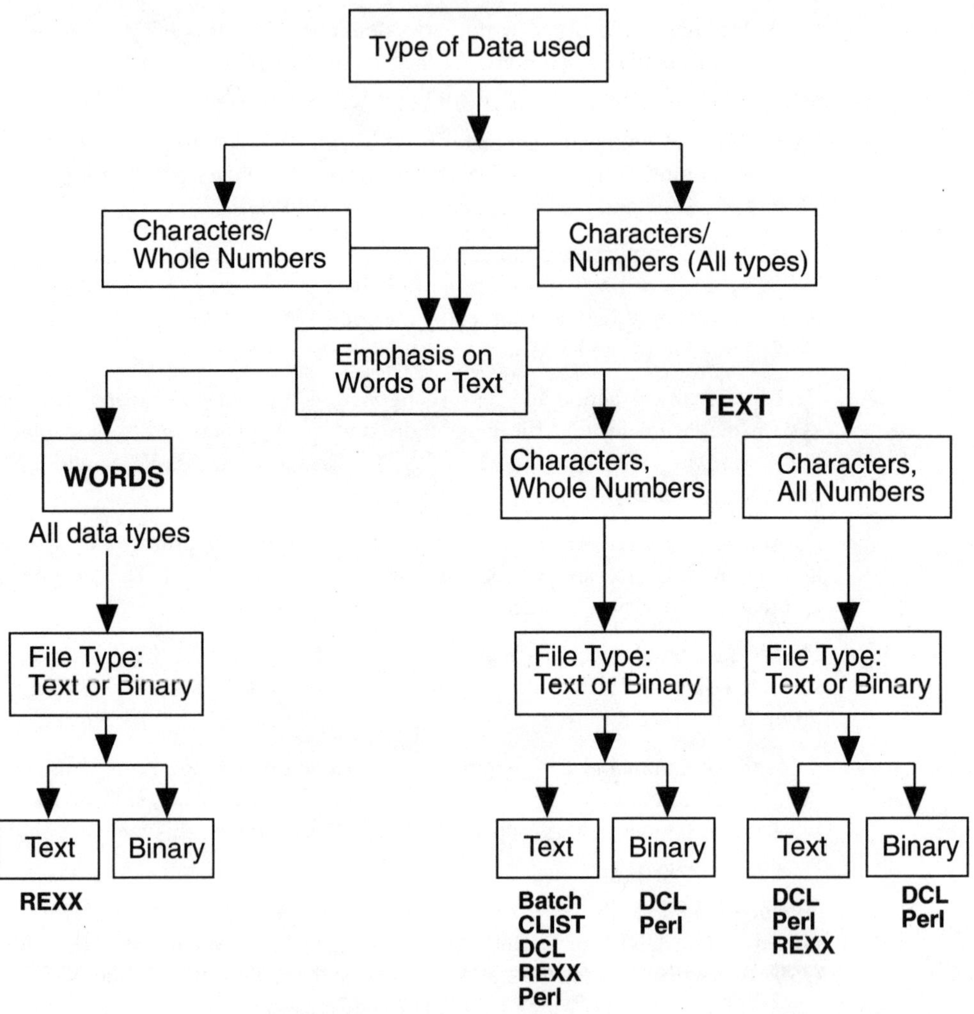

Figure 7-2 Command Language by Data/File Type

Notes

1. **Binary files** are defined as non-text files that can be created and manipulated by a command language. Two command languages, DCL and Perl, can access these types of files. DCL can perform operations on indexed files. The advantages of using indexed files are: more powerful file operation capabilities; and variable data records are supported. Perl supports binary files, which are attractive for producing smaller files because of compressed text.

2. *REXX does not explicitly support binary files.* However, some interpreters/compilers may include support. See Watts (1990, p.67) for more information on this topic.

3. **Python** (not listed in Figure 7-2) supports strings, numbers (with decimals), and arrays. It is more text-oriented than word-oriented. Text file operations are also supported.

4. **Icon** (not listed in Figure 7-2) supports strings, sets, and tables. Text file operations are supported.

5. **TCL** (not listed in Figure 7-2) supports lists, variables (strings), and associative arrays. Text and random-access files are supported.

Here is a list of data types for some of the major command languages:

Arrays (Simulated)	CLIST, DCL, DOS/OS/2 Batch Language
Arrays (True)	PERL, REXX
Associative Arrays	PERL, REXX (Compound Symbols)
Boolean	DCL, PERL, REXX
Binary Strings	DCL, REXX
Double byte characters	CLIST (TSO)
Hexadecimal strings	CLIST, DCL, PERL, REXX
Octal Strings	DCL, PERL
Scientific Notation	REXX

3) Benchmarks

Generally knowing how a command language performs can be useful in deciding if a command language is appropriate for an application. Benchmarks comparing four OS/2 command language interpreters are provided in Chapter 5. These benchmarks look at the Quercus and IBM REXX, batch, & Perl interpreters doing ordinary things — reading, writing, etc. The reader is encouraged to read that section.

4) Power by Ease-of-Use

In the *Command Language Cookbook*, an attempt was made to measure the overall strength of a command language. This involved creating two indices: One that indicated the *overall power* of a command language (including some rough measurement of a command language's popularity), and one that listed the command language's ease of use. The final scores were based on 110 items. 100 represented *power* and 10 represented *ease-of-use*.) Each item received a score of 1 if that component was a standard part of the command language. (Values less than 1 such as .25, .5, .75, and .85 were assigned based on the number of platforms for which that component was available.) Again, this approach is far from perfect, I hope it encourages others to look into this area. Note, that a casual and a power user will have different perceptions on ease-of-use and power. This index is more oriented to the casual user. See Table 7-2 for the results:

Table 7-2 Power and Ease-of-Use Rankings

Command Language	Power Score and Rank	Ease-of-Use Score and Rank	Unadjusted Total Score and Rank	*Adjusted* Total Score and Rank
Batch	44.0 (5)	75.0 (3)	59.5 (5)	54 (5)
CLIST	80.0 (4)	85.0 (1)	82.5 (2)	82 (3)
DCL	86.25 (3)	77.5 (2)	81.9 (3)	83 (2)
Perl	89.0 (1)	52.5 (4)	70.8 (4)	77 (4)
REXX	88.75 (2)	85.0 (1)	86.9 (1)	88 (1)

The three main conclusions you can draw from the above are the following:

- The power index indicates that Perl and REXX are virtually tied for the highest rating of those examined. ***Because there are only a few components to measure ease-of-use, one should rely more on the power index in choosing a command language for an application.***

- The ease-of-use index indicates that REXX and CLIST tied for the highest scores of those examined.
- REXX received the highest combined scores on ease-of-use and power. ***Thus it appears that REXX is the best overall command language for general users and Perl is the best overall command language for power users.*** *All other rankings, except for the DOS batch languages, may be the result of an inflation or deflation of the overall* **unadjusted** *score by the ease-of-use score — and should not be taken as the sole factor in choosing a command language.* The DOS batch languages received low results from both indices, an adjusted score was also calculated by giving ease-of-use a .5 weight. This minimized the effect of getting a high score on an index that has few items. This resulted in rankings similar to those produced by the power index.

5) Other Factors

Other "soft" factors may go into developing a command language application include:

1. **The expected life of the application.** A short-lived application may make sense to do using the OS/2 batch language.
2. **Your knowledge and development timeframe.** Perl may be the best "tool" to develop a particular application. But, another command language could be used if you are familiar with other command languages; not familiar with UNIX commands and concepts; and have a short development timeframe.
3. **The knowledge of those maintaining the application.** For example, a maintenance group or person will be responsible for updating and fixing the application. However, if they are not familiar with a particular command language and you have little or no time to train them, this could be a factor in your decision.
4. **The type of users and visibility for an application.** What types of users is the application being addressed to? Does the application support all of their input styles? Power users may want a command line, secretaries may want a full-screen/mouse-aware application, management may want a menu-driven application. Visibility of an application may also determine how an application should look and perform.
5. **Capabilities of a command language.** Your application may need some capability that can be done easily and flexibly in a particular command language. Examples include: capturing output from operating system commands using REXX, or the report writing capabilities of Perl. This could be the "tie breaker" in choosing a command language.

Table 7-3

Command Languages	Unique features	When to Use
Batch	No special interface needed to operating system commands.	Quick and dirty programming
	No special interface needed to retrieve values from a program.	When the string parsing needed is simple.
	Many commercial and third-party extensions/ replacements,	Emphasis is on manipulating operating system commands instead of text files.
	Ability to process ANSI/VT100 escape sequences.	When file operations needed are simple (such as browsing a file.)
		When data types (strings or numbers) and flow control structures needed are simple.
		When you want to create "personal commands" together, you can create your own "personal environment."
		When portability (except many DOS) is not a concern.
CLIST	No special interface needed to operating system and ISPF commands.	When emphasis is on short-term applications. On TSO, you use the command.
	No special interface needed to retrieve values from a program.	When you are using TSO commands that have subcommands such as EDIT.

Table 7-3 Continued

Command Languages	Unique features	When to Use
	Multiple levels of symbolic substitution.	When portability (except from TSO to MS-DOS) is not a concern.
		When multiple levels of symbolic substitution are needed.
		When the string parsing needed is simple.
		When the data is either character, numeric, or double-byte characters. And no decimals or exponents are needed.
		When a more powerful alternative to the OS/2 batch language is needed.
DCL	Strong links to the VMS operating system needed to perform system support and maintenance.	When operating system information (particularly VMS) is needed.
	Ability to process ANSI/VT100 escape sequences.	When formatted reports (including data merging) are needed.
	When indexed file operations are needed.	When you wish to create a "personal commands" that enhance existing operating system commands. By putting these commands together, you can create your own "personal environment."

Table 7-3 Continued

Command Languages	Unique features	When to Use
		When you need a stronger alternative to the DOS batch language.
		When string parsing needs are simple.
		When portability is a concern (when using a DCL emulator such as VCL.)
Perl	Good portability	When operating system and maintenance operations are needed.
	Strong ties to the UNIX operating system.	When formatted reports (including data merging) are needed.
	Strong string handling and text file capabilities.	When text file operations at any level are needed.
	Database operations searching and parsing.	When complicating operations are needed.
	Report operations	When directory operations are needed.
	Copyrighted freeware with source.	When data can be processed as scalars (such as numeric, character, integer, scientific notation, and element in an array, lists, and arrays.)
	Many extensions with ties to the major databases.	When portability is a concern.

Table 7-3 Continued

Command Languages	Unique features	When to Use
	Associative arrays	When a stronger alternative to the batch language is needed.
	Directory and file (including binary) operations	When database routines (using dbm/ndbm/ or gdbm) are needed.
REXX	Good portability parsing capabilities are	When sophisticated string needed.
	Good interface to operating system/ applications.	When portability is a concern (especially across the IBM environments.)
	Many extensions such as external function libraries.	When an application macro language is needed.
	Strong string handling (especially word) capabilities.	When a prototype for an application is needed.
	Ease of learning/ minimizing of syntax.	When date and time operations are needed.
	Natural datatyping	When you wish to build your own operating system or editor commands.
		When building a preprocessor for a compiler.

What are the Major Components of a Command Language Application?

Chapter 2, in a section called "The components of REXX", discussed the five major components in a command language. These are:

1. **Input/Output** such as output to a screen, input from the keyboard, file operations and stack operations — REXX only.
2. **Flow control** such as conditional, looping, exit/return code handling, and exception handling.
3. **General Features** (Such as debugging/trace facility, symbolic substitution, labels, non-portable global options, numeric options, and interpreter version.)
4. **Interfaces** Internal/external interfaces. Internal interfaces include: functions and subroutines.
5. **Built-in functions and system variables.**

Now comes the most crucial step in the pre-development phase of your application. By combining the three types of command language applications with the command languages' components, you can determine which commands you will be using in an application. This is shown in Table 7-4.

Table 7-4 Command language applications and components

Front-end	System/Utility	Self-contained
Operating system commands	Operating system commands	
External Interfaces	External Interfaces	External Interfaces
• Invoke executable	• Invoke executable	• Invoke external functions
• Input and output to/from an executable	• Input and output to/from an executable.	
Internal Interfaces: Utility functions	Internal interfaces: Utility functions	Internal interfaces: Functions/subprocedures
Input/Output	**Input/Output**	**Input/Output**
	• Clear a screen.	• Capture command line values
• File operations	• File operations	• File (record) operations

Table 7-4 Continued

Front-end	System/Utility	Self-contained
• Command line input	• Command line input	• User (keyboard) input/validation
	• Printer operations	
Built-in functions: system & session variables	**Built-in functions:** • System & session variables • String operations	**Built-in functions:** • Text case operations • String operations
Flow control: • Conditional	Flow control: • Loop testing and conditional.	**Flow control:** • Multi-conditional and loop testing.
• Exception & return code handling. (Emphasis on command errors.)	• Exception & return code handling. (Emphasis on command errors.)	• Exception & return code handling. (Emphasis on user input errors.)
		• Data validation (flow control)
General	**General** • Batch operations	**General** • Interactive operations
	• Arrays	• Arrays

Note that those components listed above in bold are characteristic of that particular command language application type. And, the final step for command languages other than REXX is beyond the scope of this work. For more on this refer to the *Command Language Cookbook.*

Should I Use a Programming Language Instead?

Good programmers are constantly evaluating their coding efforts and questioning their assumptions. Not doing so leads to being stuck in what Seymour Prapert (1980) called a "mini-world". This may lead to believing many false assumptions. Likewise, command languages are not ideal for all applications. Thus, good command language programmers are also experienced with at least one programming language so they can readily use the right "tool" to get the best fit. This section will attempt to give you an idea which language type may be appropriate to use.

The following is a list of some of the conditions **wherein it makes sense to use a command language** over a programming language.

- When a major part of the application is performing operating system, utility, "housekeeping" or startup functions.
- When the allowed development time for an application is short.
- When an application's processing speed and numerical precision is less of a concern. (Although the processing speed and numerical precision of command languages [particularly REXX and Perl] are more than adequate for most applications.)
- When string operations (particularly parsing) is a concern.
- When portability is a concern.

The following lists some of the conditions **when it makes sense to consider to use a programming language** instead of a command language.

- An application needs a data type that is not found in a command language such as imaginary numbers.
- An application's processing speed is a major concern.
- Greater numerical precision than provided by a command language is needed.
- A special function needs to be performed in an application that is only available as a class or function library for a programming language. (Such as building a customized communications application.)
- An application needs to be easily ported to operating systems/environments that a command language does not support.

When Should I Consider Third-party Commercial and Shareware REXX Extensions?

The following are some of the conditions when it makes sense to use a command language extension:

- When portability is not a concern.
- When various functions are needed to be performed by an application and are not available in the proposed command language interpreter such as communications, advanced operating system operations, full-screen applications, etc.
- When you can afford the cost of licensing fee of adding the run-time module to your application, this is an issue, particularly, if multiple versions of your application will be distributed.
- When an extension greatly enhances "the look and feel" of an application such as using Visual REXX over standard REXX for screen operations. This may depend on the type of users for a proposed application and its visibility.

OTHER REXX CONCERNS

The following sections looks at four interesting advanced and miscellaneous issues:

1. Portability concerns (including porting to and from OS/2 REXX).
2. The elusive, often overlooked area of REXX programming style.
3. The future of REXX — so you can take advantage of these trends in anticipating future REXX application development.
4. The future of OS/2 REXX. This will include a discussion of the forthcoming object-oriented extensions to OS/2 REXX.

Portability Concerns

On many occasions, a REXX application is designed with the purpose on running on multiple operating systems/environments. The issue of porting REXX applications raises the following questions:

- What is considered Portable REXX?
- What REXX non-standard features have equivalents on another REXX platforms?
- What REXX non-standard features have no equivalents on another REXX platforms?

Let's deal with each of these in turn.

What is Considered Portable REXX?

Portability implies the ability to run code unchanged on multiple computers running different operating systems. This is also called system-independence. REXX is a very portable language because most implementations support the commands found in Mike Cowlishaw's *The REXX Language: A Practical Approach to Programming.* (1990) (Hereafter called "standard REXX." Also known as REXX Language Version 4.0.) This standard will be tightened with the emergence of the REXX standard due out in 1994. However, IBM REXX implementations also adhere to the SAA REXX standard as outlined in the Common Programming Interface REXX Level 2 Reference. Therefore, writing portable REXX procedures implies adherence to at least one of two current standards and one future standard.

Note: When developing or maintaining your REXX procedure, place a comment next to a non-portable command or built-in function. Consider placing these commands in a subprocedure.

Standard REXX

Standard REXX supports the following:

- 27 keyword commands with 31 sub-keywords.
- 3 Special variables (RC, RESULT, SIGL)
- 67 functions

When porting a REXX procedure to another platform, focus on the following REXX components, for a more detailed list see the *Command Language Cookbook*

1. General issues:
    a. Implementation limits such as clause length.
    b. REXX filenames and file structure (e.g. ASCII vs. EBCDIC, fixed vs. variable length, REXX file extensions).
    c. How the REXX interpreter/compiler is invoked.
    d. Keys on new keyboard such as Escape versus Attention.
    e. If redirecting of output from the interpreter and operating system commands is supported. This is usually different for each REXX implementation.
    f. If a startup file can be a REXX procedure or support invoking a REXX procedure.

g. Differences in terms of developing external functions and libraries and command environments.

h. REXX instructions and built-in functions may give different return codes across implementations.

i. If external functions or environments are used, then finding an equivalent on the new platform is important.

2. Differences in keyword instructions :

a. These instructions will yield different output across implementations: PARSE SOURCE, and PARSE VERSION.

b. It is up to the REXX implementation to provide options for the OPTIONS instruction. Options are supported on SAA implementations (EXMODE and ETMODE described in Chapter 3.), DOS, Amiga, and some UNIX implementations.

c. REXX compilers such as CMS and TSO generally do not support the INTERPRET command.

d. The implementation of the stack is usually different across operating systems. Some of the differences are discussed in Mason Kelsey's 1990 article. Use PUSH, QUEUE, and PULL as much as possible.

e. The ADDRESS instruction will support different environments across operating systems. Each will also have a different default environment (such as CMD for OS/2 and TSO for TSO.) Operating system commands will have to be converted to the equivalent on the new platform.

f. As outlined in Chapter 2, some of the TRACE values, (especially with interactive tracing) may differ across implementations. The tracing output (such as showing CALL, INTERPRET or comments) may not be the same across platforms.

g. CALL ON NOTREADY is supported under OS/2 but not under other SAA environments.

h. The not signs may be different across REXX platforms.

i. Various CALL conditions such as NOTREADY may not be supported on all implementations. Generally use CALL/SIGNAL ON ERROR or FAILURE for portable code. (However, the conditions that raise these conditions may not be portable!)

j. Some implementation require a comment in the first line and column. (OS/2). Some recommend that this comment contain the word REXX (TSO).

k. PARSE LINEIN is supported only by DOS, OS/2, OS/400 and some UNIX implementations.

3. Differences in built-in functions:

a. Only DOS, OS/2, and UNIX support CHARIN, CHAROUT, CHARS LINEIN, LINES and LINEOUT. The number of operands supported and pointers to track the read/write stream position used by the interpreter in processing these commands may be different. (i.e., OS/2 supports only one read/write position where it is usual to have two.) CMS, DOS, and TSO support the EXECIO command.

b. Only OS/2 currently supports retrieving environment variables using the VALUE function. DOS, OS/2, and UNIX support and use operating system environment variables. (CMS supports an equivalent called global variables.)

c. Not all of the DATE and TIME values are supported across REXX implementations. These include Personal REXX on DOS and OS/2, and REXX on the Amiga. The L (local) date and time formats may be different across platforms.

d. Only DOS and OS/2 implementations support the STREAM function. This function, as currently written may use non-portable commands (i.e., if the C sub-keyword is used).

SAA REXX

SAA REXX is a superset of standard REXX.

- Support for twelve additional functions dealing with double-byte strings.
- Support of OPTIONS EXMODE and ETMODE.
- Support of standardized user exits (except TSO which uses a different syntax.) This may be standardized in the forthcoming REXX standard.
- Support of a standard common ADDRESS environment — CPICOMM.
- Support of the Variable Pool Interface to pass values between a REXX procedure and a compiled program. This may be supported in the forthcoming REXX standard.

Use these above components when porting to another SAA environment only.

The ANSI REXX Standard

Since the ANSI REXX standard is not finalized as of this writing, it is hard to suggest all of the changes you can make to your REXX procedure so it is "ANSI REXX-ready." Note that it will probably take most REXX implementations 1-2 years to have a version that is ANSI REXX compliant. This means that the standard may not produce code to all desired implementations for several years. Here are some of the "quick and dirty" changes that could be made once the standard is finalized and you obtain a compliant REXX interpreter or compiler.

1. At some point, your mainframe code may have to be changed from supporting EXECIO to CHARIN, CHAROUT, CHARS LINEIN, LINES and LINEOUT functions. Practice under OS/2 (or DOS or UNIX) and perhaps convert your mainframe or minicomputer code to support it.
2. Using the GivenUpper function instead of TRANSLATE to convert a string to uppercase.
3. Changing the ADDRESS instruction condition testing to use the RS special variable instead of RC. (i.e., ADDRESS 'dir c:\' ;if rs = 0...) This will probably take place in a later (1996) version of a standard.
4. Taking advantage of the new features:
   a. The enhanced ADDRESS command.
   b. GivenSourceChar, GivenSourceConverged which give lines in source program.
   c. The backslash as the only not sign.
   d. GivenCharIn, GivenCharOut, GivenStream, GivenStreamDescription, and PositionToChar. These names will probably change.
   e. OPTIONS ANSI to assure compliance (if implemented).

What REXX Non-standard Features Have Equivalents on Another REXX Platform?

The following are non-standard features that have equivalents in OS/2 REXX.

a. If going from Personal REXX for DOS to Personal REXX for OS/2 (or the reverse), you can use most of the 80 Personal REXX built-in functions (REXXLIB) in both implementations.
   1. However, these functions are available on DOS only: DOSMEM, FCNPKG, INP, OUTP, PCROMDATE, PEEK, and POKE.

2. These functions perform differently for both implementations: CURSOR, CURSORTYPE, DOSDIRCLOSE, DOSDIRPOS, DOSPID, EMSMEM, PCGAME, PCVIDEO, PRXSWAP, SCRBLINK, SCRMETHOD, SHIFTSTATE, STACKSTATUS.

3. The following functions are available on OS/2 only: DOSEALIST, DOSEASIZE, DOSISPIPE, all of the EVENTSEM functions, all of the MACRO functions, all of the MUTEXSEM functions, and all of the NMPIPE functions.

4. Personal REXX supports various REXX extensions that have direct equivalents in the CMS and TSO equivalents. (i.e., EXECIO, GLOBALV, LISTFILE).

5. The following REXXUTIL functions in Table 7-5 have Personal REXX equivalents: (Note that Personal REXX supports both.)

Table 7-5

IBM OS/2 function	Personal REXX equivalent
BEEP	SOUND
DIRECTORY	DOSCD, DOSCHDIR, and DOSDRIVE
FILESPEC	PARSEFN
RxMessageBox	RXWINDOW functions (W_ functions)
SysCurPos	CURSOR
SysCls	SCRCLEAR
SysDriveInfo	DOSDISK, PCDISK
SysDriveMap	DOSBOOTDRIVE, PCDISK,
SysFileDelete	DOSDEL
SysFileTree	DOSDIR
SysFileSearch	FILESEARCH, DOSISFILE
SysGetKey	INKEY, PRESS (command in DOS version only)
SysMkDir	DOSMKDIR

Table 7-5 Continued

IBM OS/2 function	Personal REXX equivalent
SysOS2Ver	DOSVERSION
SysRmDir	DOSRMDIR
SysSearchPath	DOSPATHFIND
SysSleep	DELAY
SysTempFileName	DOSTEMPNAME
SysTextScreenRead	SCRREAD, W_SCRREAD
SysTextScreenSize	SCRSIZE, W_SIZE

b. Table 7-6 is a list of equivalents to OS/2 REXX components on other platforms:

Table 7-6

OS/2 Command	Platform Equivalent
Beep	TONE (DOS — Kilowatt)
CHARIN, CHAROUT	READCH, WRITECH (ARexx)
LINEIN, LINEOUT	EXECIO (DOS, CMS, TSO, UNIX), OPEN, READLN, WRITELN (ARexx)
RxQueue (redirecting output from a file)	OUTTRAP (TSO)
RxQueue (stack operations)	DESBUF (CMS and DOS— Quercus) DROPBUF and MAKEBUF (CMS, DOS, and DOS — Quercus) DELSTACK, NEWSTACK, QBUF, QELEM, and QSTACK (TSO)

Table 7-6 Continued

OS/2 Command	Platform Equivalent
	EXTERNALS (CMS, DOS — Quercus and TSO) and PARSE EXTERNAL (CMS, DOS — Quercus and UNIX — Uni-REXX)
SysFileTree	FindDevice (ARexx), LISTDSI (TSO)
SysGetKey	GETKEY (DOS — Quercus)
SysFileSearch	ExistF (ARexx), SYSDSN (TSO)
SysMkDir	DOSCREAT, DOSMKDIR (DOS — Kilowatt)
SysRmDir	DOSDEL, DOSRMDIR (DOS — Kilowatt)
TRANSLATE (Upper case only — standard REXX)	LOWER/UPPER (ARexx [UPPER and ToUPPER only] MS-DOS [Quercus], UNIX)

c. Note that operating system commands can usually be converted from one platform to another. (Although the file structures may be different.)

What REXX Non-standard Features Have No Equivalents on Another REXX Platform?

The following non-standard features cannot be converted to or from OS/2 REXX:

1. All other REXXUTIL and OS/2 functions not listed in the previous section such as the "object" functions (i.e., SysCreateObject, SysRegisterObjectClass, SysDeregisterObjectClass, SysQueryObject, SysQueryClassList, SysSetObject-Data), the DLL functions (i.e., RxFuncadd, RxFuncDrop, RxFuncQuery), SysGetMessage, and SysIni have no equivalents on other REXX platforms.
2. Many of the non-standard AREXX functions have no OS/2 REXX equivalent. These include the five bit-testing functions (such as BITCLR), various Clip List functions (such as GetClip), and the over sixty AREXX system library functions.

3. Nearly all of the "CLIST look-alike" built-in functions of TSO have no equivalent under OS/2. These include EXTERNALS (available on CMS), FIND (CMS), INDEX (CMS), LINESIZE (CMS), LISTDSI (parts), MSG, OUTTRAP (parts), PROMPT, STORAGE (CMS), SYSDSN, SYSVAR, USERID (CMS, UNIX).
4. The following CMS functions have no equivalent under OS/2: CMSFLAG, CSL, DIAG, DIAGRC, EXTERNALS, FIND (TSO), INDEX (TSO), JUSTIFY (TSO), LINESIZE (TSO), STORAGE (TSO), USERID (TSO, UNIX).
5. The following OS/400 function has no OS/2 equivalent: SETMSGRC.
6. Immediate commands (Amiga, CMS and TSO) have no direct equivalent under OS/2.

REXX Style

REXX programming style is one of those "religious issues" that REXX programmers either embrace at some level or feel is a waste of time. Each person's style is uniquely individual and can reveal a lot about a person.

What is "Good" Programming Style?

Programming style is defined here as a set of procedures/rules that can be consistently applied to OS/2 REXX procedures. Many of these procedures can also be applied to any programming language. Also, look at DiIorio (1989), Kernighan and Plauger (1978), and Savit (1992) references for further information.

By using a "good" programming style, you promote the following attributes:

- Effective programs that are easy/fast to create, debug, and maintain.
- Programs that are easy to read because of a generous use of indentation, mixed case, and blank spaces.
- Ease of portability is enhanced with a set of consistent procedures across platforms.

Here are some *suggestions* for REXX style rules. Use these based on your personal and site preferences.

Making Your REXX Procedures More Readable.

1. **Minimize the number of multiple clauses appearing on the same line.** This also helps in debugging.

2. **Generally use blank space**. This could be before labels marking a new module, flow control structures, and operating system commands. Blank lines in large REXX procedures may have some effect on processing.

3. **Use meaningful names.** These include REXX procedures, labels, symbols, external files, etc.

4. **Use various cases consistently in your procedure.**

Here is a typical example:

   a. UPPER CASE for operating system and environment commands (also in quotes), labels.

   b. Mixed Case for REXX symbols.

   c. Lower Case for REXX instructions.

   Although there are studies showing that mixed case is the easiest to read, many people oppose its use especially in long symbol names (AgeOfRespondent). An alternative is using underscores (i.e., age_of_respondent). **Whatever approach you use, make sure that it is consistently applied.**

5. **Use quoting consistently in your procedures.** Unquoted strings, if written incorrectly, may lead to an unexpected concatenation. Remember the abuttal operator! So, generally quote strings. It is up to you whether this is consistently done with single or double quotes.

6. **Consistently indent at least two to three spaces** for the following.

   a. Clauses under a label.

   b. Instruction within a DO-END or THEN-DO-END or any DO structure.

   c. A PULL after a SAY.

   d. Nested flow-control structures (i.e., multiple IFs).

7. **Line up your flow control structures.** This includes all DOs and ENDs and SELECT and ENDs

8. **Break your REXX procedures into modules.** Each module should perform only one or two functions. Use meaningful label names to describe these functions and to mark their start.

9. **Develop some consistent rules to comment your REXX procedure.** In-program comments are another "religious" issue among REXX programmers. They may have some effect on the processing of the REXX procedure. Here are some comment suggestions:

a. Regardless of what style is used, make sure your comments are current.

b. If portability is a concern, comment non-portable sequences.

c. If multiple programmers are maintaining a REXX procedure, then use a "flower-box" providing a change history including dates and what was changed.) A comment on the changed line with the date and initials of the programmer should also be considered.

d. Commenting only complicated (non-obvious) modules.

e. Comment on the first line containing the word REXX, Not required for all implementations.

f. Comment with a header file that lists the procedure name, what each label (module) does, if any nested procedures are used, any global (or environment) variables used, and change history.

g. A comment next to each appropriate REXX instruction or environment command.

h. One or more comments before each label.

i. I prefer the "jump start" theory (also sometimes called the "three beer" theory). **WRITE AS MUCH DOCUMENTATION TO ALLOW YOU OR ANOTHER PERSON TO QUICKLY UNDERSTAND HOW THE PROCEDURE WORKS.**

Making Your REXX procedure More Effective

1. **Leave things as you found them:**

   a. Purge and close all queues, stack buffers, and files.

   b. Remove all temporary files.

   c. Remove or reset all global (or environment) variables.

   d. Reset your operating system and editor settings if changed.

2. **Redo a flow control structure if it is not easy to understand** — i.e., too many nesting levels. This may be a good sign to break a program into modules.

3. **Don't use SIGNAL as a GOTO** and try to prematurely exit a DO loop or other control structure (or enter in a flow control structure).

4. If you want an expression to be evaluated a certain way, **add parentheses** around mathematical terms.

5. **Never assume that a new data file or user input is correct.** Always check case, data type, if blank, if a valid value, and if in a valid range.

6. **Look for internal/external function and subroutine candidates.** If more than one procedure is using a particular REXX procedure, then consider making it into an external function or subroutine. If the same procedure is using a certain module heavily, then consider converting it into an internal function or subprocedure.

The Future of REXX

1993 marks the tenth anniversary of the public release of a REXX interpreter. The future continues to look bright for this product. Here are some of the future trends that I see:

1. **Continued porting of REXX to other machines and operating systems.** This is likely to include VSE, AIX, and the Power PCs. At this writing, Windows NT is just about to be announced and already four REXX interpreters will be available for that platform. A free MS-DOS REXX interpreter just appeared on the scene and the demand for free interpreters on other platforms will continue to be high. Also, as OS/2 is ported to other hardware platforms, (ports to HP and Sun have been rumored) so will OS/2 REXX. Having an OS/2 "personality" (emulation) means that REXX will be available on Workplace OS — IBM's next operating system. (Along with Taligent.)

2. **The forthcoming REXX ANSI standard means uncertainty for some time to come.** The first release basically clears up much of the ambiguities of "Standard REXX." The second release will consider adding extensions to the REXX language. Because many of the REXX implementation developers are active members of the Standards Committee, a high degree of implementation compliance is likely. But two major concerns remain: 1) What will be the user reaction to the standard efforts, particularly the second release? and, will REXX become a radically different language after the second release? The next several years will answer these questions.

3. **Converters to REXX will continue to increase the popularity of the language. These could be:**

   - UNIX shell scripts to REXX.
   - Perl to REXX
   - TCL to REXX
   - Python to REXX
   - DOS and OS/2 batch language to REXX.
   - DCL to REXX.

- Visual Basic to Visual REXX.
- AppleScript to REXX.
- REXX to various programming languages.

4. **An increase in the number of REXX compilers.** It is likely that someone will develop REXX compilers in addition to the ones available for CMS and TSO. See Pinter (1991) for more information on the issues of developing a REXX compiler.
5. **An increase in the full-screen interpreters debuggers (like PMREXX) across all REXX platforms** and the gradual disappearance of invoking REXX from the command-line. This is consistent with the success of the Graphical User Interface (GUI) on PC and workstation platforms.
6. **The increase of Visual REXX-like products across all REXX platforms.** This is consistent with the previous trend. Whether or not this will be bundled with the REXX interpreter to compete with Visual BASIC and the like remains to be seen.
7. **The increase of both REXX add-ons and REXX as an application macro language.** This is already happening on the Amiga and OS/2 platforms and no doubt, others will follow.
8. **REXX will have increasing ties into emerging areas such as multimedia, work group computing, and mobile communications.**
9. **The future of REXX on UNIX is particularly critical to its future popularity.** REXX has to decide how to market itself on UNIX platforms. Will it be a competitor or supplement to UNIX shells? With many scripting languages already well entrenched, even having free REXX interpreters on a UNIX system (as now available) may not make much of a difference.
10. **A general REXX marketing "attack" will take place.** This will lead by the newly-formed REXX Language Association (REXXLA). As a REXXLA member, you will receive a newsletter and more. Contact me (via VNR or hhg1@gte.com) on how to join.
11. **With the forthcoming arrival of AppleScript and Visual BASIC on the Macintosh and Intel platforms, REXX will have serious competition.** REXX suffers from the fact that there is no company responsible for marketing it. (Although IBM does a reasonably good job through its promotion of OS/2). REXX or IBM will be going against the marketing efforts of Apple and Microsoft which plan to bundle REXX in the operating systems, operating environments, and applications. Lotus is also pushing LotusScript as its cross-application macro language

and Borland will be pushing ObjectPal as theirs. Just as REXX's success is partially hinging on the selling of OS/2, Visual BASIC's success will be tied to the sales of Windows NT. Although OS/2 has had a successful first year, its being perceived as anything besides a niche product remains uncertain.

Future Trends

Here are some of the likely trends in OS/2 REXX:

1. **A Visual REXX-like product will eventually be bundled with OS/2 REXX.** Users are clamoring for this. It appears that the Visual REXX product will unlikely be enhanced but that something better (and supported) is likely.
2. **REXX will become the application macro language of choice under OS/2.** This is already true for many applications. However, it will become a "standard" feature for nearly all OS/2 applications because of user interest.
3. **REXX add-ons will continue to become available in healthy numbers.** These include dynamic link libraries of external functions, REXX debuggers, customized subcommands and user exits, and much more.
4. **OS/2 REXX will continue to be enhanced, keeping strong ties with changes in the operating system.** This includes taking full advantage of the forthcoming Distributed System Object Model (DSOM) which is the successor to the current SOM (System Object Model) paradigm that OS/2 is based on. OS/2 2.2 development is underway at this writing.

Object-Oriented REXX

One of the known enhancements to the OS/2 REXX language is the addition of enhanced object-oriented features to REXX.

A discussion of some object-oriented concepts and current REXX object support was presented in Chapter 3. The remainder of this chapter discusses some of what may be included in this product. This obviously may change before these extensions come to light.

Here are the major points of these extensions:

- REXX manipulates GUI items (such as folders) called **objects.** More than one object can run **concurrently.**
- Each object (and related objects) belong to a **class.** Each class defines sets of objects with similar **properties** (which determines how an object will behave — i.e., similar behaviors) and includes a set of **methods** to modify those properties and behaviors for specified objects.

```
calc = ~class~new('add numbers')
/* Creates the calc class */
/* Note the ~ (called a twiddle) operator that notes a message will be sent to a */
/* receiving object */
```

- Objects receive **messages** that includes a **method.**

```
calc~define('addtwo','add_sequence')
/* Creates a new object that is part of the calc class called add_sequence */
/* The first argument refers to the label below defining the method. */
```

- The method defines an object's behavior. It can be created "on the fly" and contains: an object to receive the object; the name of the method; and any accompanying argument. The method may give a result object.

```
/* define method */
addtwo: method expose summ
parse arg num1 num2
summ = num1 + num2
/* Entering something like reply summ will support concurrency */
return summ
```

- REXX **variables** are instances (a case) of a particular object.

```
numm = calc~new       /* A variable creates an instance of the calc object */
numm~addtwo(2,2)      /* A message is sent to the addtwo method */
```

REFERENCES

Cowlishaw, M. F. 1990 *The REXX Language: A Practical Approach to Programming 2nd ed.* Englewood Cliffs, N.J.: Prentice Hall

DiIorio, Frank 1989 "Good Code, Bad Code: Strategies for Program Design." *Proceedings of the Second Annual Northeast SAS Users Group Conference* pp. 260-266

German, Hallett 1991 "The Adventure Continues: Using CLIST, DOS Batch Languages, DCL, and REXX Command Languages in the SAS Development Cycle" *Proceedings of the Fourth Annual Northeast SAS Users Group Conference* pp. 145-150

German, Hallett 1992 *The Command Language Cookbook for Mainframes, Minicomputers, and PC's: DOS/OS/2 Batch Language, CLIST, DCL, Perl, REXX* New York: Van Nostrand Reinhold

Griswold, Ralph 1990 *An Overview of Version 8, the Icon Programming Language* (electronic file)

IBM 1992 *Systems Application Architecture: Common Programming Interface REXX Level 2 Reference* SC24-5549

IBM 1992 "OS/2 REXX Programming Interface" (handout) in the *OS/2 Developer Conference & Exposition* October 18-21 1992 Proceedings

Kelsey, Mason 1990 "REXX in Three Different Environments" *Proceedings of the REXX Symposium for Developers and Users.* pp. 172-230

Kerninghan, Brian W. and P. J. Plauger 1978 *The Elements of Programming Style. 2nd ed.* New York: McGraw-Hill

Nash, Simon C. 1990 "Object-Oriented REXX" *Proceedings of the REXX Symposium for Developers and Users* pp. 76-100

Ousterhoust, John K. 1993 *An Introduction to TCL and Tk Addision-Wesley* (electronic draft)

Pinter, R. Y. P. Vortman, and Z. Weiss 1991 "Partial Compilation of REXX" *IBM Systems Journal 20(3)* pp. 312-331

Prapert. Seymour 1980 *Mindstorms: Children, Computers, and Powerful Ideas Basic Books*

Savit, Jeffrey B. 1992 "REXX Programming Style" in the *REXX Handbook*, Gabriel Goldberg and Philip H. Smith III New York: McGraw-Hill pp. 47-67

Van Rossum, Guido 1993 *Python Library Reference*

Van Rossum, Guido 1993 *Python Tutorial*

Wall, Larry and Randal L. Schwartz 1991 *Programming Perl Sebastopol,* Calif.: O'Reilly & Associates

Watts, Keith 1990 "REXX Language I/O and Environment Challenges" *Proceedings of the REXX Symposium for Developers and Users* pp. 65-74

Appendix A: Your Turn

Your comments on this book are important to us. Please send them to:

Dianne Littwin c/o Van Nostrand Reinhold 115 Fifth Avenue, NY NY 10003
or hhg1@gte.com (via e-mail).

1. What sections did you find least interesting? Why?

2. What sections would like to see added or expanded?

3. Use this space to add any corrections, suggestions, examples, or changes you would like to see in the next edition of the book.

4. We would appreciate if you identify yourself:

Name ________________________________

Address ________________________________

____

E-mail Address ____________________________

Appendix B: REXX Error Messages

Here are list of the current OS/2 REXX Error Messages. (These are nearly identical to those found in Cowlisaw's *The REXX Language*.) Here is a breakdown by keyword:

Keyword	Error Number (Prefixed by REX00)
ADDRESS	29
CALL/Function	4, 16, 19, 40, 43, 44
DO-END	10, 14, 26, 27, 34
File Problems	1,3
IF-THEN-ELSE	8, 14, 18, 34
INTERPRET	47, 49
ITERATE/LEAVE	28
Label	16, 30, 43, 47
NUMERIC	26, 22
PARSE	38, 46
Queue/Stack Operations	48, 119-124

Keyword	Error Number (Prefixed by REX00)
RETURN	44, 45
SELECT	7, 8, 9, 10, 14, 21
SubCommands	114-118, 125
SIGNAL	4, 16, 19
TRACE	24, 26, 114

Error Message Number (Prefixed by REX00)	Message Text	What to do about It
01	"File Table Full"	1. Close some of the open files. 2. Get more memory.
02	NA	NA
03	"Program is unreadable"	Unlock file or see if there is another process using it.
04	"Program interrupted'	User or Error invoked a CALL ON HALT /SIGNAL ON HALT routine. Investigate why.
05	"Machine resources exhausted"	1. Rewrite procedure or 2. Get more memory or disk space.
06	"Unmatched /* or quote"	Delete the comment or literal string or add the quote or */.
07	"WHEN or OTHERWISE expected"	Correct your SELECT structure: - Add a WHEN or drop another clause. - Add an OTHERWISE. Check SELECT logic.

Error Message Number (Prefixed by REX00)	Message Text	What to do about It
08	"Unexpected THEN or ELSE"	Check WHEN or IF clauses. - Add an END. - Add a THEN or ELSE.
09	"Unexpected WHEN or OTHERWISE"	1. Missing SELECT instruction. 2. Drop WHEN or OTHERWISE clauses.
10	"Unexpected or unmatched END"	1. Drop DO or SELECT. 2. Add END
11	"Control stack full"	1. Check for a flow control structure that is not terminated (i.e. loops forever). 2. Simplify your flow control structure. (Exceeded OS/2 limit of 100 nested structures.)
12	"Clause too long"	Split into multiple clauses. (Exceeded OS/2 clause length limit of 500 characters.)
13	"Invalid character in program"	1. Not a blank or valid character. Check for this. 2. Do a TRACE R.
14	"Incomplete DO/SELECT/IF"	1. Do a TRACE R. 2. Add an END to a DO/SELECT structure. 3. Add a THEN clause to an IF structure.

Error Message Number (Prefixed by REX00)	Message Text	What to do about It
15	"Invalid hexadecimal or binary string"	1. Invalid hexadecimal (such as G-Z, g-z) or binary (such as 2-9) character. 2. X or B seen as start of hexadecimal/binary string instead of a character. Perhaps you need to concatenate (||) strings.
16	"Label not found"	1. Change CALL/SIGNAL routine name. 2. Add a label to subroutine/function. 3. Correct label typing error.
17	"Unexpected PROCEDURE"	1. Drop PROCEDURE statement (not part of subroutine/function). 2. Move the PROCEDURE to be the first statement after a subroutine or function definition.
18	"THEN expected"	Add a THEN to IF or WHEN instruction.
19	"String or Symbol expected"	Add a routine name in a CALL oe SIGNAL instruction.
20	"Symbol expected"	1. Run TRACE R. 2. Be on the lookout for incomplete CALL,DROP, END, ITERATE, LEAVE, NUMERIC, and PROCEDURE clauses.

Error Message Number (Prefixed by REX00)	Message Text	What to do about It
21	"Invalid data at the end of a clause"	Clause ends with an invalid end-of-clause character. Usually a typing error.
22	"Invalid character string"	Check if a literal string has any invalid characters.
23	"Invalid data string"	Check for invalid characters or typing errors.
24	"Invalid TRACE Request"	Check Trace option. Using TRACE S — not supported under OS/2. (But is on some REXX interpreters.)
25	"Invalid sub-keyword found"	Run TRACE R to see which instructions are incomple. Be especially wary of NUMERIC and PARSE clauses.
26	"Invalid Whole numbers"	Check DO, NUMERIC, and TRACE R clauses.
27	"Invalid DO Syntax"	Check DO clauses (particular look at TO/BY/FOR)
28	"Invalid LEAVE or ITERATE"	1. ITERATE/LEAVE not part of a loop 2. Entered within a loop (bad practice).
29	"Environment name too long"	On an ADDDRESS clause, check if the entered name is valid.
30	"Name or string too long"	Shorten label name, variable name or size of literal string. (Exceeded OS/2 limit of 250 characters.)

Error Message Number (Prefixed by REX00)	Message Text	What to do about It
31	"Name starts with a number or "." "	Check for invalid symbol names
32	NA	NA
33	"Invalid Expression Result"	Run TRACE R to look for invalid clauses.
34	"Logical Value Not 0 or 1"	Invalid *condition* in IF, DO, or WHEN structure.
35	"Invalid expression"	RUN TRACE R to look for invalid clauses (i.e. invalid expressions.)
36	"Unmatched "(" in expression.	1. Add right parenthesis. 2. Drop left parenthesis.
37	"Unexpected "," or ")"	1. Drop comma or right parenthesis. 2. Add left parenthesis.
38	"Invalid template or pattern"	Check statements with parsing templates such as ARG, PARSE, and PULL.
39	"Evaluation stack overflow"	Simplify/Make fewer nested expressions.
40	"Incorrect call to routine"	1. Check routine name in CALL/SIGNAL/ function/label. 2. Too many invalid arguments.

Error Message Number (Prefixed by REX00)	Message Text	What to do about It
41	"Bad arithmetic conversion"	1. Check for invalid numbers. 2. Increase NUMERIC settings.
42	"Arithmetic overflow/ underflow"	1. Dividing by 0. 2. Invalid exponent.
43	"Routine not found"	Check/subroutine name in both invocation and definition clauses (i.e. CALL, SIGNAL, label)
44	"Function did not return data"	Functions, by definition, are supposed to return a result. Check your function invocation and definition clauses (usually for external functions).
45	"No data specified or function RETURN"	Functions, by definition, are supposed to return a result. Check your function invocation and definition clauses (usually for internal functions).
46	"Invalid variable reference"	1. Mistyped symbol name. 2. Missing parethesis. 3. Run TRACE R to look for invalid instructions. (Be on the look out for invalid DROP, PARSE, or PROCEDURE clauses.)
47	"Unexpected label" **Not part of Standard REXX**	Take the Label out of the INTERPRET or other instruction.

Error Message Number (Prefixed by REX00)	Message Text	What to do about It
48	"Failure in system service"	Check queue/stack/stream operations clauses. If invoked by a C program, check syntax of the exit handlers.
49	"Interpretation error"	1. Check syntax. 2. Simplify expression
50	NA	NA
102-113	"January" (102) - "December " (113) **Not part of Standard REXX**	Nothing but fun to show to friends.
114	"Interactive Trace. TRACE OFF to end. Enter to continue". **Not part of Standard REXX**	Normal interactive trace message (CHECK)
115	"The RXSUBCOM parameters are incorrect." **Not part of Standard REXX**	Check RXSUBCOM syntax.
116	"The RXSUBCOM parameter REGISTER are incorrect" **Not part of Standard REXX**	Check RXSUBCOM syntax.

Error Message Number (Prefixed by REX00)	Message Text	What to do about It
117	"The RXSUBCOM parameter DROP is incorrect" **Not part of Standard REXX**	Check RXSUBCOM syntax.
118	"The RXSUBCOM parameter LOAD is incorrect" **Not part of Standard REXX**	Check RXSUBCOM syntax.
119	"REXX queuing system not initialized" **Not part of Standard REXX**	- System Bug. Contact IBM. - System corrupted/ missing files. May need reinstall.
120	"Size of data incorrect" **Not part of Standard REXX**	RXQUEUE can only have records ranging between 0 and 65,472 characters.
121	"Storage for data queues is exhausted." **Not part of Standard REXX**	1. Add more memory 2. Delete uneeded data in queues.
122	The name is not a valid queue name. **Not part of Standard REXX**	Change name to include only letters, numbers, period, exclamation point, and question mark.

Error Message Number (Prefixed by REX00)	Message Text	What to do about It
123	The queue access mode is not correct. **Not part of Standard REXX**	1. Files may be corrupted or missing. 2. System bug — contact IBM.
124	The Queue does not exist. **Not part of Standard REXX**	Create queue or use an existing queue.
125	"The RXSUBCOM parameter QUERY is incorrect" **Not part of Standard REXX**	Check RXSUBCOM syntax.

Appendix C: REXX BBSes

The following are phone numbers of BBSes that contain general REXX procedures or vendors who support OS/2 REXX products. These have not been tested by the author — including how virus-free they are:

Blue Edge BBS (has REXXLIB software)	in Maryland (301) 526-7243 (look in REXXLIB).
Mansfield Software	in Connecticut (203) 429-3784, 300-9600 8-N-1.
Oberon Software	in Minnesota 507-388-1154. (TE/2)
Quercus Systems (has REXXLIB software)	in California (408) 867-7488 1200 or 2400 8-N-1
REXXpert Systems, Inc.	in Rocklin, CA. (916) 783-4739, 7am-7pm Pacific time, Mon-Fri, 2400-8-N-1.

The following are BBSes that are oriented to OS/2. These may contain some REXX procedures: (Those in Bold are official IBM sites — such as for patches):

Fernwood [Connecticut]	203-483-0348
Blue BBS [California]	213-494-6168
Optical Illusion [Pennsylvania]	215-879-3310
Medlantic BBS[Maryland]	301-680-7792

IBM BBS [Atlanta]	**404-835-6000** **800-547-1283 (BBS Info)**
IBM Canada BBS {Toronto]	**416-946-4255 (2400 baud)** **416-946-4244 (9600 baud)**
Comu-Plane BBS [Oregon]	503-759-3811
Bay Area OS/2 BBS [California]	510-657-7948
Logistique LMM [Montreal, Canada]	514-374-9422
IBM Canada BBS [Montreal]	**514-938-3022 (2400 baud)**
IBM Canada BBS [Vancover]	**604-664-6466 (2400 baud)** **604-664-6464 (9600 baud)**
OS/2 Shareware BBS [Virginia]	703-385-4325
Life's like that [Virginia]	703-560-5616
Greater Chicago Online [Illinois]	708-895-4042
Omega-Point BBS [California]	714-963-8517
Magnum BBS [California]	805-582-9306
OS/2 Magazine [California]	805-684-0589
WSI BBS [Tennessee]	901-386-4712
Wizard's Opus [Florida]	904-682-1620
Programmer's Oasis [North Carolina]	919-226-6984
IBM South Africa	**27-11-224-2000**
IBM Belgium	**32-2-725-6010**
OS/2 Mania [France]	33-1-64-090460
IBM UK	**44-256-336655**

Usrsus Fremens Rexx [UK]	44-772-828975
Josti-BBS [Denmark]	45-47-380120 -380524
IBM Germany	**49-711-785-7777**
Checkpoint OS/2	49-733-168221
IBM Australia	**61-2-241-2466**
3M Australia	61-2-498-9184
OZ - Share OS/2 BBS [Australia]	61-7-398-3759
OS/2 Centre [Singapore]	65-274-0577

Appendix D: Anonymous FTP sites

The following are the names of some OS/REXX anonymous ftp sites. Files are accessed using the following sequence:

1. Enter *ftp site_name* to access these files.
2. Then enter *anonymous* as your userid and your *mail address* as the password.
3. Then, you usually enter *cd \pub* to access the public file area. ls will list the directories/files .
4. Then *cd* to the appropriate directory (usually os2). Don't forget to enter *binary* first if transferring "zip" or non-text files.
5. Enter *bye* to close the session and exit ftp.

Site_name	Comments
access.usask.ca	
rexx.uwaterloo.ca	Use only between 6pm-8am Pacific Time on weekdays
ftp-os2.nmsu.edu	
pftp.urz.uni-heidelberg.de	
funic.funet.fi	
luga.latrobe.edu.au	
mims-iris.waterloo.edu	
mtsg.ubc.ca	in os2:
novell.com	8am-5:30 pm Pacific Time only
software.watson.ibm.com	The official IBM ftp site. Mirrored at cdrom.com
vega.hut.fi	

Appendix E: Other OS/2 Electronic Resources

1. Usenet News Groups of interest:

bit.listserv.os2-l	Bitnet OS/2 newsgroup
comp.lang.rexx	A general REXX discussion newsgroup. Includes articles from Dave Gomberg and IBM support. An archive of past articles can be found in the /pub/rexx directory of flipper.pvv.unit.no using anonymous ftp.
comp.os.os2.programming	Discussion group on all OS/2 programming questions including REXX.

2. Bitnet mailing lists. Send a message to LISTSERV@*host* (listed below). The message should contain the words SUBSCRIBE *list_name your_full_name* (listed below).

List name	Hosts	Topics
OS2-L	HEARN	OS/2 and OS/2 REXX
PC-REXX	UCF1VM	Personal REXX
REXX-L	U1UCVMD	REXX General Language
	UALTAVM	
REXXLIST	DEARN	REXX General Language Same as REXX-L
	EBOUB011	

List name	Hosts	Topics
	FINHUTC	
	HEARN	
	OHSTVMA	
	POLYGRAF	
	TWNMOE10	
	UALTAVM	
	UCF1VM	
	UGA	

3. To access a ftp mail server (if no ftp capability), send a message to bitftp@pucc.bitnet or ftpmail@decwrl.dec.com. The message should contain the word help.

4. REXXLIB is a list of REXX programs with documentation for all platforms. Send a message to REXXLIB@PSUVM to find out further information. This is also available on Blue Edge BBS and Quercus System's BBS.

5. As mentioned throughout the book, there are various REXX resources available on on-line services such as BIX and CompuServe.

   For CompuServe, check the following areas:

GO BORLAND	Look in ObjectVision
GO IBMPRO	Look in Other languages
GO OS2DF1	Look at REXX and other languages.
GO OS2USER	Look in Application questions.
GO OS2SUP	Look in REXX and other languages
GO PCVENA	Look in Mansfield, Quercus
GO QUERCUS	Personal REXX

6. If you do not have ftp access, you can still purchase the ftp-os2 OS/2 archives on CD-ROM:

   Bob Bruce
   Walnut Creek CDROM
   1547 Palos Verdes Mall, Suite 260
   Walnut Creek, Ca 94596
   Phone: 800-786-9907
   Fax:510-947-1644

7. There is both a Gopher (Info Retrieval) Server and client for OS/2 The OS/2 client has built-in access to the Almaden IBM Gopher site with much info. Gopher clients and servers can be obtained from most OS/2 BBSes and Anonymous FTP sites.

8. Once connected to a Gopher Server, use Veronica with the keyword REXX to find other Gopher sites with REXX files. A quick search found the REXX Standard Minutes, and SHARE REXX Project abstracts on-line.

Appendix F: OS/2 Vendors

Here is a list of the OS/2 vendors mentioned in this book.

Vendor	Address/Product
Borland International Inc.	Phone: 408-438-5300 Address: 1800 Green Hills Road POB 66001, Scotts Valley, CA 95067-001 Product: **ObjectVision** (See Chapter 6.)
CTC (Command Technology Corporation)	Phone: 510-521-5900 Fax: 510-521-0369 Orders: 800-336-3320 Address: 1040 Marina Village Parkway Alameda, CA 94501 Product: **SPF/PC** (See Chapter 6.)
DeScribe Inc.	Phone: 916-646-1111 Address: 4234 N. Freeway Blvd., STE 500 Sacramento, CA 95834 Product: **DeScribe**. Word processor used for this book.
Hockware	Phone: 919-387-0757, 0616 Address: POB 336, Cary, NC 27512-0336 Product: **Visual Programming With REXX** Also in CompuServe OS2AUER forum.

Vendor	Address/Product
IBM Corporation	OS2 Orders: 800-3-IBM-OS2 General: 800-426-2255 or 914-765-1900 Fax: 303-440-1639 Product: **OS/2** Developer Support: 407-982-6408 Address: Old Orchard Road Armonk NY 10504
Mansfield Software Group Inc.	Phone: 203-429-8402 Fax: 203-487-1185 Address: P.O.B. 532 Storrs, CT 06268 Product: **KEDIT** (See chapter 6)
Mark Hessling	Phone: 61-7-875-7691 Fax: 61-7-875-5314 Mail: M.Hessling@gu.edu.au Address: DBA,ITS Griffith University Nathan, Brisbane QLD 4111 Australia Software: **THE** (See chapter 6) and **PDCurses** (window libraries).
Oberon Software	Phone: 507-388-7001 Fax: 507-388-7568 Address: 518 Blue Earth Street Mankato, Minnesota 56001-2142 Product: **TE/2** (See chapter 6.) and **FSHL** (a shell alternative to CMD.EXE)
Quercus Systems	Phone: 408-867-REXX Fax: 408-867-7489 Address: POB 2157 Saratoga, CA 95070 Product: **Personal REXX** and **REXXTERM.** (See chapters 4 and 6.)
Ruddock & Associates Inc	Phone: 416-340-0887 Fax: 416-340-7373 Address: Anthony Green 74 McGill St Toronto, Ontario M5B 1H2 Product: **REXXTACY**

Vendor	Address/Product
SourceLine Software, Inc.	Phone: 619-587-4713 Address: 7770 Regents Road #113-502 San Diego CA 92122 Product: **SourceLink** (See chapter 6)
Tritus, Inc.	Phone: 800-321-2100 or 512-794-5800 Fax: 512-794-3833 Address: 6034 W. Courtyard Drive, Suite 120, Austin, Texas 78730-5014 Product: **Tritus SPF** (See chapter 6)
Watcom International Corporation	Phone: 800-265-4555 or 519-886-3700 Fax: 519-747-4971 Address: 415 Philip Street Waterloo Ontario Canada N2L 3X2 Product: **VX-REXX** (See Appendix I) CompuServe: GO PCVENH

Appendix G: OS/2 REXX Shareware

The following is a list of some of the available OS/2 REXX software. The names may be slightly different on your on-line service or anonymous ftp site.

ACTS11.ZIP

Description: REXX procedure to dial NIST Automated Computer Time Service for setting PC date and time. Can optionally adjust for daylight savings time.

ATRGF.ZIP

Description: ATRGF is similar to the AT command on UNIX. It runs a command at a time specified. Unlike CRONRF, there is no control file and usually there is only a single execution of the command.

BBSREX.ZIP

Description: This is an 800+ line REXX HLLAPI procedure that logons to IBM's OS2BBS on IBMLink. It then retrieves all or the new notes from selected forums and saves them into a file Or uploads new notes from files on the PC. Also included are some useful HLLAPI routines (e.g. HostScreenToStem).

BDSOM1.ZIP

Description: This REXX procedure generates a description language that uses SysCreateObject to create OS/2 folder and program objects. It automatically resolves path names and nesting of objects within folders.

BROWSE.ZIP

Description: A BROWSE REXX procedure for OS/2 2.0 including search and edit.

CHGCAS.ZIP

Description: Simple REXX procedure that changes the name of one or more OS/2 files to upper/lower case.

CRTOBJ.TXT

Description: Tips, techniques and samples for using the Rexx Workplace Shell functions. Many useful tips and information about using SysCreateObject, SysIni and related functions to manipulate the Workplace Shell.

DEFPRN.CMD

Description: A simple REXX procedure that shows how to use SysIni to query the system for the default printer port.

DELDIR.CMD

Description: REXX procedure (uses REXXUTIL) that deletes directories and files at same time.

DHRGCD.ZIP

Description: Use this REXX procedure to change a directory for all hard disks. It is identical to Norton NCD. It Includes a DLL (similar to REXXUTIL) that returns information from a DosQuerySysInfo request such as the boot disk (and more.)

EAPREP.CMD

Description: A REXX procedure that creates command files to automate the backup and restoration of extended attributes, for use with DOS backup programs that are not aware of extended attributes.

EVX.ZIP

Description: Ben Chi's external algebraic and transcendental functions. Also look at RXMATH.

FACTOR.ZIP

Description: A Rexx procedure that factors a positive integer by entering "factor nnnnnn."

GENFLD.CMD

Description: Creates folder and program objects (if a user has rights. Based on NetWare group program objects.) Or destroys objects for which they no longer have rights. This update adds initialization commands options and multi-value strings like DOS_DEVICE and DOS_VERSION.

GOPHER.ZIP

Description: The client for distributed information retrieval. **Part of IBM Employee-Written Software Program.** An OS/2 Gopher server is also available.

HLP2IN.CMD

Description: A simple REXX procedure to create an INF file from a HLP file.

ICNTLK.ZIP

Description: This utility allows .CMD files to update the ICON and TITLE text with a message. It is useful for updates, or just to add interesting comments to your batch procedures. This works with fullscreen or windowed OS/2 sessions.

I265.ZIP

Description: This is the handout (in PostScript format) and all the sample programs from the Using REXX Procedure Language in the OS/2 Environment' session at SHARE 79 in Atlanta. (Sessions I265-I266).

INIT_A.ZIP

Description: This procedure is an example of Dialog Manager with REXX. Shows HELP, MSG Popup, Grayed choices, etc. GML is included so you can change dialogs. If you don't have DM runtime (it's shipped with the toolkit), download INIT_D.ZIP instead. (Which includes DM runtime and source.)

INIT_D.ZIP

Description: Download this file if you DO NOT have the Dialog Manager Runtime.

MNET10.ZIP

Description: This REXX procedure makes NET.CFG files. It uses driver definitions stored in a simple text file format. Useful for many installations of OS/2 and the NetWare Requester.

MONDAY.ZIP

Description: The Monday Adventure game, by Mikel Rice. Originally coded on CMS.

MSTDSK.ZIP

Description: Reads a text file and create objects on the desktop.

PMCOMM.ZIP

Description: A working demo of Pmcomm 1.10 is a commercial OS/2 Presentation Manager Asynchronous communication program. Includes sample scripts. This version requires OS/2 1.2 or later. Pmcomm also allows you to use a modem pool, under OS/2 LAN Server.

PMGLOBE.ZIP

Description: A program (written by Mike Cowlishaw) that simulates the motion of the Earth. Uses REXX as an application macro language. **Part of IBM Employee-Written Software Program.**

PMSW.ZIP

Description: Use either as a REXX external function or an executable. Tests if a task is active or makes a task active. With C source.

PRXUT1.ZIP

Description: A DLL of macrospace, date,virtual i/o functions.

QDATE.CMD

Description: QDATE - Query Date Program. A Mike Cowlishaw's REXX procedure (one of the earliest) that provides the date and corresponding phase of the moon.

QTIME.CMD

Description: QTIME — Query Time Program. Another Mike Cowlishaw REXX procedure (one of the earliest) that provides the time of day in English.

RD!.CMD

Description: RD! deletes entire directory structures (either HPFS and FAT.) This is a a simple but effective example of how REXX can enhance OS/2 by solving a common problem.

REXXEA.ZIP

Description: A DLL of REXX callable functions for handling Extended Attributes of a file/directory. Exceeds the REXXUTIL capabilities.

REXMAZ.ZIP

Descriptions: This REXX procedure draws a maze on your screen using the IBM graphics character set.

REXXOV.ZIP

Description: Two examples demonstrating the ObjectVision REXX connection. SEEK.OVD is a simple clone of the OS/2 Seek and Scan applet. ADDTYPE.OVD adds new associated types to the system and displays the currently defined associated types. Neither of these are particlarly sophisticated

REXXPA.ZIP

Description: RexxPack v1.0 — RexxPack optimizes a REXX procedure to run faster (and reduces it to one line),and stops user modifications to a REXX procedure.

REXXTA.ZIP

Description: The latest version of the REXXTACY compiler. It has been re-written to increase run-time performance, and to address a number of the reported bugs. REXXTACY is a REXX-to-C compiler — generating Microsoft C Version 6 compatible source code from your REXX procedures.

REXXTR.ZIP

Description: DLL with these functions RxBootDrive, RxVolumeLabel, RxRead, RxWrite, RxVarDump, RxStemCopy, RxSort, RxSwitchTo and RxExtras (to load and drop the function set).

RGF.ZIP

Description: Contains a DLL and REXX sample files that encode/decode files (such as for electronic mailings). The DLL was recompiled with MS C 6.0 — to run 30% faster. Sample REXX procedures include: 1) MAKE_XXD.CMD — encoding example. 2) DECODE.CMD — Recreates executables from XX/UU-encoded files. 3) LSPLIT.CMD — Splits a file into multiple chunks. 4) CODE_IT.CMD — Encodes/Decodes executables using REXX.

RGFREX.ZIP

Description: Author-Rony G. Flatscher A fairly complete set of REXX date/time functions. Includes: DATERGF.CMD — date/time conversions & arithmetics, DATE2STR.CMD — date string formating, ATRGF.CMD — Delay command execution, and TIMEIT.CMD — Time commands.

RMODEM.CMD

Description: RMODEM Version .45 is a REXX based Hayes compatible modem handler and communications script utility. Part of a larger package to be released. Also demonstrates how to use OS/2 REXX to control a a modem attached to a COM port.

RSCOPY.ZIP

Description: Alternative to BACKUP/RESTORE. Copies files only when source file is newer than target file, or source doesn't exist in target.

RXCALC.ZIP

Description: A set of sample C programs on using REXX as an application macro language. The example application is a very simple PM-based calculator. Various levels of REXX support are shown: from program function keys to an extremely integrated macro environment with tracing and I/O support.

RXD.ZIP

Description: A full-screen REXX debugger. **Part of the IBM Employee-Written Software Program.**

RXINFO.ZIP

Description: Provides a readable/printable (ASCII) version of the on-line REXX file. Section numbers and section dividing lines have been added to make it easier for reading/searching.

RXMATH.ZIP

Description: DLL of mathematical and trigonometric functions. **Part of the IBM Employee-Written Software Program.**

RXMNU2.ZIP

Description: RexxMenu is an OS/2 REXX procedure for prompting user selection from a choice list. Useful for quick access to commonly used programs or calls, and for choosing options from among any file list.

RXPRIO.ZIP

Description: A DLL (with source and a REXX sample) that can be invoked from REXX (using the SysSetPriority system call) to change its priority. It must be copied to one of the directories listed in LIBPATH.

RXSHIP.ZIP

Description: REXXShip Version 2.5 by Timothy F. Sipples. Sends any binary file as a self extracting plain ASCII file (that is a REXX procedure). Recipient can decode file with OS/2 1.3/2.0's REXX (or xxdecode on any other platform). Useful for sending binary file through any text-only link (such as mail).

SERVER.CMD

Description: A simple REXX procedure (less than 10 lines) that creates a private REXX queue in one session which can retrieve data queued by another session. (The data came from another REXX procedure or some utility which can pipe its output to the RXQUEUE utility.)

SHWINI.ZIP

Description: A large REXX procedure to perform operations on .INI files such as (displaying, backup, and modifying .INI values)

STONE.ZIP

Description: Search for the Sacred Stone, an adventure game written in REXX. Originally coded on CMS.

TIMESE.ZIP

Description: OS/2 REXX Utility to dial the Naval Observatory and set your system time to their time.

UPPRT.ZIP

Description: REXX command files to print 2UP in landscape mode or 1UP in portrait mode on laser printers using PPDS or HPLJ commands. Will number lines or support ANSI control characters. Suppresses multiple blank lines and page ejects. Includes VREXX versions. Supports A4 [European] paper size. Version 1.6.

VMB10.ZIP

Description: Issues a DosStartSession for a DOS program or .BAT file that defines DOS session parameters to tailor a session, such as DOS_BACKGROUND_EXECUTION, DPMI_DOS_API etc. using an ASCII text file. Especially useful on LANs or with mountable disks to test for access prior to starting a program. Source available.

VREXX.ZIP

Description: Visual REXX as described in Chapter 4. **Part of the IBM Employee-Written Software Program.**

WPSGEN.ZIP

Description: REXX procedure that easily builds Workplace Shell Objects. Created by Blue Bird Computing Inc.

Appendix H: Glossary of Terms

Here are some of the terms used in this book.

CL (See Command Language)

Command Language or **CL**

1. Uses English-like commands and offers the user an easy means to "ask" the operating system to perform one or more tasks.

2. A language spoken on an obscure island in the South Pacific which is nothing other than a series of orders.

Comment

1. For OS/2 REXX, required on the first line and column of a procedure.

   Begins with a /* and ends with a */. May slow down processing on some operating systems. Many different commenting style exists.

2. What a programmer has after inheriting someone else's REXX procedure that is not indented and lacks comments.

Dynamic Link Library or DLL

1. In REXX, A compiled package of external REXX functions.

Edit macro (see macro)

Exec (see Procedure)

Expressions

1. In REXX, sets of data that an explicit arithmetic, string, boolean,or relational operation(s) is to be performed on. One or more expressions may be found in a REXX clause.

2. What Judy has on her face when being woken up from a sound sleep at 2 a.m.

External Command

1. In REXX, a command that is recognized as not being a REXX command and is passed to the external operating system or application.
2. A command given outside the home.

Extended Attributes

1. In OS/2, a set of additional data (such as file type or a comment) that is attached to a file. REXX can process these.

Instruction

1. A REXX statement containing a keyword.

2. Used in education circles. Such as in signs outside schools saying "Instruction ahead."

Macro or Edit Macro

1. A specialized REXX procedure that performs one or more edit operations.

2. A new diet to try out.

Macrospace

1. In REXX, where procedures reside (in memory) for faster execution.

2. An undeveloped large tract of land.

Object

1. Everyday things you use such as folders and programs.

2. Something that can't write a REXX program because it lacks a breathing mechanism.

Parsing

1. The ability to break up a string into two or more specified substrings.

2. What the more expensive food processors can do.

Procedure

1. What an OS/2 REXX program is called. (Sometimes called script, macro, or exec).

2. The series of steps needed to successfully program a VCR.

Queue

1. In REXX, used to store and retrieve output from commands and the keyboard.

2. Whatever forms whenever you are in a hurry to cash a check at the bank.

REXX

1. The **RE**structured e**X**tended e**X**ecutor command language created by Mike Cowlishaw of IBM in 1979.

2. The name of some forgotten person's dog. Not the name of some large, forgotten dinosaur.

SAA or **Systems Application Architecture**

1. The series of rules and guidelines that IBM used for generating portable applications across their entire hardware line. REXX was selected as the SAA command (procedures) language. Its future is uncertain.

2. The name of a banned rock group from the 1970s. They are best remembered for having badly coded REXX programs displayed on their record.

Signal

1. In REXX, a routine used for exception handling. Sometimes misused as a GOTO.

2. What Tommy was ignoring when he drove through the intersection.

SQL

1. **Structured Query Language** (Prononunced either "see-kwel" or "ess-queue-ell.") is a standardized language (defined by ISO, ANSI, and SAA standards) that allows you to perform operations on relational databases. (A simplified definition is a collection of related data that is maintained in a two-dimensional table. This is sometimes called "a flat file" such as a phone listing.), SQL calls allow portability across the entire SAA line. Note that vendors often put in extensions to the SQL language.

Stem

1. Part of a compound symbol that identifies the "array" such as a. (letter[s] and a period). Operations performed on a stem affect the entire "array."

Stream

1. In REXX, a series of data from a device (such as a keyboard or serial port) or a file.

2. What formed in the house after two-year old Lucy left the faucet running.

Subprograms

1. "Modules" of REXX code that perform a series of tasks and return a result.

2. Bad code that is not worthy of being called a program.

Symbol

1. In REXX, includes labels and keyword **instructions** and simple or compound symbols (variables with values).

Tail

1. The part of the compound symbol "array" that identifies the element (may be numbers or letters) .0 usually has a value of the number of elements in the "array.

2. What Billy had after his first experience with compound symbols, i.e., a tail to tell.

Token

1. In REXX, types of data such as strings, symbolic variables, and operators that are delimited by blanks.

2. What you have to deposit to use rapid transit in many cities. Colors vary.

Trace

1. In REXX, the means used to debug a REXX procedure. May be fully interactive.

2. What children like to do on clear pieces of paper.

Appendix I: VX-REXX from Watcom

INTRODUCTION

This is a "bonus" section. It was written during the final days between proofing and typesetting. (My thanks to Dianne and the Campbells for giving it the green light.) It includes the essential information needed to get you up and running with VX-REXX. Time does not permit inclusion of coding examples. In future editions, this appendix will be expanded to a full chapter. Competitors to this product such as Hockware's Visual Programming With REXX will also be looked at as well.

Note that this product is relatively new (available since late June 1993) and bears a release version of 1.0. No doubt, it will be enhanced in future releases and interim updates. (One was planned for September 1993.)

Overview

VX-REXX has the following features:

- SOM and CUA '91 compliance
- Interfaces to standard IBM OS/2 REXX extensions like REXXUTIL, Communications manager, and Database Manager.
- Interfaces to Standard OS/2 procedures and application macros.
- 15 Basic tools (Also called controls or objects) that can be placed on an application window.
- 72 different properties that can be assigned to an object (such as bordertype.)

- 42 different VX-REXX functions to manipulate objects and perform system operations.
- And much more...

Invoking VX-REXX

Use any of the following two approaches to start VX-REXX:

The Direct Approach

1. From the Workplace shell, double-click on the "Watcom VX-REXX" icon (red & yellow lightening bolt).
2. The Watcom VX-REXX Icon view (or the default view) should appear. Double-click on the VX-REXX icon. (A notepad with a pencil). Other files in the directory include on-line help and sample programs.
3. The VX-REXX logo screen should briefly be shown. This is followed by the main screen of VX-REXX. You may then perform any valid operation with VX-REXX.

The New Project Approach

Each new application requires its own VX-REXX project. This is a collection of all of the related files for an application. To create a new project and access VX-REXX, use the following approach: (Note that projects can also be created within VX-REXX.)

1. From the Workplace shell, double-click on the "Watcom VX-REXX" icon (red & yellow lightening bolt).
2. The Watcom VX-REXX Icon view (or the default view) should appear. Double-click on the Projects folder icon.
3. Drag the "VX-REXX Project" template icon anywhere in the icon view window.
4. A new folder named "VX-REXX Project 1" is created. Double-click on this icon.
5. The project folder should have three empty items: Window1.VRX/Window1.VRY (various source files), and Project.VRP (the project file). Click on the Project.VRP (the Notepad with a pencil) icon.
6. The VX-REXX logo screen should briefly be shown. This is followed by the main screen of VX-REXX. You may then perform any valid operation with VX-REXX.

Exiting VX-REXX

Simply click on the system menu in the top-left hand corner of the VX-REXX window. Then select Close. (Either Enter just C, click on Close, or press Alt-F4.) Some of the things that you can do once in VX-REXX are covered in a later section.

Getting Help about VX-REXX

Use any of the following means to get more help on VX-REXX:

1. Once in VX-REXX, you may access the on-line help by clicking on the Help menu option or entering H. Then select "General Help" to access the VX-REXX on-line help. Information is available on: 1) the VX-REXX menu options, 2) using the VX-REXX debugger and much more.
2. Within the Watcom VX-REXX folder are four on-line references:

   (These are all in the directory where VX-REXX resides. The default name is VXREXX)

Name In Window (Actual File Name)	What it is
Reference (a2z.inf)	Reference Same as the printed version — list of functions.
Programmer's Guide (progguid.inf)	Programmer's Guide. Same as the printed version.— information on programming VX-REXX.
Read Me First (readme.inf)	Readme First Same as the printed version. Provides release notes, installation instructions, and other general information.
REXX Information (rexx.inf)	OS/2 REXX Language Reference The standard IBM REXX reference and tutorial. REXXUTIL functions are also included.

3. VX-REXX includes some sample applications: (Found in the \VXREXX\SAMPLES directory.)

BUTTON	Turns any of four buttons to red.
CALC	A calculator program.
HINTHELP	An example of how to build context-sensitive help in a VX-REXX application.
MINDGAME	A version of MasterMind.
MOVIES	Uses the Multimedia Presentation Manager to run software-driven video.
SAMPLEDB	An example of a database viewer using Extended Services or DB2/2.
SCAN	Uses the OS/2 Enhanced Editor discussed earlier to build a customized edit command. This command displays all labels in a REXX procedures and can then go to that label in the procedure (and display the procedure.)
THREADS	An example of coding a multi-threaded application using VX-REXX. This allows you to take full advantage Of OS/2.

4. VX-REXX includes some utilities. These are the following:

BPATCH.EXE	A program to apply patches to VX-REXX.
BUILDVRX.CMD	A REXX procedure that restores the Watcom VX-REXX folder if damaged or erased. Has some good examples of using REXXUTIL's SysCreateObject.
CONVERT.EXE	A VX-REXX procedure that converts from VX-REXX projects to the current (1.0) format.
TECHINFO.EXE	Provides information on your system for Watcom Tech support. (Version is 1.3) Output is placed in a file called TECHINFO.OUT This includes: Environment variables, free memory, OS/2 version, CONFIG.SYS, AUTOEXEC.BAT, and microprocessor type.

5. For additional help on VX-REXX, try the following sources:
   a. CompuServe — Enter GO WATCOM which is library 5 in PCVENH. This includes tech notes, patches, and updates.
   b. The anonymous ftp site of rexx.uwaterloo.ca. Call between 6 p.m. and 8 a.m. Pacific Time on weekdays.
   c. Tech Support phone at 519-884-0702, regular fax 519-747-4971, WATFAX 519-747-2693, BBS —519-884-2103 (nearly all baud rates).
   d. Internet support at tech@watcom.on.ca

Basic Operations

Once in VX-REXX, the project window appears. It contains three parts:

a) The menu

b) The project window which appears on the user's display when running an application.

c) The tools palette (in Visual BASIC this is called the toolbox).

Each of these will be briefly looked at.

The Menu

The menu offers the following operations: (Main menu names are in boldface)

- **Project** —(Create, open and save) and file (Create a window or code file) operations. Create a EXE (self-executable binary version of a VX-REXX project) file, or a REXX macro to be used with applications.
- **Tools** — (In Visual BASIC also called controls). You may select the particular tool from the menu or use the tool palette on the right-hand side of the project window. These include 14 tools (or objects) such as Descriptive Text, Check Box, Combo Box, Radio Buttons, etc. Once a tool is selected, the mouse pointer changes to a plus (or cross-hair). Then, you may drag the mouse to the desired location and determine the size of the tool.
- **Windows** — Makes active any of these following windows used while creating and maintaining a project. These include errors (useful when debugging a problem), file list (lists all the files of a project which can be then copied, renamed, viewed, etc.), section list (lists all of the sections of a file which then can be created, viewed, or deleted), tool palette (see below), and window (lists all windows in a window file which then can be created, deleted, etc.).

- **Run**. Used to either run or debug a project.
- **Options**. Allows you to customize your VX-REXX session. These include setting the default editor (The OS/2 Enhanced Editor [EPM] is the default.), run or debug project options (Such as the working directory, command-line arguments, and the main window file).), and performing object library operations. (Object libraries end with a .VRL extension and are supplied by Watcom or third-parties. They provide more tools and functions to VX-REXX.)
- On-line **Help**

The Tools Palette and Project Window

The tools palette performs an identical function as the Tools menu option — it allows you to select a control to be placed on the project window. (Except the tool names are represented by icons instead of by text.) Once a tool is selected, the mouse pointer changes to a plus (or cross-hair). Then, you may drag the mouse to the desired location and determine the size of the tool.

The project window is the window where your tools (or objects) are placed — the user-viewable part of the application. Rows of dots appear in this window to help you align your tool.

Extending VX-REXX

You can use any of the following methods to extend VX-REXX:

1. Obtaining additional object libraries from Watcom and third-parties that allow additional objects (tools) to be used projects.
2. You can also build external VX-REXX functions. A technical note and example on how to do this is available on the Compuserve and anonymous ftp site mention above. Look for a file called vxtech.zip.
3. VX-REXX has interfaces to many of the OS/2 API and applications:
   a. You can use VX-REXX to build and run application macros (such as enhanced editor [EPM], PMGLOBE, GOPHER, etc.) or standard OS/2 REXX procedures.

      To do this, use the following procedure:

      1. Create a new project folder as mentioned above.
      2. Since most application macros and standard REXX procedures have no windows, select the Project menu and the *New Code File* submenu selection.
      3. Add the REXX instructions (if not done already).

4. Select the Project menu and the *Make Macro* subcommand option.

5. If an application macro, run the application and invoke the macro.

OR

5. If a standard REXX application. Enter VRX *procedure_name* arguments (This executes VRX.EXE)

b. VX-REXX has also ties to Extended Service's Database Manager (now DB2/2). Running the Sample project SAMPLEDB will show you an example of how to do this. (Don't forget to run sqlampl first.)

c. Look at the MOVIE sample project to see an example of interfacing VX-REXX with the Multimedia Presentation Manager/2 software.

d. VX-REXX should also work with other IBM extensions such as Communications Manager.

Debugging VX-REXX Projects

Use the following to debug VX-REXX procedures:

a. If an error is encountered when running a VX-REXX procedure, then the Errors window will be displayed. It will show which section and line caused the error and a trace of the same.

b. Selecting Debug project from the Run menu will provide an interactive trace session. You can set breakpoints to further customize your debugging session.

c. Setting up a variable window during a debug session will allow you to track the values of a variable during processing.

d. See also the section in Chapter 2 on REXX debugging for other techniques to use.

Index

A

B

C

D

E

F

G

H

I

K

L

M

N

O

P

Q

R

S

T

U

W

X

INTERESTED IN:

- Learning more about the REXX language through local courses and an information-packed newsletter?
- Influencing the direction of REXX interpreters/compilers and REXX add-on products?
- Accessing on-line databases filled with REXX resources?

Then join **RexxLA** (REXX Language Association)

Send to: VNR c/o Dianne Littwin, 115 Fifth Avenue, NY, NY 10003

Name: ______________________________

Company: ______________________________

Address: ______________________________

____

____

We'd also like to help serve you better. Can you let us know:

Where you purchased your book:

❏ bookstore, ❏ VNR, ❏ IBM, ❏ Other ____________

What OS/2 topics would you like VNR to publish books on?

What other areas are you interested in books on?

❏ IBM Mainframe ❏ IBM Midrange ❏ IBM PC's ❏ Artificial Intelligence

❏ Automation in Manufacturing ❏ Computer Security ❏ Databases

❏ DEC, VAX, VMS ❏ MIS ❏ Networking and Communications

❏ Software Engineering ❏ UNIX ❏ Other ____________

Please give us your comments about the book you purchased and any suggestions for future editions.